# JUS AD BELLUM

This work expounds, for those in practice and beyond, the rules of international law governing the inter-state use of force. *Jus ad bellum* determines when a state – or group of states – may lawfully use force against, or on the territory of, another state, and when such action violates international law. The bedrock of the law is found in the Charter of the United Nations, but the interpretation and application of many of the rules codified in the Charter, particularly by the International Court of Justice, are contested. Accordingly, the book seeks to clarify the law as it stands today, explaining its many complexities and controversies, such as when non-state actors may be attacked in another state and when consent is validly given to intervention by a forcible foreign state. The interrelationships between *jus ad bellum* and the law of armed conflict/international humanitarian law, the law of neutrality, and international human rights law are also illuminated, along with important concepts such as the 'responsibility to protect' and humanitarian intervention.

# Jus ad Bellum

*The Law on Inter-State Use of Force*

Stuart Casey-Maslen

·HART·

OXFORD · LONDON · NEW YORK · NEW DELHI · SYDNEY

HART PUBLISHING

Bloomsbury Publishing Plc

Kemp House, Chawley Park, Cumnor Hill, Oxford, OX2 9PH, UK

1385 Broadway, New York, NY 10018, USA

HART PUBLISHING, the Hart/Stag logo, BLOOMSBURY and the Diana logo are
trademarks of Bloomsbury Publishing Plc

First published in Great Britain 2020

A catalogue record for this book is available from the British Library.

Library of Congress Cataloging-in-Publication data

Names: Casey-Maslen, Stuart, author.

Title: Jus ad bellum : the law on inter-state use of force / Stuart Casey-Maslen.

Description: Oxford ; New York : Hart, 2020.  |  Includes bibliographical references and index.

Identifiers: LCCN 2020009685 (print)  |  LCCN 2020009686 (ebook)  |
ISBN 9781509930692  |  ISBN 9781509930708 (Epub)

Subjects: LCSH: Just war doctrine.

Classification: LCC KZ6396 .C37 2020 (print)  |  LCC KZ6396 (ebook)  |  DDC 341.6—dc23

LC record available at https://lccn.loc.gov/2020009685

LC ebook record available at https://lccn.loc.gov/2020009686

| ISBN: | PB: | 978-1-50993-069-2 |
| | ePDF: | 978-1-50993-071-5 |
| | ePub: | 978-1-50993-070-8 |

Typeset by Compuscript Ltd, Shannon

To find out more about our authors and books visit www.hartpublishing.co.uk.
Here you will find extracts, author information, details of forthcoming events
and the option to sign up for our newsletters.

# TABLE OF CONTENTS

Table of Cases ................................................................................................ *ix*
Table of Treaties Etc ...................................................................................... *xvii*
Table of National Instruments ....................................................................... *xxv*

**Introduction** ...................................................................................................1
    I.   War and the Foundations of International Law .......................................2
    II.  A History of the Regulation of War under International Law ...............6
    III. *Jus ad bellum* and Contemporary International Law ...........................13

**1.  The General Prohibition on the Use of Force** ...............................................16
    I.   Introduction ........................................................................................16
    II.  The Status of the Prohibition under International Law .......................17
    III. The Scope and Content of the Prohibition on the Use of Force ...........21
    IV. The Content of the Prohibition on the Threat of Force ........................34

**2.  Consenting to a Use of Force by Another State** ...........................................39
    I.   Introduction ........................................................................................39
    II.  The Lawful Donor of Consent ..............................................................40
    III. The Expression of Valid Consent ..........................................................51
    IV. Withdrawal of Consent ........................................................................53
    V.  Consent has no Bearing on the Duty to Respect Other Rules
        of International Law ..............................................................................54

**3.  Use of Force in Self-defence** ........................................................................56
    I.   Introduction ........................................................................................56
    II.  The Right of the State to Use Force in Self-defence ............................56
    III. Use of Force in Defence of Other States ...............................................75

**4.  United Nations Security Council Authorisation to Use Force** ...................76
    I.   Introduction ........................................................................................76
    II.  The Role of the UN Security Council ...................................................77
    III. The Form and Content of a Council Authorisation to Use Force .........83
    IV. Respect for the Terms of the Authorisation .........................................85
    V.  Security Council Authorisation and Regional Organisations ..............87

5. Use of Force and the Law of Neutrality ................................................90
   I.    Introduction ...............................................................................90
   II.   The Origins of the Law of Neutrality .........................................91
   III.  The Modern Law of Neutrality ...................................................93

6. The Legality of Humanitarian Intervention ..................................... 108
   I.    Introduction .............................................................................108
   II.   The Notion of Humanitarian Intervention ..............................109
   III.  Humanitarian Intervention under International Law .............110
   IV.   The Content and Consequence of 'Responsibility to Protect' .............117
   V.    Rescue of Nationals as Humanitarian Intervention? .............118

7. Responsibility for Aggression ........................................................... 120
   I.    Introduction .............................................................................120
   II.   The Definition of Aggression ...................................................122
   III.  State Responsibility for Acts of Aggression ............................124
   IV.   Individual Responsibility for Aggression under
         International Criminal Law .......................................................130
   V.    Concluding Remarks .................................................................139

8. Use of Force in United Nations Peacekeeping Operations ....................... 140
   I.    Introduction .............................................................................140
   II.   The Evolution in Peacekeeping Use of Force:
         From Self-defence to the Protection of Civilians ....................141
   III.  The International Legal Basis for Use of Force by
         UN Peacekeepers ......................................................................152

9. Rights and Obligations of Non-state Actors *ad Bellum*
   and *in Bello* .......................................................................................... 154
   I.    Introduction .............................................................................154
   II.   'Non-state Actor' and 'Non-state Armed Groups' Defined .............155
   III.  Non-state Actors' Rights and Obligations under
         International Law ......................................................................157

10. The Interrelationship between *Jus ad Bellum* and *Jus in Bello* ................. 166
   I.    Introduction .............................................................................166
   II.   The Relevance of *ad Bellum* Rules to an Application
         of *Jus in Bello* ...........................................................................167
   III.  Neutrality *ad Bellum* and *in Bello* ..........................................169
   IV.   Proportionality *ad Bellum* and *in Bello* .................................170
   V.    The Legality of Targeting under *Jus in Bello* and its
         Influence on the Legality of Action in Self-defence ...............171

**11. The Interrelationship between International Human Rights Law**
  **and *Jus ad Bellum*** ............................................................................................ **175**
  I.  Introduction ....................................................................................................175
  II.  The Substantive Prohibition under the Right to Life ...........................175
  III.  Identifying and Remedying a Violation of the Right to
        Life *ad Bellum* ...............................................................................................180

*Bibliography* ...............................................................................................................*183*
*Index* .............................................................................................................................*201*

# TABLE OF CASES

**Court of Justice of the European Union**

Council v Front Polisario Case C-104/16 P, ECLI:EU:C:2016:973,
21 December 2016, CJEU (Grand Chamber)
para 89 ............................................................................................................32
para 92 ............................................................................................................33
R (on the application of Western Sahara Campaign UK) v HMRC
and DEFRA Case C-266/16, ECLI:EU:C:2018:1, Opinion of
Ad-Gen Wathelet, 10 January 2018, CJEU ..........................................................33


**Eritrea-Ethiopia Claims Commission**

Eritrea-Ethiopia Claims Commission, Partial Award: Jus Ad
Bellum – Ethiopia's Claims 1–8, 19 December 2005
para 10 ............................................................................................................27
para 11 ...................................................................................................... 58, 75


**European Court of Human Rights**

Banković v Belgium 52207/99, (2007) 44 EHRR SE5..............................................179
Cyprus v Turkey, Judgment (Grand Chamber), 10 May 2001...............................129
Georgia v Russia (II) App No 38263/08 (Grand Chamber hearing),
30 May 2018...................................................................................................179
Loizidou v Turkey, Judgment (Merits) (Grand Chamber),
18 December 1996...........................................................................................129
para 52 ...................................................................................................... 178, 180
Loizidou v Turkey, Judgment (Preliminary Objections)
(Grand Chamber), 23 March 1995
para 62 ............................................................................................................178
Ukraine v Russia App No 20958/14 (Grand Chamber hearing),
11 September 2019 ..........................................................................................179

## International Court of Justice

*Contentious Cases*

Application of the Convention on the Prevention and Punishment
of the Crime of Genocide (Bosnia and Herzegovina v Yugoslavia
(Serbia and Montenegro)), Application Proceedings Submitted
by the Republic of Bosnia and Herzegovina, 20 March 1993
 para 123 ................................................................................................................79
 para 125 ................................................................................................................79
 para 135(o) ...........................................................................................................79
Application of the Convention on the Prevention and Punishment
of the Crime of Genocide (Bosnia and Herzegovina v Yugoslavia
(Serbia and Montenegro)), Order (Further Requests for the Indication
of Provisional Measures), 13 September 1993, ICJ Rep 1993, p 325
 para 41 ..................................................................................................................79
Armed Activities on the Territory of the Congo (Democratic
Republic of Congo v Rwanda), Judgment, 19 December 2005,
ICJ Rep 2005 p 168................................................................................................40
 paras 45–47 ..........................................................................................................40
 para 52 ..................................................................................................................53
 para 53 ..................................................................................................................53
 para 135 ................................................................................................................65
 para 146 ................................................................................................................65
 para 147 ..............................................................................................................170
 para 148 ......................................................................................................... 14, 66
 para 149 ................................................................................................................54
 para 153 ................................................................................................................54
 paras 178–180 ......................................................................................................54
 Separate Opinion of Bruno Simma, para 11.......................................................63
Corfu Channel Case (United Kingdom v Albania), Judgment (Merits),
 9 April 1949, ICJ Rep 1949, p 4 ..........................................................................56
 35 .................................................................................................... 36, 116, 168
East Timor (Portugal v Australia), Judgment, 30 June 1995, ICJ
Rep 1995 p 90
 para 29 ..................................................................................................................30
Fisheries Jurisdiction Case (Spain v Canada), Jurisdiction of the Court,
Judgment 4 December 1998, ICJ Rep 1998, p 432
 para 84 ..................................................................................................................24
Gabčikovo-Nagymaros Project (Hungary v Slovakia), Judgment,
 25 September 1997, ICJ Rep 1997, p 7 ................................................................65
 para 54 ..................................................................................................................66

Land and Maritime Boundary Between Cameroon and Nigeria
(Cameroon v Nigeria: Equatorial Guinea intervening), Judgment,
10 October 2002, ICJ Rep 2002, p 303
  para 311 ........................................................................................................28
  para 314 ........................................................................................................28
  para 319 ........................................................................................................29
Legality of Use of Force (Yugoslavia v Belgium), Request for
the indication of provisional measures, Public sitting on
10 May 1999, Vice-President Weeramantry, Verbatim Record,
ICJ doc 99/15 (1999), ICJ
  15 .......................................................................................................... 114, 115
  16 .......................................................................................................... 115, 116
Military and Paramilitary Activities in and against Nicaragua
(Nicaragua v United States of America), Judgment (Merits),
27 June 1986, ICJ Rep 1986, p 14 ...............................................50, 56, 64, 74, 156
  para 92 ...........................................................................................................36
  para 115 ........................................................................................................156
  para 176 ...................................................................................................... 57, 73
  para 186 ...........................................................................................................20
  para 188 ...........................................................................................................18
  para 190 ...........................................................................................................19
  para 191 ...........................................................................................................58
  para 194 ...................................................................................37, 69, 167, 170
  para 195 ...................................................................................58, 61, 69, 75, 156
  para 200 ...........................................................................................................74
  para 202 ...................................................................................................... 17, 111
  para 206 ...........................................................................................................51
  para 209 ........................................................................................................160
  para 218 ........................................................................................................165
  para 227 ...................................................................................................... 20, 36
  para 228 ...................................................................................................... 22, 23
  para 235 ...................................................................................................... 57, 75
  para 246 ...................................................................................................... 39, 160
  para 268 ........................................................................................................111
  para 276 ...........................................................................................................68
  para 282 ...........................................................................................................85
  Dissenting Opinion of Judge Sir Robert Jennings, 530 ...................................75
  Dissenting Opinion of Judge Sir Robert Jennings, 544–45 ............................75
  Separate Opinion of ICJ President Nagendra Singh, 153 ................................19
Nuclear Tests Case (New Zealand v France), Judgment,
20 December 1974, ICJ Rep 197, p 457 .................................................................14
  paras 45–49 ....................................................................................................14

Oil Platforms (Islamic Republic of Iran v United States
    of America), Judgment (Merits), 6 November 2003,
    ICJ Rep 2003, p 161..........................................................................19, 56, 171, 173
    para 43 ...............................................................................................................69
    para 51 ........................................................ 37, 58, 69, 71, 72, 167, 172
    para 61 ...............................................................................................................71
    para 64 ................................................................................... 58, 59, 71, 73
    para 72 ...............................................................................................................59
    para 73 ...............................................................................................................69
    para 76 ...............................................................................................................37
    Separate Opinion of Bruno Simma, para 6.........................................19
    Separate Opinion of Judge Buergenthal, para 41 .............................71
    Separate Opinion of Judge Higgins, para 30........................................71
    Separate Opinion of Pieter Kooijmans, para 46.................................19
Questions of Interpretation and Application of the 1971 Montreal
    Convention arising from the Aerial Incident at Lockerbie
    (Libyan Arab Jamahiriya v United Kingdom), Order (Request
    for the Indication of Provisional Measures), 14 April 1992, ICJ
    Rep 1992, p 3
    para 39 ...............................................................................................................79
Questions of Interpretation and Application of the 1971 Montreal
    Convention arising from the Aerial Incident at Lockerbie
    (Libyan Arab Jamahiriya v United Kingdom), Memorial by the
    Libyan Arab Jamahiriya, 20 December 1993
    para 6.34 ............................................................................................................79
United States Diplomatic and Consular Staff in Tehran (United
    States v Iran), Judgment, 24 May 1980, ICJ Rep 1980, p 3
    paras 29–32 ....................................................................................................154
    para 57 .................................................................................................... 25, 62
    para 63 .............................................................................................................154

*Advisory Opinions*

Accordance with International Law of the Unilateral Declaration
    of Independence in Respect of Kosovo, Advisory Opinion,
    22 July 2010, ICJ Rep 2010, p 403 ................................................129
    para 79 .............................................................................................................50
    para 80 .............................................................................................................129
    para 84 .............................................................................................................114
Certain Expenses of the United Nations (Article 17, Paragraph 2,
    of the Charter), Advisory Opinion, 20 July 1962, ICJ Rep 1962, p 151 ...........77
Interpretation of the Agreement of 25 March 1951 Between the
    WHO and Egypt, Advisory Opinion, 20 December 1980,

ICJ Rep 1980, p 73
   para 37 .............................................................................................. 77, 78
Legal Consequences of the Construction of a Wall in the Occupied
   Palestinian Territory, Advisory Opinion, 9 July 2004,
   ICJ Rep 2004, p 136.................................................................... 30, 56
   para 87 .......................................................................................31
   para 115 .....................................................................................31
Legality of the Threat or Use of Nuclear Weapons, Advisory
   Opinion 8 July 1996, ICJ Rep 1996, p 226 .............................34, 36, 56, 104, 177
   para 25 ......................................................................................177
   para 47 .......................................................................................37
   para 48 .......................................................................................35
   paras 78, 79.................................................................................172
   para 88 .......................................................................................97
   para 89 .................................................................................. 97, 105
Reparation for Injuries for Injuries Suffered in the Service of
   the United Nations, Advisory Opinion, 11 April 1949,
   ICJ Rep 1949, p 179.........................................................................77
Western Sahara, Advisory Opinion, 16 October 1975, ICJ Rep
   1975, p 12
   para 79 .......................................................................................31
   para 162 .....................................................................................31

**International Criminal Tribunal for the Former Yugoslavia (ICTY)**

Case No IT-94-1 *Prosecutor v Tadić (aka 'Dule')*, Decision on the
   Defence Motion for Interlocutory Appeal on Jurisdiction
   (Appeals Chamber), 2 October 1995
   para 70 .................................................................................. 155, 156
   para 73 ......................................................................................162
   para 98 ......................................................................................165
   para 117 .....................................................................................165
   para 136 .....................................................................................162
Case No IT-94-1-A *Prosecutor v Duško Tadić*, Judgment
   (Appeals Chamber), 15 July 1999
   para 296 ......................................................................................77
Case No IT-95-17/1-T *Prosecutor v Anto Furundžija*, Judgment,
   10 December 1998
   para 153 ......................................................................................19
Final Report to the Prosecutor by the Committee Established
   to Review the NATO Bombing Campaign Against the Federal

Republic of Yugoslavia, 13 June 2000
    para 48 ......................................................................................................171


## International Military Tribunals

International Military Tribunal for the Far East; Charter dated
    19 January 1946, bit.ly/2SbfWAa
        Art 5(a) ...................................................................................................132
International Military Tribunal for the Far East, Judgment,
    4 November 1948
        49,588–89 ..................................................................................................52
        1946, 27......................................................................................................132
Trial of the Major War Criminals before the International Military
    Tribunal
    vol 1, Nuremberg, 1947
        pp 36–37.....................................................................................................52
        p 222 ........................................................................................................132
        p 223 ........................................................................................................130
    vol 22, Nuremberg, 1948
        p 427 ........................................................................................................121
Trial of Von Leeb and Thirteen others (High Command Case) 1948,
    US Military Tribunal, Nuremberg ...................................................................134


## Permanent Court of Arbitration

Guyana/Suriname. Arbitral Tribunal Constituted Pursuant to
    Article 287, and in Accordance with Annex VII, of the United
    Nations Convention on the Law of the Sea in the Matter of an
    Arbitration Between Guyana and Suriname, Award of the
    Arbitral Tribunal, The Hague, 17 September 2007, PCA.................................21
*Naulilaa* arbitration (Portugal/Germany). See Responsabilité
    de l'Allemagne a raison des dommages causés dans les colonies
    portugaises du sud de l'Afrique
Responsabilité de l'Allemagne a raison des dommages causés dans
    les colonies portugaises du sud de l'Afrique (sentence sur le
    principe de la responsabilité) (Portugal c Allemagne), (1928)
    RIAA, 31 July 1928, vol II 1011
        1028–29 .....................................................................................................96

Savarkar – 'Arrest and Return of Savarkar (France/Great Britain)',
  undated, PCA.................................................................................................53
Savarkar Case Award Delivered on 24 February 1911 by the Arbitral
  Tribunal Appointed to Decide the "Case of Savarkar", – PCA...........................52

## Permanent Court of International Justice

*Contentious Cases*

SS Lotus (France v Turkey), Judgment, 7 September 1927
  18–19, PCIJ ...................................................................................................10

*Advisory Opinions*

Status of the Eastern Carelia, Advisory Opinion No 5, 23 July 1923
  para 33, PCIJ Adv Op .......................................................................................10

## Special Court for Sierra Leone (SCSL)

Case Nos SCSL-2004-15-AR72(E) and SCSL-2004-16-AR72(E)
  Prosecutor v Morris Kallon and Brima Buzzy Kamara, Decision
  on Challenge to Jurisdiction: Lomé Accord Amnesty (Appeals
  Chamber), 13 March 2004
    para 9 ........................................................................................................163
    paras 42 et seq.............................................................................................161
    paras 45–47 ...............................................................................................165
    para 46 ......................................................................................................162
    paras 48, 49................................................................................................161
Case No SCSL-2004-14-AR72(E) Prosecutor v Sam Hinga Norman,
  Decision on Preliminary Motion Based on Lack of Jurisdiction
  (Appeals Chamber), 31 May 2004
    para 22 ......................................................................................................164
Case No SCSL-04-15-T Prosecutor v Issa Hassan Sesay, Morris Kallon,
  and Augustine *Gbao*, Judgment (Trial Chamber), 2 March 2009
    para 1906 ..................................................................................................153
    para 1908 ..................................................................................................153
    para 1925 ..................................................................................................153

**National Jurisprudence**

*United Kingdom*

Al Rabbat v Tony Blair and others. See R (on the application of
    Al Rabbat) v Westminster Magistrates' Court (HM Attorney
    General intervening)
R v Jones (Margaret) [2006] UKHL 16, [2007] 1 AC 136 ............................. 138, 181
R (on the application of Al Rabbat) v Westminster Magistrates'
    Court (HM Attorney General intervening) [2017] EWHC
    1969 (Admin) ........................................................................................ 138, 181

*France*

Dreyfus Case (1901) .................................................................................................41

# TABLE OF TREATIES ETC

Adana Agreement signed on 20 October 1998 by the Republic of Turkey
and the Syrian Arab Republic...........................................................................46
Agreement for the Prosecution and Punishment of the Major War
Criminals of the European Axis; signed at London, 8 August 1945 ...............121
Annex: Charter of the International Military Tribunal 1945 ................. 130, 131
Art 6(a)............................................................................... 121, 131
Agreement on Principles of Settlement of the Georgian–Ossetia
Conflict of 24 June 1992 (Sochi Agreement)................................... 158, 159, 160
Agreement 'On the further development of the process of the
peaceful regulation of the Georgian-Ossetian conflict and
on the Joint Control Commission' (1994).................................................. 158, 159
Arms Trade Treaty; adopted at New York, 2 April 2013; entered
into force, 24 December 2014........................................................................ 91, 106
Art 5(1) ................................................................................................107
Art 6(1), (2) ........................................................................................106
Art 6(3) ................................................................................................107
Art 7(1) ................................................................................................107
Art 7(1)(a) ...........................................................................................107
Art 7(1)(b)(i), (ii) ...............................................................................107
Art 7(3) ................................................................................................107
Bosnia and Herzegovina, Agreement No 1 of 22 May 1992 ..................................162
Charter of the Organization of American States; signed at Bogota,
30 April 1948; entered into force, 13 December 1951
Art 18 ............................................................................................ 17, 111
Art 29 ....................................................................................................60
Commission on the Responsibility of the Authors of the War and
on Enforcement of Penalties, Report presented to the Preliminary
Peace Conference, 29 March 1919
Conclusions, Point 4 ..........................................................................120
Conference on Security and Co-operation in Europe
Final Act (Helsinki, 1975) Part I, s II.................................................158
Congress of Vienna 1815.........................................................................94
Constitution of the Socialist Federal Republic of Yugoslavia 1974.......................112
Constitution of France 1791 ....................................................................120

Convention for the Protection of Human Rights and Fundamental
    Freedoms; adopted at Rome by the Council of Europe,
    4 November 1950; entered into force, 3 September 1953 .........67, 178, 179, 181
    Art 1 ................................................................................................ 139, 179, 180
    Art 2 ...........................................................................................................178
    Art 2(2) .......................................................................................................178
    Art 2(2)(c) ..................................................................................................178
    Art 15(2) .....................................................................................................178
    Art 41 .........................................................................................................181
    Art 46(1) .....................................................................................................181
Convention on the Law of the Sea; adopted at Montego Bay,
    10 December 1982; entered into force, 16 November 1994
    (UNCLOS) ............................................................................................ 18, 101
    Art 17 ....................................................................................................91, 101
    Art 19(2) ................................................................................................91, 101
    Art 25(3) .....................................................................................................103
    Art 76(1) .....................................................................................................101
    Art 301 .........................................................................................................18
    Art 309 .........................................................................................................18
Convention on the Rights of the Child
Optional Protocol to the Convention on the Rights of the Child
    on the involvement of children in armed conflict; adopted at
    New York, 25 May 2000; entered into force, 12 February 2002 .....................155
    Art 4(1) .......................................................................................................155
Covenant of the League of Nations 1919; adopted at Paris,
    28 June 1919; entered into force, 10 January 1920.................................. 9, 10, 11
    Art 10 ......................................................................................................9, 10
    Art 12 ..........................................................................................................10
    Art 14 ..........................................................................................................10
European Convention on Human Rights 1950. See Convention
    for the Protection of Human Rights and Fundamental Freedoms
Friendship Treaty between Japan and Thailand 12 July 1940................................52
General Treaty for Renunciation of War as an Instrument of
    National Policy (Kellogg–Briand Pact) (Pact of Paris);
    adopted at Paris, 27 August 1928; entered into force,
    24 July 1929........................................................................ 11, 12, 13, 14, 131, 132
    Art 1 ............................................................................................................11
    Art 2 ............................................................................................................11
    Art 3 ............................................................................................................11
Geneva Convention (I) for the Amelioration of the Condition
    of the Wounded and Sick in Armed Forces in the Field;
    adopted at Geneva, 12 August 1949; entered into force,
    21 October 1950 1949 ..................................................... 107, 160, 161, 162, 165
    Art 1 ............................................................................................................54

Art 2 ...................................................................................................8, 52
Art 3 ................................................................ 160, 161, 162, 164, 165
Geneva Convention (II) for the Amelioration of the Condition
   of Wounded, Sick and Shipwrecked of Armed Forces at Sea;
   adopted at Geneva, 12 August 1949; entered into force,
   21 October 1950 ......................................................107, 160, 161, 162
   Art 1 ....................................................................................................54
   Art 2 .....................................................................................................8
   Art 3 .............................................................. 160, 161, 162, 164, 165
Geneva Convention (III) relative to the Treatment of
   Prisoners of War; adopted at Geneva, 12 August 1949;
   entered into force, 21 October 1950 ..........................107, 160, 161, 162
   Art 1 ....................................................................................................54
   Art 2 .....................................................................................................8
   Art 3 .............................................................. 160, 161, 162, 164, 165
   Art 4 ..................................................................................................155
   Art 4(6) ..............................................................................................173
   Art 4(A)(3) ..........................................................................................42
Geneva Convention (IV) relative to the Protection of Civilian
   Persons in Time of War; adopted at Geneva, 12 August 1949;
   entered into force, 21 October 1950 ..........................107, 160, 161, 162
   Art 1 ....................................................................................................54
   Art 2 .....................................................................................................8
   Art 3 ..................................................................... 160, 161, 162,
                                                     164, 165
Geneva Protocol for the Pacific Resolution of International
   Disputes 1924........................................................................................131
Hague Conventions 1899
   Russian Memorandum of 30 December 1898/11 January 1899 ........................7
Hague Convention I on the Pacific Settlement of International
   Disputes 1899; adopted at The Hague, 29 July 1899; entered
   into force, 4 September 1900 ..............................................................7
   preamble, para (1) .................................................................................7
   Art II ...................................................................................................7
Hague Convention (II) with Respect to the Laws and Customs of
   War on Land and its annex: Regulations concerning the Laws
   and Customs of War on Land; adopted at The Hague, 29 July 1899;
   entered into force, 4 September 1900 ....................................................95
   Annex: Regulations....................................................................... 96, 97
      Art 57..............................................................................................95
Hague Convention III Relative to the Opening of Hostilities;
   adopted at The Hague, 18 October 1907; entered into force,
   26 January 1910 ...............................................................................8, 36
   Art 1 ...............................................................................................8, 36

Hague Convention (V) respecting the Rights and Duties of
    Neutral Powers and Persons in Case of War on Land;
    adopted at The Hague, 18 October 1907; entered into
    force, 26 January 1910 .................................................................95, 96, 97, 98, 131
    Art 1 ........................................................................................................................96
    Art 2 ........................................................................................................................96
    Art 5 ........................................................................................................................96
    Art 10 ....................................................................................................................103
Hague Convention (XIII) concerning the Rights and Duties
    of Neutral Powers in Naval War; adopted at The Hague,
    18 October 1907; entered into force, 26 January 1910 ......................... 95, 97, 98
    Art 1 ........................................................................................................................96
    Art 2 ........................................................................................................................96
    Art 10 ....................................................................................................................103
    Art 25 ........................................................................................................... 101, 104
Helsinki Principles on the Law of Maritime Neutrality adopted
    within the International Law Association in 1998............................................103
    para 2.3 .................................................................................................................103
International Covenant on Civil and Political Rights; adopted
    at New York, 16 December 1966; entered into force,
    23 March 1976 (ICCPR) 1966 ................................................................. 55, 175
    Art 2(1) ....................................................................................................................55
    Art 6 ................................................................................................................ 55, 175
    Art 6(1) ......................................................................................................... 175, 176
    Optional Protocol
        Art 5(4).............................................................................................................181
Kellogg–Briand Pact. See General Treaty for Renunciation of
    War as an Instrument of National Policy
League of Nations Draft Treaty of Mutual Assistance 1923....................................131
"Lome Agreement". See Peace Agreement between the Government
    of Sierra Leone and the Revolutionary United Front of Sierra
    Leone (RUF/SL)
Memorandum on Measures to Provide Security and Strengthen
    Mutual Trust between Sides in the Georgian–South Ossetian
    Conflict of 16 May 1996 ....................................................................................159
Military Technical Agreement Between the International Security
    Force ('KFOR') and the Governments of Federal Republic of
    Yugoslavia and the Republic of Serbia, concluded at Kumanovo,
    North Macedonia (then the former Yugoslav Republic of
    Macedonia), 9 June 1999; entered into force, 10 June 1999.............................113
    Art I(4)(a)..............................................................................................................129

Montevideo Convention on Rights and Duties of States 1933;
    signed at Montevideo, 26 December 1933; entered into force,
    26 December 1934........................................................................................13
    Art 8....................................................................................................108
    Art 11.....................................................................................................13
Montreal Convention 1971 – Convention for the Suppression
    of Unlawful Acts against the Safety of Civil Aviation; adopted
    at Montreal, 23 September 1971; entered into force, 26 January 1973..............79
North Atlantic Treaty; signed at Washington DC, 4 April 1949;
    entered into force, 24 August 1949
    Art 5.......................................................................................................62
Pact of Paris. See General Treaty for Renunciation of War as an
    Instrument of National Policy
Paris Declaration on Maritime Law 1856...............................................................95
    preamble................................................................................................95
Paris Peace Conference 1919 ..............................................................................120
Peace Agreement between the Government of Sierra Leone and
    the Revolutionary United Front of Sierra Leone (RUF/SL),
    Lome, 7 July 1999 ("Lome Agreement") ...................................160, 161, 162, 163
Potsdam Declaration (Proclamation Defining Terms for
    Japanese Surrender) July 26, 1945.......................................................132
Protocol Additional to the Geneva Conventions of 12 August 1949,
    and relating to the Protection of Victims of International
    Armed Conflicts (Protocol I); adopted at Geneva, 8 June 1977;
    entered into force, 7 December 1978......................................................32
    Art 1(4)....................................................................................................32
    Art 48.....................................................................................................172
    Art 51(6)..................................................................................................174
    Art 52(2)..................................................................................37, 72, 172
    Art 96(3)..................................................................................................32
Protocol Additional to the Geneva Conventions of 12 August 1949,
    and relating to the Protection of Victims of Non-International
    Armed Conflicts (Protocol II); adopted at Geneva, 8 June 1977;
    entered into force, 7 December 1978 ...........................................164, 165
Resolution of the Assembly of the League of Nations 1927.....................................131
    preamble...............................................................................................131
Rome Statute of the International Criminal Court; adopted
    at Rome, 17 July 1998; entered into force, 1 July 2002
    (ICC Statute)......................................................................18, 82, 130, 133,
                                                                                              135, 137, 139
    preamble para (7) .....................................................................................18
    Art 8bis ..........................................................................................133, 137

Art 8bis (1) ............................................................................ 133, 134, 139
Art 8bis (2) ................................................................................. 133, 134
Art 8bis(2)(a) .................................................................................. 26, 133
Art 8bis(2)(b) ................................................................................... 26,133
Art 8bis(2)(c) .................................................................................. 22, 133
Art 8bis(2)(d)–(f) .................................................................................133
Art 8bis(2)(g) ........................................................................ 61, 133, 134
Art 13(b) ...............................................................................................136
Art 15bis ...............................................................................................136
Art 15bis(5), (6) ...................................................................................136
Art 15bis(7) .................................................................................... 82, 136
Art 15bis(8), (9) ...................................................................................136
Art 15ter ...............................................................................................136
Art 15ter(4) ..........................................................................................136
Art 120 .....................................................................................................18
Amendments on the crime of aggression to the Rome Statute
    of the International Criminal Court; adopted at Kampala,
    11 June 2010; entered into force, 8 May 2013 ......................... 133, 135
Second Hague Peace Conference ................................................................95
Sochi Agreement. See Agreement on Principles of Settlement
    of the Georgian–Ossetia Conflict of 24 June 1992
Statute of the International Court of Justice 1945
    Art 38 .................................................................................................14
    Art 38(1)(d) .......................................................................................15
Treaty of Friendship, Commerce and Navigation between
    Nicaragua and the United States 1956 ................................................85
Treaty of London 1839 – Treaty between Great Britain, Austria,
    France, Prussia, and Russia, on the one part, and Belgium,
    on the other; signed at London, 19 April 1839 .................................94
    Art VII ...............................................................................................94
Treaty of Versailles 1919; signed at Versailles, 28 June 1919;
    entered into force, 10 January 1920 ............................................. 9, 120
    Art 227 ...................................................................................... 121, 131
Treaty of Westphalia 1648 .........................................................................6
UN Charter 1945 adopted at San Francisco, 26 June 1945;
    entered into force, 24 October 1945 ....................................6, 7, 11, 13, 14, 19, 20,
                                                                         21, 24, 26, 27, 32, 34, 36,
                                                                         38, 54, 56, 58, 61, 63, 69, 76,
                                                                         78, 81, 82, 84, 85, 87, 90, 97,
                                                                         98, 99, 105, 108, 109, 114, 115,
                                                                         123, 127, 129, 133, 134, 137,
                                                                         139, 140, 152, 157, 158, 159,
                                                                         177, 178, 179
    preamble ............................................................................................16

preamble, para (6) ...................................................................................7

preamble, para (7) ..................................................................................16

Art 1 ............................................................................................... 13, 30

Art 1(1) ..................................................................................................77

Art 1(2) ..................................................................................................30

Art 1(3) ........................................................................................... 77, 116

Art 2 ...................................................................................................157

Art 2(3) ...................................................................................... 14, 157, 180

Art 2(4) .......................................................... 14, 16, 18, 20, 21, 23, 24, 25,
26, 27, 29, 30, 33, 34, 37,
38, 39, 54, 58, 60, 68, 80,
91, 99, 102, 108, 114, 115,
116, 118, 123, 128, 129,
134, 138, 153, 157, 160,
168, 170, 176, 180

Art 2(7) ...............................................................................................108

Art 7 .....................................................................................................77

Art 24 ..................................................................................................128

Art 24(1) .................................................................................. 76, 77, 79, 126

Art 24(2) ................................................................................................77

Art 25 .............................................................................................. 79, 97

Art 26 ....................................................................................................30

Ch VI Pacific Settlement of Disputes (Arts 33–38) .......... 14, 117, 140, 143, 152

Art 33(1) ................................................................................................14

Art 36(3) ................................................................................................14

Ch VII Action with respect to threats to the peace,
    breaches of the peace, and acts of aggression
    (Arts 39–51) ................................................... 14, 51, 76, 78, 79, 80, 82,
84, 99, 105, 106, 109, 110,
113, 114, 117, 136, 140,
144, 145, 153, 176

Art 39 ...................................................................................78, 80, 83, 106

Art 41 ............................................................................................. 90, 99

Art 42 .................................................................................14, 37, 76, 90, 99

Art 43(1) ..............................................................................................152

Art 51 ................................................................................6, 14, 27, 39, 54, 56, 57,
58, 61, 62, 63, 65, 66,
67, 68, 74, 75, 79, 102,
115, 160, 176

Ch VIII Regional Arrangements (Arts 52–54) ........................................ 87, 117

Art 52(1) ................................................................................................87

Art 52(2) ......................................................................................... 87, 88

Art 53 ..................................................................................................128

Art 53(1) ..................................................................................................................88
Art 103 ............................................................................................................... 79, 97
UN Charter 1945 – Charte des Nations Unies; adopted
   at San Francisco, 26 June 1945; entered into force,
   24 October 1945
Art 51 ......................................................................................................................61
Vienna Convention on the Law of Treaties 1969; adopted
   at Vienna, 23 May 1969; entered into force, 27 January
   1980 (VCLT) ................................................................................ 18, 159, 163
Art 31(3)(b) ..........................................................................................................159
Art 52 ............................................................................................................. 34, 128
Art 53 ......................................................................................................................19
Art 60(1) ...............................................................................................................163
XVII Ministerial Conference of the Non-Aligned Movement,
   Algiers, 26–29 May 2014, Final Document
para 25.2 ................................................................................................................57
para 26.5 ................................................................................................................66
para 673 ...............................................................................................................116

# TABLE OF NATIONAL INSTRUMENTS

Russian Constitution
    Art 72(n)......................................................................................................159
Ukrainian Constitution 1996................................................................................48

## United Nations Documents and Materials

Basic Principles on the Use of Force and Firearms by Law
    Enforcement Officials, welcomed by UN General Assembly
    Resolution 45/166, adopted without a vote on 14 December 1990................143
Basic Principle 9 ................................................................................................143

## Human Rights Committee

An Agenda for Peace (1993), UN Secretary-General............................................143

### Concluding Observations

Concluding Observations on the Fourth Periodic Report of the
    United States of America, UN doc CCPR/C/USA/CO/4,
    23 April 2014
    para C.....................................................................................................55

### General Comments

General Comment No 6 (1982)
    para 1 ....................................................................................................175
    para 2 ....................................................................................................176
    para 70 ..................................................................................................180
General Comment No 14 (1984)
    para 2 ....................................................................................................175
General Comment No 36 (2018) on Article 6 of the International
    Covenant on Civil and Political Rights, on the Right to Life,
    UN doc CCPR/C/GC/36, 30 October 2018............................................ 55, 176
    para 2 ....................................................................................................175
    para 12 ..................................................................................................176

para 68 ...............................................................................................78
para 70 ...............................................................................................175


**General Assembly Decisions and Documents**

*Resolutions*

Resolution 290 (IV) (1949) ('Essentials of Peace'), adopted
   on 1 December 1949 ......................................................................16
Resolution 377A ('Uniting for Peace') (1950) adopted
   on 3 November 1950 ....................................................................140
   para 1 ........................................................................................141
Resolution 380 (V) (1950) ('Peace through Deeds') (1950)
   adopted by consensus on 17 November 1950
   para 1 ........................................................................................121
Resolution 998 (ES – 1) (1956) adopted on 2 November 1956 ...........141
Resolution 1514 (XV) (1960), 14 December 1960 ..................................31
   Declaration on the Granting of Independence to Colonial
      Countries and Peoples
         para 4 ...................................................................................31
Resolution 2625 (XXV), adopted without a vote, 24 October 1970 ....111
   Annex – 'Declaration on Principles of International Law
      concerning Friendly Relations and Co-operation
      among States in accordance with the Charter of the
      United Nations'..................................................15, 17, 18, 32, 111
         Principal 1..............................................................................18
         Principal 1, para 6..................................................................30
         Principal 1(7)..........................................................................50
         Principal 1, para 9..................................................................31
Resolution 3070 (XXVIII) ('Importance of the universal
   realization of the right of peoples to self-determination
   and of the speedy granting of independence to colonial
   countries and peoples for the effective guarantee and
   observance of human rights'), adopted on 30 November 1973
   paras 2, 3....................................................................................51
Resolution 3314 (XXIX); adopted without a vote on
   14 December 1974.........................................................118, 123, 133, 176
   Annex – Definition of Aggression ...........................29, 124, 134
      preamble, para (5).........................................61, 123, 176
      Art 1 ................................................................123, 177
      Art 2 ......................................................59, 123, 177
      Art 3 ..............................................................................124
      Art 3(a) ....................................................... 26, 177

Art 3(b) ................................................................................... 26, 177
Art 3(c) ................................................................................... 22, 177
Art 3(d) .................................................................................. 29, 177
Art 3(e) ................................................................................... 54, 177
Art 3(f) .................................................................................... 64, 177
Art 3(g) ........................................................................ 61, 156, 157, 177
Art 4 ...................................................................................... 123, 124
Art 5(1) .................................................................................. 118, 121
Art 5(2) .................................................................................. 121, 124
Art 5(3) ......................................................................................... 127
Art 7 ............................................................................................. 124
Resolution 34/47 (Services of the Secretariat concerned with
   Human Rights), adopted on 21 November 1979
   paras 5, 6 ..................................................................................... 32
Resolution 38/7 (The Situation in Grenada), adopted on
   2 November 1983 .......................................................................... 41
Resolution 45/166 (1990) (Human rights in the administration
   of Justice) adopted without a vote on 14 December 1990 .............................. 143
Resolution 50/80A (1995) (Permanent neutrality of Turkmenistan),
   adopted without a vote on 12 December 1995 ......................................... 99
   preamble para (2) .......................................................................... 99
   preamble para (7) .......................................................................... 99
Resolution 56/83 (2001) (Responsibility of States for
   internationally wrongful acts) of 12 December 2001 ................. 78, 91, 105, 124
Resolution 60/1 (2005 World Summit Outcome') (2005),
   adopted without a vote on 16 September 2005
   para 4 ........................................................................................ 54
   para 139 ............................................................................... 117, 118
Resolution 66/253B (The situation in the Syrian Arab Republic),
   adopted on 7 August 2012
   preamble, para (16) ......................................................................... 83
Resolution 67/1 (2012) ('Declaration of the High-level Meeting
   of the General Assembly on the Rule of Law at the National
   and International Levels') adopted on 24 September 2012 ............................ 77
   para 2 ........................................................................................ 78
Resolution 68/262 (2014) ('Territorial Integrity of Ukraine')
   adopted on 27 March 2014
   para 2 ....................................................................................... 127
   para 6 ....................................................................................... 127

*Reports of the Secretary-General*

'Note by the Secretary-General', UN doc S/5653, 11 April 1964,
   para 16 ..................................................................................... 143

'Report of the Secretary-General Pursuant to General Assembly
    Resolution 53/35: The Fall of Srebrenica', UN doc A/54/549,
    15 November 1999
    para 131 ...........................................................................................................88


**International Law Commission Documents**

Addendum to the Eighth Report on State Responsibility
    (1980) II(1) United Nations Yearbook of the International
    Law Commission – Ago, R, ILC Special Rapporteur
    69, para 120 .....................................................................................................70
    69, para 121 ............................................................................................. 73, 170
Draft Articles on Responsibility of States for Internationally
    Wrongful Acts, with commentaries, UN doc A/56/10
    (New York, 2001) ..............................................................................................91
    Ch III .................................................................................................................124
    Art 1 ...................................................................................................................125
        commentary para 5 ......................................................................................125
    Art 2 ...................................................................................................................154
    Art 2(a) ..............................................................................................................154
    Art 5(3) ..............................................................................................................127
    Art 8 ...................................................................................................................156
        commentary para 3 ......................................................................................156
    Art 14 .......................................................................................................... 48, 50
        commentary para 3 .............................................................................. 48, 50
    Art 16 .................................................................................................................129
    Art 20 .................................................................................................. 34, 51, 52, 53
        commentary paras 3, 4 ..................................................................................51
        commentary para 6 ............................................................................... 52, 53
    Art 26 ...................................................................................................................30
        commentary para 5 ........................................................................................78
    Art 31
        commentary para 12 ....................................................................................154
    Art 31(1) .............................................................................................................125
    Art 40 ................................................................................................ 91, 100, 126
        commentary .....................................................................................................91
        commentary para 4 ......................................................................................106
    Art 40(2) .............................................................................................................124
    Art 41 ................................................................................................ 91, 100, 105
        commentary .....................................................................................................91
        commentary para 2, 3 ..................................................................................126
        commentary para 7 ......................................................................................127

commentary para 11...................................................................................129
commentary para 12...................................................................................130
Art 41(1)................................................................................... 106, 126
Art 41(2)........................................................................... 126, 127, 129
Art 50(1)(a)...............................................................................................19
Draft Articles on Responsibility of International Organizations,
    Art 26 in Report of the International Law Commission,
    Sixty-third session (26 April–3 June and 4 July–12 August 2011),
    UN doc A/66/10/Add.1 (New York, 2011) .............................................77
Draft Articles on the Law of Treaties 1966 (ILC).....................................19
Draft Code of Offences against the Peace and Security of Mankind,
    Text adopted by the ILC at its sixth session in 1954 and
    submitted to the UN General Assembly ...........................................121
    Arts 1, 2 ......................................................................................122
Draft Code of Crimes against the Peace and Security of Mankind,
    Text adopted by the ILC at its forty-eighth session in 1996 and
    submitted to the UN General Assembly ...........................................122
    Art 2(2) ........................................................................................122
    Art 16............................................................................................122
    commentary para 4.....................................................................122
First Report on *Jus Cogens* by Dire Tladi, Special Rapporteur,
    UN doc A/CN.4/693, 8 March 2016
    para 61 ..........................................................................................19
Second Report on a Draft Code of Offences Against the Peace and
    Security of Mankind by Mr. J Spiropoulos, Special Rapporteur,
    ILC, UN doc A/CN.4/44, 12 April 1951...............................................122
    p 69................................................................................................123
Third Report on Peremptory Norms of General International Law
    (*Jus Cogens*) by Dire Tladi, Special Rapporteur, International Law
    Commission, UN doc A/CN.4/714, 12 February 2018
    para 81 ..........................................................................................56
    paras 90–91 ................................................................................106
    paras 90–94 ................................................................................126
    paras 95–102 ..............................................................................130
Fourth Report on Peremptory Norms of General International Law
    (*Jus Cogens*) by Dire Tladi, Special Rapporteur, UN doc
    A/CN.4/727, 31 January 2019
    paras 117–121 ............................................................................172
Peremptory Norms of General International Law (*Jus Cogens*).
    Text of the draft Conclusions and Draft Annex Provisionally
    Adopted by the Drafting Committee on First Reading',
    UN doc A/CN.4/L936, 29 May 2019
    Conclusion 19(1), (2)...................................................................106

'Report of the 53rd Session' (2001) II(2) United Nations Yearbook
of the International Law Commission
73 ............................................................................................................................52


## Security Council Decisions and Documents

*United Nations Security Council Resolutions*

Resolution 47 (1948) adopted on 21 April 1948......................................................147
Resolution 50 (1948) adopted on 29 May 1948.......................................................147
Resolution 82 (1950) adopted on 25 June 1950..........................................................81
    preamble, paras (3), (4) ........................................................................................81
Resolution 143 (1960) adopted on 14 July 1960......................................................142
    para 2 ....................................................................................................................142
Resolution 161 (1960) adopted on 14 July 1960......................................................142
    para 1 ....................................................................................................................142
Resolution 169 (1961) adopted on 24 November 1961
    para 4 ....................................................................................................................142
Resolution 186 (1964) adopted unanimously on 4 March 1964 ............................146
Resolution 218 (1965) of 23 November 1965 on the Portuguese colonies ..........130
Resolution 350 (1974) of 31 May 1974 ...................................................................146
Resolution 404 (1977) of 8 February 1977 ................................................................62
Resolution 405 (1977) adopted by consensus on 14 April 1977
    para 2 ......................................................................................................................62
Resolution 418 (1977) of 4 November 1977 on South Africa................................130
Resolution 419 (1977) adopted without a vote on 24 November 1977
    para 1 ......................................................................................................................62
Resolution 487 (1981) adopted unanimously on 19 June 1981
    preamble, para (8) ..................................................................................................66
    para 1 ......................................................................................................................66
    para 2 ......................................................................................................................26
Resolution 502 (1982) adopted on 3 April 1982........................................................81
Resolution 569 (1985) of 26 July 1985 on South Africa .......................................130
Resolution 573 (1985) adopted on 4 October 1985 .................................................82
    para 1 ..............................................................................................................82, 168
    para 2 ......................................................................................................................20
    para 3 ....................................................................................................................168
Resolution 611 (1988) adopted on 25 April 1988 .....................................................82
    preamble para 3 .....................................................................................................135
    para 1 ......................................................................................................................82
Resolution 660 (1990), adopted on 2 August 1990 .................................... 43, 81, 83
    preamble, paras (1), (2) ..........................................................................................81

Letter dated 9 October 2019 from the Permanent Representative
of Turkey to the United Nations addressed to the President
of the Security Council, UN doc S/2019/804, 9 October 2019,
bit.ly/37yrvc9 ................................................................................................ 45, 46
Letter to the President of the UN Security Council from John D
Negroponte, US Permanent Representative to the United
Nations in New York, UN doc S/2001/946, 7 October 2001 ...................... 63, 72
Report of the Security Council Special Mission to the People's
Republic of Benin Established under Resolution 404 (1977),
UN doc S/12294/Add.1, 8 March 1977 ................................................................62
    Annex I: Statement of the President and Head of State and
    Government of the People's Republic of Benin
    p 1 .................................................................................................................62
Statement of the President of the UN Security Council, UN doc
S/PV.3225, 28 May 1993
    p 3 ................................................................................................................143
UN doc S/PV.2615, 4 October 1985, 87.................................................................168
UN doc S/19791, 18 April 1988...............................................................................73
UN doc S/PV.2938, 25 August 1990, 55 .................................................................84
UN doc S/PV.3989, 26 March 1999
    p 4 ................................................................................................................114
    p 5–7.............................................................................................................115
UN doc S/PV.6498, 17 March 2011
    p 6 .................................................................................................................85
    p 10 ...............................................................................................................85
UN doc S/PV.7125, 3 March 2014
    Statement of Sir Mark Lyall Grant before the UN Security Council ...............47
    Statement of Stephanie Power before the UN Security Council.......................47
    Statement of Vitaly Churkin before the UN Security Council................... 46, 47

### Press Releases

'Belarus, India and Russian Federation: draft resolution',
    UN doc S/1999/328, 26 March 1999, bit.ly/2Ygkqqw. ....................................128
'General Assembly Adopts Resolution Calling upon States
    Not to Recognize Changes in Status of Crimea Region',
    Information Note, UN doc GA/11493, 27 March 2014,
    bit.ly/2OExDq5.................................................................................................127
General Assembly Special Committee on Decolonization,
    'Ensuring Non-Self-Governing Territories Can Address
    Challenges Key to Moving Decolonization Efforts Forward,
    Secretary-General Tells Regional Seminar', UN doc
    GA/COL/3320, 10 May 2018, bit.ly/2DsZqFm ......................................................30

"'Intervention Brigade" Authorized as Security Council
   Grants Mandate Renewal for United Nations Mission
   in Democratic Republic of Congo', UN doc SC/10964,
   28 March 2013, bit.ly/2r8WZ8b ..........................................................................148
'Security Council Rejects Demand for Cessation of Use of Force
   against Federal Republic of Yugoslavia', Press Release,
   26 March 1999, bit.ly/2JYh0no ..........................................................................128

## United Nations Claims Commission

UNCC Governing Council Decision 11 ......................................................................125
UNCC, 'Recommendations Made By the Panel of Commissioners
   Concerning Individual Claims for Serious Personal Injury
   or Death (Category "B" Claims)', UN doc S/AC26/1994/1,
   26 May 1994
   pp 14–15 ...............................................................................................................125

## Other UN Documents

'A More Secure World: Our Shared Responsibility', Report of
   the High-level Panel on Threats, Challenges and Change,
   UN doc A759/565, 2 December 2004
   para 203 ...............................................................................................................118
*Capstone Doctrine*, United Nations Peacekeeping Operations
   Principles and Guidelines, UN, New York, 2008, bit.ly/2P709kQ .................152
   p 34 ......................................................................................................................152
Code of Conduct for Law Enforcement Officials 1979
   Art 1 .....................................................................................................................152
Department of Peace Operations, *The Protection of Civilians in
   United Nations Peacekeeping*, DOP Policy doc 2019.17,
   1 November 2019 ...............................................................................................150
   para16 fn 2 ...........................................................................................................145
   para 22 .................................................................................................................151
   para 27 .................................................................................................................151
   para 29 .................................................................................................................148
   para 30 .................................................................................................................151
   para 50 .................................................................................................................151
   para 57 .................................................................................................................151
   para 61 .................................................................................................................148
*Minnesota Protocol on the Investigation of Potentially Unlawful
   Death* (2016), Office of the UN High Commissioner for
   Human Rights, New York/Geneva, 2017 .........................................................150

'Principles of Peacekeeping', undated, bit.ly/2VTa7t6 ............................................148
'Protection of Civilians Mandate', undated, bit.ly/2Bqhdf2 ...................................148
*Report of the Panel on United Nations Peace Operations,*
    UN doc A/55/305 and S/2000/809, 2000
    para 62 ........................................................................................................................153
'Summary Study of the Experience Derived from the Establishment
    and Operation of the Force: Report of the Secretary-General',
    UN doc A/3943, 9 October 1958, bit.ly/2MyvlBT
    para 70 ........................................................................................................................141


**African Commission on Human and Peoples' Rights**

*General Comments*

General Comment No 3 on the African Charter on Human and
    Peoples' Rights: The Right to Life (Article 4); adopted during the
    57th Ordinary Session of the African Commission on Human
    and Peoples' Rights, held from 4 to 18 November 2015 in
    Banjul, The Gambia
    para 5 ...........................................................................................................................78
    para 12 .......................................................................................................................176


**African Union**

'African Union decision on the peaceful resolution of the
    Libyan crisis', Extraordinary Session of the Assembly
    of the Union, Addis Ababa, 25 May 2011
    para 7 ...........................................................................................................................86
Communiqué of the 883rd meeting of the African Union PSC
    at the Ministerial Level, held on 27 September 2019, on the
    Situation in Libya (last updated 4 October 2019), bit.ly/35LXSSI
    para 2 ...........................................................................................................................87
Constitutive Act of the African Union 2000
    Art 4(h)........................................................................................................................88


**Independent International Fact-Finding Mission on the
Conflict in Georgia**

Independent International Fact-Finding Mission on the Conflict
    in Georgia, Report, Vol II, September 2009............................................. 117, 118
    p 232.................................................................................................................... 35, 36

p 235.................................................................................................................38
p 236.........................................................................................................38, 157
p 238.................................................................................................................38
p 240......................................................................................................158, 159
p 241......................................................................................................159, 160
p 242........................................................................................................23, 160
p 243.................................................................................................................33
p 244.................................................................................................................60
p 245.................................................................................................................58
p 248.................................................................................................................69
p 249........................................................................................................73, 170
p 254.................................................................................................65, 66, 67
p 257.................................................................................................................54
p 261................................................................................................................157
p 264.................................................................................................................29
p 266.................................................................................................................59
p 272.................................................................................................................73
p 272 fn 163...................................................................................................166
p 283................................................................................................................110
p 284......................................................................................................111, 117
p 286................................................................................................................118
p 287................................................................................................................119
p 288................................................................................................................119

## International Committee of the Red Cross (ICRC)

Commentary on 1949 Geneva Convention I, 2016
  para 260, bit.ly/2NVube4 ..............................................................................169
  para 263 ...........................................................................................................52
  para 842 .........................................................................................................161
  para 860 .........................................................................................................162
Commentary on Article 3 of the 1949 Geneva Convention I (2016)
  fn 819, bit.ly/2DNLYvH..................................................................................162
  para 505, bit.ly/2OQn9Wf...............................................................................165
  para 507, bit.ly/2OQn9Wf...............................................................................165
  para 508, bit.ly/2OQn9Wf...............................................................................165
Commentary on the Additional Protocols of 8 June 1977
  to the Geneva Conventions of 12 August 1949 (Geneva,
  ICRC/Dordrecht, Martinus Nijhoff, 1987)
  p 1345.............................................................................................................164
Customary Study of International Humanitarian Law
  Rule 5 (Definition of Civilians) .....................................................................172

Rule 8 (Definition of Military Objectives) ........................................................172
Rule 14 (Proportionality in Attack) ......................................................... 167, 171
Final Act of the International Peace Conference. The Hague,
    29 July 1899 (Geneva, ICRC, 2016), bit.ly/2Fa2ycF.
Increasing Respect for International Humanitarian Law in
    Non-International Armed Conflicts', Geneva, February 2008
    p 16 ................................................................................................................161
International Committee of the Red Cross (ICRC), 'Final Act
    of the International Peace Conference. The Hague, 29 July 1899' .....................7
Jus ad Bellum and Jus in Bello (29 October 2010), bit.ly/2NxAB0u ...................166

## International Criminal Court (ICC)

ICC doc RC/Res 6, Annex III, Understanding No 6, adopted on
    11 June 2010 by consensus, bit.ly/2OFt14t ....................................................134
Special Working Group on the Crime of Aggression – ICC doc
    ICC-ASP/6/20/Add.1
    Annex II: Report of the Special Working Group on the
        Crime of Aggression (June 2008)
        para 31 ...................................................................................................123

## Media Articles, Press Releases, Reports and Manuals

Independent International Commission on Kosovo, The Kosovo
    Report: Conflict, International Response, Lessons Learned
    (Oxford, Oxford University Press, 2000) esp 166–74 .......................................128
'Legal Basis for UK Military Action in Syria', Briefing
    Paper No 7404 (London, House of Commons Library,
    1 December 2015) 21 .......................................................................................116
'Report of the Dutch Committee of Inquiry on the War in Iraq,
    ch 8 ("The Basis in International Law for the Military
    Intervention in Iraq")' (May 2010) 57(1) Netherlands
    *International Law Review* 81, 136 .......................................................................139
Sixth International Conference of American States 1928
    Resolution – Papers relating to the foreign relations of the
    United States, 1928, vol I, 204
        preamble ..................................................................................................131
Statement of President George W Bush, 'National Security
    Strategy of the United States of America' (Washington DC,
    September 2002) iii ...........................................................................................65

UK Prime Minister's Office, 'Syria Action – UK Government
   Legal Position', Policy Paper (10 Downing Street, 14 April 2018),
   bit.ly/2LT7owG ...................................................................................................110

*Manuals*

*Joint Service Manual of the Law of Armed Conflict*, Joint Service
   Publication
383 (UK Ministry of Defence, 2004)
   para 1.42 ............................................................................................... 90, 169
   para 1.42.2 .......................................................................................................90
   para 1.43 ..........................................................................................................98
   para 1.43(a) ....................................................................................................100
   para 1.43(b) ............................................................................................. 100, 101
*Law of Armed Conflict Manual*, Joint Service Regulation
   (ZDv) 15/2 (German Ministry of Defence, Berlin, 2013)
   para 210 .........................................................................................................155
*Law of War Manual* (Washington DC, June 2015, updated
   December 2016, US Department of Defense)
   para 5.12.4 .....................................................................................................171
   para 13.2.2.4 ..................................................................................................104
   para 15.1.1 ............................................................................................. 90, 169
   para 15.1.4 .......................................................................................................98
   para 15.2 ................................................................................................ 90, 105
   para 15.2.1.2 ....................................................................................................98
   para 15.2.3 .......................................................................................................97
   para 15.2.3.1 ........................................................................................ 99, 102, 105
   para 15.3.1.1 ....................................................................................................96
   para 15.3.1.2 ..................................................................................................100
   para 15.3.2 ............................................................................................. 90, 169
   para 15.4.1 .....................................................................................................107
   para 15.4.3 .....................................................................................................102
   para 15.5 ........................................................................................................100
   para 15.7.1 .....................................................................................................101
   para 15.10 ......................................................................................................101
   para 15.16 ......................................................................................................101
*Leuven Manual on the International Law Applicable to Peace
   Operations* (2017)
   Rule 12.3 ........................................................................................................152
   Rule 12.6 ........................................................................................................153
*Tallinn Manual on the International Law Applicable to Cyber
   Warfare* (2013)
   Rule 93 ...........................................................................................................101
      commentary paras 6, 7 ................................................................................102

Rule 94
    commentary paras 3, 4................................................................................102
    commentary para 5...................................................................................103
Rule 95
    commentary para 3...................................................................................105

# Introduction

Much is made in current security discourse of the importance of a rules-based international order.[1] *Jus ad bellum* – the branch of international law that governs when one state may use force against, or on the territory of, another – is at the heart of such an international order. For while contemporary international law admits that force may still be used between states, those circumstances are limited. They are also sharply disputed: the use of force is undoubtedly one of the most controversial areas of international law.[2]

This work is devoted to identifying the rules of international law that govern the interstate use of force. It is therefore more normative than discursive in style and tone, seeking to expound the law as it is (*lex lata*). It is not a work of political science, much less one that attempts to apply moral principles to any decision to use force (or to justify opposition to such a decision). Accordingly, where the law is not settled or may be changing (*lex ferenda*), this is made explicit.

For sure, *jus ad bellum* is a branch of international law that has come under pressure as never before in the modern, post-Second World War era. But reports of its demise are greatly exaggerated. In late 2018, one jurist wrote that international law 'cannot save the rules-based order', even asserting that the very search for the rules of law is an 'unattainable holy grail'.[3] Readers will decide for themselves whether they believe those claims. But if either is true, we live in dark times indeed.

---

[1] In late 2018, at a G20 summit in Buenos Aires, the leaders of the world's largest economies felt constrained to include in a joint communiqué a renewal of their commitment 'to work together to improve a rules-based international order that is capable of effectively responding to a rapidly changing world': 'G20 Leaders' Declaration: Building Consensus for Fair and Sustainable Development', 1 December 2018, para 5, bit.ly/37uUz3X. In early December 2019, celebrating 70 years as a military alliance, the leaders of NATO (North Atlantic Treaty Organization) members declared that 'the rule of law' was one of the values they shared and that 'State and non-state actors challenge the rules-based international order': Heads of State and Government participating in the meeting of the North Atlantic Council in London, 3–4 December 2019, 'London Declaration', NATO Press Release (2019) 115 (4 December 2019) para 3. See also, eg M Chalmers, 'Which Rules? Why There is No Single "Rules-Based International System"', RUSI Occasional Paper (London, Royal United Services Institute for Defence and Security Studies, April 2019), bit.ly/2OeuMWe.

[2] C Gray, *International Law and the Use of Force*, 4th edn (Oxford, Oxford University Press, 2018) 10.

[3] M Jorgensen, 'International Law Cannot Save the Rules-Based Order', *The Interpreter*, 18 December 2018, bit.ly/2OGm2HD.

# I.  War and the Foundations of International Law

Warfare has played a critical role in the history and evolution of humankind from time immemorial.[4] The first recorded war in history is said to have taken place in Mesopotamia in 2700 BCE between Sumer and Elam; the Sumerians defeated the Elamites and, it is chronicled, 'carried away as spoils the weapons of Elam'.[5] Certainly, though, warfare occurred much earlier, a fact to which the heavy fortification of the city of Jericho circa 7000 BCE attests.[6]

As Ian Brownlie observed, among ancient civilisations, 'even societies which had achieved a high degree of civilization were ready to resort to war against other societies and groups for reasons which were often very slight'.[7] Indeed, while thousands of wars would rage over the course of the subsequent millennia, laws, to the extent they sought to govern warfare at all, would serve rather to curb its worst excesses – applying prohibitions on the use of certain weapons or tactics *in bello* (during armed conflict) – but not, for the most part, calling into question the legality of war itself.

## A.  Religious Justification for War

Justification for warfare in antiquity tended to depict war as a manifestation of divine will. One commentator traces 'Just War' theory all the way back to fifth century BCE India and the *Mahabharata*.[8] In the Roman Republic, the focus was on legal formalities rather than legality: a *justum bellum* began with the approval of the college of *fetiales*: priests devoted to Jupiter, the God of the sky and of lightning.[9] It is true that the waging of war needed the approval (express or implied) of the gods.[10] That said, the theory of *jus bellum justum* is most closely associated with Christianity, and particularly the works of Augustine of Hippo

---

[4] R Wrangham and D Peterson, *Demonic Males: Apes and the Origins of Human Violence* (London, Bloomsbury, 1996).

[5] JJ Mark, 'War: Definition', *Ancient History Encyclopedia*, 2 September 2009, bit.ly/2qzIPsM.

[6] R O'Connell, *Of Arms and Men. A History of War, Weapons, and Aggression* (New York, Oxford University Press, 1990).

[7] I Brownlie, *International Law and the Use of Force by States* (Oxford, Oxford University Press, 1963) 3, citing R Numelin, *The Beginnings of Diplomacy* (New York, Copenhagen, 1950).

[8] E Harris, 'Pain but not Harm: Some Classical Resources toward a Hindu Just War Theory' in P Robinson (ed), *Just War in Comparative Perspective* (London, Routledge, 2016). In the case of ancient Egypt, Rory Cox argues that the creation of a pre-potent *jus ad bellum* doctrine – based on universal and absolutist claims to justice – hindered the development of *jus in bello* norms in Egyptian warfare: R Cox, 'Expanding the History of the Just War: The Ethics of War in Ancient Egypt' (2017) 61(2) *International Studies Quarterly* 371.

[9] Brownlie, *International Law and the Use of Force by States*, 4, citing inter alia C Phillipson, *The International Law and Custom of Ancient Greece and Rome* (London, Macmillan & Co, 1911) vol II, 180. See also vol I, 96–98.

[10] Brownlie, *International Law and the Use of Force by States*, 4. Cicero argued that no war was just unless it was wrought after a formal demand for satisfaction or warning was made and a formal declaration of war was made. MT Cicero, *De Officiis*, Book I, s XI, 34–36.

and Thomas Aquinas.[11] Augustine condemned wars of conquest,[12] but in his early fifth century CE work, *De civitate Dei contra paganos* ('The City of God against the Pagans'), he asserted that:

> They who have waged war in obedience to the divine command, or in conformity with His laws, have represented in their persons the public justice or the wisdom of government, and in this capacity have put to death wicked men; such persons have by no means violated the commandment, 'Thou shalt not kill.'

Writing eight centuries later, Thomas Aquinas built on Augustine's work and thought. In the second part of his *Summa Theologiae*, he delimited the conditions under which he believed war could be justified. First, a just war is one that is waged on behalf of God (though under the authority of a 'sovereign'). Second, war must be prosecuted for a legitimate purpose (such as to repair or punish an earlier evil) and not for self-gain. Third, the securing of peace must be a central motivation, even amid the violence inherent in warfare.[13] Writing in the fourteenth century, Giovanni da Legnano, Professor of Civil and Canon Law at the University of Bologna, would even laud war as a divine remedy for the diseases of the world.[14] In her *Book of Deeds of Arms and of Chivalry* of 1410, Christine da Pizan, the 'mother' of international law, agreed that wars could be waged (when authorised by God) in order to 'maintain law and justice'; to 'counteract evildoers who befoul, injure, and oppress the land and the people'; and to recover stolen lands. She further affirmed, though, that vengeance for 'any loss or damage incurred' and territorial acquisition by force were also permissible.[15] Writing in the early sixteenth century, however, Franciscus de Victoria, the intellectual founder of the natural law School of Salamanca, argued that, since warfare wrought such misery, only a serious wrong could justify recourse to war.[16] Forgivingly, though, he believed that a mistake made in good faith would exculpate a belligerent.[17]

Just war doctrine persists within contemporary Catholicism; most recently, it was enunciated during the reign of Pope Jean Paul II in the *Catechism of the Catholic Church*. The 1992 Catechism supports the right of lawful self-defence – once all peace efforts have failed – but sets four conditions for 'legitimate' defence by military force: the damage inflicted by the aggressor on a state must be lasting, grave, and certain; all other means of putting an end to it must have been shown to be impractical or ineffective; there must be serious prospects of success; and the

---

[11] This is so even though early Christianity before Augustine condemned all war. See, eg CJ Cadoux, *The Early Christian Attitude to War* (London, Headley Bros, 1919) 96ff.

[12] Brownlie, *International Law and the Use of Force by States*, 5.

[13] See, eg 'St Thomas Aquinas Discusses the Three Conditions for a Just War (1265–74)', *The Portable Library of Liberty*, 2013, bit.ly/2PSWvNO.

[14] Brownlie, *International Law and the Use of Force by States*, 7.

[15] F. Latty, 'Founding "Fathers" of International Law: Recognizing Christine de Pizan', *EJIL: Talk!*, Blog post published on 15 January 2019, bit.ly/3a8hH9h.

[16] ibid 9; see F de Victoria, *De Indis & De Jure Belli Relectiones*, a 1917 translation of a large part of the *Relectiones Theologicae* of 1557.

[17] Brownlie, *International Law and the Use of Force by States*, 9.

use of arms must not produce evils and disorders that are more grave than the evil to be eliminated.[18]

Early Islam also accepted the legality of war on certain grounds, notably in self-defence, but also later as punishment for apostasy.[19] A number of verses in the Quran give Muslims permission to go to war,[20] though as one author cautions, 'it is of utmost importance that these verses are understood in their original context'.[21] Qureshi claims that Islam 'has become the most misunderstood religion and Jihad the most misinterpreted activity of Islam in the post 9/11 era'.[22] *Jihad*, which means struggle, can be pursued by forceful and peaceful means. Its different forms include a personal struggle against one's own sinful desires (*Jihad bil Nafs*) as well as defensive *jihad* to protect Muslims from attack and offensive *jihad* in support of the oppressed (*Jihad bis Saif – jihad* with the sword, commonly known as *Qital*).[23]

Modern Islam encompasses a range of views on the use of force both between and within the Sunni and Shia sects. In contrast to Sunni doctrine, the Shia sect of Islam embraces *jihad* as the seventh pillar of Islam. Qureshi argues that the notion of *Jihad bis Saif* is 'more violent' in Shia thought than in Sunni doctrine, and includes, once the last Shia imam is revealed, a right to wage war on Sunnis to cause them to follow the Shia path.[24] In the Sunni sect of Islam, the Hanbali school of thought advocates use of force against only those who either threaten the spread of Islam or resist its path.[25] It is asserted that Osama Bin Laden, and more recently Islamic State adherents, misinterpreted the works of renowned Hanbali jurist, Ahmed Ibn Taymiyyah, to justify their attacks on civilians.[26]

Indeed, one of the main criticisms of Just War theory is that it is sometimes invoked to excuse violations of international law *in bello* on the basis of the transgressor's righteous aim of wreaking warfare.[27] Thus, in his landmark work, *Just and Unjust Wars*, Michael Walzer remarked that the argument 'fight all-out or not at all' is 'universal in the history of war'.[28] But he rejects this argument on the basis that

> we cannot forget that the rights violated for the sake of victory are genuine rights, deeply founded and in principle inviolable. And there is nothing asinine about this principle: the very lives of men and women are at stake. So the theory of war, when it is fully understood, poses a dilemma, which every theorist (though, fortunately, not every

---

[18] *Catechism of the Catholic Church* (1992) paras 2308, 2309, bit.ly/2AXYuYM.

[19] See, eg M Khadduri, *The Law of War and Peace in Islam* (London, Luzac & Co, 1940).

[20] SH Hashmi, 'War and Peace' in R Peters and P Bearman (eds), *Ashgate Research Companion to Islamic Law*, (London, Routledge, 2014) 194.

[21] WA Qureshi, *The Use of Force in Islam* (Islamabad, National Book Foundation, 2017) 91, citing WB Hallaq, *Sharia: Theory, Practice, Transformations* (Cambridge, Cambridge University Press, 2009) 524.

[22] Qureshi, *The Use of Force in Islam*, 43, citing SS Ali and J Rehman, 'The Concept of Jihad in Islamic International Law' (2005) I *Journal of Conflict and Security Law* 321.

[23] Qureshi, *The Use of Force in Islam*, 43–54.

[24] ibid 63–64.

[25] ibid 61, citing H Mutalib, *Islam in Malaysia: From Revivalism to Islamic State?* (Singapore, NUS Press, 1993) 72.

[26] Qureshi, *The Use of Force in Islam*, 62–63.

[27] Brownlie, *International Law and the Use of Force by States*, 406–07.

[28] M Walzer, *Just and Unjust Wars*, 2nd edn (London, Basic Books, 1992) 227.

soldier) must resolve as best he can. And no resolution is serious unless it recognizes the force of both *jus ad bellum* and *jus in bello.*[29]

## B. Secular International Law and Grotius' Law on War and Peace

Not until the seventeenth century CE would a systematic attempt be made to assess the legality of war other than under religious tenets. Alberico Gentili is credited with the development of 'a system of norms for state relations which was secular and legal in origin'.[30] His work of 1612, *De Iure Belli Libri Tres*, is a foundational text of historical *jus ad bellum*. Therein he materially expanded the notion of self-defence to cover pre-emptive attacks, advocating that: 'No one ought to wait to be struck, unless he is a fool.'[31] But Hugo de Groot (better known to the world as Grotius), not Gentili, is typically regarded as the 'father' of international law. In his *Law on War and Peace* of 1625, Grotius argued for the legitimacy of war under certain circumstances even though his masterpiece was written and published amid the ravaging of continental Europe by the Thirty Years' War in the Holy Roman Empire.[32] Drawing on the works of Gentili, da Legnano, and de Victoria, among others, he claimed that to use force where necessary was 'in no way contrary to the first principles of nature, since all animals are endowed by nature with strength, in order to protect and defend themselves'.[33]

There were, Grotius reasoned, just legal bases for the waging of war: self-defence, reparation for injury, and even punishment of an unjust act.[34] He cautioned, though, that it was 'proper' that sovereigns have 'the sole authority to devise and execute the operations of war'.[35] This stance on *jus ad bellum* would be reflected, at least partially, in the first international treaties of the modern world.

---

[29] ibid 228.

[30] Brownlie, *International Law and the Use of Force by States*, 11, citing GHJ Van der Molen, *Alberico Gentili and the Development of International Law* (Amsterdam, HJ Paris, 1937). In Theodor Meron's view, Gentili was an original, enlightened, and eloquent writer 'who has not been given as much credit as his works clearly deserve': T Meron, 'Common Rights of Mankind in Gentili, Grotius and Suarez' (1991) 85 *American Journal of International Law* 110, 116.

[31] For a brief but thoughtful essay on Gentili's contribution to international law, including *jus ad bellum*, see C Kenny, 'Alberico Gentili, De Jure Belli Libri Tres (1588–1599)', *Classics of Strategy and Diplomacy*, 7 July 2015, bit.ly/2L91CaR.

[32] Brownlie was critical of Grotius' work as being 'not original' and was rather dismissive of his conclusions as 'those of any writer of the era before probabilism'. He did, though, concede that Grotius 'properly receives great respect for his achievement in writing the first comprehensive and systematic treatise on the law of nations': Brownlie, *International Law and the Use of Force by States*, 13.

[33] H de Groot, *De Jure Belli ac Pacis* (1625) (trans AC Campbell, London, 1814) Book I, Ch 2, §I, bit.ly/3aDTmJo.

[34] See, eg C Kenny, 'Hugo Grotius, The Law of War and Peace (1625)', *Classics of Strategy and Diplomacy*, 27 July 2015, bit.ly/2Pm2rPQ.

[35] H Grotius, *De Jure Belli ac Pacis*, 1625 (trans AC Campbell, London, 1814) Book II, Ch2, §II and Ch 3, §IV, bit.ly/2DxuDcs.

# II. A History of the Regulation of War under International Law

## A. International Law and the 1648 Treaty of Westphalia

If Grotius was truly the father of international law, then the 1648 Treaty of Westphalia, a collection of peace agreements that nominally ended the Thirty Years' War as well as the Eighty Years' War between Spain and the Dutch Republic,[36] is justly viewed as the genesis of modern international law.[37] In jurisprudential terms, the Treaty of Westphalia holds particular significance for two of the principles espoused therein: respect for the territory of sovereign states and a concomitant duty of non-interference in domestic affairs. These are the legal cornerstones for the future outlawing of war, and the notion of sovereignty remains central to the rule of law on the international plane to this day, even though human rights and other branches of international law have more tightly circumscribed its outer frontiers.

Yet one must not exaggerate the respect for territorial integrity demanded by international law prior to the adoption of the 1945 Charter of the United Nations[38] (UN Charter). As James Crawford observes, in the practice of states in nineteenth-century Europe, 'the prevailing view' was that 'resort to war was an attribute of statehood' and further that 'conquest produced title'.[39]

## B. State Practice and the Exercise of Self-defence

Customary law governing lawful self-defence by a state is often said to derive from a diplomatic exchange between Great Britain and the United States that arose following the killing of two US citizens in an incident in 1837.[40] The Americans were part of a broader attack by Canadian rebels on British forces in Canada, which was at that time a British colony. After a nautical skirmish, British naval forces, which had crossed into the United States, sent the steamship *Caroline* over the Niagara Falls within US territory.[41] Under the so-called *Caroline* test, enunciated primarily in a letter dated 27 July 1842 from the US Secretary of State Daniel Webster to Baron Ashburton of Great Britain, there must exist 'a necessity' of

---

[36] R Cavendish, 'The Treaty of Westphalia' (1998) 48(10) *History Today* 1, bit.ly/2POh6Tr.

[37] G Heathcote, 'Feminist Perspectives on the Law on the Use of Force' in M Weller (ed), *The Oxford Handbook of the Use of Force in International Law* (Oxford, Oxford University Press, 2015) 127.

[38] Art 51 of the Charter of the United Nations; adopted at San Francisco, 26 June 1945; entered into force, 24 October 1945.

[39] J Crawford, *Brownlie's Principles of Public International Law*, 9th edn (Oxford, Oxford University Press, 2019) 717.

[40] See, eg the discussion in C Henderson, *The Use of Force and International Law* (Cambridge, Cambridge University Press, 2018) 226–27.

[41] A Clapham, *Brierly's Law of Nations*, 7th edn (Oxford, Oxford University Press, 2012) 468–69.

self-defence that is 'instant, overwhelming, leaving no choice of means, and no moment of deliberation'.

Much – indeed, too much – is made of the *Caroline* test as the basis for modern rules governing the 'inherent' right of states to self-defence codified in the UN Charter. It did not, as some claim, address pre-emptive self-defence given that hostilities were already underway,[42] and in any event the tenets of the modern concept of necessity in self-defence are substantially different. At best, it could describe the principles underpinning what Yoram Dinstein terms 'interceptive' self-defence, particularly when a massive first strike, such as one that involves the use of nuclear weapons, has just been launched.[43]

## C. The Hague Peace Conferences of 1899 and 1907

At the end of the nineteenth into the early twentieth century, as tensions mounted across Europe as well as in parts of Asia, the two Hague Peace Conferences sought to reduce armaments and restrict interstate use of force. In 1899, representatives of some two dozen of the states existing at the time[44] met, on the initiative of the Russian tsar, 'with the object of seeking the most effective means of ensuring to all peoples the benefits of a real and lasting peace, and, above all, of limiting the progressive development of existing armaments'.[45]

The First Hague Peace Conference adopted three conventions and several declarations (all treaties as the term is understood under international law). Most of the instruments agreed upon by the delegates concerned *jus in bello*. The 1899 Hague Convention I on the Pacific Settlement of International Disputes,[46] however, was an early treaty of *jus ad bellum*. It committed its states parties, whenever they were involved in a serious dispute between themselves, to call upon the good offices or mediation of friendly states before any 'appeal to arms'.[47] This obligation, though, applied only 'as far as circumstances allow'.[48]

---

[42] Y Dinstein, *War, Aggression and Self-defence*, 6th edn (Cambridge, Cambridge University Press, 2017) para 589.

[43] ibid paras 606–10; see also paras 652, 656, and 746–47.

[44] Austria-Hungary, Belgium, Bulgaria, China, Denmark, France, Germany, Greece, Iran, Italy, Japan, Luxembourg, Mexico, Montenegro, the Netherlands, Norway, Portugal, Romania, Russia, Serbia, Spain, Sweden, Switzerland, Thailand (then Siam), Turkey, UK, and the United States.

[45] Russian memorandum of 30 December 1898/11 January 1899. See International Committee of the Red Cross (ICRC), 'Final Act of the International Peace Conference. The Hague, 29 July 1899' (Geneva, ICRC, 2016), bit.ly/2Fa2ycF.

[46] Convention for the Pacific Settlement of International Disputes; adopted at The Hague, 29 July 1899; entered into force, 4 September 1900. The same language was included in the treaty's 1907 counterpart, which replaced the 1899 Convention.

[47] See Dinstein, *War, Aggression and Self-Defence*, para 228.

[48] 1899 Hague Convention I on the Pacific Settlement of International Disputes, Art II. The sentiment of 'strong desire', evinced in the first preambular paragraph of the 1899 Convention 'to concert for the maintenance of the general peace', would be reflected in the preamble to the UN Charter. In the sixth preambular paragraph, the peoples of the United Nations express the determination 'to unite our strength to maintain international peace and security'.

Given the limited progress achieved at the First Hague Peace Conference, diplomats agreed to convene a second. This was held in 1907, again in The Hague, this time with 44 participating states.[49] The Second Peace Conference adopted one treaty that instituted new rules on the use of force *ad bellum*: the 1907 Hague Convention III on the Opening of Hostilities. The Convention obliged its states parties not to initiate hostilities between themselves 'without previous and explicit warning, in the form either of a declaration of war, giving reasons, or of an ultimatum with a conditional declaration of war'.[50] Its negotiation had been prompted by the 1904 war between Russia and Japan – grandiloquently termed by some 'World War Zero'[51] – which erupted when Japan attacked the Russian navy at Port Arthur in Manchuria on 8 February 1904.[52] Japan's formal declaration of war against the Russian Empire was made on the day of the attack, but Russia's leaders did not receive notice of it until several hours after the attack had already begun.[53]

Although the 1907 Hague Convention III remains nominally in force today,[54] since the end of the Second World War *opinio juris* has dictated that this international legal obligation has fallen into desuetude.[55] Instead of a formalistic duty to declare war, an attack by one state on another without either prior UN Security Council authorisation or in legitimate response to an armed attack launched by the state now being assailed, with or without prior warning, will violate the rules of modern *jus ad bellum*. That said, there is, of course, no international legal bar to a declaration of war. Further, it remains accepted that no bellicose acts need be committed before a state of war exists between two (or more) states.[56]

---

[49] Argentina, Austria-Hungary, Belgium, Bolivia, Brazil, Bulgaria, Chile, China, Colombia, Cuba, Denmark, Dominican Republic, Ecuador, El Salvador, France, Germany, Greece, Guatemala, Haiti, Iran, Italy, Japan, Luxembourg, Mexico, Montenegro, the Netherlands, Nicaragua, Norway, Panama, Paraguay, Peru, Portugal, Romania, Russian Federation, Serbia, Spain, Sweden, Switzerland, Thailand (then Siam), Turkey, UK, United States, Uruguay, and Venezuela.

[50] Art 1 of the 1907 Hague Convention (III) Relative to the Opening of Hostilities; adopted at The Hague, 18 October 1907; entered into force, 26 January 1910.

[51] See, eg JW Steinberg, 'Was the Russo-Japanese War World War Zero?' (2008) 67(1) *The Russian Review* 1; JW Steinberg, 'Russo-Japanese War', *History*, 2018, bit.ly/2QA75GR.

[52] War as a legal construct has long been defined under international law in predominantly formalistic terms as one nation state declaring war on another. A century ago, the great publicist Arnold McNair asserted that war 'is a state or condition of affairs, not a mere series of acts of force': AD McNair, 'The Legal Meaning of War, and the Relation of War to Reprisals' (1925) 11 *Transactions of the Grotius Society* 29, 33, bit.ly/2JLQFIw. Lord McNair was a judge at the International Court of Justice and subsequently the first president of the European Court of Human Rights.

[53] D Schindler and J Toman, *The Laws of Armed Conflicts* (Dordrecht, Martinus Nijhoff, 1988) 57–59.

[54] The following 36 states are party to the Convention: Austria, Belarus, Belgium, Bolivia, Brazil, China, Denmark, El Salvador, Ethiopia, Fiji, Finland, France, Germany, Guatemala, Haiti, Hungary, Japan, Liberia, Luxembourg, Mexico, the Netherlands, Nicaragua, Norway, Panama, Poland, Portugal, Romania, Russia, South Africa, Spain, Sweden, Switzerland, Thailand (then Siam), Ukraine, UK, and the United States. South Africa was the last to adhere, in 1978.

[55] M Mancini, 'The Effects of a State of War or Armed Conflict' in Weller, *The Oxford Handbook of the Use of Force in International Law*, 997. Art 2 common to the four 1949 Geneva Conventions determines their application, inter alia, in 'all cases of declared war'. See, eg Art 2 of Convention (I) for the Amelioration of the Condition of the Wounded and Sick in Armed Forces in the Field; adopted at Geneva, 12 August 1949; entered into force, 21 October 1950.

[56] Mancini, 'The Effects of a State of War', 989.

# D. The 1919 Treaty of Versailles and the League of Nations

The Treaty of Versailles was 'the first peace treaty among sovereigns that broke with the tradition of silence over the justice of war'.[57] While it formally ended the First World War, its terms humiliated Germany,[58] imposing crippling economic penalties that sowed the seeds for the outbreak of the global conflagration that would formally begin 20 years later.[59] John Maynard Keynes, who had travelled to the Paris Peace Conference negotiating the Treaty as the British Treasury's chief representative, wrote to the British Prime Minister, David Lloyd George, informing him that he was resigning his post in protest of the impending 'devastation of Europe'. In *The Economic Consequences of the Peace*, published in December 1919, Keynes derided the Treaty of Versailles as a 'Carthaginian' peace, stating that:

> If we aim at the impoverishment of Central Europe, vengeance, I dare say, will not limp. Nothing can then delay for very long the forces of Reaction and the despairing convulsions of Revolution, before which the horrors of the later German war will fade into nothing, and which will destroy, whoever is victor, the civilisation and the progress of our generation.[60]

In stark contrast, Marshal Ferdinand Foch, the French commander (and, in the latter stages of the First World War, also the commander of all Allied Forces), thought the Treaty of Versailles too lenient on Germany. Yet he too offered a grim prophecy of the future. As the Treaty was being signed on 28 June 1919, he presciently declared: 'This is not a peace. It is an armistice for twenty years.'[61]

The peace conferences that negotiated the Treaty of Versailles also adopted the 1919 Covenant of the League of Nations, which included *ad bellum* provisions in a number of its articles. In particular, under Article 10, the League's members undertook

> to respect and preserve as against external aggression the territorial integrity and existing political independence of all Members of the League. In case of any such aggression or in case of any threat or danger of such aggression the Council shall advise upon the means by which this obligation shall be fulfilled.[62]

---

[57] R Lesaffer, 'From War as Sanction to the Sanction of War' in Weller, *The Oxford Handbook of the Use of Force in International Law*, 50.

[58] *The Times* reported in May 1919 that Ministerpräsident Philipp Scheidemann, the head of the German government, told the German Peace Commission in Berlin that Germany had 'drunk the last dregs of degradation': 'Enemy Tactics at Versailles', *The Times*, 10 May 1919, bit.ly/2JhahH1. A month later, Scheidemann resigned in protest at the harshness of the peace terms imposed on Germany.

[59] JM Keynes, *The Economic Consequences of the Peace. Collected Writings of JM Keynes* (Cambridge, Cambridge University Press, 1971) vol II, 23; Dinstein, *War, Aggression and Self-Defence*, paras 109 and 322.

[60] JM Keynes, *The Economic Consequences of the Peace* (reprinted by Freeland Press, 2017).

[61] W Murray and J Lacey, *The Making of Peace: Rulers, States, and the Aftermath of War* (New York, Cambridge University Press, 2009) 209.

[62] Art 10 of the Covenant of the League of Nations; adopted at Paris, 28 June 1919; entered into force, 10 January 1920 (hereinafter 1919 Covenant of the League of Nations).

This provision 'was perhaps the most revolutionary element in the Covenant'.[63] Brownlie refers to the intervention by Earl Curzon in the House of Lords on 3 July 1919, who averred that: 'Aggressive war, aiming at territorial aggrandisement or political advantage, is expressly forbidden under the guarantee of the members of the League'.[64]

The Covenant did not, though, even seek to outlaw all waging of war, focusing instead on efforts to prevent its outbreak by obliging states in dispute to pursue settlement by peaceful means. Article 12 stipulated a three-month 'cooling-off period' during which states could not initiate war; thereafter, such action would only be unlawful if the Council of the League agreed unanimously on the pacific actions to be taken. During the Manchurian crisis that began in 1931, state practice is taken to suggest that 'Article 10 was violated only if the attacking state formally annexed territory'.[65] The League of Nations was, though, the first permanent international organisation whose principal aim was to maintain world peace 'as well as the first attempt at a legal regime of collective security'.[66]

In the interregnum between the First World War and the Second World War, an 'immense number' of treaties provided for 'conciliation, arbitration, judicial settlement, commissions of inquiry, or other forms of peaceful settlement'.[67] The Permanent Court of International Justice (PCIJ), the forerunner to the International Court of Justice, was a non-mandatory mechanism empowered to adjudicate disputes between consenting states on the basis of international law.[68] Even though the PCIJ itself is long defunct, some of its rulings remain authoritative (or at least influential) statements of the law. In its judgment in the *Lotus* case, the Court held that a state is not permitted to exercise its power 'in any form' outside its territory unless a treaty or customary international law allows it to do so. This prohibition on the extraterritorial exercise of power would encompass recourse to the use of force.[69]

At the same time, international law does not prohibit a state 'from exercising jurisdiction in its own territory, in respect of any case which relates to acts which have taken place abroad, and in which it cannot rely on some permissive rule of international law'.[70] Moreover, in its earlier Advisory Opinion in the *Eastern Carelia* case, the Court had noted that it 'is well established in international law that no State can, without its consent, be compelled to submit its disputes with other States either to mediation or to arbitration, or to any other kind of pacific settlement'.[71]

---

[63] Brownlie, *International Law and the Use of Force by States*, 62.
[64] ibid; see also Statement of Earl Curzon of Kedleston, *Hansard*, HL Vol 35, §174 (3 July 2019), bit. ly/2XE9QhG.
[65] Brownlie, *International Law and the Use of Force by States*, 65.
[66] Henderson, *The Use of Force and International Law*, 14.
[67] Brownlie, *International Law and the Use of Force by States*, 67.
[68] 1919 Covenant of the League of Nations, Art 14.
[69] PCIJ, *SS Lotus (France v Turkey)*, Judgment, 7 September 1927, 18–19.
[70] ibid 19.
[71] PCIJ, *Status of the Eastern Carelia*, Advisory Opinion No 5, 23 July 1923, para 33, text of the Opinion at bit.ly/2QwnqvZ.

# E. The 1928 Kellogg–Briand Pact

Prior to the outbreak of the Second World War, the most significant treaty govern-ing *jus ad bellum* was the General Treaty for Renunciation of War as an Instrument of National Policy (more commonly known as the Kellogg–Briand Pact).[72] Indeed, owing to the importance of the Pact in prohibiting aggressive warfare, 1928 – the year of its adoption – has been described as a 'watershed date in the history of the legal regulation of the use of inter-State force'.[73] As has been remarked, the need for the Pact points to the 'limited character' of the restrictions on war in the Covenant of the League of Nations.[74]

The Pact comprises three articles, of which only two are substantive rules *ad bellum*.[75] In the first article, which condemns recourse to war as a 'solution of international controversies', states parties formally renounce its conduct 'as an instrument of national policy' in their mutual relations. The second article stipu-lates that purely 'pacific means' shall be 'sought' to settle 'all disputes or conflicts of whatever nature or of whatever origin they may be'.[76]

While emphasising its importance, Dinstein makes four criticisms of the Kellogg–Briand Pact. First, it did not address the right of self-defence (although formal notes were exchanged by a number of states in connection with the Pact's adoption, explicitly preserving this right).[77] Second, limits were not set on the legality of war as an instrument of international policy, such as one conducted 'for the maintenance of international law'.[78] Third, the abnegation of war did not extend to every state, since states parties were not precluded from waging war on those that did not adhere to the Pact. And fourth, forcible measures 'short of war' were not considered.[79] But perhaps graver still was the lack of a mechanism to enforce the Pact's provisions *contra bellum*.[80] An editorial in the *Manchester Guardian* that

---

[72] General Treaty for Renunciation of War as an Instrument of National Policy; adopted at Paris, 27 August 1928; entered into force, 24 July 1929. The Pact's name comes from reference to the French Foreign Minister Aristide Briand (1862–1932) and his US counterpart, Secretary of State Frank B Kellogg (1856–1937), both of whom were highly influential in its elaboration. See R Lesaffer, 'Kellogg–Briand Pact (1928)', *Max Planck Encyclopedia of Public International Law* (last updated October 2010), bit.ly/2YrjnEX.

[73] Dinstein, *War, Aggression and Self-Defence*, 87, para 236.

[74] Brownlie, *International Law and the Use of Force by States*, 57. Less persuasively, Brownlie also claimed that the Pact 'simply complemented the Covenant and continued a development inherent in it'.

[75] The third article pertains only to the treaty's entry into force.

[76] As Brownlie observes, the wording of the provisions suggests that the nature of the duty is to seek but not necessarily to settle disputes peacefully. Brownlie, *International Law and the Use of Force by States*, 90.

[77] Henderson, *The Use of Force and International Law*, 15. While the US Senate ratified the Pact by a vote of 85 to 1, it did so only after insisting on a reservation whereby US participation did not limit its right to self-defence (nor require it to act against adherents that violated the Pact's provisions): 'The Kellogg–Briand Pact, 1928', Milestones in the History of US Foreign Relations, Office of the Historian, US Department of State, bit.ly/2DuSIAr.

[78] H Kelsen, *Principles of International Law* (New York, Rinehart & Co, 1952) 43.

[79] Dinstein, *War, Aggression and Self-Defence*, para 238.

[80] N Schrijver, 'The Ban on the Use of Force in the UN Charter' in Weller, *The Oxford Handbook of the Use of Force in International Law*, 468. According to Brownlie, however, 'Whether or not this is a defect in the instrument, the argument is a *non sequitur*, many treaties or other sources of law provide no sanctions': Brownlie, *International Law and the Use of Force by States*, 83.

marked the signature of the Pact observed that: 'The Pact does not automatically turn the world into a Garden of Eden. It does not even take us automatically out of Bedlam.'[81]

Nonetheless, at the outbreak of the Second World War, most states of the day had adhered to the Kellogg–Briand Pact;[82] among those generally recognised as states at the time, Argentina, Bolivia, El Salvador, and Uruguay were not party.[83] Brownlie acknowledges that it can be argued that a comprehensive prohibition on the use of force other than in self-defence had not been conclusively established by 1939.[84] But he concludes that state practice between 1920 and 1945 – and more particularly since 1928 – provides 'adequate evidence' that custom had evolved to outlaw aggressive war (meaning the use of force other than in self-defence and for an unlawful purpose, such as the annexation of foreign lands).[85]

That much may well be true. But serious doubts persevere as to whether the Pact (or customary international law) had criminalised aggression by 1939.[86] In 1927, the Assembly of League of Nations had affirmed, in a resolution adopted unanimously, that 'all wars of aggression are, and shall always be, prohibited', but a reference to a war of aggression as an international crime was tucked away in the preamble.[87] Nonetheless, at the post-war Nuremburg trials, the Kellogg–Briand Pact, adopted a year after the resolution, would be used as the primary international

---

[81] Reproduced in 'The Kellogg–Briand Pact: World Treaty to Outlaw War – Archive, 1928', *The Guardian*, 14 June 2018, bit.ly/2STqP9T.

[82] Afghanistan, Albania, Australia, Austria, Belgium, British India, Bulgaria, Canada, Chile, China, Costa Rica, Cuba, Czechoslovakia, Danzig, Denmark, Dominican Republic, Egypt, Estonia, Ethiopia, Finland, France, Germany, Greece, Honduras, Guatemala, Hungary, Iceland, the Irish Free State, Italy, Japan, Latvia, Liberia, Lithuania, Luxembourg, the Netherlands, New Zealand, Nicaragua, Norway, Panama, Peru, Persia, Poland, Portugal, Romania, Russia, the Kingdom of the Serbs, Croats, and Slovenes, Siam, South Africa, Spain, Sweden, Switzerland, Turkey, the UK, the United States, and Venezuela.

[83] M Frostad, 'The Kellogg–Briand Pact – Nearing the 90th Anniversary for the Outlawing of War' (Kellogg College Oxford, 3 July 2017), bit.ly/2DbrRbM. Brownlie also refers to states not party to the Pact – San Marino, Nepal, and Yemen – though he concedes that the latter two took little part in international life at that time: Brownlie, *International Law and the Use of Force by States*, 75, fn 5.

[84] As he noted, the Nuremberg Tribunal found that peaceful invasion following a threat of force did not constitute aggression. Thus, the invasion of Austria in March 1938 (the Anschluss) and the invasion of Czechoslovakia in March 1939 were not deemed to be aggressive wars (though they were held to be part of Germany's common plan for aggression). Brownlie, *International Law and the Use of Force by States*, 211.

[85] ibid 66, 107, 110.

[86] R Cryer, H Friman, D Robinson, and E Wilmshurst, *An Introduction to International Criminal Law and Procedure*, 2nd edn (Cambridge, Cambridge University Press, 2010) 112–13; T Taylor, *The Anatomy of the Nuremberg Trials*, Bloomsbury, London, 1993, 581.

[87] Moreover, the Polish representative to the League of Nations observed that the resolution would not constitute a juridical instrument, but was more one of 'moral and educational' significance: Brownlie, *International Law and the Use of Force by States*, 72. A Draft Treaty of Mutual Assistance, in which the High Contracting Parties 'solemnly declare[d]' in Article I, that 'aggressive war is an international crime', was proffered to members of the League of Nations in 1923 by the Commission on Armaments, but it was not approved and never entered into force. The rejection of the draft treaty by the League's Assembly is said to have come after objections from Great Britain, which feared that it would be called upon to commit troops to respond to aggression, which were needed to defend the Empire.

legal basis for prosecuting senior Nazi figures for the waging by Germany of a war of aggression (a 'crime against peace').

The failure of the Kellogg–Briand Pact to prevent the Second World War, including the 55 million or more deaths that would occur as a result, demonstrates that its practical flaws were critical.[88] Ironically (in light of what would follow a decade later), Frank Kellogg, the US Secretary of State, was awarded the Nobel Peace Prize in 1929 for his work on the Pact.[89] The Pact remains nominally in force today,[90] with Barbados acceding in 1971, the last state to do so, but as binding international law its tenets have been comprehensively superseded by the *ad bellum* provisions of the UN Charter.

## F. The 1933 Montevideo Convention on Rights and Duties of States

Five years after the adoption of the Kellogg–Briand Pact, the Montevideo Convention on Rights and Duties of States presaged certain provisions in the UN Charter, providing that: 'The territory of a state is inviolable and may not be the object of military occupation nor of other measures of force imposed by another state directly or indirectly or for any motive whatever even temporarily.'[91] It was further stipulated that states parties

> definitely establish as the rule of their conduct the precise obligation not to recognize territorial acquisitions or special advantages which have been obtained by force whether this consists in the employment of arms, in threatening diplomatic representations, or in any other effective coercive measure.[92]

## III. *Jus ad bellum* and Contemporary International Law

As chapter one of this book describes in more detail, the UN Charter is the foundational treaty governing *jus ad bellum* in the modern world. Indeed, Article 1 of the

---

[88] For a passionate defence of the virtues of the Pact, see the first few pages of David Koplow's 2014 article. Therein he argues colourfully that it has had a 'bum rap': DA Koplow, 'Nuclear Kellogg–Briand Pact: Proposing a Treaty for the Renunciation of Nuclear Wars as an Instrument of National Policy' (2014–15) 42 *Syracuse Journal of International Law and Commerce* 123.

[89] Frostad, 'The Kellogg–Briand Pact – Nearing the 90th Anniversary'.

[90] The UK Foreign and Commonwealth Office held the Pact to be in force as recently as 2013: Frostad, 'The Kellogg–Briand Pact – Nearing the 90th Anniversary'. See also Lesaffer, 'Kellogg–Briand Pact (1928)'.

[91] Art 11 of the Convention on Rights and Duties of States; signed at Montevideo, 26 December 1933; entered into force, 26 December 1934.

[92] ibid.

Charter determines that the suppression of acts of aggression or other breaches of the peace are among the explicit purposes of the United Nations. Under Article 2(3), all UN member states are obligated 'to settle their international disputes by peaceful means in such a manner that international peace and security, and justice, are not endangered'.[93] Article 2(4) then institutes a corresponding, general prohibition on the interstate use of force.[94] This rule is the cornerstone both of the UN Charter and of modern *jus ad bellum*.[95]

Chapter VII of the Charter, which is entitled 'Action with respect to threats to the peace, breaches of the peace, and acts of aggression', redresses the two greatest failings of the Kellogg–Briand Pact. First, Article 51 overtly protects the 'inherent' right of states under customary law to take forcible action in self-defence when it suffers an 'armed attack'. Second, Article 42 empowers the UN Security Council to take 'such action by air, sea, or land forces as may be necessary to maintain or restore international peace and security'. These two provisions are the lawful exceptions to the general prohibition on interstate use of force.

Aside from treaty law, the other primary sources of international law (and subsidiary means for determining rules of international law binding on the world's 197 states[96]) are set out in Article 38 of the 1945 Statute of the International Court of Justice. Each is also relevant to contemporary *jus ad bellum*. Customary international law has been noted in relation to the right of self-defence where it continues to operate in parallel with treaty law. Among general principles of law (the third primary source of international law, along with treaty and custom),[97] the duty

---

[93] Ch VI of the UN Charter, entitled Pacific Settlement of Disputes, reiterates the duty on member states 'to seek a solution by negotiation, enquiry, mediation, conciliation, arbitration, judicial settlement, resort to regional agencies or arrangements, or other peaceful means of their own choice' to any dispute that is likely to endanger international peace and security: UN Charter, Art 33(1). The International Court of Justice is cited as having a primary role in settling legal disputes: UN Charter, Art 36(3).

[94] As Christine Gray observes, the drafters of the UN Charter deliberately chose to use the wider term 'use of force' than 'war' in Art 2(4): Gray, *International Law and the Use of Force*, 9.

[95] ICJ, *Case Concerning Armed Activities on the Territory of the Congo (Democratic Republic of Congo v Rwanda)*, Judgment, 19 December 2005, para 148.

[96] As recognised by the UN Secretary-General in his capacity as depositary of more than 500 multilateral treaties. See 'Depositary of Treaties', UN Treaty Collection, bit.ly/2S6xzku. Many global treaties concluded today use the 'all states' formula for adherence. For the UN Secretary-General, this currently allows all 193 UN member states to either sign and ratify or accede along with the two UN observer states (Holy See and Palestine) and two other states (Cook Islands and Niue), for a total of 197 states. The Sahrawi Arab Democratic Republic is a member of the African Union (and therefore recognised by the African Union as a state), but is not similarly accepted as such by the UN Secretary-General. In 2015, Kosovo fell three votes short of the two-thirds majority it needed in a vote in the General Assembly of the UN Educational, Scientific and Cultural Organization (UNESCO) to be able to join that organisation. If it had reached the requisite threshold, it would have been recognised by the UN Secretary-General as the world's 198th state. For a discussion of the constitutive versus declaratory views on recognition of statehood, see BR Roth, *Governmental Illegitimacy in International Law* (Oxford, Oxford University Press, 2000) ch 5.

[97] Since the adoption of the Statute, the ICJ has also held that a unilateral declaration by a state can also be a source of an international legal rule, albeit only in exceptional circumstances: ICJ, *Nuclear Tests Case (New Zealand v France)*, Judgment, 20 December 1974, paras 45–49.

to seek pacific resolution of a dispute before any resort to armed force may be considered a strong contender.

Both subsidiary means for the determination of rules of law[98] have influenced *ad bellum* rules. Judicial decisions have, in particular, delineated the contours of and conditions for the lawful exercise of self-defence, while the views of the most highly qualified publicists of the various nations (ie public international lawyers) have addressed all aspects of *jus ad bellum*. Finally, soft law (eg politically binding instruments), such as the Declaration on Principles of International Law on Friendly Relations among States, endorsed by the UN General Assembly in 1970,[99] as well as other pertinent UN General Assembly resolutions, contains norms that are nowadays reflective of customary international law.

---

[98] 1945 Statute of the ICJ, Art 38(1)(d).

[99] UN General Assembly Resolution 2625 (XXV), 'Declaration on Principles of International Law concerning Friendly Relations and Co-operation among States in accordance with the Charter of the United Nations'; adopted without a vote, 24 October 1970.

# 1

# The General Prohibition
# on the Use of Force

## I. Introduction

In the preamble to the 1945 Charter of the United Nations[1] (UN Charter), the peoples of the United Nations agreed 'to ensure, by the acceptance of principles and the institution of methods, that armed force shall not be used, save in the common interest'.[2] The bedrock of what is occasionally termed the 'Universal Security System'[3] is thus a general prohibition on the use of force by one state against another. This prohibition, which was instituted under Article 2(4) of the UN Charter, was, at the time, a progressive development of *jus ad bellum*. It reads in full as follows:

> All Members shall refrain in their international relations from the threat or use of force against the territorial integrity or political independence of any state, or in any other manner inconsistent with the Purposes of the United Nations.

Within 'the most solemn pact of peace in history',[4] Article 2(4) is the cornerstone of contemporary *jus ad bellum*. Robert Kolb describes the emergence of the prohibition on the use of force as the 'beginning of modern international law', though he traces it back to the League of Nations.[5] The sweeping prohibition of the use or threat of force by one state against another is underpinned by the duty of non-intervention. This principle of international law dictates that no state shall interfere in the affairs of another, in particular (but not only) through the medium

---

[1] Charter of the United Nations; adopted at San Francisco, 26 June 1945; entered into force, 24 October 1945.

[2] UN Charter, seventh preambular paragraph.

[3] M Chalmers, 'Which Rules? Why There is No Single "Rules-Based International System"', RUSI Occasional Paper (London, Royal United Services Institute for Defence and Security Studies, April 2019) 3, bit.ly/2OeuMWe.

[4] UN General Assembly Resolution 290 (IV) ('Essentials of Peace'), adopted on 1 December 1949 by 53 votes to 5 with 1 abstention.

[5] R Kolb, *International Law on the Maintenance of Peace: Jus Contra Bellum* (Cheltenham, Edward Elgar, 2019), 321–22.

of armed intervention.[6] As expressed in the 1970 Declaration on the Principles of International Law:

> No State or group of States has the right to intervene, directly or indirectly, for any reason whatever, in the internal or external affairs of any other State. Consequently, armed intervention and all other forms of interference or attempted threats against the personality of the State or against its political, economic, and cultural elements, are in violation of international law.[7]

Citing the 1970 Declaration in its 1986 judgment on the merits in the *Nicaragua* case, the International Court of Justice (ICJ) considered that the principle of non-intervention is 'part and parcel of customary international law'.[8] This is so even though, as the Court acknowledged, 'examples of trespass against this principle are not infrequent'.[9] These instances of trespass include non-forcible interference in other states. For example, if it is true that Russia hacked into the Democratic Party computer systems during the 2016 US presidential election with a view to influencing the outcome of that election,[10] this would amount to unlawful intervention in the US political system.[11] It would not, though, be an instance of unlawful use of force.

# II. The Status of the Prohibition under International Law

Before addressing their content in detail, the legal status of the two core prohibitions *ad bellum* is considered in turn. First, the international legal significance of

---

[6] As Louise Doswald-Beck affirmed, 'the doctrine of belligerency may well have fallen into desuetude' and this 'old formulation has been totally replaced by the new law of non-intervention in internal affairs': L Doswald-Beck, 'The Legal Validity of Military Intervention by Invitation of the Government' (1985) 56(1) *British Yearbook of International Law* 189, 252.

[7] The Declaration on Principles of International Law concerning Friendly Relations and Co-operation among States, annexed to UN General Assembly Resolution 2625, adopted by the UN General Assembly without a vote on 24 October 1970. For similar language, see inter alia Art 18 of the 1948 Charter of the Organization of American States; signed at Bogotá, 30 April 1948; entered into force, 13 December 1951.

[8] ICJ, *Case Concerning Military and Paramilitary Activities in and against Nicaragua (Nicaragua v United States of America)*, Judgment (Merits), 27 June 1986, para 202 (hereinafter ICJ, *Nicaragua* judgment).

[9] ibid.

[10] In January 2017, the US Central Intelligence Agency, the Federal Bureau of Investigation, and the National Security Agency jointly agreed, with 'high confidence', that Russian state agents, under orders from President Vladimir Putin, conducted a sophisticated campaign to influence the election. 'Assessing Russian Activities and Intentions in Recent US Elections', Doc ICA 2017-01D, 6 January 2017, Key Judgments, in Office of the Director of National Intelligence, 'Background to "Assessing Russian Activities and Intentions in Recent US Elections": The Analytic Process and Cyber Incident Attribution' (Washington DC, 6 January 2017) ii, bit.ly/2Lx1SAm. See also J Masters, 'Russia, Trump, and the 2016 US Election', Council on Foreign Relations, United States (last updated 26 February 2018), on.cfr.org/2M1xOws.

[11] C Henderson, *The Use of Force and International Law* (Cambridge, Cambridge University Press, 2018) 52.

the prohibition of interstate use of force is determined. Then the normative value of the prohibition on the threat of force by one state against another is assessed. The former – the general outlawing of interstate use of force – is a peremptory norm of international law. The prohibition on the threat of force may also be a customary norm, but it does not similarly enjoy the status of *jus cogens*.

## A. The International Legal Status of the Prohibition on the Use of Force

First and foremost, the general prohibition on the interstate use of force is a rule that applies *in toto* as a matter to treaty law to all UN member states. The substantive terms of the prohibition in Article 2(4) of the UN Charter are also reflected in the 1982 UN Convention on the Law of the Sea.[12] The prohibition is further reaffirmed in the preamble to the 1998 Rome Statute of the International Criminal Court.[13] These two global treaties, wherein no reservations are possible to the relevant provisions,[14] have been widely ratified by states.[15]

In its judgment on the merits in the *Nicaragua* case, the ICJ held that the prohibition on the use of force set out in Article 2(4) of the UN Charter had already become a rule of customary international law prior to 1986.[16] It adduced as evidence the practice of states in adopting without a vote the 1970 Declaration on Principles of International Law.[17] In their pleadings in the *Nicaragua* case, both Nicaragua and the United States asserted that the prohibition was of a customary nature. The customary status of the prohibition is accepted by other states and only exceptionally does any publicist contest this.[18] Moreover, in proclaiming the general prohibition on use of force as a 'principle' of international law, Principle 1 of the 1970 Declaration on the Principles of International Law broadens its scope to encompass the actions of all states, not merely those of UN members.

But such is the fundamental nature of the general prohibition on the use of force, it is also widely considered to be a *jus cogens* norm. In the 1969 Vienna Convention on the Law of Treaties, a *jus cogens* norm is described as one that is 'accepted and recognized by the international community of States as a whole as a norm from which no derogation is permitted and which can be modified only

---

[12] Art 301 of the UN Convention on the Law of the Sea; adopted at Montego Bay, 10 December 1982; entered into force, 16 November 1994 (UNCLOS).

[13] Rome Statute of the International Criminal Court; adopted at Rome, 17 July 1998; entered into force, 1 July 2002 (ICC Statute), seventh preambular paragraph.

[14] UNCLOS, Art 309; ICC Statute, Art 120.

[15] As at 1 May 2020, 168 states were party to UNCLOS and 123 states were party to the ICC Statute.

[16] ICJ, *Nicaragua* judgment, para 188.

[17] ibid.

[18] Most notably, T Franck: 'Who Killed Article 2(4)? or: Changing Norms Governing the Use of Force by States' (1970) 64(5) *American Journal of International Law* 809. Franck returned to the charge after the United States-led invasion of Iraq: 'What Happens Now? The United Nations After Iraq' (2003) 97(3) *American Journal of International Law* 607.

by a subsequent norm of general international law having the same character'.[19] A peremptory norm 'enjoys a higher rank in the international hierarchy than treaty law and even "ordinary" customary rules', as the International Criminal Tribunal for the former Yugoslavia (ICTY) has since remarked.[20]

That the prohibition is indeed a peremptory norm of international law appears, implicitly, to be the position of the ICJ. In its judgment in the *Nicaragua* case, the Court cited the view of the International Law Commission (ILC), in the course of the ILC's work on the codification of the law of treaties, that 'the law of the Charter concerning the prohibition of the use of force in itself constitutes a conspicuous example of a rule in international law having the character of *jus cogens*'.[21] This was also the position of the two litigants in the *Nicaragua* case: Nicaragua and the United States.[22] It is also the overt position of most leading publicists.[23]

One of the consequences of a customary norm having the character of *jus cogens* is that any treaty which, at the time of the treaty's conclusion, conflicts with such a norm is void.[24] Thus, for instance, states could not contract under a military alliance to use armed force against any state that instituted a trade embargo against one of its members. Such a treaty would be void *ab initio*. In addition, the ILC's 2001 'Draft Articles on the Law of State Responsibility for Internationally Wrongful Acts' stipulates that countermeasures shall not affect the 'obligation to refrain from the threat or use of force as embodied in the Charter of the United Nations'.[25] As a rule of customary international law, this precludes a state that is

---

[19] Art 53 of the Vienna Convention on the Law of Treaties; adopted at Vienna, 23 May 1969; entered into force, 27 January 1980 (VCLT). As at 1 May 2020, only 116 states were party to the Vienna Convention, although most of its provisions are today reflective of customary law. This includes the provisions in Art 53, which contains the 'basic elements of *jus cogens*'. ILC, 'First Report on *Jus Cogens* by Dire Tladi, Special Rapporteur', UN doc A/CN.4/693 (8 March 2016) para 61.

[20] ICTY, Case No IT-95-17/1-T *Prosecutor v Anto Furundžija*, Judgment, 10 December 1998, para 153.

[21] ICJ, *Nicaragua* judgment, para 190, citing para 1 of the commentary of the Commission to Art 50 of its Draft Articles on the Law of Treaties, *ILC Yearbook*, 1966-II, 247.

[22] ICJ, *Nicaragua* judgment, para 190.

[23] See, in particular, ICJ, *Nicaragua* judgment, Separate Opinion of ICJ President Nagendra Singh, 153; *Case Concerning Oil Platforms (Islamic Republic of Iran v United States of America)*, Judgment (Merits), 6 November 2003 (hereinafter ICJ, *Oil Platforms* judgment), Separate Opinion of Bruno Simma, para 6; *Oil Platforms* judgment, Separate Opinion of Pieter Kooijmans, para 46; Y Dinstein, *War, Aggression and Self-defence*, 6th edn (Cambridge, Cambridge University Press, 2017) para 302; A Orakhelashvili, *Akehurst's Modern Introduction to International Law*, 8th edn (London, Routledge, 2018) 54; O Corten, *The Law Against War* (Oxford, Hart Publishing, 2010) 200*ff*. André de Hoogh 'assumed' that the prohibition on the use of armed forces is a *jus cogens* norm: A de Hoogh, 'Jus Cogens and Armed Force' in M Weller (ed), *The Oxford Handbook of the Use of Force in International Law* (Oxford, Oxford University Press, 2015) 1164. Christine Gray does not pronounce directly on the matter with her own view, but does observe that 'States and commentators generally agree that the prohibition is not only a treaty obligation but also customary law and even *ius cogens*': C Gray, *International Law and the Use of Force*, 4th edn (Oxford, Oxford University Press, 2018) 32. James Green is one of the few publicists who question the finding of *jus cogens* in relation to the prohibition on the use of force: JA Green, 'Questioning the Peremptory Status of the Prohibition of the Use of Force' (2011) 32 *Michigan Journal of International Law* 215.

[24] VCLT, Art 53.

[25] *Draft Articles on Responsibility of States for Internationally Wrongful Acts, with commentaries*, UN doc A/56/10 (New York, 2001), Art 50(1)(a).

the object of a use of force by another state, where that does not amount to an armed attack, from itself using force in response. A lawful countermeasure must be either pacific in nature or of such limited extent as to not violate the tenets of Article 2(4).[26]

## B. The International Legal Status of the Prohibition on the Threat of Force

Whether the prohibition on the interstate threat of force is a customary rule is not settled, but it is assuredly not a peremptory norm of international law. Indeed, a number of leading publicists have argued that the threat of force may even play a valuable role in the settlement of disputes.[27]

The ICJ has not explicitly affirmed that the treaty prohibition on the threat of force is of a customary nature, though at one point in its judgment in 1986 in the *Nicaragua* case it implied that this might be the case.[28] There is, though, relatively little evidence of threats by one state to use force against another being treated as breaches of a customary rule of international law, especially in recent years.[29] That said, the ICJ also noted its judgment in the *Nicaragua* case that it

> does not consider that, for a rule to be established as customary, the corresponding practice must be in absolutely rigorous conformity with the rule. In order to deduce the existence of customary rules, the Court deems it sufficient that the conduct of States should, in general, be consistent with such rules, and that instances of State conduct inconsistent with a given rule should generally have been treated as breaches of that rule, not as indications of the recognition of a new rule.[30]

In fact, to the extent that, under the UN Charter at least, threats to use unlawful force are illegal, the prohibition appears to be widely flouted and rarely decried.[31]

---

[26] For possible examples of such a measure, see the discussion below on the minimum threshold of force under the prohibition on use of force codified in Art 2(4) of the UN Charter.

[27] J Crawford, *Brownlie's Principles of Public International Law*, 9th edn (Oxford, Oxford University Press, 2019) 717, citing A Randelzhofer and O Dörr, 'Article 2(4)' in B Simma, D-E Khan, G Nolte and A Paulus (eds), *The Charter of the United Nations: A Commentary*, 3rd edn (Oxford, Oxford University Press, 2012) vol I, 218. Kolb observes that 'international practice is relatively tolerant with regard to threats in general'. Kolb, *International Law on the Maintenance of Peace: Jus Contra Bellum*, 333.

[28] ICJ, *Nicaragua* judgment, para 227; see also N Stürchler, *The Threat of Force in International Law* (Cambridge, Cambridge University Press, 2007) 62–63.

[29] For details of a number of UN Security Council resolutions in 1964–85 that addressed threats of force, see A Lagerwall, 'Threats of and Actual Military Strikes against Syria – 2013 and 2017' in T Ruys and O Corten with A Hofer (eds), *The Use of Force in International Law: A Case-Based Approach* (Oxford, Oxford University Press, 2018) 846. In only one of the six cited resolutions, however, did the Council effectively condemn unlawful threats as violations of international law. In its Resolution 573 of 4 October 1985, the Security Council demanded 'that Israel refrain from perpetrating such acts of aggression or from threatening to do so': UN Security Council Resolution 573 (1985), adopted on 4 October 1985 by 14 votes to 0, with 1 abstention (United States) para 2. See also R Sadurska, 'Threats of Force' (1988) 82(2) *American Journal of International Law* 239, 246.

[30] ICJ, *Nicaragua* judgment, para 186.

[31] See, eg D Kritsiotis, 'Close Encounters of a Sovereign Kind' (2009) 20(2) *European Journal of International Law* 299.

Over the last few years, for example, the United States and the Democratic People's Republic of Korea (DPRK) have traded threats to use nuclear weapons against each other in circumstances that are unlawful, but without subsequent legal or political censure. In March 2016, in reaction to the initiation of a US–South Korean military exercise, the DPRK threatened a 'pre-emptive nuclear strike of justice' and to turn Washington and Seoul into 'flames and ashes'.[32] Such a use of force would amount to the commission of a number of international crimes, including but not only aggression. In August 2017, US President Donald Trump contended that the DPRK 'best not make any more threats to the United States', adding that if it does so it 'will be met with fire and fury and frankly power, the likes of which this world has never seen before'.[33] This statement can be interpreted as the United States threatening to use nuclear and conventional weapons against the DPRK in the absence of a prior armed attack. Another threatening statement by the DPRK in 2017, announced via the government news agency, called for the 'four islands' of the Japanese archipelago to be 'sunken into the sea by the nuclear bomb of Juche'.[34]

In its 2007 Award in the Arbitration between Guyana and Suriname,[35] a case which concerned allegedly unlawful threats of force in the maritime environment, the Permanent Court of Arbitration did not need to address the customary nature or otherwise of the prohibition as it could rely on the rule contained within the UN Charter. In his 2007 work on the threat of force, Nikolas Stürchler affirmed that 'the legal regime governing threats of force still eludes rigid legal taxonomy'.[36] That said, the prohibition of the threat of force 'against the territorial integrity or political independence of any state, or in any other manner inconsistent with the Purposes of the United Nations', is not a norm of *jus cogens*.[37]

# III. The Scope and Content of the Prohibition on the Use of Force

On the basis that the general prohibition on interstate use of force, as codified in Article 2(4) of the UN Charter, is a peremptory norm of international law, but that the corresponding prohibition on the threat of force is not, both the scope and content of the rules are discussed below. The discussion considers what conduct

---

[32] Reported by Associated Press, 'North Korea Threatens to Reduce US and South Korea to "flames and ash"', *The Guardian*, 7 March 2016, bit.ly/2FNlzi6.

[33] See, eg P Baker and C Sang-Hun, 'Trump Threatens "Fire and Fury" against North Korea if It Endangers US', *New York Times*, 8 August 2017, bit.ly/2Ew8ooq.

[34] Juche is the ideology of self-reliance pioneered by Kim Il-sung, the country's founder and the grandfather of the current leader, Kim Jong-un.

[35] Permanent Court of Arbitration, *Arbitral Tribunal Constituted Pursuant to Article 287, and in Accordance with Annex VII, of the United Nations Convention on the Law of the Sea in the Matter of an Arbitration Between Guyana and Suriname*, Award of the Arbitral Tribunal, The Hague, 17 September 2007.

[36] Stürchler, *The Threat of Force in International Law*, 92.

[37] Dinstein, *War, Aggression and Self-defence*, para 302.

amounts to a use of force, the minimum threshold of force encompassed by the prohibition, and what constitutes an unlawful threat of force.

## A. The Nature of Force

The general prohibition on the use of force is limited to curbing a use of *armed* force.[38] Economic measures by one state against another, including trade embargoes and the unlawful imposition of tariffs upon foreign goods, do not constitute a prohibited use of force.[39] Even the provision of funds to an unauthorised non-state actor in another state does not violate the general prohibition on interstate use of force (though it is a form of unlawful intervention).[40]

Force may be employed from or on land, from or at sea, from or in the air, from or in space, and from or in cyberspace. The notion of force is not limited in scope to the use of weapons and ammunition that act through the application of kinetic energy, such as bullets, bombs, and missiles. Other weapons also deliver force: by transmitting electricity, diffusing toxic chemicals, biological agents, or sound, or directing electromagnetic energy.[41] The term 'weapon' also encompasses cyber operations that damage or interrupt the normal operation of computer systems and networks. This includes – but is not limited to – when those operations result in physical harm to people or objects.[42] Similarly, a naval blockade may cause no physical damage but it is clearly a use of force. Under the 1974 Definition of Aggression, for instance, it is explicit that the blockade of the ports or coasts of one state by the armed forces of another may constitute an act of aggression.[43]

In contrast, unauthorised reconnaissance flights and other unauthorised penetration of airspace by a military aircraft or of territorial waters by a military vessel are better considered per se as a threat of force than an actual use of force.[44] That said, as Brownlie recalled in 1963, on earlier occasions such acts had been

---

[38] ibid para 247.

[39] Crawford, *Brownlie's Principles of Public International Law*, 717.

[40] 'In particular, the Court considers that the mere supply of funds to the *contras*, while undoubtedly an act of intervention in the internal affairs of Nicaragua, … does not in itself amount to a use of force': ICJ, *Nicaragua* judgment, para 228.

[41] S Casey-Maslen (ed), *Weapons Under International Human Rights Law* (Cambridge, Cambridge University Press, 2014) xx.

[42] A cyber attack that precluded the operation of another state's missile defences, for instance, would amount to a use of force, even though no physical damage occurred to the weapons themselves. See also, eg M Roscini, 'Cyber Operations as a Use of Force' in N Tsagourias and R Buchan (eds), *Research Handbook on International Law and Cyberspace* (Cheltenham, Edward Elgar, 2015) 233–54. For a different view, arguing that such attacks would violate instead the principle of non-intervention, see R Buchan, 'Cyber Attacks: Unlawful Uses of Force or Prohibited Interventions?' (2012) 17(2) *Journal of Conflict & Security Law* 211. See also Henderson, *The Use of Force and International Law*, 59, who suggests that, without physical damage, 'the use of the Stuxnet worm in Iran would not by itself have constituted a prohibited use of force'. This is not persuasive.

[43] Art 3(c), of the Definition of Aggression, annexed to UN General Assembly Resolution 3314 (XXIX); adopted without a vote on 14 December 1974 (hereinafter, 1974 Definition of Aggression). See also ICC Statute, Art 8*bis*(2)(c).

[44] I Brownlie, *International Law and the Use of Force by States* (Oxford, Oxford University Press, 1963) 148. Brownlie does, though, leave the door open to these acts being a use of force instead.

referred to as 'acts of aggression'. He referred in particular to the Soviet reaction to the actions of the US Air Force U-2 aerial reconnaissance plane, which the Soviet Union Air Force shot down in 1960.[45] With the advent of high-resolution satellite imagery, such a determination today is neither sensible nor coherent, at least insofar as the intelligence gathering is concerned.

A refusal by one state to supply weapons to another does not constitute a use of force, but the international transfer of weapons may be: specifically when arms are delivered to a non-state actor that is not authorised by the territorial state and which is engaged in violence against it.[46] Henderson suggests this is an 'indirect use of force',[47] whereas, in its judgment on the merits in the *Nicaragua* case, the ICJ termed it the 'threat or use of force':

> In the view of the Court, while the arming and training of the *contras* can certainly be said to involve the threat or use of force against Nicaragua, this is not necessarily so in respect of all the assistance given by the United States Government.[48]

Until the weapons supplied are actually used, however, their provision to an unauthorised non-state actor operating in another state is better understood as a threat of force than as an actual use of force.

## B. A Low Minimum Threshold for a Prohibited Use of Force

The minimum threshold of force applicable to Article 2(4) of the UN Charter and the corresponding rule under customary international law is low. Thus, the Independent International Fact-Finding Mission on the Conflict in Georgia affirms that prohibition on use of force 'covers all physical force which surpasses a minimum threshold of intensity'.[49] Dinstein's out-of-hand rejection of this assertion by the Fact-Finding Mission is not persuasive.[50] For instance, it is not seriously suggested that two soldiers from the armed forces of different states throwing stones against each other across the international border is a violation of Article 2(4).[51] Moreover, as chapter five discusses, the law of neutrality may even impose certain forcible actions by a territorial state against another state's armed forces.

---

[45] ibid 363. On 1 May 1960, the U-2 aerial reconnaissance plane was shot down by a Soviet surface-to-air missile while taking photographs over Soviet territory. See, eg 'U-2 Overflights and the Capture of Francis Gary Powers, 1960', Milestones in the History of US Foreign Relations, Office of the Historian, US Department of State, bit.ly/2LVj4PA.

[46] ICJ, *Nicaragua* judgment, para 228.

[47] Henderson, *The Use of Force and International Law*, 29.

[48] ICJ, *Nicaragua* judgment, para 228.

[49] Independent International Fact-Finding Mission on the Conflict in Georgia, Report (September 2009) vol II 242. See also Corten, *The Law Against War*, 55.

[50] Dinstein, *War, Aggression and Self-defence*, para 247. See also in this vein T Ruys, 'The Meaning of "Force" and the Boundaries of the *Jus ad Bellum*: Are "Minimal" Uses of Force Excluded from UN Charter Article 2(4)?' (2014) 108(2) *American Journal of International Law* 159.

[51] In May 2020, four Indian soldiers and seven Chinese soldiers were reportedly injured in a border fist fight. Although both nations send out patrols that often engage in physical stand-offs, no bullet has been fired over the border in the last four decades. BBC, 'Indian and Chinese troops "clash on border" in Sikkim', 10 May 2020, bbc.in/3g45w0L.

In its 1998 judgment on jurisdiction in the *Fisheries Jurisdiction* case, the ICJ found that

> the use of force authorized by the Canadian legislation and regulations falls within the ambit of what is commonly understood as enforcement of conservation and management measures … This is so notwithstanding that the reservation does not in terms mention the use of force. Boarding, inspection, arrest and minimum use of force for those purposes are all contained within the concept of enforcement of conservation and management measures according to a 'natural and reasonable' interpretation of this concept.[52]

The ICJ did not suggest that such a use of force would somehow violate the UN Charter.

Indeed, Olivier Corten describes a limited number of law enforcement measures conducted by one state on the territory of another without that territorial state's express consent which arguably would not violate the prohibition on interstate use of force.[53] This is particularly so when the aim of an extraterritorial law enforcement operation is to arrest a fugitive from justice, but it would not be the case where the intent is a targeted killing.[54] In this regard, in relation to the attempted assassination in March 2018 by Russian operatives of a Russian military intelligence defector resident in the UK, the UK Government claimed that this had violated Article 2(4) of the UN Charter. The UK Prime Minister, Theresa May, addressed the House of Commons as follows: 'There is no alternative conclusion other than that the Russian state was culpable for the attempted murder of Mr Skripal and his daughter, and for threatening the lives of other British citizens in Salisbury, including Detective Sergeant Nick Bailey.' This represents, the Prime Minister declared, 'an unlawful use of force by the Russian state against the United Kingdom'.[55]

In exceptional circumstances, an action may even be lethal or potentially lethal in nature and not violate Article 2(4). One such instance is where a state engages in a small-scale extraterritorial hostage rescue.[56] If the territorial state is holding the individuals hostage, or is at least complicit in their unlawful detention, a limited and targeted rescue operation conducted with a view to preserving life may not amount to unlawful use of force. Henderson cites as a further instance of lawful action the UK operation to extract its nationals from Libya in 2011 as the country descended into civil war.[57] Such a limited law enforcement

---

[52] See ICJ, *Fisheries Jurisdiction case (Spain v Canada)*, Judgment (Jurisdiction of the Court), 4 December 1998, para 84.

[53] Corten, *The Law Against War*, 52–55.

[54] See Kolb, *International Law on the Maintenance of Peace: Jus Contra Bellum* 336–37. Kolb further suggests that the forcible abduction of an individual or even the interception of a single aircraft may also fall below the threshold. If true, whether this was the case or not would depend on the individual who was being killed or abducted and the nature of the aircraft and its payload.

[55] 'Salisbury Incident', Statement by the Prime Minister (Mrs Theresa May), in *Hansard* HC Vol 637 (14 March 2018), bit.ly/2Q8Ol1L.

[56] See Kolb, *International Law on the Maintenance of Peace: Jus Contra Bellum*, 440.

[57] Henderson, *The Use of Force and International Law*, 70.

operation must be clearly distinguished from a broader one seeking to 'protect' nationals abroad.[58] A major rescue operation where the hostages are state officials will rather constitute a possible act of self-defence against a prior armed attack.[59]

In addition, there may be countermeasures (acts of retaliation) that fall below the Article 2(4) threshold. In mid-July 2019, Iran's Revolutionary Guards boarded and seized a UK-flagged oil tanker, the *Stena Impero*, in Omani waters, claiming that it had collided with an Iranian fishing boat. In fact, the act seemed to be as much a retaliatory response to the prior seizure, by the UK, of an Iranian vessel two weeks before, in an action taken ostensibly to enforce European Union sanctions. Indeed, in relation to the seizure of the *Stena Impero*, a spokesman for Iran's Guardian Council was quoted as saying that 'the rule of reciprocal action is well-known in international law' and that Tehran had made the decision in the face of an 'illegitimate economic war and seizure of oil tankers'.[60] Penny Mordaunt, then the UK Secretary of State for Defence, described the incident to a journalist as a 'hostile and aggressive act'.[61] But in a letter to the UN Security Council the same day, the UK complained only of 'illegal interference'.[62] Upon the vessel's release in September 2019, then UK Secretary of State for Foreign and Commonwealth Affairs, Dominic Raab, declared: 'The *Stena Impero* was unlawfully seized by Iran. It is part of a pattern of attempts to disrupt freedom of navigation. We are working with our international partners to protect shipping and uphold the international rule of law'.[63]

## C. Use of Force against a State's Territorial Integrity

Article 2(4) explicitly prohibits use of force by a UN member state against the territorial integrity of any state. General international law[64] extends that prohibition to encompass a use of force by all states. Bombardment of the territory of

---

[58] Dinstein, *War, Aggression and Self-defence*, para 577.

[59] In its 1980 judgment in the *United States v Iran* case, the ICJ called the attack on the US Embassy in Tehran by militants on 4 November 1979, the overrunning of its premises, the seizure of its 'inmates' as hostages, the appropriation of its property and archives, and the conduct of the Iranian authorities in the face of those occurrences an armed attack: ICJ, *Case Concerning United States Diplomatic and Consular Staff in Tehran (United States v Iran)*, Judgment, 24 May 1980, para 57.

[60] J Ensor, P Sawer, and A Vahdat, 'British Warship Was an Hour from Tanker Seized by Iran in "Hostile Act"', *Daily Telegraph*, 20 July 2019, bit.ly/2xXueeD.

[61] 'UK Defence Sec: "This Was a Hostile Act"', *Sky News*, 20 July 2019, bit.ly/2xX6Y0h; see also T Wyatt and S Osborne, 'Iran Tensions: UK Oil Tanker Was Seized in Oman Waters in "Hostile Act"', *The Independent*, 20 July 2019, bit.ly/2YkPYzA.

[62] 'UK Tells UN: Iran's Seizure of British-Flagged Tanker "Constitutes Illegal Interference"', *Sky News*, 20 July 2019, bit.ly/2M3E0UM; see also M Nichols, 'Britain Says Iran Approached Tanker in Omani Waters: Letter to UN', *Reuters*, 21 July 2019, reut.rs/2ZcpkGF.

[63] UK Government, 'Release of the Stena Impero', Press Release, 27 September 2019, bit.ly/33hJbFg.

[64] The term 'general international law' is often used in contradistinction to particular (treaty) law where the treaty rules are binding only upon the states parties. But see also G Tunkin, 'Is General International Law Customary Law Only?' [1993] 4 *European Journal of International Law* 534.

another state or the use of weapons on or against that territory ordinarily violates the international legal prohibition on the use of force. Thus, the definition of aggression annexed to UN General Assembly Resolution 3314 cites as an act of aggression the 'Bombardment by the armed forces of a State against the territory of another State or the use of any weapons by a State against the territory of another State'.[65] Such action may involve the firing of bullets, rockets, shells, or missiles, or the dropping of a bomb, and occurs irrespective of whether the force is delivered directly, remotely, or autonomously.

Anthony D'Amato sought to argue that the Israeli Air Force bombing of an Iraqi nuclear research centre at Osirak in 1981 did not affect Iraq's territorial integrity because no portion of Iraq's territory 'was taken away from Iraq by the bombardment'.[66] His postulate that the bombing only 'interfered with' a 'use of the territory – namely, to construct a nuclear reactor'[67] – is not credible.[68] Indeed, in its Resolution 487, adopted unanimously on 19 June 1981, the UN Security Council strongly condemned 'the military attack by Israel in clear violation of the Charter of the United Nations and the norms of international conduct'.[69] Decades later, Amato sought, unpersuasively, to explain away the resolution and dismiss its explicit wording as 'a gentle pat on the wrist'.[70]

Military occupation by one state of part of the territory of another also violates the prohibition on use of force. According to the text annexed to UN General Assembly Resolution 3314, an act of aggression includes:

> The invasion or attack by the armed forces of a State of the territory of another State, or any military occupation, however temporary, resulting from such invasion or attack, or any annexation by the use of force of the territory of another State or part thereof ...[71]

There is no need for the territorial state to react militarily to an occupation for that occupation to constitute an unlawful interstate use of force. When foreign military units 'premeditatedly make an unauthorized crossing of the frontier of a State, this may be deemed as an incipient use of force – prompting the application of the prohibition in Article 2(4) – even if no hostilities have erupted as yet'.[72]

---

[65] 1974 Definition of Aggression, Art 3(b). See also ICC Statute, Art 8*bis*(2)(b).

[66] A D'Amato, 'Israel's Airstrike upon the Iraqi Nuclear Reactor' (1983) 77(3) *American Journal of International Law* 584, 585, bit.ly/2CIfXFl.

[67] ibid.

[68] O Schachter, 'The Legality of Pro-democratic Invasion' (1984) 78(3) *American Journal of International Law* 645.

[69] UN Security Council Resolution 487, adopted unanimously on 19 June 1981, para 2.

[70] A D'Amato, 'Israel's Air Strike Against the Osiraq Reactor: A Retrospective', Faculty Working Papers, Northwestern University School of Law (Chicago, 2010) 3, bit.ly/2FGuDW9.

[71] 1974 Definition of Aggression, Art 3(a). See also ICC Statute, Art 8*bis*(2)(a).

[72] Dinstein, *War, Aggression and Self-defence*, para 248.

## (i) Military Occupation in Contested Areas

Whether the placement of military forces in areas where sovereignty is contested amounts to unlawful military occupation depends on a number of factors. If there is a dispute about the precise delineation of a border line, parties to the dispute may not be *ipso facto* violating the prohibition on the use or threat of force by retaining their forces if they are already stationed there. If, on the other hand, forces are moved into an area by a state that has no legitimate claim to that area or if there are competing claims to it, or alternatively if a state acts to prevent or impede a people's exercise of its right to self-determination,[73] this will violate the prohibition on the interstate use of force.

In any event, the duty to resolve disputes without recourse to the use of force persists. In the Eritrea-Ethiopia Claims Commission Award on *jus ad bellum* issues, the Commission condemned Eritrea for using force to secure an area (in and around Badme) to which Eritrea 'had a valid claim'. The Commission noted that

> border disputes between States are so frequent that any exception to the prohibition of the threat or use of force for territory that is allegedly occupied unlawfully would create a large and dangerous hole in a fundamental rule of international law.[74]

This decision is criticised on two grounds. First, that prior use of force by Ethiopian soldiers was dismissed as a 'relatively minor' border incident not giving rise to the right of self-defence.[75] Second, that the area in and around Badme was subsequently held to have been Eritrean territory (so Eritrean forces were, in effect, acting forcibly to secure their own territory).[76]

In relation to the first issue, the application of the right of self-defence, it is clear that the threshold of an armed attack (giving rise to the right of a state to act forcibly in self-defence) is higher than is the minimal threshold contained in the general prohibition of the use of force. That this is so is generally (though not universally) uncontested.[77] It may be deduced not only from ICJ jurisprudence, but also from the terms of the UN Charter. As discussed further in chapter three, it is not by accident that the terms used in Article 2(4) and Article 51 differ.

In relation to the second issue, the taking of Badme, Eritrean forces were not in control of the town when hostilities erupted. Eritrea had maintained consistently that, since securing independence from Ethiopia in 1993, Badme was Eritrean territory. It cited colonial treaties between Italy and Ethiopia in justification of

---

[73] See the discussion on this issue below.

[74] Eritrea-Ethiopia Claims Commission, *Partial Award: Jus Ad Bellum – Ethiopia's Claims 1–8*, 19 December 2005, para 10.

[75] Dinstein, *War, Aggression and Self-defence*, para 547.

[76] Gray, *International Law and the Use of Force*, 36, 129.

[77] Even Yoram Dinstein, who sets the bar for an armed attack at a very low level of force, appears to concede that there may be a use of force in violation of Art 2(4) that does not rise to the level of an armed attack. See Dinstein, *War, Aggression and Self-defence*, paras 548–53.

its position on this point. It had also, however, acknowledged 'that the Badme area had been continuously under Ethiopian authority for a considerable period of time, both before and after independence in 1993'.[78] During the conflict, the Organization of African Unity's Ministerial Committee had stated that Badme and the surrounding area were under Ethiopian administration prior to May 1998 and had demanded that Eritrea withdraw its forces from the area.[79]

Thus, for instance, Argentina continues to claim sovereignty over the Malvinas/Falkland Islands. Any renewed attempt to seize the islands by force would, though, once again violate the prohibition on interstate use of force, even if Argentina were subsequently granted sovereignty over the islands.

In March 1994, Cameroon instituted proceedings against Nigeria in the ICJ with respect to sovereignty over the Bakassi Peninsula. Cameroon asked the Court to determine the course of the maritime frontier between the two states insofar as that frontier had not been established in 1975. In its application, Cameroon referred to 'an aggression by the Federal Republic of Nigeria, whose troops are occupying several Cameroonian localities on the Bakassi Peninsula', and asked the Court to declare that, under international law, sovereignty over the Peninsula was Cameroonian.

Nigeria argued that it was not only in peaceful possession of the Lake Chad area and the Bakassi region at the time of the alleged invasions, but also that it had been lawfully present since independence. It claimed that the military deployment was for the purpose of resolving internal problems 'and responding to Cameroon's campaign of systematic encroachment on Nigerian territory'. Nigeria claims to have acted in self-defence. It contended that,

> even if the Court were to find that Cameroon has sovereignty over these areas, the Nigerian presence there was the result of a 'reasonable mistake' or 'honest belief'. Accordingly, Nigeria cannot be held internationally responsible for conduct which, at the time it took place, Nigeria had every reason to believe was lawful ...[80]

In its judgment on the merits in *Cameroon v Nigeria*, the ICJ held that Nigeria was under an obligation 'expeditiously and without condition to withdraw its administration and its military and police forces from that area of Lake Chad which falls within Cameroon's sovereignty and from the Bakassi Peninsula'.[81] It further determined that 'by the very fact of the present Judgment and of the evacuation of the Cameroonian territory occupied by Nigeria, the injury suffered by Cameroon

---

[78] M Plaut, 'The Conflict and Its Aftermath' in D Jacquin-Berdal and M Plaut (eds), *Unfinished Business: Ethiopia and Eritrea at War* (Trenton, NJ, Red Sea Press, 2004, 93; see also SD Murphy, 'The Eritrean-Ethiopian War (1998–2000)' (Washington DC, George Washington University Law School, 2016) 2, bit.ly/2KPyqUu.

[79] Murphy, 'The Eritrean-Ethiopian War (1998–2000)', 2.

[80] ICJ, *Case Concerning the Land and Maritime Boundary Between Cameroon and Nigeria (Cameroon v Nigeria, Equatorial Guinea intervening)*, Judgment, 10 October 2002, para 311.

[81] ibid para 314.

by reason of the occupation of its territory will in all events have been sufficiently addressed'. The Court would 'not therefore seek to ascertain whether and to what extent Nigeria's responsibility to Cameroon has been engaged as a result of that occupation'.[82]

## D. Use of Force against a State's Political Independence

An attack that takes place outside the territory of a state may also violate the prohibition on use of force in Article 2(4) of the UN Charter and customary international law where it targets another state's political independence. An obvious example, which is included in the 1974 Definition of Aggression, is an attack by the armed forces of one state against the land, sea, or air forces of another but which takes place outside the territory of the victim state.[83] As the Report of the Independent International Fact-Finding Mission on the Conflict in Georgia observed, the wording of the 1974 Definition of Aggression 'cannot be interpreted narrowly so as to exclude military bases *outside* the territory of the victim state, because a systematic interpretation of this provision shows that land forces outside their own state are the very object of this provision'.[84]

Another clearly unlawful use of force against a state's political independence would be the assassination of the head of another state or a senior state official anywhere outside that state's metropolitan or non-metropolitan territory. Also encompassed within this rubric would be the detention of a foreign head of state with the demand that he or she resign (for instance, so that a leader deemed more amenable might be invested in his/her place).

## E. Use of Force in Any Other Manner Inconsistent with UN Purposes

Under customary international law, the use of force by any state (not just a UN member state) in its international relations in any manner inconsistent with the Purposes of the United Nations is unlawful. This element of the provision is a catch-all that broadens, not narrows, the scope of the general prohibition on the use or threat of force. Its most obvious consequence is to confirm the prohibition on use of force such as to deprive a people of its right to self-determination. This is especially the case where a colonial state uses force to seek to prevent a people under its suzerainty from formally attaining independence.

---

[82] ibid para 319.
[83] 1974 Definition of Aggression, Art 3(d).
[84] Independent International Fact-Finding Mission on the Conflict in Georgia, Report, vol II, 264 (original emphasis).

## (i)  Use of Force to Deprive a People of its Right to Self-determination

Article 1 of the UN Charter sets out the purposes of the United Nations, one of which is to develop 'friendly relations among nations based on respect for the principle of equal rights and self-determination of peoples'.[85] It could be argued that the limitation of the scope of the provision to a state's 'international relations' restricts the reach of the general prohibition on the use of force, but that would be to denude the *jus cogens* right of a people to self-determination[86] of its normative effect. Indeed, the elaboration of the UN Charter is ascribed not to its states parties, as is the case with most treaties, but explicitly to the 'peoples of the United Nations'. Thus, the reference to 'any manner inconsistent with the Purposes of the United Nations' in the general prohibition on use of force is not restricted to action against another existing state, as is the case with respect to the prohibitions on use of force against either the territorial integrity or political independence. In the 1970 Declaration on the Principles of International Law's first principle, which is dedicated to the rules laid down in Article 2(4) of the UN Charter, it is stipulated that: 'Every State has the duty to refrain from any forcible action which deprives peoples ... of their right to self-determination and freedom and independence.'[87] This includes the use of force against peoples under colonial, racist, or alien domination, most notably those identified by the United Nations as non-self-governing territories.[88]

In the context of the ICJ's 2004 Advisory Opinion on the Legal Consequences of the Construction of a Wall in the Occupied Palestinian Territory, the Palestine Liberation Organization affirmed in a legal memorandum that 'The construction of the Barrier is an attempt to annex the territory contrary to international law', and further that 'The de facto annexation of land interferes with the territorial sovereignty and consequently with the right of the Palestinians to self-determination'. Its view was, the ICJ noted, echoed in certain of the written statements submitted

---

[85] UN Charter, Art 1(2).

[86] Para 5 of the commentary to Art 26 in ILC, 'Draft Articles'. Art 26 states that: 'Nothing in this chapter precludes the wrongfulness of any act of a State which is not in conformity with an obligation arising under a peremptory norm of general international law.' In its 1995 judgment in *East Timor (Portugal v Australia)*, the ICJ described it as 'one of the essential principles of contemporary international law'. ICJ, *Case Concerning East Timor (Portugal v Australia)*, Judgment, 30 June 1995, para 29. See also 'Fourth Report on Peremptory Norms of General International Law (*Jus Cogens*) by Dire Tladi, Special Rapporteur', UN doc A/CN.4/727 (31 January 2019) paras 108–15.

[87] 1970 Declaration on Principles of International Law, Principle 1, para 6.

[88] As of 2018, the UN General Assembly Special Committee on Decolonization's list of Non-self-governing Territories comprised American Samoa, Anguilla, Bermuda, British Virgin Islands, Cayman Islands, Falkland Islands (Malvinas), French Polynesia, Gibraltar, Guam, Montserrat, New Caledonia, Pitcairn, Saint Helena, Tokelau, Turks and Caicos Islands, United States Virgin Islands, and Western Sahara. Their respective administering powers were France, New Zealand, the UK, and the United States. UN General Assembly Special Committee on Decolonization, 'Ensuring Non-Self-Governing Territories Can Address Challenges Key to Moving Decolonization Efforts Forward, Secretary-General Tells Regional Seminar', UN doc GA/COL/3320 (10 May 2018), bit.ly/2DsZqFm.

to the Court and in the views expressed at the oral hearings convened by the Court. Among other contentions, it was said that 'The wall severs the territorial sphere over which the Palestinian people are entitled to exercise their right of self-determination and constitutes a violation of the legal principle prohibiting the acquisition of territory by the use of force'.[89] In its Advisory Opinion, the ICJ recalled the principle from the 1970 Declaration on the Principles of International Law whereby 'No territorial acquisition resulting from the threat or use of force shall be recognized as legal'.[90] The Court reaffirmed that the prohibition of territorial acquisition resulting from a threat or use of force amounted to customary international law.[91]

With respect to Western Sahara, in 1975, after decolonisation by Spain, the ICJ determined in an Advisory Opinion that Western Sahara was not *terra nullius* (ie territory belonging to no state), meaning that it was not open to acquisition through the legal process of 'occupation'.[92] The Court referred to the 1960 Declaration on the Granting of Independence to Colonial Countries and Peoples adopted by the UN General Assembly, wherein it is stated that:

> All armed action or repressive measures of all kinds directed against dependent peoples shall cease in order to enable them to exercise peacefully and freely their right to complete independence, and the integrity of their national territory shall be respected.[93]

At the end of its analysis, the Court did not find, with respect to either Morocco or Mauritania,

> legal ties of such a nature as might affect the application of resolution 1514 (XV) in the decolonization of Western Sahara and, in particular, of the principle of self-determination through the free and genuine expression of the will of the peoples of the Territory.[94]

The Court therefore concluded that the people of Western Sahara could exercise their right to self-determination.

On 31 October 1975, however, Morocco invaded Western Sahara from the north-east and sought to annex the territory. In late February 1976, the Saharan Arab Democratic Republic (SADR) was declared by the Polisario Front, the military force of the Saharawi people. A 16-year-long insurgency ended with a

---

[89] ICJ, *Legal Consequences of the Construction of a Wall in the Occupied Palestinian Territory*, Advisory Opinion, 9 July 2004, para 115.

[90] 1970 Declaration on Principles of International Law, Principle 1, para 9.

[91] ICJ, *Legal Consequences of the Construction of a Wall in the Occupied Palestinian Territory*, Advisory Opinion, 9 July 2004, para 87.

[92] ICJ, *Western Sahara*, Advisory Opinion, 16 October 1975, para 79.

[93] Para 4 of the Declaration on the Granting of Independence to Colonial Countries and Peoples; adopted under UN General Assembly Resolution 1514 (XV) by 90 votes to 0 with 9 abstentions (Australia, Belgium, the Dominican Republic, France, Portugal, Spain, the Union of South Africa, the UK, and the United States), 14 December 1960.

[94] ICJ, *Western Sahara*, Advisory Opinion, 16 October 1975, para 162.

UN-brokered truce in 1991, but a promised referendum on independence has still to take place.[95] The SADR is a member of the African Union, but is not recognised as a state by the United Nations. Nonetheless, in 1979, the UN General Assembly adopted Resolution 34/47 by majority vote in which it deeply deplored 'the aggravation of the situation resulting from the continued occupation of Western Sahara by Morocco' and urged Morocco to 'terminate the occupation of the Territory of Western Sahara'.[96]

Morocco has continued to assert that Western Sahara is sovereign territory. In June 2011, however, Morocco adhered to the 1977 Additional Protocol I to the four Geneva Conventions, which concerns international armed conflicts under *jus in bello*. Article 1(4) of the Protocol provides that international armed conflicts include those

> in which peoples are fighting against colonial domination and alien occupation and against racist régimes in the exercise of their right of self-determination, as enshrined in the Charter of the United Nations and the Declaration on Principles of International Law concerning Friendly Relations and Co-operation among States in accordance with the Charter of the United Nations.[97]

On 21 June 2015, the Polisario Front made a declaration on behalf of the people of Western Sahara that it undertook to apply the 1949 Geneva Conventions and 1977 Additional Protocol I to the conflict between it and the Kingdom of Morocco. This was made in accordance with Article 96(3) of the Protocol, which provides:

> The authority representing a people engaged against a High Contracting Party in an armed conflict of the type referred to in Article 1, paragraph 4, may undertake to apply the Conventions and this Protocol in relation to that conflict by means of a unilateral declaration addressed to the depositary.

This was the first time the Swiss Federal Council, as depository of the Protocol, had accepted such a declaration by a national liberation movement and a non-state entity under international law.[98]

In 2016, the Court of Justice of the European Union (CJEU) found that the customary principle of self-determination 'forms part of the rules of international law applicable to relations between the European Union and the Kingdom of Morocco'.[99] The Court further held that, in 'view of the separate and distinct

---

[95] UN Office for the Coordination of Humanitarian Affairs, 'Western Sahara', undated, bit. ly/2MnmzPW; BBC, 'Western Sahara Profile', 14 May 2018, bbc.in/2NcxpYA.

[96] UN General Assembly Resolution 34/47, adopted on 21 November 1979 by 85 votes to 6 with 41 abstentions, paras 5 and 6.

[97] Protocol Additional to the Geneva Conventions of 12 August 1949, Art 1(4); Relating to the Protection of Victims of International Armed Conflicts (Protocol I), of 8 June 1977 (hereinafter 1977 Additional Protocol I).

[98] K Fortin, 'Unilateral Declaration by Polisario Under API Accepted by Swiss Federal Council', 2 September 2015, bit.ly/2NcA0lb.

[99] CJEU, Case C-104/16 P, Judgment (Grand Chamber), 21 December 2016, para 89, bit.ly/2z55sJR.

status accorded to the territory of Western Sahara by virtue of the principle of self-determination', the words 'territory of the Kingdom of Morocco' cannot 'be interpreted in such a way that Western Sahara is included' in the territorial scope of the agreement at issue in the case.[100]

The norm of 'self-determination of peoples' also acts to render as unlawful the perpetuation of rule by a 'local elite', whether that is maintained by force implicitly or overtly.[101] Roth is, though, wrong to assert that a general rule of international law exists whereby states 'are privileged to provide arms and other assistance to rebel groups' where they represent the aspirations of the 'vast majority of the population'.[102]

## F. Use of Force is Only Prohibited in 'International' Relations

The use of force *ad bellum* is only prohibited between states (or between a state and a putative state where a people is being prevented from exercising its right of self-determination). In other respects, therefore, use of force by a state against one or more of its citizens or one or more regional authorities within its own territory will not fall within the scope of the *ad bellum* prohibition on the use of force.[103] Use of force against foreign nationals on its own soil may be encompassed, but this will not be the case where the state is engaged in ordinary law enforcement action. A state is also not precluded under *ad bellum* rules from using armed force in internal conflicts against insurgents or against territorial entities fighting for secession,[104] unless, of course, force is being employed against a 'people' engaged in a struggle for self-determination.

In contrast, the Report of the Independent International Fact-Finding Mission on the Conflict in Georgia argues that attacks by the armed forces of Georgia against the city of Tskhinvali in South Ossetia and surrounding villages by means of heavy weapons 'might even be qualified as acts of aggression' on the basis that they were against 'the territory of an entity short of statehood outside the jurisdiction of the attacking state'.[105] This is incorrect on two grounds. First and foremost, South Ossetia is neither a state nor a people exercising its right of self-determination and therefore the *ad bellum* prohibition on use of force does not apply. Second, Georgia has jurisdiction over all sovereign territory, including South Ossetia, unless and

---

[100] ibid para 92. See also CJEU, *R (on the application of Western Sahara Campaign UK) v HMRC and DEFRA*, Opinion of Advocate-General Wathelet, 10 January 2018, bit.ly/30kO5kw.

[101] BR Roth, *Governmental Illegitimacy in International Law* (Oxford, Oxford University Press, 2000) 13.

[102] ibid.

[103] Henderson, *The Use of Force and International Law*, 22.

[104] A Randelzhofer, 'Article 2(4)' in B Simma (ed), *The Charter of the United Nations: A Commentary* (Oxford, Oxford University Press, 2002) vol 1, para 28.

[105] Independent International Fact-Finding Mission on the Conflict in Georgia, Report, vol II, 243.

until the region is allowed to secede by the government in Tbilisi. Such consent must be freely given, not granted under forcible duress.[106]

# IV. The Content of the Prohibition on the Threat of Force

## A. A Threat of Force Defined

There is surprisingly little agreement among international lawyers as to what amounts to a threat of force. Certainly, acts and omissions, statements, and implicit warnings *may* all constitute a threat of force. But when they do so has never been the subject of either clarity or consensus. Brownlie asserted that a threat of force 'consists in an express or implied promise by a government of a resort to force conditional on non-acceptance of certain demands of that government'.[107] This is too narrowly construed. A threat could equally well be gratuitous, vindictive, or punitive, pledging a certain course of action at the whim of a sovereign, without making either general or specific demands on another state.[108]

The ICJ has, to date, done little to clarify what amounts to a threat. In its 1996 Advisory Opinion on the Legality of the Threat or Use of Nuclear Weapons, the Court said: 'Whether a signalled intention to use force if certain events occur is or is not a "threat" within Article 2, paragraph 4, of the Charter depends upon various factors.'[109] It did not identify what the elements of 'a signalled intention to use force' might be, nor did it elucidate the factors that would be determinative. Brownlie suggests that a threat of force might be the unauthorised entry of a military aircraft into the airspace of another state, or a warship of one state entering the territorial waters of another or staging a demonstration of strength.[110]

Writing in the 1980s, Romana Sadurska described a threat as 'an act that is designed to create a psychological condition in the target of apprehension, anxiety and eventually fear, that will erode the target's resistance to change or will pressure it toward preserving the status quo'.[111] The nature of the threat may be implicit as well as explicit. Sadurska describes an explicit threat as one that is

---

[106] Under Art 52 of the VCLT, 'A treaty is void if its conclusion has been procured by the threat or use of force in violation of the principles of international law embodied in the Charter of the United Nations'. Moreover, under Art 20 of the ILC Draft Articles on State Responsibility, 'Valid consent by a State to the commission of a given act by another State precludes the wrongfulness of that act in relation to the former State to the extent that the act remains within the limits of that consent'. These rules have the status of customary international law.

[107] Brownlie, *International Law and the Use of Force by States*, 364.

[108] Dinstein, *War, Aggression and Self-defence*, para 252.

[109] ibid.

[110] Brownlie, *International Law and the Use of Force by States*, 148. Brownlie does, though, leave the door open to these acts being a use of force instead.

[111] R Sadurska, 'Threats of Force' (1988) 82(2) *American Journal of International Law* 239, 241.

'articulated ... orally or in a document or communiqué'.[112] But so too, of course, may be a threat that is implicit.[113]

More debatably, Sadurska suggests that adherence to a military alliance may in and of itself amount to such a threat.[114] Of course, it may be that a military alliance – and, by extension, its members – threatens the use of force in particular circumstances. It is not, however, the membership per se of that alliance that constitutes the threat, just as the possession of weapons does not automatically amount to a threat of the use of force under international law. Here, too, the ICJ's analysis in its 1996 Advisory Opinion on the Legality of the Threat or Use of Nuclear Weapons disappoints. The Court stated:

> Some States put forward the argument that possession of nuclear weapons is itself an unlawful threat to use force. Possession of nuclear weapons may indeed justify an inference of preparedness to use them. In order to be effective, the policy of deterrence, by which those States possessing or under the umbrella of nuclear weapons seek to discourage military aggression by demonstrating that it will serve no purpose, necessitates that the intention to use nuclear weapons be credible.[115]

But an intention is not a synonym for a threat: intention is substantially broader in scope. Thus, a threat to use, for instance, a nuclear weapon occurs when it is credibly averred or implied, by declaration or deed, that the weapon will be used proximately in time against or on the territory of another state.[116] This is so whether or not action is required of the target state if use is to be averted. Kolb suggests, credibly, that a declaration of war that is not followed by an outbreak of actual hostilities also amounts to a threat.[117]

A threat must, however, also be credible. A state that is clearly engaging in empty political gesturing (for instance, because it does not itself have a nuclear weapon nor holds sway over the use of one by another state) does not breach its international legal obligations. In the words of the Report of the Independent International Fact-Finding Mission on the Conflict in Georgia: 'Overall, the emphasis of the practice of states is on credibility. A threat is credible when it appears rational that it may be implemented, when there is a sufficient commitment to run the risk of armed encounter.'[118]

A tacit threat may exist through a demonstration of military capability in a provocative manner.[119] This would not, however, normally occur in a routine

---

[112] ibid 242.

[113] With respect to implicit threats, see Permanent Court of Arbitration, *Award in the Arbitration Regarding the Delimitation of the Maritime Boundary Between Guyana and Suriname*, 17 September 2007, paras 432–39. Surprisingly, however, the Court of Arbitration designated the rather opaque statement 'the consequences will be yours' as an overt threat to use force.

[114] Sadurska, 'Threats of Force', 243.

[115] ICJ, *Legality of the Threat or Use of Nuclear Weapons*, Advisory Opinion, 8 July 1996, para 48.

[116] S Casey-Maslen, *The Treaty of the Prohibition of Nuclear Weapons: A Commentary* (Oxford, Oxford University Press, 2019) para 1.82.

[117] Kolb, *International Law on the Maintenance of Peace: Jus Contra Bellum*, 331.

[118] Independent International Fact-Finding Mission on the Conflict in Georgia, Report, vol II, 232.

[119] Dinstein, *War, Aggression and Self-defence*, para 253.

military operation or exercise.[120] In its judgment in the *Nicaragua* case, the ICJ held that US military exercises conducted jointly with Honduras near the border with Nicaragua 'in the circumstances in which they were held' did not constitute an unlawful threat of force.[121] Similarly, in 1949, in the *Corfu Channel* case, the Court did not consider that the actions of the British Navy at the time had amounted to 'a demonstration of force for the purpose of exercising political pressure' on Albania, but considered them to be a legitimate protective measure.[122] A clear instance of where acts related to nuclear weapons might amount to an implicit – and potentially unlawful – threat of force was the nuclear tests conducted by India and Pakistan in 1998. While, arguably, India's tests were also intended as a warning to China,[123] India and Pakistan were sending a clear signal to each other through those multiple explosive tests.

Accordingly, under international law, a threat of force is to be understood as a credible expression of intent by one state, whether explicit or implicit, to use force against another specific state or states, or on the territory of a foreign state without its valid consent. The threat exists when the purported action is to be taken within a proximate period of time and in a specific set of circumstances. This is so whether or not action is demanded of the state or states targeted by the threat.

Whether any given threat of force is unlawful is now discussed.

## (i)  Unlawful Threats of Force: The 'Brownlie Formula'

There is general (though not universal) acceptance as to what constitutes an unlawful threat of force.[124] In its narrow articulation, the so-called Brownlie formula on the legality of a threat of force holds that if a state vows to use force 'in conditions for which no justification for the use of force exists, the threat itself is illegal'.[125] The Brownlie formula (understood in broader terms) has been endorsed by the ICJ. In its 1996 Advisory Opinion on the Legality of the Threat or Use of Nuclear Weapons, the Court stated: 'If the envisaged use of force is itself unlawful, the stated

---

[120] ibid, citing Independent International Fact-Finding Mission on the Conflict in Georgia, Report, vol II, 232.

[121] ICJ, *Nicaragua* judgment, paras 92 and 227.

[122] ICJ, *Corfu Channel case (United Kingdom v Albania)*, Judgment (Merits), 9 April 1949, 35.

[123] See, eg Z Keck, 'India's Nuclear Blunder', *The National Interest*, 26 August 2013, bit.ly/2WAyI5m.

[124] See, eg the discussion by Nobuo Hayashi in 'Legality under *Jus ad Bellum* of the Threat of Use of Nuclear Weapons' in G Nystuen, S Casey-Maslen and A Golden Bersagel (eds), *Nuclear Weapons under International Law* (Cambridge, Cambridge University Press, 2014) 45–46.

[125] Brownlie, *International Law and the Use of Force by States*, 364. In fact, Brownlie himself cites *Oppenheim's International Law* in support of this assertion. L Lauterpacht (ed), *Oppenheim's International Law: A Treatise, vol II: Disputes, War and Neutrality*, 7th edn (1952) 133, 295–98. Lauterpacht discusses the interrelationship between, on the one hand, the 1907 Hague Convention III on the Outbreak of Hostilities, and on the other, the *ad bellum* provisions in the UN Charter. The Convention obligates each state party to issue either 'a declaration of war, giving reasons', or an 'ultimatum with conditional declaration of war', prior to the opening of hostilities against another state party: Art 1 of the Convention (III) Relative to the Opening of Hostilities; adopted at The Hague, 18 October 1907; entered into force, 26 January 2010.

readiness to use it would be a threat prohibited under Article 2, paragraph 4.'[126] Later in the same paragraph of its Advisory Opinion, the Court returned to the theme, affirming that:

> The notions of 'threat' and 'use' of force under Article 2, paragraph 4, of the Charter stand together in the sense that if the use of force itself in a given case is illegal – for whatever reason – the threat to use such force will likewise be illegal. In short, if it is to be lawful, the declared readiness of a State to use force must be a use of force that is in conformity with the Charter.[127]

Most obviously, therefore, 'it would be illegal for a State to threaten force to secure territory from another State, or to cause it to follow or not follow certain political or economic paths'.[128] In contrast, a threat by one state to defend itself by all lawful means following an armed attack by another state would not violate Article 2(4) of the UN Charter.[129] As chapter three describes, such lawful exercise of the right of self-defence demands compliance with the *ad bellum* principles of necessity and proportionality.[130] Accordingly, to be lawful, the threat must be of only necessary or proportionate forcible action in the exercise of self-defence.[131] This is substantively broader than Brownlie's enunciation of the formula, which, as noted above, limited an unlawful threat to one where force was foreseen in conditions for which no justification for the use of force exists.[132]

The Report of the Independent International Fact-Finding Mission on the Conflict in Georgia found that the actions of both Georgia and Russia in the lead-up to the 2008 conflict between the two states amounted to a threat of force. It suggested that a 'substantial risk' of Russian military intervention in Georgia made the threat a credible one:

> By any reasonable definition, the sum of actions undertaken by Russia by mid-2008 amounted to a threat of force vis-à-vis Georgia. For Tbilisi, both official statements by Moscow and the military operations it authorised on the border and within Georgian territory generated a definite sense that, within the context of earlier experiences and of the latest developments, Georgia ran a substantial risk of Russian military intervention.

---

[126] ICJ, *Legality of the Threat or Use of Nuclear Weapons*, Advisory Opinion, 8 July 1996, para 47.
[127] ibid.
[128] ibid.
[129] Dinstein, *War, Aggression and Self-defence*, para 249.
[130] ICJ, *Nicaragua* judgment, para 194.
[131] A Randelzhofer, 'Article 42' in Simma, *The Charter of the United Nations: A Commentary*, vol I, para 8.
[132] In addition, if the dicta of the ICJ in the *Oil Platforms* case are correct, any threatened targets of force must also be lawful military objectives under the law of armed conflict (*jus in bello*). ICJ, *Oil Platforms case (Iran v United States of America)*, Judgment (Merits), 6 November 2003, paras 51 and 76. With respect to the definition of a lawful military objective, see 1977 Additional Protocol I, Art 52(2). Dinstein dismisses without caveat the stance of the ICJ on the grounds that it wrongly crosses the frontier between international legal rules *ad bellum* and *in bello* (see Dinstein, *War, Aggression and Self-defence*, para 490), but there is a certain logic in the Court's approach. For more on this issue, see ch 10 of the present work.

This risk involved the *de facto* partition of Georgia and thus a re-definition of its territorial boundaries.[133]

The Fact-Finding Mission concluded that both Georgia and Russia employed military threats that were 'inconsistent' with Article 2(4) of the UN Charter, qualifying them later in the report as 'illegal'.[134]

The possession of weapons, including nuclear weapons, does not, per se, constitute a prohibited threat of force under international law. For a threat to exist in violation of the UN Charter, there must be an overt or implicit intent to use weapons in an unlawful manner. This concerns a credible threat to use weapons against or on the territory of a particular state or states, either within a defined period of time or in a certain set of circumstances. Empty posturing does not constitute a prohibited threat under international law.

---

[133] Independent International Fact-Finding Mission on the Conflict in Georgia, Report, vol II, 235.
[134] ibid 236 and 238.

# 2

# Consenting to a Use of Force by Another State

## I. Introduction

One state may lawfully confer upon another, either by treaty or on an ad hoc basis, a right to use armed force on its territory or in any other place under its sovereign jurisdiction.[1] Consent may be in the form of a request[2] or invitation by the territorial state; it may be through an acceptance to a request by a foreign state; or potentially it may result from the lease of sovereign land to a foreign state. Where one state lawfully consents to a use of force by another, consequent military action does not violate the *jus cogens* prohibition on the use of force, codified in Article 2(4) of the 1945 Charter of the United Nations[3] (UN Charter). This is so as long as the action remains within the bounds of the consent and that consent has not been withdrawn. In some cases, however, 'the right to give such consent is curtailed by obligations in treaties with other states or by international guarantee, for example of the status of neutrality'.[4]

But who is entitled to give consent on behalf of a state can be controversial. During a high-intensity armed conflict, when different parts of sovereign territory are effectively controlled by political and military adversaries, who represents the state for the purpose of granting consent? And within a single state in peacetime, who is the lawful donor of consent? In the United States, for instance, is it the US President or the US Congress, or both? In Pakistan, is it the president, the prime minister, the parliament, or the Inter-Services Intelligence (or all four)? What happens if they disagree? This chapter discusses who can give valid consent under

---

[1] I Brownlie, *International Law and the Use of Force by States* (Oxford, Oxford University Press, 1963) 317.

[2] Famously, the International Court of Justice (ICJ) held in its judgment on the merits in the *Nicaragua* case in 1986 that foreign intervention was 'already allowable at the request of the government of a State'. ICJ, *Case Concerning Military and Paramilitary Activities in and against Nicaragua (Nicaragua v United States of America)*, Judgment (Merits), 27 June 1986, para 246 (hereinafter ICJ, *Nicaragua* judgment).

[3] Art 51 of the Charter of the United Nations; adopted at San Francisco, 26 June 1945; entered into force, 24 October 1945.

[4] ibid. See ch 5 on the issue of neutrality.

international law, including: how inconsistent statements from state representatives are to be reconciled; how valid consent is to be given; and how consent may be withdrawn (along with a description of the consequences of such withdrawal).

# II. The Lawful Donor of Consent

The granting of consent to foreign use of force is a sovereign decision by a state. The lawful donor of consent is the authority that effectively controls the state on whose territory force is to be used. Thus, consent must normally emanate from the functional head of state, such as the president, or, in a ceremonial monarchy, the head of the serving government, such as the prime minister.

It may also be the case that a military junta effectively controls the state: its power to grant consent is not tempered by any domestic illegality that occurred in its seizure of power, even if that amounted to a *coup d'état*. Likewise, a deposed sovereign may no longer grant consent to a foreign power to use force, unless he or she was removed as the result of an armed attack; removal by forces within the state, even if (as is highly likely) that action violates national law, precludes the former sovereign from validly inviting foreign intervention.

That said, it remains potentially open to the UN Security Council to mandate the removal of an illegitimate leader in order to restore international peace and security. This it did in 1994 in the case of Haiti,[5] even though it was stressed at the time that this was an exceptional and potentially even unique case.[6]

## A. The Highest Ranking State Official Should Give Consent

Whichever entity is authorised to give consent on behalf of a state to foreign intervention, it must be the highest ranking official in the presiding civilian or military structure who does so. Or, at the least, the hierarchical superior must have approved the formal decision to grant consent where that is rendered by a subordinate (such as through the conclusion and ratification of a treaty). This is consonant with the findings of the International Court of Justice (ICJ) in its 2005 judgment in the *Armed Activities* case between the Democratic Republic of Congo and Uganda.[7]

---

[5] UN Security Council Resolution 940, adopted on 31 July 1994 by 12 votes to 0 with 2 abstentions (Brazil and China), Rwanda not present, para 4.

[6] C Gray, *International Law and the Use of Force*, 4th edn (Oxford, Oxford University Press, 2018) 344.

[7] See ICJ, *Case Concerning Armed Activities on the Territory of The Congo (Democratic Republic of the Congo v Uganda)*, Judgment, 19 December 2005, esp paras 45–47.

A president or sovereign who holds a ceremonial position as head of state is not a sufficient authority. Thus, for example, in the UK, Queen Elizabeth II (or her successor) could not lawfully grant such consent; it would need to be the prime minister of the day. Similarly, in Ireland, President Michael D Higgins (or his successor) could not do so; it would have to be the Taoiseach. This is so, even though the Taoiseach is appointed by the Irish President[8] while the British Prime Minister is formally appointed by the Queen.

In the case of the military operation in Grenada in 1983, the United States claimed that they had been invited to intervene. However, their legal basis was an invitation from the Governor-General, a ceremonial head of state[9] and 'a post without executive powers',[10] and not the Revolutionary Military Council that was ruling and in effective control at the time.[11] This purported consent to foreign military intervention was therefore invalid,[12] and accordingly the invasion of Grenada was unlawful under *jus ad bellum*. The illegality of Operation Urgent Fury was duly affirmed at the time by the UN General Assembly. In its Resolution 38/7, adopted by overwhelming majority, UN member states 'deeply deplore[d] the armed intervention in Grenada, which constitutes a flagrant violation of international law and of the independence, sovereignty and territorial integrity of that State'.[13] Only the use of the US veto had prevented the adoption of a prior resolution in the UN Security Council that similarly decried 'a flagrant violation of international law'.[14]

## B.  A Functioning Regime will Trump a Recognised but Impotent Government

To represent the state under international law, the central authorities must have effective control over the territory and the armed forces.[15] As Hans Kelsen stated:

> a national legal order begins to be valid as soon as it has become – on the whole – efficacious; and it ceases to be valid as soon as it loses this efficacy ... The government

---

[8] This appointment is made upon the nomination of the Dáil Éireann, the lower house of the Oireachtas (Irish Parliament).

[9] BR Roth, *Governmental Illegitimacy in International Law* (Oxford, Oxford University Press, 2000) 304.

[10] Gray, *International Law and the Use of Force*, 94.

[11] Roth, *Governmental Illegitimacy in International Law*, 307; see also J Quigley, 'The United States Invasion of Grenada: Stranger than Fiction' (1986–87) 18(2) *University of Miami Inter-American Law Review* 271.

[12] Roth, *Governmental Illegitimacy in International Law*, 319.

[13] UN General Assembly Resolution 38/7, adopted on 2 November 1983 by 108 votes to 9 with 27 abstentions.

[14] Roth, *Governmental Illegitimacy in International Law*, 307.

[15] Louise Doswald-Beck cites the *Dreyfus* case of 1901, in which the arbitrator stated: 'According to a principle of international law ... today universally admitted, the capacity of a government to represent the State in its international relations does not depend in any degree upon the legitimacy of its origin, so that ... the usurper who in fact holds power with the consent express or tacit of the nation acts ... validly in the name of the State': L Doswald-Beck, 'The Legal Validity of Military Intervention by Invitation of the Government' (1985) 56(1) *British Yearbook of International Law* 189, 192.

brought into permanent power by a revolution or *coup d'état* is, according to international law, the legitimate government of the State, whose identity is not affected by these events.[16]

In 1980, the UK's Secretary of State for Foreign and Commonwealth Affairs declared that the British government would

> continue to decide the nature of our dealings with regimes which come to power unconstitutionally in the light of our assessment of whether they are able ... to exercise effective control of the territory of the State concerned, and seem likely to continue to do so.[17]

Thus, while under international law the government whose leader may give consent to foreign intervention will normally be the government that is internationally recognised, this is not necessarily so. Different branches of international law endorse the effective control doctrine. Within *jus in bello*, for instance, combatant members of regular armed forces who profess allegiance to a government or an authority not recognised by the Detaining Power are nonetheless entitled to prisoner-of-war status in an international armed conflict under the 1949 Geneva Convention III.[18] The same principle applies *ad bellum*. Sovereignty is a factual as well as a legal status. A purported sovereign who controls neither the sovereign territory nor the armed forces (broadly understood) is not a sovereign for the purpose of granting valid consent under international law. The case of Afghanistan is illustrative in this regard.

## (i)   *The Case of Afghanistan (October 2001)*

In 2001, the Islamic Emirate of Afghanistan under the ruling Taliban regime was recognised internationally by only three states: Pakistan, Saudi Arabia, and the United Arab Emirates.[19] In its Resolution 1333 (2000), the UN Security Council strongly condemned 'the continuing use of the areas of Afghanistan under the control of the Afghan faction known as Taliban, which also calls itself the Islamic Emirate of Afghanistan'.[20] A year later, however, Taliban forces were in control of around 90 per cent of the country, making them both the *de facto* and *de jure* sovereign of Afghanistan. The Northern Alliance, formally known as the United Islamic Front for Salvation of Afghanistan, was nominally headed in 1996–2001 by Burhanuddin Rabbani, the President of Afghanistan from 1992 to 1996; its

---

[16] H Kelsen, *General Theory of Law and State* (trans A Wedberg, New York, Russell & Russell, 1961) 220–21; see Roth, *Governmental Illegitimacy in International Law*, 137–42.

[17] *Hansard*, HL Vol 408, cols 1121–22 (28 April 1980).

[18] Art 4(A)(3) of the Convention (III) relative to the Treatment of Prisoners of War; adopted at Geneva, 12 August 1949; entered into force, 21 October 1950.

[19] K Gannon, 'Pakistan, Saudis, UAE join US–Taliban Talks', *AP News*, 17 December 2018, bit. ly/2y9tMtO.

[20] UN Security Council Resolution 1333, adopted on 19 December 2000 by 13 votes to 0 with 2 abstentions (China and Malaysia), seventh preambular paragraph.

forces held the remaining 10 per cent of the country prior to the 9/11 attacks in the United States and the subsequent US invasion.

When the United States initiated its bombardment of Afghanistan on 7 October 2001, this therefore amounted to an international armed conflict between the two states under *jus in bello*. Consent for the US intervention would have had to come from the Taliban, in particular its leader, Mullah Omar, known domestically as the 'Supreme Leader of the Muslims'. The Northern Alliance, whether through Burhanuddin Rabbani or its military commander, Ahmad Shah Massoud, could not have lawfully granted that consent, its widespread international recognition as the *legitimate* government of Afghanistan notwithstanding.[21]

## (ii)  A Leader Deposed by Domestic Forces may no Longer Grant Valid Consent to Foreign Intervention

A leader that has already been deposed by domestic forces is not entitled under international law to grant consent to a foreign military intervention. Only a leader that has been removed as a result of an armed attack by a foreign state may do so. That is the essence of the inherent right of a state to self-defence. Thus, Iraq's invasion of Kuwait on 2 August 1990, and the subsequent announcement that Iraq had 'annexed' Kuwait,[22] did not preclude the Emir from lawfully calling other states to his aid in furtherance of Kuwait's right of collective self-defence. The installation of a puppet regime by the aggressor, as occurred in the case of Kuwait in 1990 after the Iraqi invasion,[23] cannot be used to override valid consent previously granted nor constitute a valid new consent to the illegal occupier.

The 1990 intervention by the Economic Community of West African States (ECOWAS) Monitoring Group (ECOMOG) in Liberia occurred where claims of a prior granting of lawful consent were, at the least, highly questionable. ECOMOG, composed largely of Nigerian troops, entered Liberia with the aim of ending fighting between forces loyal to the former President, Samuel Doe, and the force led by Charles Taylor, the National Patriotic Front of Liberia (NPFL), which had led a military uprising against President Doe. While there were 'some reports that President Doe had provided his consent, Charles Taylor and the NPFL which controlled 90 per cent of the country had not done so'.[24] Thus, the foreign intervention in Liberia, which otherwise would have amounted to an armed attack, could not be justified by reference to any legitimacy of the former president under

---

[21] Whether the US-led military intervention was lawful *ad bellum* is discussed in ch 3.

[22] See, eg (1990) 36 *Keesing's Record of World Events* 37634.

[23] Gray notes the claim of invitation from the 'Free Provisional Government of Kuwait', a purported consent which was implicitly but firmly rejected by the UN Security Council in its Resolutions 660 and 662 (1990): Gray, *International Law and the Use of Force*, 93. See also, eg Y Dinstein, *War, Aggression and Self-defence*, 6th edn (Cambridge, Cambridge University Press, 2017) para 262; 'Superpowers Unite over Iraqi Invasion of Kuwait – Archive, 1990', *The Guardian*, 3 August 1990, bit.ly/2pSEKDq.

[24] C Henderson, *The Use of Force and International Law* (Cambridge, Cambridge University Press, 2018) 151.

international law. In fact, neither ECOWAS nor the participants in the UN Security Council debate that addressed the intervention referred to Doe's invitation.[25] Indeed, the best case that can be made to sustain a position that ECOMOG did not breach the general prohibition on interstate use of force is on the basis of retrospective Security Council authorisation.[26] But such an scenario is not generally recognised by international law as it stands. Kolb believes there is a little wiggle room in this regard: 'there can be but little room for *ex post* authorisations'.[27]

### (iii) Competing Claims to Represent the State

As has been duly observed, 'in many cases the status of the consenting government is problematic'.[28] Indeed, if different state entities appear to give different views on whether consent has been lawfully given or competing individuals and groups purport to represent the state, the situation is consequentially complicated, but the same principles apply. Ashley Deeks suggests giving greater weight to domestic law in assessing the validity of consent,[29] but that would be intensely problematic in practice and does not reflect extant international law. The cases of Syria, Ukraine, and Yemen over the last decade exemplify the key issues.

### (iv) The Case of Syria

'Perhaps the most dramatic illustration of the principle that a government may invite outside assistance is that of Syria.'[30] Thus, in applying the rules of international law, Iran and Russia were both validly invited by the Assad regime to use force on the territory of Syria, despite loss by the government of considerable swathes of territory to opposition armed groups.[31] President Bashar al-Assad was not replaced by another sovereign, although it appeared at one point in 2015 that a tipping point was soon to be reached; before this could occur, however, Russia intervened with the consent of the Syrian president.[32] In contrast, the apparent

---

[25] Z Vermeer, 'Intervention with the Consent of a Deposed (but Legitimate) Government? Playing the Sierra Leone Card', *EJIL: Talk!*, 6 March 2014, bit.ly/35Dt0Ea. See also O Corten, *The Law Against War* (Oxford, Hart Publishing, 2010) 379.

[26] U Villani, 'The ECOWAS Intervention in Liberia – 1990–97' in T Ruys and O Corten with A Hofer (eds), *The Use of Force in International Law: A Case-Based Approach* (Oxford, Oxford University Press, 2018) 446–54.

[27] R. Kolb, *International Law on the Maintenance of Peace: Jus Contra Bellum* (Cheltenham, Edward Elgar, 2019), 185.

[28] J Crawford, *Brownlie's Principles of Public International Law*, 9th edn (Oxford, Oxford University Press, 2019) 743.

[29] A Deeks, 'Consent to the Use of Force and International Law Supremacy' (2013) 54(1) *Harvard International Law Journal* 3.

[30] Gray, *International Law and the Use of Force*, 107.

[31] ibid 114, 197. See also K Bannelier-Christakis, 'Military Interventions against ISIL in Iraq, Syria and Libya, and the Legal Basis of Consent' (2016) 29(3) *Leiden Journal of International Law* 743, §4.1.1, bit.ly/37AEgmn.

[32] See, eg BBC, 'Syrian President Bashar al-Assad: Facing down rebellion', 3 September 2018, bbc. in/34htIGG.

provision of weapons or other military support to non-state armed groups by Qatar, Saudi Arabia, Turkey, the UK, and the United States was done without the consent of the Syrian government and was therefore an unlawful threat or use of force.[33] Gray notes in particular that Syria 'sent hundreds of letters protesting about Turkey's intervention, but Turkey offered no legal justification for its support for armed opposition forces'.[34]

In August 2014, the United States began air strikes against Islamic State and the al-Nusra Front on Syrian territory.[35] On 17 October 2014, the US Department of Defense formally established the Combined Joint Task Force – Operation Inherent Resolve with a view to formalising 'ongoing military actions against the rising threat' posed by Islamic State in both Iraq and Syria. More than 15,000 coalition air strikes were conducted as part of Operation Inherent Resolve.[36] All of the air strikes were conducted without the consent of the Syrian government.[37] Syria stated that

> if any State invokes the excuse of counterterrorism to be present in Syrian territory without the consent of the Syrian government, whether on the country's land or in its airspace or territorial waters, its actions shall be considered a violation of Syrian sovereignty.[38]

On 9 October 2019, Turkey invaded Syria after President Recep Erdogan had reportedly secured 'consent' to go ahead from US President Donald Trump.[39] Turkey said the purpose of Operation Peace Spring was to remove Kurdish fighters from the border region and to establish a 'safe zone' to resettle some of the refugees living in Turkey.[40] In a letter to the UN Security Council, Turkey invoked the right of self-defence

> to counter the imminent terrorist threat, to ensure Turkey's border security, to neutralize terrorists starting from along the border regions adjacent to Turkish territory and to liberate Syrians from the tyranny of PKK's Syrian branch, PKK/PYD/YPG, as well as Deash [sic].[41]

---

[33] Gray, *International Law and the Use of Force*, 113, 114, 115. Dinstein argues, unpersuasively, that action by foreign states in Syria amounts to state practice that 'prominently upholds' the 'unable or unwilling' test for forcible action in self-defence against non-state actors operating on the territory of another state. Dinstein, *War, Aggression and Self-defence*, para 768.

[34] Gray, *International Law and the Use of Force*, 116.

[35] ibid 117.

[36] 'Combined Joint Task Force Operation Inherent Resolve', Doc APO AE 09306, 1, bit.ly/2OHg2ye.

[37] ibid 117.

[38] 'Identical Letters dated 17 September 2015 from the Permanent Representative of the Syrian Arab Republic to the United Nations addressed to the Secretary-General and the President of the Security Council', UN doc S/2015/719, 21 September 2015, bit.ly/34lNPUb.

[39] C Mills, 'Operation Peace Spring: A Timeline', *Geopolitical Monitor*, 18 October 2019, bit.ly/2KUyRgl.

[40] U Uras, 'Turkey's Operation Peace Spring in Northern Syria: One Month On', *Al Jazeera*, 8 November 2019, bit.ly/33prvIc.

[41] Letter dated 9 October 2019 from the Permanent Representative of Turkey to the United Nations addressed to the President of the Security Council, UN doc S/2019/804, 9 October 2019, 1, bit.ly/37yrvc9.

Turkey further wrote that

> the Adana agreement signed on 20 October 1998 by the Republic of Turkey and the
> Syrian Arab Republic constitutes a contractual basis for my country to fight all kinds of
> terrorism emanating from Syrian territory in its hideouts and in an effective and timely
> manner.[42]

Under the 1998 Agreement, Syria, 'on the basis of the principle of reciprocity',
undertook not to 'permit any activity which emanates from its territory aimed
at jeopardizing the security and stability of Turkey'.[43] The Agreement did not,
however, provide consent for forcible foreign intervention on either state's territory. Thus, without consent and in the absence of an armed attack, 'it is impossible
to see how Operation "Peace Spring" could be justified under international law.'
Indeed, as Claus Kreß has further observed 'There is the very serious possibility
that Operation "Peace Spring" could constitute a manifest violation of the prohibition of the use of force.'[44] One should remove the caveats. This was a clear act of
aggression.[45]

## (v)   Ukraine: The Case of Crimea

Russia offered, both directly and indirectly, several legal justifications for its use
of force in Crimea, including a request for military intervention, but none was
persuasive.[46] A resolution adopted by the Russian Parliament initially authorised
the use of force on the basis of a threat to Russian personnel stationed at existing Russian military bases in Ukraine. At a meeting of the UN Security Council
on 1 March 2014, however, Russia cited a request for intervention from the
Government of Crimea. As this was clearly inadequate, two days later Russia's
representative to the Security Council, Vitaly Churkin, presented a letter dated
1 March 2014 from deposed Ukrainian President Victor Yanukovych inviting
Russian military intervention. There are strong arguments to sustain the argument
that Yanukovych was removed from power in a manner that did not comply with
Ukrainian law. The letter stated as follows:

> As the legitimately elected President of Ukraine, I wish to inform you that events in my
> country and capital have placed Ukraine on the brink of civil war. Chaos and anarchy

---

[42] ibid 2.

[43] Turkish Ministry of Foreign Affairs, 'Minutes of the Agreement Signed by Turkey and Syria in
Adana (Unofficial Translation) – 20 October 1999', bit.ly/37ye2kl. See also S Cengiz, 'Why Is the
1998 Adana Pact between Turkey and Syria Back in the News?', *Arab Monitor*, 25 January 2019,
bit.ly/2XKbwDf.

[44] C Kreß, 'A Collective Failure to Prevent Turkey's Operation "Peace Spring" and NATO's Silence on
International Law', *EJIL: Talk!*, 14 October 2019, bit.ly/35D1LJx.

[45] Vito Todeschini implies, but does not make explicit, that he believes that this is the case.
V Todeschini, 'Turkey's Operation "Peace Spring" and International Law', Blog post, *Opinio Juris*,
21 October 2019, bit.ly/2YpQHx8.

[46] See, eg V Bílkov, 'The Use of Force by the Russian Federation in Crimea' (2015) 75 *ZaöRV* 27,
bit.ly/2rpTcmR.

reign throughout the country. The lives, security and rights of the people, particularly in the south-east and in Crimea, are under threat. Open acts of terror and violence are being committed under the influence of Western countries. People are being persecuted on the basis of their language and political beliefs. I therefore call on President Vladimir Vladimirovich Putin of Russia to use the armed forces of the Russian Federation to establish legitimacy, peace, law and order and stability in defence of the people of Ukraine.[47]

In response, Stephanie Power, the US representative to the UN Security Council, addressed the invitation by the leader of the Crimean regional authority:

I note that Russia has implied a right to take military action in the Crimea if invited to do so by the Prime Minister of Crimea. As the Government of Russia well knows, that has no legal basis. The prohibition on the use of force would be rendered moot were subnational authorities able to unilaterally invite military intervention by a neighbouring State. Under the Ukrainian Constitution, only the Ukrainian Rada [the unicameral parliament of Ukraine] can approve the presence of foreign troops.[48]

She further affirmed that:

Russian military action is not a human rights protection mission. It is a violation of international law and of the sovereignty and territorial integrity of the independent nation of Ukraine and a breach of Russia's Helsinki commitments and its United Nations obligations.[49]

Sir Mark Lyall Grant, the UK representative to the Council, addressed the legality of the request by former Ukrainian President Victor Yanukovych in the following terms:

The Russian representative claims that Mr. Yanukovych has called for Russian military intervention. We are talking about a former leader who abandoned his office, his capital and his country; whose corrupt governance brought his country to the brink of economic ruin; who suppressed protests against his Government leading to over 80 deaths; and whose own party has abandoned him. The idea that his pronouncements now convey any legitimacy whatsoever is far-fetched and in keeping with the rest of Russia's bogus justification for its actions. The Government in Kyiv is legitimate and has been overwhelmingly endorsed by the Ukrainian Parliament.[50]

He concluded that Russian military action 'is against the express wishes of the legitimate Ukrainian Government. It is a clear and unambiguous violation of the sovereignty, independence and territorial integrity of Ukraine, and is a flagrant breach of international law.'[51]

---

[47] Statement of Vitaly Churkin before the UN Security Council, UN doc S/PV7125, 3 March 2014, 3–4.
[48] Statement of Stephanie Power before the UN Security Council, UN doc S/PV7125, 3 March 2014, 5.
[49] ibid 4.
[50] Statement of Sir Mark Lyall Grant before the UN Security Council, UN doc S/PV7125, 3 March 2014, 7.
[51] ibid 6.

On 18 March 2014, Russia went a step further by announcing it was annexing Crimea. Crimea had already been annexed by the Russian Empire in 1783 during the reign of Catherine the Great. It remained part of Russia until 1954, when it was transferred to Ukraine under the then Soviet leader, Nikita Khrushchev.[52] The 1996 Ukrainian constitution stipulated that Crimea would have the status of an autonomous republic within Ukraine, but required that Crimean legislation be in alignment with that of the rest of Ukraine.[53] On 16 March 2014, a referendum was held in Crimea on whether to call for reincorporation within the Russian Federation or to have greater autonomy within Ukraine; an overwhelming majority of those who voted supported returning to Russia. The referendum was not, though, authorised by the Ukrainian government. The European Union said in a statement that the vote was 'illegal and illegitimate and its outcome will not be recognised'.[54] In the commentary to the 2001 International Law Commission (ILC) Draft Articles on the Law of State Responsibility for Internationally Wrongful Acts, an example of a continuing wrongful act is unlawful occupation of part of the territory of another state or stationing armed forces in another state without its consent.[55]

## (vi)  *The Case of Yemen*

Following widespread protests against Ali Abdullah Saleh in 2011, who had been in power in Yemen since 1978, first as president of North Yemen and then as president of Yemen following reunification with the south in 1990, he stepped down. His deputy and successor, Abdrabbuh Mansur Hadi, took office on 27 February 2012, having been elected in an election in which he was the only candidate. President Hadi remained in power beyond the expiration of his mandate, but, on 22 January 2015, handed in his resignation under pressure from Houthi forces who were taking control of the capital.[56]

Hadi fled to Aden in the south of the country, whereupon he sought to rescind his resignation,[57] and then subsequently travelled to Riyadh. On 24 March 2015, he wrote to the Gulf Cooperation Council (GCC) to request its forcible intervention in Yemen in response to 'aggression' by Houthi forces and 'Houthi coup

---

[52] BBC, 'Crimea Profile', 17 January 2018, bbc.in/2DfPmz4.

[53] ibid.

[54] BBC, 'Crimea Referendum: Voters "Back Russia Union"', 16 March 2014, bbc.in/33m9fPR. See also, eg L Ragozin, 'Annexation of Crimea: A Masterclass in Political Manipulation. Ukraine's Revolution Had the Potential to Dig Putin's Political Grave, but he Managed to Turn the Situation on Its Head', *Al Jazeera*, 16 March 2019, bit.ly/35AUObY.

[55] ILC, *Draft Articles on Responsibility of States for Internationally Wrongful Acts, with commentaries*, UN doc A/56/10 (New York, 2001) commentary para 3 to Art 14 ('Extension in time of the breach of an international obligation').

[56] 'Yemeni President Hadi Resigns from Office', *Al Arabiya*, 22 January 2015, bit.ly/33fOZ23.

[57] 'Yemen's President Retracts Resignation after Escape from House Arrest', *The Guardian*, 24 February 2015, bit.ly/2KTDC9I.

orchestrators' who were (unnamed) 'regional powers'. The letter was forwarded to the President of the Security Council, informing him that

> He [Hadi] has requested from the Cooperation Council for the Arab States of the Gulf and the League of Arab States to immediately provide support, by all necessary means and measures, including military intervention, to protect Yemen and its people from the continuing aggression by the Houthis.

The wording of the request was also subsequently forwarded in letters to the UN Security Council by Bahrain, Kuwait, Qatar, Saudi Arabia, and the United Arab Emirates (UAE),[58] coincidentally delivered on the same day Hadi arrived in Riyadh.[59]

On 26 March 2015, a military intervention named Operation Decisive Storm was initiated by Saudi Arabia and the UAE, with the participation of Bahrain, Egypt, Jordan, Kuwait, Morocco, Pakistan, Qatar (for a while), and Sudan.[60] There was no prior armed attack in Yemen, whether by Iran or anyone else, so the plea of self-defence must fail.[61] This therefore brings into question the legality of the military operation, particularly whether valid consent had been given by Yemen to the GCC.

By the time Hadi left the Yemeni capital, Sana'a, his forces were no longer in effective control of the north. The UN Security Council has recognised Hadi as the legitimate president of Yemen,[62] which is a significant (though not decisive) factor, but has not authorised the use of force to restore Hadi to power. Indeed, in 2017, he was even said to be under 'a form of house arrest' in Riyadh.[63] And while Houthi forces do not dominate Yemen to the same extent that the Taliban controlled Afghanistan in 2001, they certainly controlled most of the country in 2015 and continue to do so. As Gray remarked, in 2017 the Panel of Experts found that the (then two-year-long) aerial campaign was 'devastating to Yemeni infrastructure and civilians', but also that it 'had failed to dent the political will of the Houthis to continue the conflict'.[64]

In sum, the legality of the GCC intervention in Yemen was and remains highly questionable. Valid consent does not appear to have been given by the sovereign

---

[58] 'Identical Letters dated 26 March 2015 from the Permanent Representative of Qatar to the United Nations addressed to the Secretary-General and the President of the Security Council', UN doc S/2015/217, 27 March 2015.

[59] 'Saudi Arabia: Yemen's President Hadi Arrives in Saudi Capital Riyadh', *Huffington Post*, 26 March 2015.

[60] G Shabaneh, 'Operation Decisive Storm: Objectives and Hurdles', Report (Al Jazeera Centre for Studies, 12 April 2015) 3, bit.ly/37umCk6. See also E Buys and A Garwood-Gowers, 'The (Ir)Relevance of Human Suffering: Humanitarian Intervention and Saudi Arabia's Operation Decisive Storm in Yemen' (2019) 24(1) *Journal of Conflict and Security Law* 1.

[61] Gray, *International Law and the Use of Force*, 99.

[62] For instance, UN Security Council Resolution 2216, adopted on 14 April 2015 by 14 votes to 0 with 1 abstention (Russia), eighth preambular paragraph.

[63] 'Officials Tell AP Ban Prompted by Enmity between Hadi and UAE, Which Is Part of Saudi-Led Coalition Fighting Yemen War', *Al Jazeera*, 7 November 2017, bit.ly/34jZAuo.

[64] Gray, *International Law and the Use of Force*, 100.

power prevailing in Yemen in March 2015. As the UK had correctly stated in the Security Council a year earlier (albeit in relation to a different head of state and a different conflict), there can be no valid invitation by a 'former leader who abandoned his office, his capital and his country'.[65] By late August 2019, Hadi was even calling on Saudi Arabia to intervene to stop 'aerial bombardment of our armed forces' by its coalition partner, the UAE.[66] The Southern Transitional Council, backed by the UAE, had seized control of the port of Aden in the south, 'leaving the Saudi- and UN-backed government led by President Abd Rabbu Mansour Hadi in possession of little land or effective power'.[67]

## C.  Consent and the Right of a People to Self-determination

As the ICJ opined in its 2010 Advisory Opinion on Kosovo's unilateral declaration of independence:

> During the second half of the twentieth century, the international law of self-determination developed in such a way as to create a right to independence for the peoples of non-self-governing territories and peoples subject to alien subjugation, domination and exploitation.[68]

In the commentary to the 2001 ILC Draft Articles on the Law of State Responsibility for Internationally Wrongful Acts, an example of a continuing wrongful act is maintenance by force of colonial domination.[69] That said, although it is prohibited for a state to use force to suppress a national liberation movement through which a people exercises its *jus cogens* right of self-determination,[70] external support for such a movement is also unlawful. This is not, as might appear, internally inconsistent.

In its 1986 judgment in the *Nicaragua* case, the ICJ declared that it was constrained to consider

> whether there might be indications of a practice illustrative of belief in a kind of general right for States to intervene, directly or indirectly, with or without armed force, in

---

[65] Statement of Sir Mark Lyall Grant before the UN Security Council, UN doc S/PV7125, 3 March 2014, 7.

[66] 'Hadi Urges Saudi Intervention to Stop UAE Support for Separatists', *Al Jazeera*, 29 August 2019, bit.ly/2XKEOBy.

[67] P Wintour, 'Saudi Arabia Brokers Deal between Warring Sides in South Yemen', *The Guardian*, 25 October 2019, bit.ly/2OgbOhU.

[68] ICJ, *Accordance with International Law of the Unilateral Declaration of Independence in Respect of Kosovo*, Advisory Opinion, 22 July 2010, para 79.

[69] ILC, *Draft Articles on Responsibility of States for Internationally Wrongful Acts, with commentaries*, Commentary para 3 to Art 14.

[70] Under the 1970 Declaration on Principles of International Law, 'Every State has the duty to refrain from any forcible action which deprives peoples referred to in the elaboration of the principle of equal rights and self-determination of their right to self-determination and freedom and independence': Principle 1(7) of *The Declaration on Principles of International Law concerning Friendly Relations and Co-operation among States*, annexed to UN General Assembly Resolution 2625, adopted by the UN General Assembly without a vote on 24 October 1970. For further on this issue, see ch 1.

support of an internal opposition in another State, whose cause appeared particularly worthy by reason of the political and moral values with which it was identified.[71]

For 'such a general right to come into existence', the ICJ held, 'would involve a fundamental modification of the customary law principle of non-intervention'.[72]

James Crawford has suggested that it 'would appear that intervention in support of an insurgency must be in accordance with Chapter VII' of the UN Charter.[73] It is possible to be unequivocal on this issue. Under extant international law, a national liberation movement does not possess an inherent right of individual, much less collective, self-defence. It may seek to exercise its right of self-determination using all lawful means, but there is no right under international law to use force. It cannot lawfully request foreign military intervention and, in the absence of Chapter VII authorisation by the UN Security Council, a foreign state is precluded from intervening or even assisting an armed struggle.[74]

# III. The Expression of Valid Consent

As the 2001 Draft Articles on the Law of State Responsibility for Internationally Wrongful Acts stipulate, 'Valid consent by a State to the commission of a given act by another State precludes the wrongfulness of that act in relation to the former State to the extent that the act remains within the limits of that consent'.[75] This is, the commentary on the draft article says, a reflection of 'the basic international law principle of consent'.[76] Such consent must be 'valid' under international law.[77] This means, among other criteria, that consent to foreign military intervention must be freely given.

As Brownlie has observed, 'some difficulty may be experienced' in determining whether the granting of consent is truly voluntary.[78] As an example of unlawful

---

[71] ICJ, *Nicaragua* judgment, para 206.

[72] ibid.

[73] Crawford, *Brownlie's Principles of Public International Law*, 744.

[74] For a contrary view on this latter point, see Roth, *Governmental Illegitimacy in International Law*, 214–15. His argument grounded in the 'prevalence' of state support to national liberation movements does not persuade. UN General Assembly Resolution 3070 (XXVIII) does refer to the 'legitimacy' of 'armed struggle' and call for 'moral, material and any other assistance' to a national liberation movement, but the resolution was adopted by majority vote, not consensus, falling short of the general *opinio juris* among states needed for a rule of customary law, let alone that which could overturn the *jus cogens* prohibition on use of force. Moreover, the assistance is to be provided in accordance with the UN Charter. See UN General Assembly Resolution 3070 (XXVIII) ('Importance of the universal realization of the right of peoples to self-determination and of the speedy granting of independence to colonial countries and peoples for the effective guarantee and observance of human rights'), adopted on 30 November 1973 by 97 votes to 5 with 28 abstentions, paras 2 and 3.

[75] 2001 Draft Articles on States Responsibility, Art 20 ('Consent').

[76] ILC, *Draft Articles on Responsibility of States for Internationally Wrongful Acts, with commentaries,* Commentary para 3 to Art 20.

[77] ibid Commentary para 4.

[78] Brownlie, *International Law and the Use of Force by States*, 317.

pressure, he cites the *Anschluss*. Germany had claimed that the incorporation of Austria in 1938 was consensual, but the Nuremberg Tribunal rejected this assertion.[79] In contrast, the International Criminal Tribunal for the Far East surprisingly rejected the charge of aggressive war by Japan against Thailand on the basis that consent was lawfully given to the passage of Japanese forces through Thailand.[80] On 12 July 1940, a Friendship Treaty was signed between Japan and Thailand. On 8 December 1941, however, Japan invaded Thailand and after several hours of fighting between Japanese and Thai troops, the Thai Government acceded to Japanese demands for passage through the country for its forces invading Burma and Malaya.[81] It is very hard to see how this amounted to consent freely given.

To be valid, consent to the use of force must also be explicit, but it does not need to be made public. For instance, consent may be validly established through the act of a state agent, where it is clear from the circumstances that the agent has the support of the sovereign. This does not, though, occur through an omission, in particular where acquiescence in the forcible act of a foreign state is perceived to have occurred. Thus, the International Committee of the Red Cross (ICRC) was wrong to claim in its 2016 commentary on Article 2 of the 1949 Geneva Convention I that consent to use of force on the territory of a state by a foreign state may be established 'tacitly'.[82]

One of the sources the ICRC proffers in support of its position is the Rapporteur's commentary to the ILC 2001 draft articles on the law of state responsibility for internationally wrongful acts.[83] The commentary cites the *Savarkar* case,[84] which was the subject of an arbitral decision in 1911 between Great Britain and France. But this case did not concern interstate use of force, addressing

---

[79] *Trial of the Major War Criminals before the International Military Tribunal*, vol I, Nuremberg, 1947, 36–37; see Brownlie, *International Law and the Use of Force by States*, 317.

[80] International Military Tribunal for the Far East, Judgment, 4 November 1948, 49,588–89: 'we are left without reasonable certainty that the Japanese advance into Thailand was contrary to the wishes of the Government of Thailand and the charges that the defendants initiated and waged a war of aggression against the Kingdom of Thailand remain unproved'.

[81] See, eg HA Fine, 'The Liquidation of World War II in Thailand' (1965) 34(1) *Pacific Historical Review* 65.

[82] 'Where a territorial State consents to the actions of an intervening State, thereby removing the existence of a parallel international armed conflict, the consent given must have been previously expressed or established (explicitly or tacitly)': ICRC commentary on 1949 Geneva Convention I, para 263, bit.ly/2NVube4. The ICRC cites, in support of its assertion, ILC, 'Report of the 53rd Session' (2001) II(2) *United Nations Yearbook of the International Law Commission* 73, and also A Cassese, *International Law*, 2nd edn (Oxford, Oxford University Press, 2005) 370–71. The ICRC further asserts that the absence of protest by the territorial State 'is a strong indicator of the existence of – at least – tacit consent'.

[83] ILC, *Draft Articles on Responsibility of States for Internationally Wrongful Acts, with commentaries*, Commentary para 6 on Draft Article 20 ('Consent').

[84] Permanent Court of Arbitration, 'Award Delivered on 24 February 1911 by the Arbitral Tribunal Appointed to Decide the "Case of Savarkar"', bit.ly/30BsYtP.

rather a law enforcement action and an alleged unlawful extradition.[85] As the ILC commentary also observed:

> Who has authority to consent to a departure from a particular rule may depend on the rule. It is one thing to consent to a search of embassy premises, another to the establishment of a military base on the territory of a State.[86]

## IV. Withdrawal of Consent

What has been given may also be taken away. As noted above, for consent to remain valid, the foreign state must ensure its conduct 'remains within the limits of that consent'.[87] In its 2005 judgment in the *Armed Activities* case, the ICJ explicitly drew attention 'to the fact that the consent that had been given to Uganda to place its forces in the DRC, and to engage in military operations, was not an open-ended consent'.[88] The DRC had validly granted consent to Uganda 'to act, or assist in acting, against rebels on the eastern border and in particular to stop them operating across the common border'.[89] But this was the limit of the consent. At the Victoria Falls Summit, which took place on 7 and 8 August 1998, the DRC accused both Rwanda and Uganda of invading its territory. Thus, it appeared 'evident' to the Court that 'consent by the DRC to the presence of Ugandan troops on its territory had at the latest been withdrawn by 8 August 1998, i.e. the closing date of the Victoria Falls Summit'.[90]

Subsequently in its judgment in the *Armed Activities* case, the ICJ held that, 'from 7 August 1998 onwards, Uganda engaged in the use of force for purposes

---

[85] The case centred on the events that followed the attempted escape of a British-Indian subject, Mr Vinayak Damodar Savarkar, who was detained aboard a British commercial vessel harboured at Marseille. He was en route to India, where he was to be prosecuted for having abetted a murder. Mr Savarkar swam ashore with a view to escaping, but was arrested by a brigadier of the French maritime gendarmerie. Acting under the mistaken belief that the escapee was a member of the crew, the brigadier took him back on board and handed him over to British agents. The next morning, the ship left Marseille with Mr Savarkar on board. The French government demanded his restitution to France, on the grounds that his delivery to British authorities amounted to a defective extradition. The British government argued that, according to arrangements made with France for the security of the prisoner while the ship was in port, the French authorities had been obliged to prevent his escape. The Tribunal found that all those agents who had taken part in the incident had demonstrated good faith. It concluded that despite irregularities in the arrest of Mr Savarkar, these did not result in any obligation on the British government to restore Mr Savarkar to the French Government. Permanent Court of Arbitration, 'Arrest and Return of Savarkar (France/Great Britain)', undated but accessed 1 July 2019, bit.ly/2LICnBY.

[86] ILC, *Draft Articles on Responsibility of States for Internationally Wrongful Acts, with commentaries*, Commentary para 6, on Draft Article 20 ('Consent').

[87] 2001 Draft Articles on States Responsibility, Art 20 ('Consent').

[88] ICJ, *Case Concerning Armed Activities on the Territory of the Congo (Democratic Republic of Congo v Uganda)*, Judgment, 19 December 2005, para 52.

[89] ibid.

[90] ibid para 53.

and in locations for which it had no consent whatever.[91] The Court stated that the evidence demonstrated that the Ugandan People's Defence Force (UPDF) 'traversed vast areas of the DRC, violating the sovereignty of that country. It engaged in military operations in a multitude of locations, including Bunia, Kisangani, Gbadolite and Ituri, and many others.' These were, the Court said, 'grave violations' of Article 2(4) of the UN Charter.[92]

Indeed, where the conduct of the foreign state is in serious violation of the consent that has been granted to it, this is likely to amount to aggression.[93] Thus, under Article 3(e) of UN Resolution 3314, an act of aggression includes the

> use of armed forces of one State which are within the territory of another State with the agreement of the receiving State, in contravention of the conditions provided for in the agreement or any extension of their presence in such territory beyond the termination of the agreement.[94]

According to the Report of the Independent International Fact-Finding Mission on the Conflict in Georgia, in legal scholarship, Article 3(e)

> tends to be interpreted restrictively. That means that minor violations of stationing agreements are not sufficient to reach the threshold of an 'armed attack'. The breach of the agreement must have the effect of an invasion or occupation in order to equal an armed attack.[95]

# V. Consent has no Bearing on the Duty to Respect Other Rules of International Law

Finally, it is worth reaffirming that even if valid consent to forcible intervention by a foreign power is secured, this obviates only a charge that the general prohibition of interstate use of force has been violated. This has no bearing on the foreign state's other duties under international law which persist – notably, those to respect and protect human rights[96] and to respect and ensure respect for international humanitarian law.[97] Referring to the invitation by Bahrain to Saudi Arabia and other members of

---

[91] ibid para 149.

[92] ibid para 153.

[93] Dinstein, *War, Aggression and Self-defence*, para 645.

[94] Consent can, of course, be withdrawn. The parliaments in the two countries could, of course, hold a vote of no confidence in their respective prime ministers and appoint someone who did not maintain that consent.

[95] Independent International Fact-Finding Mission on the Conflict in Georgia, Report, vol II, September 2009, 257, citing A Randelzhofer, 'Article 51' in B Simma (ed), *The Charter of the United Nations: A Commentary* (Oxford, Oxford University Press, 2002) vol 1, para 28.

[96] See, eg ICJ, *Case Concerning Armed Activities on the Territory of the Congo (Democratic Republic of Congo v Uganda)*, Judgment, 19 December 2005, paras 178–80; see also UN General Assembly 60/1 ('2005 World Summit Outcome'), adopted without a vote on 16 September 2005, para 4.

[97] See, eg Art 1 common to the four Geneva Conventions of 12 August 1949. The Conventions have been ratified by 196 states. The 197th state, Niue, is said by the ICRC to remain bound by virtue of New Zealand's adherence in May 1959.

the GCC in 2011 to assist in the repression of peaceful protests by its Shia minority, Gray affirms that 'an invitation cannot justify unlawful action in violation of human rights or international humanitarian law by the intervening state'.[98]

This legal reality deals with part of the concern expressed by Deeks in her paper, 'Consent to the Use of Force and International Law Supremacy'.[99] But problems arise in practice where a state avers that it does not have extraterritorial obligations to respect, in particular, the rights to life and to freedom from torture. In its 2014 Concluding Observations on the fourth periodic report of the United States under the 1966 International Covenant on Civil and Political Rights (ICCPR), the Human Rights Committee expressed its regret that the United States

> continues to maintain the position that the Covenant does not apply with respect to individuals under its jurisdiction, but outside its territory, despite the interpretation to the contrary of article 2, paragraph 1, supported by the Committee's established jurisprudence, the jurisprudence of the International Court of Justice and State practice.[100]

The Committee called on the United States to: 'Interpret the Covenant in good faith, in accordance with the ordinary meaning to be given to its terms in their context, including subsequent practice, and in the light of the object and purpose of the Covenant, and review its legal position so as to acknowledge the extraterritorial application of the Covenant under certain circumstances'.[101] In its General Comment No 36 on the right to life, issued at the end of October 2018, the Human Rights Committee stated that, in light of Article 2(1) of the ICCPR, a state party has an obligation to respect and to ensure the rights under Article 6 of 'all persons over whose enjoyment of the right to life it exercises power or effective control'.[102] This, the Committee affirms, 'includes persons located outside any territory effectively controlled by the State, whose right to life is nonetheless impacted by its military or other activities in a direct and reasonably foreseeable manner'.[103]

---

[98] Gray, *International Law and the Use of Force*, 92.

[99] Deeks, 'Consent to the Use of Force and International Law Supremacy'.

[100] Human Rights Committee, Concluding Observations on the Fourth Periodic Report of the United States of America, UN doc CCPR/C/USA/CO/4, 23 April 2014, para C.

[101] ibid.

[102] Human Rights Committee, 'General Comment No 36 (2018) on Article 6 of the International Covenant on Civil and Political Rights, on the Right to Life', UN doc CCPR/C/GC/36, 30 October 2018, para 63.

[103] ibid.

# 3

## Use of Force in Self-defence

### I. Introduction

This chapter describes the right of every state under customary international law and Article 51 of the 1945 Charter of the United Nations[1] (UN Charter) to defend itself and others 'if an armed attack occurs'. It considers what constitutes an armed attack that justifies the use of force and how, in particular, the principles of necessity and proportionality affect the exercise of the right. The right to self-defence is 'clearly relevant to the question of the responsibility of a State for the use of force since the use of force in self-defence would not be a breach of the *jus cogens* norm'.[2]

Discussion is informed by international jurisprudence, in particular the *Corfu Channel*, *Nicaragua*, and *Oil Platforms* cases before the International Court of Justice (ICJ), as well as the *Nuclear Weapons* and *Wall* Advisory Opinions. The range of views of leading publicists is also assessed in establishing the normative content of the right.

### II. The Right of the State to Use Force in Self-defence

The right of the state to use force in self-defence is codified in Article 51 of the UN Charter. This article provides in full that:

> Nothing in the present Charter shall impair the inherent right of individual or collective self-defence if an armed attack occurs against a Member of the United Nations, until the Security Council has taken the measures necessary to maintain international peace and security. Measures taken by Members in the exercise of this right of self-defence shall be immediately reported to the Security Council and shall not in any way affect the authority and responsibility of the Security Council under the present Charter to take at any time such action as it deems necessary in order to maintain or restore international peace and security.

---

[1] Charter of the United Nations; adopted at San Francisco, 26 June 1945; entered into force, 24 October 1945.

[2] 'Third Report on Peremptory Norms of General International Law (*Jus cogens*) by Dire Tladi, Special Rapporteur', International Law Commission (ILC), UN doc A/CN.4/714, 12 February 2018, para 81.

The burden of proving the legality of the resort to force rests on the state engaging or seeking to engage in forcible self-defence.[3] The level of this burden is considered below.

## A. An Inherent Right of States

The right of self-defence exists only for states. The reference in Article 51 to the right being 'inherent' indicates that it also exists under customary international law.[4] In this regard, while views continue to differ on the matter, as Brownlie asserted back in 1963, 'there is considerable justification for conclusion that the right of self-defence, individual or collective, which has received general acceptance in the most recent period has a content identical with the right expressed in Article 51 of the Charter'.[5] That said, while Article 51 limits the scope of the right to an armed attack against a UN member state, the customary right extends to all states.[6] In addition, as discussed below, the failure of a UN member state to report to the Security Council as required by Article 51 is not fatal to the exercise of self-defence under customary law.[7] It is unclear whether a state that is not a UN member is bound by custom to make such a report.

As Dinstein observes, it is 'by no means clear' that the right to self-defence is also a *jus cogens* norm.[8] Moreover, there is also strong evidence that the customary right should be interpreted narrowly. In 2014, the Seventeenth Ministerial Conference of the Non-Aligned Movement, whose membership numbered at the time more than 110 states, determined that 'consistent with the practice of the UN and international law, as pronounced by the ICJ, Article 51 of the UN Charter is restrictive and should not be re-written or re-interpreted'.[9]

## B. The Notion of an 'Armed Attack'

### (i) The Minimum Threshold of Force

Not every interstate use of force amounts to an armed attack.[10] Thus, the notion of an armed attack is narrower than the scope of the use of force prohibited in

---

[3] I Brownlie, *International Law and the Use of Force by States* (Oxford, Oxford University Press, 1963) 214.

[4] ICJ, *Case Concerning Military and Paramilitary Activities in and against Nicaragua (Nicaragua v United States of America)*, Judgment (Merits), 27 June 1986 (hereinafter ICJ, *Nicaragua* judgment), para 176.

[5] Brownlie, *International Law and the Use of Force by States*, 280.

[6] Y Dinstein, *War, Aggression and Self-defence*, 6th edn (Cambridge, Cambridge University Press, 2017) para 727.

[7] ICJ, *Nicaragua* judgment, para 235.

[8] Dinstein, *War, Aggression and Self-defence*, para 525.

[9] XVII Ministerial Conference of the Non-Aligned Movement, Algiers, 26–29 May 2014, Final Document, para 25.2.

[10] Dinstein, *War, Aggression and Self-defence*, para 552.

Article 2(4) of the Charter.[11] As the ICJ held in its judgment on the merits in the *Nicaragua* case, the 'most grave' forms of the use of force, which constitute an armed attack, must be distinguished from 'less grave' forms.[12] The Court reaffirmed this holding in its judgment in the *Oil Platforms* case.[13] Thus, there can be military operations which amount to an unlawful use of force but which do not constitute an armed attack in the sense of Article 51 of the UN Charter.[14] At the same time, the ICJ has accepted (in theory) that a series of minor attacks, each falling below the minimum threshold, may cumulatively constitute an armed attack.[15]

Whether incidents are taken individually or cumulatively, to meet the threshold for an armed attack military action must have a minimum of 'scale and effects'.[16] In its judgment in the *Nicaragua* case, the ICJ distinguished an armed attack from a mere 'frontier incident', which would not give rise to the right to self-defence.[17] Similarly, the Eritrea-Ethiopia Claims Commission, in its 2005 Award on *jus ad bellum* issues, stated that: 'Localized border encounters between small infantry units, even those involving the loss of life, do not constitute an armed attack for purposes of the Charter.'[18] This is controversial. As Christine Gray recalls, the Legal Adviser of the US Department of State, following its judgment in the *Oil Platforms* case, appeared to accept that a frontier incident might not amount to an armed attack.[19] However, Taft limited the definition of such an incident to 'an isolated instance in which border forces may be acting without authority' and presumed that this was the intent of the ICJ in its finding in the *Nicaragua* case.[20] He concluded that 'there is no support in international law or practice for the suggestion that missile and mine attacks carried out by a State's regular armed forces on civilian or military targets of another State do not trigger a right of self-defense' and warned that 'if the United States is attacked with deadly force by the military personnel of another State, it reserves its inherent right preserved by the UN Charter to defend itself and its citizens'.[21]

---

[11] ibid para 543.

[12] ICJ, *Nicaragua* judgment, para 191.

[13] ICJ, *Case Concerning Oil Platforms (Islamic Republic of Iran v United States of America)*, Judgment (Merits), 6 November 2003 (hereinafter ICJ, *Oil Platforms* judgment), para 51.

[14] Independent International Fact-Finding Mission on the Conflict in Georgia, Report, vol II, September 2009, 245.

[15] ICJ, *Oil Platforms* judgment, para 64.

[16] ICJ, *Nicaragua* judgment, para 195.

[17] ibid.

[18] Eritrea-Ethiopia Claims Commission, *Partial Award: Jus Ad Bellum – Ethiopia's Claims 1–8*, 19 December 2005, para 11. But see on this finding Dinstein, *War, Aggression and Self-defence*, para 551.

[19] C Gray, *International Law and the Use of Force*, 4th edn (Oxford, Oxford University Press, 2018) 157; see WH Taft IV, 'Self-defense and the Oil Platforms Decision' (2004) 29 *Yale Journal of International Law* 302, bit.ly/2YkzO9o.

[20] Taft, 'Self-defense and the Oil Platforms Decision', 302.

[21] ibid.

Nonetheless, the 1974 Definition of Aggression, which was endorsed by all UN member states at the General Assembly, noted that the UN Security Council

> may, in conformity with the Charter, conclude that a determination that an act of aggression has been committed would not be justified in the light of other relevant circumstances, including the fact that the acts concerned or their consequences are not of sufficient gravity.[22]

The precise relationship between an act of aggression and an armed attack is discussed below, but what is certain is that the threshold of an armed attack is not lower than that for an act of aggression.

It is claimed that the sinking of a warship 'would palpably amount to an armed attack'.[23] In its judgment in the *Oil Platforms* case, however, the ICJ stated that even if it were the case that the mine that hit the US warship and the missile that was fired against the US-flagged oil tanker, the *Sea Isle City*, were attributable to Iran,

> these incidents do not seem to the Court to constitute an armed attack on the United States, of the kind that the Court, in the case concerning Military and Paramilitary Activities in and against Nicaragua, qualified as a 'most grave' form of the use of force.[24]

The Court did not, though, 'exclude the possibility' that 'the mining of a single military vessel' might be sufficient to 'bring into play' the inherent right of self-defence.[25]

Accordingly, as Gray observes, 'considerable doubt' exists as to whether a single attack on a merchant vessel could constitute an armed attack.[26] That said, Yoram Dinstein correctly asserts that for the purpose of establishing the existence of an armed attack, whether the target of the attack is military or civilian in nature is not per se determinative.[27]

An armed attack may occur on sovereign territory or extraterritorially. But when a third state is harmed during a conflict between two other states, there must be a specific intention to target the state which claims self-defence.[28] Thus, when NATO (North Atlantic Treaty Organization) forces mistakenly hit the Chinese Embassy in Belgrade during the 1999 conflict over Kosovo, this did not give China the right to use force in self-defence.

An attack on a visiting head of state would, though, amount to an armed attack.[29] Given the symbolism, this would be the case whether or not the role of head of state was primarily – or even purely – ceremonial. Thus, an assassination

---

[22] Art 2 of the 1974 Definition of Aggression, annexed to UN General Assembly Resolution 3314 (XXIX), adopted without a vote on 14 December 1974 (hereinafter 1974 Definition of Aggression).

[23] Dinstein, *War, Aggression and Self-defence*, para 531.

[24] ICJ, *Oil Platforms* judgment, para 64. The *Oil Platforms* case concerned action that occurred during the Gulf War between Iraq and Iran in the 1980s.

[25] ibid para 72.

[26] Gray, *International Law and the Use of Force*, 151. This assertion (made also in an earlier edition of Gray's work) was approved by the Independent International Fact-Finding Mission on the Conflict in Georgia (Report, vol II, 266, fn 140).

[27] See, eg Dinstein, *War, Aggression and Self-defence*, para 573.

[28] Independent International Fact-Finding Mission on the Conflict in Georgia, Report, vol II, 266.

[29] D Kritsiotis, 'The Legality of the 1993 US Missile Strike on Iraq and the Right of Self-defence in International Law' (1996) 45(1) *International and Comparative Law Quarterly* 162.

of, or an unsuccessful attempt against the life of, for instance, Queen Elizabeth II or President Michael D Higgins would be an armed attack against, respectively, the UK or Ireland. It could also be so where the attempt was made against a former head of state. When Iraqi agents sought to kill former US President George HW Bush in Kuwait in 1993, the United States invoked its right of self-defence, 'a claim that was generally accepted by other states'.[30]

In contrast, as the Independent International Fact-Finding Mission on the Conflict in Georgia claimed, attacks on citizens acting as private persons cannot, 'according to state practice and prevailing doctrine, trigger self-defence', although it concedes that this 'is subject to some scholarly debate'.[31] Indeed, as noted in chapter one with respect to the attack by Russian operatives against Sergei Skripal, a Russian national and former military intelligence officer who had defected and was living in Salisbury, the UK claimed that this had violated Article 2(4) of the UN Charter. But whereas the UK alleged that this incident had occurred along with a 'pattern of Russian aggression elsewhere',[32] it did not assert that the attempted assassination was an armed attack or even an act of aggression against the UK.

## (ii) Armed Attack versus Aggression

There is no consensus as to whether the notions of 'armed attack' and 'aggression' are synonyms. The better view is that they are not.[33] The Report of the Independent International Fact-Finding Mission on the Conflict in Georgia averred that the threshold of violence of an armed attack is higher than that for aggression; hence, 'not every "aggression" is considered an "armed attack"'.[34] If true, however, this would act to preclude the victim state of its right to protect itself using force against certain manifestations of the 'supreme' international crime. While this is hard to accept conceptually, there is clear state practice to support the assertion. As Jan Klabbers recalls,[35] the 1948 Charter of the Organization of American States explicitly refers to 'an act of aggression that is not an armed attack'.[36]

---

[30] C Henderson, *The Use of Force and International Law* (Cambridge, Cambridge University Press, 2018) 59.

[31] ibid 266.

[32] "Salisbury Incident', Statement by the Prime Minister (Mrs Theresa May), in *Hansard* HC Vol 637 (14 March 2018), bit.ly/2Q8Ol1L.

[33] Henderson claims it is 'perhaps safe to conclude' that the notion of aggression is broader than that of armed attack: Henderson, *The Use of Force and International Law*, 65, citing M Roscini, *Cyber Operations and the Use of Force in International Law* (Oxford, Oxford University Press, 2004) 71. Stephen Schwebel has held a similar position in the past: SM Schwebel, 'Aggression, Intervention and Self-defence in Modern International Law' (1972 – II) 136 *Hague Recueil des Cours* 463. On this issue, see also Gray, *International Law and the Use of Force*, 137.

[34] Independent International Fact-Finding Mission on the Conflict in Georgia, Report, vol II, 244.

[35] J Klabbers, 'Intervention, Armed Intervention, Armed Attack, Threat to Peace, Act of Aggression, and Threat or Use of Force – What's the Difference?' in M Weller (ed), *The Oxford Handbook of the Use of Force in International Law* (Oxford, Oxford University Press, 2015) 492.

[36] Art 29 of the 1948 Charter of the Organization of American States; signed at Bogotá, 30 April 1948; entered into force, 13 December 1951. See also K Trapp, 'Can Non-state Actors Mount an Armed Attack?' in Weller, *The Oxford Handbook of the Use of Force in International Law*, 682, 683.

That said, aggression was defined in 1974 as 'the most serious and dangerous form of the illegal use of force'.[37] That does not leave a lot of room between what might constitute an act of aggression and an armed attack. Indeed, the authentic French version of the UN Charter uses the formulation of '*agression armée*' for 'armed attack' in Article 51.[38] On this basis, Dinstein argues that the two concepts 'may at least partly coincide',[39] an assertion that is certainly accurate. One substantive difference exists where a state, in responding forcibly to a prior armed attack against it, uses disproportionate force. In such a case, that state may be committing an act of aggression, but its disproportionate use of force would not itself be a new armed attack.

## (iii) An Armed Attack Must be Attributable to a State

The preponderance of *opinio juris* holds that only armed attacks attributable to a state give rise to the right of self-defence under international law.[40] The notion of armed attack does, however, include the 'sending by or on behalf of a State of armed bands, groups, irregulars or mercenaries, which carry out acts of armed force against another State of such gravity as to amount to' an act of aggression, 'or its substantial involvement therein'.[41] In its judgment on the merits in the *Nicaragua* case, the ICJ declared that this rule 'may be taken to reflect customary international law'.[42] The fact of sending an armed group suffices to render the non-state armed group an agent of the state *ad bellum*.[43] A state may also become responsible for an armed attack through its conduct following the use of force against another state by a non-state armed group. That is so where the group is present on its territory or is one over which it exercises effective control and it declines to take appropriate action against the group.

In contrast, the financing, training, and/or arming of non-state armed groups by a state are not, in and of themselves, sufficient to constitute an armed attack. As the ICJ puts it,

> assistance to rebels in the form of the provision of weapons or logistical or other support ... may be regarded as a threat or use of force, or amount to intervention in the internal or external affairs of other States.[44]

---

[37] 1974 Definition of Aggression, fifth preambular paragraph.

[38] Art 51 of the Charte des Nations Unies; adopted at San Francisco, 26 June 1945; entered into force, 24 October 1945, text at bit.ly/30HXCBF. The Spanish version of the UN Charter, however, uses the formula '*ataque armado*'. Kolb suggests that the French text is a simple mistranslation. R. Kolb, *International Law on the Maintenance of Peace: Jus Contra Bellum* (Cheltenham, Edward Elgar, 2019), 394.

[39] Dinstein, *War, Aggression and Self-defence*, para 549.

[40] For a contrary view, see, eg Trapp, 'Can Non-state Actors Mount an Armed Attack?'.

[41] 1974 Definition of Aggression, Art 3(g). See also Art 8*bis*(2)(g) of the Rome Statute of the International Criminal Court; adopted at Rome, 17 July 1998; entered into force, 1 July 2002 (ICC Statute).

[42] ICJ, *Nicaragua* judgment, para 195.

[43] For more on this issue, see ch 10.

[44] ICJ, *Nicaragua* judgment, para 195.

With respect to the use of the term in Article 5 of the North Atlantic Treaty,[45] in 1949 the Committee on Foreign Relations of the United States Senate declared that 'the words "armed attack" clearly do not mean an incident created by irresponsible groups or individuals, but rather an attack by one state upon another'.[46] The discussions further clarified that this was 'just' as Article 51 of the Charter 'clearly contemplates'.[47]

That said, Brownlie reserved judgement on a situation where 'a coordinated and general campaign by powerful bands of irregulars, with obvious or easily proven *complicity* of the government of a state from which they operate, would constitute an "armed attack"'.[48] In its 1980 judgment in the *United States v Iran* case, the ICJ termed the attack on the US Embassy in Tehran by 'militants' on 4 November 1979, the overrunning of its premises, the seizure of its 'inmates' as hostages, the appropriation of its property and archives, and the conduct of the Iranian authorities in the face of those occurrences as an armed attack.[49]

Dinstein cites as evidence for his contention that non-state actors may launch an armed attack a number of UN Security Council resolutions, beginning with the attack on Benin by a group of mercenaries in 1977.[50] He refers to Resolutions 405 and 419, which do indeed refer to an 'act of armed aggression' without citing state involvement.[51] That said, during prior discussions in the Security Council, reference was made to a '*de facto* aggression'.[52] Moreover, in his statement to the Security Council Special Mission to the People's Republic of Benin Established under Resolution 404, the President of Benin referred to mercenaries 'in the pay of rich countries which want to preserve in the countries of the third world their domination, oppression and exploitation of man by man'.[53]

It is suggested that the attempted coup in Benin was supported by Morocco, resulting from anger by King Hassan II at President Kérékou's official recognition of Western Sahara as an independent nation, combined with tacit approval from

---

[45] North Atlantic Treaty; signed at Washington DC, 4 April 1949; entered into force, 24 August 1949.

[46] US Senate, Report of the Committee on Foreign Relations on the North Atlantic Treaty, Executive Report No 8; see Brownlie, *International Law and the Use of Force by States*, 278.

[47] RH Heindel, TV Kalijarvi and FO Wilcox, 'The North Atlantic Treaty in the United States Senate' (1949) 43(4) *American Journal of International Law* 633, 645.

[48] Brownlie, *International Law and the Use of Force by States*, 279 (emphasis added). He thought it more conceivable, though, that this would occur where the use of force was with a view to settling a dispute or acquiring territory.

[49] ICJ, *Case Concerning United States Diplomatic and Consular Staff in Tehran (United States v Iran)*, Judgment, 24 May 1980, para 57.

[50] Dinstein, *War, Aggression and Self-defence*, para 645.

[51] UN Security Council Resolution 405, adopted by consensus on 14 April 1977, para 2; UN Security Council Resolution 419, adopted without a vote on 24 November 1977, para 1.

[52] See summary report of discussion during the 1986th meeting of the Security Council on 7 February 1977 and the proposal by Mauritius, bit.ly/2qSC3SP.

[53] *Report of the Security Council Special Mission to the People's Republic of Benin Established under Resolution 404 (1977)*, UN doc S/12294/Add.1, 8 March 1977, Annex I: Statement of the President and Head of State and Government of the People's Republic of Benin, 1.

the French intelligence services.[54] During December 1976, the mercenaries are said to have travelled in small groups to the Ben Guerir airbase in Morocco, where they underwent intensive training, particularly in the use of firearms.[55]

In the case of 9/11 attacks in the United States by al-Qaeda, Dinstein argues that the Taliban became 'accessories after the fact'.[56] As he notes, the 'original outrage of 9/11 could not be imputed to Afghanistan *ex post facto*'.[57] He therefore affirms that UN Security Resolutions 1368 and 1373, which refer to 'the inherent right of individual or collective self-defence in accordance with the Charter',[58] demonstrate that an armed attack can be mounted by non-state actors operating without the support of a state.[59] Bruno Simma made similar comments in his Separate Opinion to the ICJ judgment in 2005 in the *Armed Activities* case: 'Security Council resolutions 1368 (2001) and 1373 (2001) cannot but be read as affirmations of the view that large-scale attacks by non-State actors can qualify as 'armed attacks' within the meaning of Article 51.'[60]

Of course, while attention turned swiftly to al-Qaeda as the source of the 9/11 attacks, the extent of foreign state involvement was very unclear in the days and weeks following 11 September 2001. Indeed, US Vice-President Dick Cheney subsequently sought to link Iraq with the 9/11 attacks.[61]

In its letter to the UN Security Council on 7 October 2001, announcing that it was taking forcible action in Afghanistan, the United States stated that it had 'obtained clear and compelling information that the Al-Qaeda organization, which is supported by the Taliban regime in Afghanistan, had a central role in the attacks'. It further affirmed that the

> attacks on 11 September 2001 and the ongoing threat to the United States and its nationals posed by the Al-Qaeda organization have been made possible by the decision of the Taliban regime to allow the parts of Afghanistan that it controls to be used by this organization as a base of operation.[62]

It conceded, though, that: 'There is still much we do not know. Our inquiry is in its early stages.'[63]

---

[54] T Cooper and A Fontanellaz, 'In 1977, 80 Mercenaries Nearly Took Over Benin', *War is Boring*, 25 January 2018, bit.ly/2OSGyVg.

[55] ibid.

[56] Dinstein, *War, Aggression and Self-defence*, para 639. See also Kolb, *International Law on the Maintenance of Peace: Jus Contra Bellum*, 106.

[57] Dinstein, *War, Aggression and Self-defence*, paras 639, 640.

[58] Both resolutions were adopted by unanimous votes in favour: Resolution 1368 on 12 September 2001 and Resolution 1373 on 28 September 2001.

[59] Dinstein, *War, Aggression and Self-defence*, para 647. See also Trapp, 'Can Non-state Actors Mount an Armed Attack?', 690.

[60] ICJ, *Armed Activities* case, Separate Opinion of Bruno Simma, para 11.

[61] See, eg JS Landay, WP Strobel and J Walcott, 'Doubts Cast on Efforts to Link Saddam, al-Qaida', *Knight-Ridder*, 3 March 2004, bit.ly/2KZH4j9.

[62] Letter dated 7 October 2001 from the Permanent Representative of the United States of America to the United Nations addressed to the President of the Security Council, UN doc S/2001/946, 7 October 2001, 1.

[63] ibid.

Gray observes that the references to the right of self-defence in UN Security Resolutions 1368 and 1373 are 'unusual', and especially so given their rarity in the broader practice of the Council.[64] Michael Byers carefully reviews the significant state practice that exists in the aftermath of the 9/11 attacks in favour of the US claim that it was entitled, under international law, to use force in self-defence against an armed attack from a non-state actor and to attack a country that was harbouring but not controlling it.[65] He affirms that the US claim 'was unsupported by international law as it existed prior to 11 September 2001'.[66] He argues, though, that what is effectively instantaneous customary law developed whereby a state harbouring a non-state actor 'who had already committed acts of violence amounting to an armed attack' was entitled to take action in self-defence.[67] This reflects Dinstein's stance that the ruling Taliban regime in Afghanistan became 'accessories after the fact'. It is also 'a much smaller step' in the development of general international law 'than if the United States had claimed a right to attack terrorists who simply happened to be within another country's territory'.[68]

While the ICJ had been clear in its judgment in the earlier *Nicaragua* case that the sending of an armed group by one state to attack another could, depending on the circumstances, amount to an armed attack, it did not expressly consider whether a lesser level of state involvement would suffice. Gray argues, though, that it is implicit that it would not.[69] Where, however, a state knowingly hosts an armed group on its territory and is aware that they are preparing a significant attack on the territory of, or otherwise against, another state and does nothing to prevent it, this may serve to give rise to the right of the state that is attacked to self-defence.[70] Where a state knowingly hosts an armed group on its territory and that group launches operations amounting in scale and effects as an armed attack against another state, the territorial state must take action against the group that is

---

[64] Gray, *International Law and the Use of Force*, 127.

[65] M Byers, 'The Intervention in Afghanistan – 2001–' in T Ruys and O Corten with A Hofer (eds), *The Use of Force in International Law: A Case-Based Approach* (Oxford, Oxford University Press, 2018) 628–31.

[66] ibid 631 and see also 632–34.

[67] ibid 634. Byers does not underplay the controversial nature of this assertion nor disregard opposition among a number of leading publicists to this position. As he recalls, there was both time and opportunity to secure UN Security Council authorisation to use force; the decision by the United States not to do so 'can only undermine the international system of collective security centred in the United Nations'.

[68] Byers, 'The Intervention in Afghanistan – 2001–', 634.

[69] Gray, *International Law and the Use of Force*, 139.

[70] Dinstein refers to a duty of due diligence to prevent attacks by non-state actors against foreign state: Dinstein, *War, Aggression and Self-defence*, para 761. See also Trapp, 'Can Non-state Actors Mount an Armed Attack?', 695. The 1974 Definition of Aggression determines that an act of aggression includes the 'action of a State in allowing its territory, which it has placed at the disposal of another State, to be used by that other State for perpetrating an act of aggression against a third State'. While the actor of the aggression differs, the principle relating to use of territory is fully consistent: 1974 Definition of Aggression, Art 3(f).

appropriate in the circumstances. A failure to do so may bring into play the inherent right of self-defence for the state that has been attacked.

But the scenario where the state is able but *unwilling* to act must be clearly distinguished from one where a state is *unable* in the circumstances to act effectively.[71] This was the situation in the *Armed Activities* case between the Democratic Republic of Congo and Uganda, adjudged by the ICJ in 2005. As the Court observed in its judgment, an International Crisis Group report of August 1998 cited by Uganda, 'North Kivu, into the Quagmire', spoke of the Allied Democratic Forces (ADF) that were engaged in attacks against Ugandan forces

> as being financed by Iran and the Sudan. It further states that the ADF is '[e]xploiting the incapacity of the Congolese Armed Forces' in controlling areas of North Kivu with neighbour Uganda. This independent report does seem to suggest some Sudanese support for the ADF's activities. It also implies that this was not a matter of Congolese policy, but rather a reflection of its inability to control events along its border.[72]

The inability to control events along its border – the 'unable to act' standard – was certainly not enough for the DRC's responsibility to be engaged in that case. Subsequently, the Court concluded that there was 'no satisfactory proof of the involvement in these attacks, direct or indirect, of the Government of the DRC'.[73] The Court was therefore implicitly accepting that indirect involvement might suffice. Indirect involvement could comprise action to create the conditions and opportunity for an armed group to launch its attacks.

## (iv)  An Imminent Armed Attack is not Sufficient

The wording of Article 51 is clear: 'if an armed attack occurs'.[74] It is not written if an armed attack 'is imminent', much less if one is probable. Thus, despite assertions by certain states[75] and other authorities,[76] an 'imminent' or temporally proximate[77]

---

[71] Kimberley Trapp argues that either scenario is sufficient to give rise to the right of self-defence, where the extent of the attack is such that it reaches the threshold of an armed attack: Trapp, 'Can Non-state Actors Mount an Armed Attack?', 695. This is not persuasive: Byers, 'The Intervention in Afghanistan – 2001–', 636–37.

[72] ICJ, *Case Concerning Armed Activities on the Territory of The Congo (Democratic Republic of the Congo v Uganda)*, Judgment, 19 December 2005, para 135.

[73] ibid para 146.

[74] J Crawford, *Brownlie's Principles of Public International Law*, 9th edn (Oxford, Oxford University Press, 2019) 723.

[75] See, eg the 2002 National Security Strategy of the United States of America, which claimed the right to self-defence including in response to abstract and putative dangers: 'as a matter of common sense and self-defense, America will act against … emerging threats before they are fully formed': Statement of President George W Bush, 'National Security Strategy of the United States of America' (Washington DC, September 2002) iii and see also 15–16, bit.ly/2Xrp9p6.

[76] See the discussion of this issue in Gray, *International Law and the Use of Force*, 174–75. According to the Independent International Fact-Finding Mission on the Conflict in Georgia (Report, vol II, 254), it is 'controversial whether self-defence against future attacks is permitted'.

[77] The two terms are not synonyms for the purpose of the use of force. In this regard, the ICJ dicta to the contrary in its judgment in the *Gabčikovo-Nagymaros* case should be distinguished: ICJ,

armed attack is not sufficient to allow for forcible action in self-defence.[78] The Non-Aligned Movement, whose membership today numbers 120 states, has rejected the assertion that a pre-emptive use of force is lawful: in 2014, the NAM explicitly 'oppose[d] and condemn[ed] … the adoption of the doctrine of pre-emptive attack'.[79] As the ICJ declared in its 2005 judgment in the *Armed Activities* case,

> Article 51 of the Charter may justify a use of force in self-defence only within the strict confines there laid down. It does not allow the use of force by a State to protect perceived security interests beyond these parameters.[80]

A fortiori, a 'merely presumed threat of an armed attack'[81] is manifestly insufficient. In its Resolution 487, adopted unanimously on 19 June 1981, the UN Security Council expressed its deep concern about 'the danger to international peace and security created by the premeditated Israeli air attack on Iraqi nuclear installations on 7 June 1981' and 'strongly' condemned it as a 'clear violation of the Charter of the United Nations'.[82] While a small number of states may have changed their minds on the matter, there is no general *opinio juris* that would change the prevailing rule of international law.

Indeed, as Brownlie observed, as a matter of principle and policy, any anticipatory use of force in self-defence is open to numerous objections:

> It involves a determination of the certainty of attack which is extremely difficult to make and necessitates an attempt to ascertain the intention of a government. This process may lead to a serious conflict if there is a mistaken assessment of a situation. Furthermore, even if a state is preparing an attack it still has a *locus poenitentiae* prior to launching its forces against the territory of the intended victim …
>
> Another consideration which is usually ignored is the effect of the proportionality rule … [I]n the great majority of cases[,] to commit a state to an actual conflict when there is only circumstantial evidence of impending attack would be to act in a manner which disregarded the requirement of proportionality.[83]

An armed attack does not occur even when preparations for it are ongoing. Thus, the Independent International Fact-Finding Mission on the Conflict in Georgia was not correct when it affirmed that 'not only the entry of Russian forces into Georgia, but also the mere preparation of this operation might have constituted

---

*Case Concerning the Gabčikovo-Nagymaros Project (Hungary v Slovakia)*, Judgment, 25 September 1997, para 54.

[78] Brownlie, *International Law and the Use of Force by States*, 278.

[79] XVII Ministerial Conference of the Non-Aligned Movement, Algiers, 26–29 May 2014, Final Document, para 26.5.

[80] ICJ, *Case Concerning Armed Activities on the Territory of The Congo (Democratic Republic of the Congo v Uganda)*, Judgment, 19 December 2005, para 148.

[81] Independent International Fact-Finding Mission on the Conflict in Georgia, Report, vol II, 254.

[82] UN Security Council Resolution 487, adopted unanimously on 19 June 1981, eighth preambular paragraph and operative para 1.

[83] Brownlie, *International Law and the Use of Force by States*, 259.

an armed attack on Georgia'.[84] Depending on the circumstances, such preparation may constitute an unlawful threat of force (and may be a threat to peace that entitles the Security Council to authorise intervention), but it is not an armed attack.

That said, an armed attack is not underway only when its impact is actually felt. It begins when, for instance, missiles are launched by or from one state against another. In such circumstances, if it is certain that missiles are going to hit the territory or forces of a state, that state is entitled to intercept and destroy them in flight as well as prevent further launches. The notion of interceptive self-defence advocated by Yoram Dinstein[85] is in keeping with the letter and spirit of Article 51.[86]

## (v) A Threat of Force is not an Armed Attack

As an imminent or proximate armed attack is not sufficient to ground the exercise of the right of self-defence, so a fortiori is the threat of the use of force. In the Suez Crisis, France and the UK resorted to the use of force following the nationalisation, on 26 July 1956, by the Egyptian President, Gamal Abdel Nasser, of the Suez Canal Company, the joint British–French enterprise which had owned and operated the Suez Canal since its construction in 1869.[87] One of the arguments proffered by the then Lord Chancellor, Lord Kilmuir,[88] in the course of discussions within the British Cabinet, was that the unilateral ending 'by threat of force' of an international waterway gave rise to the use of force in self-defence.[89] Lord Kilmuir's assertion was an incorrect assessment of the state of international law at the time and remains incorrect today. Indeed, as the lawyer at the Foreign and Commonwealth Office (FCO) of the time, Sir Gerald Fitzmaurice, declared in an internal FCO memorandum to a senior colleague on 10 August 1956:

> We are already on an extremely bad wicket legally as regards using force in connexion with the Suez Canal. Indeed, whatever illegalities the Egyptians may have committed in nationalising the Suez Canal Company, these do not in any way, as things stand at present, justify forcible action on our part.[90]

---

[84] Independent International Fact-Finding Mission on the Conflict in Georgia, Report, vol II, 254.

[85] Dinstein, *War, Aggression and Self-defence*, paras 598, 606–10.

[86] Though in relation to Israel's opening of fire in the 1967 'Six-Day War' he appears to confuse his own notion of interceptive self-defence – where an armed attack has begun – with that of the imminent threat of such an attack. Dinstein, *War, Aggression and Self-defence*, para 555.

[87] Office of the Historian, United States Department of State, 'The Suez Crisis, 1956', Milestones in the History of US Foreign Relations, undated, bit.ly/2NOdNMq. For detail on the background to the Crisis, see, eg L Milner, 'The Suez Crisis', *BBC* (last updated 3 March 2011), bbc.in/2LJyDKd.

[88] Lord Kilmuir was David Maxwell Fyfe, one of the prosecutors at the Nuremberg Trials (notably conducting the cross-examination of Hermann Göring) and an important contributor to the drafting of the 1950 European Convention on Human Rights.

[89] Lord Kilmuir, *Political Adventures: The Memoirs of the Earl of Kilmuir* (London, Weidenfeld & Nicolson, 1964) 268.

[90] Cited in G Marston, 'Armed Intervention in the 1956 Suez Canal Crisis: The Legal Advice Tendered to the British Government' (1998) 37(4) *International and Comparative Law Quarterly* 773, 783.

## (vi) Economic Impact is not an Armed Attack

Lord Kilmuir had also referred to the economic impact of the nationalisation of the Suez Canal as justifying a use of force. He received scant support from publicists in this claim at the time, aside from Professor Arthur Goodhart of the University of Oxford, who, in a letter to *The Times*, averred that the use of force was lawful 'to protect a vital economic interest that is imperilled'.[91] Professor Goodhart subsequently argued that Article 51 would not preclude use of force 'when an act of force threatens to deprive the States of the Western world of the essential oil on which their economic life depends'.[92] Also sympathetic would presumably have been Derek Bowett, who, in his 1958 treatise, *Self-defence in International Law*, argued that forcible action undertaken by a state with a view to protecting its economic independence was not a violation of Article 2(4) of the Charter.[93]

In fact, use of economic power, even if it is exploited malignly, does not even violate Article 2(4) of the UN Charter, much less amount to an armed attack. In its judgment in the *Nicaragua* case, the ICJ stated that: 'A State is not bound to continue particular trade relations longer than it sees fit to do so, in the absence of a treaty commitment or other specific legal obligation.'[94] As Henderson recalls, in the negotiation of Article 2(4), Brazil had proposed that the provision read 'the threat or use of force *and the threat or use of economic measures* in any manner inconsistent with the purposes of the Organization'.[95] This proposal was not accepted.[96]

## (vii) Reprisals ad Bellum are Unlawful

If the use of force by one state against another does not amount to an armed attack, the use of force ostensibly in self-defence will also be unlawful. Such responsive use of force is often referred to as a reprisal (as a form of 'self-help').[97]

---

See also generally A Hofer, 'The Suez Crisis – 1956' in Ruys and Corten with Hofer, *The Use of Force in International Law: A Case-Based Approach*, 36–47.

[91] Cited in Marston, 'Armed Intervention in the 1956 Suez Canal Crisis: The Legal Advice Tendered to the British Government', 778.

[92] Cited in ibid 779.

[93] DW Bowett, *Self-defence in International Law* (Manchester, Manchester University Press, 1958) 185–86.

[94] ICJ, *Nicaragua* judgment, para 276.

[95] Henderson, *The Use of Force and International Law*, 53 (emphasis added).

[96] The wording demonstrates that economic measures were not considered a use of force even by Brazil. Had it read 'including the threat or use of economic measures', that could have been used as evidence that state practice in interpretation of the notion of force was less consistent.

[97] The term 'reprisal' should not be confused with its *in bello* equivalent, which remains potentially lawful in certain, limited circumstances during a situation of armed conflict. See, eg S Casey-Maslen with S Haines, *Hague Law Interpreted: The Conduct of Hostilities under the Law of Armed Conflict* (Oxford, Hart Publishing, 2018) 337–43. The issue is touched upon in ch 10 of the present work.

As Brownlie observed in 1963, the provisions of the UN Charter relating to peaceful settlement of disputes and the general duty to refrain from the use of force by one state against another 'are universally regarded as prohibiting reprisals which involve the use of force'.[98] In assessing the use of force by France and the UK during the Suez Crisis, Alexandra Hofer remarked that: 'Ultimately, the Suez Canal Crisis taught the French and British an invaluable lesson: the decision to resort to force must be made within the framework of the UN Charter.'[99]

## C. Other Conditions for the Lawful Exercise of Self-defence

If a state has been the victim of an armed attack, it may exercise its right of self-defence.[100] There are, however, conditions that it must meet if a forcible response is to be lawful: compliance with the principles of necessity and proportionality.[101] These substantive elements dictate that a use of force in self-defence must be both necessary in the circumstances and proportionate to the aim of repelling the armed attack. A further, procedural element of the exercise by a state of its right of self-defence lawful concerns the duty to notify the UN Security Council that it is so acting.

### (i) Necessity for Use of Force

According to the principle of necessity, it must be objectively and strictly necessary that force be used to respond to an armed attack.[102] Necessity *ad bellum*[103] comprises at least three elements, and possibly a fourth. First, there must be no pacific alternative reasonably available to the use of force, such as dispute resolution, mediation, and the securing of adequate measures of reparation. Second, the responding state must be certain of the identity of the attacker – it is not permitted to make a mistake (as it is, for example, in certain circumstances under *jus in bello*).[104] Third, the UN Security Council must not have already

---

[98] Brownlie, *International Law and the Use of Force by States*, 281. Brownlie cites the statement of the FCO, which observed that the British Government 'deplore all reprisals ... which have been repeatedly condemned by the Security Council': ibid 282, quoting the statement as reported in *The Times* of 27 September 1956.

[99] Hofer, 'The Suez Crisis – 1956', 47.

[100] ICJ, *Nicaragua* judgment, para 195.

[101] ibid para 194; approved by the ICJ in the *Oil Platforms* case, paras 43 and 51.

[102] Independent International Fact-Finding Mission on the Conflict in Georgia, Report, vol II, 248; ICJ, *Oil Platforms* judgment, para 73.

[103] This element should not be confused with the principle of military necessity under the law of armed conflict/international humanitarian law; the principle of necessity under international human rights law; or the principle of necessity (for the use of force) under the law of law enforcement. In each of these three cases, the meaning of necessity differs materially from that *ad bellum*. See chs 10 and 11.

[104] See, eg Casey-Maslen with Haines, *Hague Law Interpreted*, 117–18.

taken 'the measures necessary to maintain international peace and security'. Fourth, and most controversially, it is arguably the case that the targets of action in self-defence must also be lawful military objectives under *jus in bello*.

### (a) Pacific Alternatives

Roberto Ago argued that the state attacked 'must not, in the particular circumstances, have had any means of halting the attack other than recourse to armed force':[105]

> In other words, had it been able to achieve the same result by measures not involving the use of armed force, it would have no justification for adopting conduct which contravened the general prohibition against the use of armed force. The point is self-evident and is generally recognized; hence it requires no further discussion.[106]

Thus, there must be 'no realistic alternative means of redress available'.[107] An obvious instance where the requirement of necessity for the use of force in self-defence is not met is where the original attack was launched by mistake or the victim of the attack was mistakenly targeted.[108] If due reparation is made by the attacker, this would obviate the need for any forcible response.

There is no set period for the exploration of pacific alternatives. In addition, a state that is attacked is entitled to explore peaceful resolution of a dispute while also preparing its armed forces, should they be needed. Henderson cites the example of the UK's response to the April 1982 invasion of the Falkland Islands by Argentina,[109] where a period of 23 days passed before the UK launched an action in self-defence.[110] After the 9/11 attacks, the United States demanded, in particular, that the Taliban close al-Qaeda's training camps in Afghanistan and hand over Osama bin Laden for trial. It did not immediately launch a military attack on Afghanistan. The Taliban, however, demanded evidence of bin Laden's guilt before they would countenance such a move.[111] Had the Taliban handed over bin Laden and pushed the al-Qaeda forces out of the country, the attack by the United States would assuredly have been unlawful.

---

[105] R Ago, ILC Special Rapporteur, 'Addendum to the Eighth Report on State Responsibility' (1980) II(1) *United Nations Yearbook of the International Law Commission* 69, para 120.

[106] ibid.

[107] T Ruys, '*Armed Attack' and Article 51 of the UN Charter: Evolutions in Customary Law and Practice* (Cambridge, Cambridge University Press, 2010) 98.

[108] Henderson, *The Use of Force and International Law*, 215.

[109] For details of the invasion (named Operation Rosario by Argentina) and the subsequent battles between Argentine and British forces on and around the Islands, see, eg L Freedman, 'The Falklands War Explained', *History Extra*, text originally published in 2007, bit.ly/2SzLQqf.

[110] Henderson, *The Use of Force and International Law*, 230.

[111] For the longer term background, see, eg JR Hammond, 'Newly Disclosed Documents Shed More Light on Early Taliban Offers, Pakistan Role', *Foreign Policy Journal*, 20 September 2010, bit.ly/2YaDt5v.

### (b) Certainty of the Attacker

In its judgment in the *Oil Platforms* case, the Court held that an alleged attack by Iran on a US military vessel in the Gulf did not give rise to the right of self-defence on the part of the United States against Iran. This was so because the claim that Iran had specifically aimed at the United States was not proven; nor, even, was the charge that mines had been laid – by whichever party – with the specific intention of harming US vessels.[112]

The burden of proof on the state alleging it is acting in self-defence is extremely high. Where force is concerned, the international rule of law demands certainty: 'to establish in a definite manner than an armed attack was launched by a particular country against which it is forcibly responding' in Dinstein's words.[113] The standard of evidence should therefore be one of 'beyond a reasonable doubt'.

In the *Oil Platforms* judgment, the ICJ held that

> in order to establish that it was legally justified in attacking the Iranian platforms in exercise of the right of individual self-defence, the United States has to show that attacks had been made upon it for which Iran was responsible; and that those attacks were of such a nature as to be qualified as 'armed attacks'.[114]

It further concluded that 'the burden of proof of the existence of an armed attack by Iran on the United States, in the form of the missile attack on the Sea Isle City, has not been discharged'.[115]

In his separate opinion, Judge Buergenthal criticised the approach taken by the Court. He asks what is meant by the Court's reference to US evidence being 'insufficient': 'Does the evidence have to be "convincing", "preponderant", "overwhelming" or "beyond a reasonable doubt" to be sufficient? The Court never spells out what the here relevant standard of proof is.'[116] He complained that each piece of evidence adduced by the United States was analysed separately. Taken together, he argued, the evidence might establish 'that it was not unreasonable' for the United States to assume that the missile was fired by Iran.[117] This low threshold – 'not unreasonable' – cannot be accepted as the standard for the exercise of self-defence.

Judge Higgins also criticised the lack of a clear enunciation in the Court's judgment of the standard of proof to be met.[118] But that the Court referred to the burden of proof being upon the United States was, she observed, 'commonplace, well-established in the Court's jurisprudence'.[119] This must be the case when the

---

[112] ICJ, *Oil Platforms* judgment, para 64.
[113] Dinstein, *War, Aggression and Self-defence*, para 654.
[114] ICJ, *Oil Platforms* judgment, para 51.
[115] ibid para 61.
[116] ICJ, *Oil Platforms* judgment, Separate Opinion of Judge Buergenthal, para 41, bit.ly/2JFyHJg.
[117] ibid.
[118] ICJ, *Oil Platforms* judgment, Separate Opinion of Judge Higgins, para 30, bit.ly/2M3P1VO.
[119] ibid.

use of force is concerned, given both the consequences of the use of force and the *jus cogens* prohibition on its exercise under international law.

Henderson[120] refers to the letter of 7 October 2001 to the President of the UN Security Council in which John D Negroponte, the US Permanent Representative to the United Nations in New York, stated that the US Government had 'obtained *clear and compelling* information that the Al-Qaeda organization, which is supported by the Taliban regime in Afghanistan, had a central role in the attacks'.[121] This, though, is considerably higher than the standard of proof that the United States believes to be necessary for forcible action in self-defence.

### (c)  Effective Action by the UN Security Council

Once the UN Security Council 'has taken the measures necessary to maintain international peace and security', no forcible action by the state that has suffered an armed attack will be lawful. This is a clear reflection of the principles of necessity (prior to the use of force in self-defence) and of proportionality (once action in self-defence is already underway). It is 'plainly not enough' for the Council to 'adopt just any resolution, in order to divest Member States of the right to continue to resort to armed force in self-defence against an armed attack'.[122] The imposition of binding economic sanctions on the state responsible for an armed attack is similarly not sufficient,[123] nor is a demand for reparative action, such as withdrawal from land unlawfully occupied, unless and until that demand has been met.[124]

### (d)  Lawful Targets under *Jus in Bello*

In its judgment in the *Oil Platforms* case, the ICJ seemingly appended a further condition for the exercise of self-defence: that the targets of the use of force in self-defence be lawful military objectives under *jus in bello*.[125] Thus, according to one appreciation of the Court's dicta, attacking the civilian population of a state or civilian objects cannot be necessary and proportionate as an act of self-defence. This issue is discussed further in chapter ten. Suffice to note here that this putative condition is controversial, and is strongly opposed by a number of leading publicists.

---

[120] Henderson, *The Use of Force and International Law*, 213.

[121] Letter to the President of the UN Security Council from John D Negroponte, US Permanent Representative to the United Nations in New York, UN doc S/2001/946, 7 October 2001, 1 (emphasis added).

[122] Dinstein, *War, Aggression and Self-defence*, para 676.

[123] ibid.

[124] Gray, *International Law and the Use of Force*, 131–32.

[125] ICJ, *Oil Platforms* judgment, para 51. See also Art 52(2) of the Protocol Additional to the Geneva Conventions of 12 August 1949, and Relating to the Protection of Victims of International Armed Conflicts (Protocol I), of 8 June 1977: 'In so far as objects are concerned, military objectives are limited to those objects which by their nature, location, purpose or use make an effective contribution to military action and whose total or partial destruction, capture or neutralization, in the circumstances ruling at the time, offers a definite military advantage.'

## (ii)  Proportionality of Force

When the use of force is necessary in self-defence, such force as is reasonably necessary to halt and repel the attack will not be disproportionate.[126] Thus, as the Independent International Fact-Finding Mission on the Conflict in Georgia affirmed, a 'reaction is proportionate if there is a reasonable relationship between the measures employed and the objective, the only permissible objective being the repulsion of the armed attack'.[127] According to Ago, 'what matters in this respect is the result to be achieved by the "defensive action", and not the forms, substance and strength of the action itself'.[128]

That said, the 'operation needed to halt and repel the attack may well have to assume dimensions much greater than the attack suffered, and may still be proportionate to the objective of countering the attack'.[129] Moreover, 'the reaction need not be confined to the space where the armed attack was launched'.[130] As the Independent International Fact-Finding Mission on the Conflict in Georgia also observed, it was proportionate for the United States to use force against Afghanistan in reaction to an armed attack on US soil on 9/11.[131]

In its judgment in the *Oil Platforms* case, the ICJ stated that the United States had to show that its actions were 'proportional to the armed attack made on it'.[132] This largely replicated its formulation in the *Nicaragua* case ('proportional to the armed attack').[133] This view has some support in the literature,[134] but is largely – and better – reflected in the notion of the legitimate aim of a forcible response: such force as is necessary in the circumstances to repel the attack. A less extensive attack ordinarily demands a less extensive military response. But proportionality cannot be reduced to a simplistic response in kind or a tit-for-tat action.

The United States has proposed a slightly different formula for proportionality in self-defence. The Permanent Representative of the United States to the United Nations in New York wrote to the UN Security Council in April 1988, reporting that United States forces had

> exercised their inherent right of self-defence under international law by taking defensive action in response to an attack by the Islamic Republic of Iran against a United States naval vessel in international waters of the Persian Gulf. The actions taken are necessary and are *proportionate to the threat posed by such hostile Iranian actions.*[135]

This is a more subjective approach, and one that the ICJ was right not to endorse.

---

[126] Gray, *International Law and the Use of Force*, 159.
[127] Independent International Fact-Finding Mission on the Conflict in Georgia, Report, vol II, 249.
[128] Ago, 'Addendum to the Eighth Report on State Responsibility', 69, para 121.
[129] Independent International Fact-Finding Mission on the Conflict in Georgia, Report, vol II, 249.
[130] ibid 272.
[131] ibid 272, note 160.
[132] ICJ, *Oil Platforms* judgment, para 64.
[133] ICJ, *Nicaragua* judgment, para 176.
[134] R Kolb, *Ius contra bellum. Le droit international relatif au maintien de la paix*, 2nd edn (Basel, Helbing Lichtenhahn/Brussels, Bruylant, 2009) 294–95.
[135] UN Security Council, UN doc S/19791, 18 April 1988 (emphasis added).

As the legitimate aim of action in self-defence is to repel the attack and/or invasion, regime change in the attacking state is generally an unlawful objective for the use of force in self-defence, as is the annihilation of the enemy. Purely retaliatory or punitive actions are also unlawful.[136] That said, the 'general practice of States attests that the completion of an armed attack is no impediment to the victim responding with a war of self-defence'.[137] Moreover, although regime change is generally an unlawful aim in the exercise of self-defence, '[o]nce war is raging, the exercise of self-defence may bring about the "destruction of the enemy's army", regardless of the condition of proportionality'.[138] This needs to be clearly distinguished as a legal standard wherein the state acting in self-defence does not need to back down if the aggressor persists in fighting from a scenario where the initial aim is annihilation of the enemy. Dinstein is right to say that states may choose, in practice, to use force 'tenaciously, with a view to bringing about the utter collapse of the aggressor's armed forces'.[139] That choice does not, however, elevate such practice into a lawful international norm *ad bellum*.

## (iii)  *The Duty to Notify the UN Security Council*

Under Article 51 of the UN Charter, measures taken by member states in the exercise of their right of self-defence 'shall be immediately reported' to the UN Security Council. A failure to respect this procedural obligation does not automatically negate a claim to lawful self-defence,[140] although the absence or presence of a report to the Security Council 'may be one of the facts indicating whether the State in question was itself convinced that it was acting in self-defence'.[141]

This had already been raised by the ICJ in its judgment in the *Nicaragua* case in the following terms:

> There is also an aspect of the conduct of the United States which the Court is entitled to take into account as indicative of the view of that State on the question of the existence of an armed attack. At no time, up to the present, has the United States Government addressed to the Security Council, in connection with the matters the subject of the present case, the report which is required by Article 51 of the United Nations Charter in respect of measures which a State believes itself bound to take when it exercises the right of individual or collective self-defence. The Court, whose decision has to be made on the basis of customary international law, has already observed that in the context of

---

[136] A Randelzhofer, 'Article 51' in B. Simma (ed), *The Charter of the United Nations: A Commentary*, 2nd edn (Oxford, Oxford University Press, 2002) vol I, para 42.

[137] Dinstein, *War, Aggression and Self-defence*, para 741.

[138] ibid para 743, citing D Alland, 'International Responsibility and Sanctions: Self-defence and Countermeasures in the ILC Codification of Rules Governing International Responsibility' in M Spinedi and B Simma (eds), *United Nations Codification of State Responsibility* (New York, Oceana Publications, 1987) 183.

[139] Dinstein, *War, Aggression and Self-defence*, para 749.

[140] Gray, *International Law and the Use of Force*, 128.

[141] ICJ, *Nicaragua* judgment, para 200.

that law, the reporting obligation enshrined in Article 51 of the Charter of the United Nations does not exist. It does not therefore treat the absence of a report on the part of the United States as the breach of an undertaking forming part of the customary international law applicable to the present dispute. But the Court is justified in observing that this conduct of the United States hardly conforms with the latter's avowed conviction that it was acting in the context of collective self-defence as consecrated by Article 51 of the Charter. This fact is all the more noteworthy because, in the Security Council, the United States has itself taken the view that failure to observe the requirement to make a report contradicted a State's claim to be acting on the basis of collective self-defence ... [142]

The absence of a report by Eritrea to the Security Council in 1998 was also taken into account by the Eritrea-Ethiopia Claims Commission in its Award on *jus ad bellum* issues.[143]

# III.  Use of Force in Defence of Other States

Collective self-defence or defence of other states is lawful, subject to the same conditions that exist for individual self-defence. In 1945, it was seemingly a 'novel concept',[144] although, whether or not that was the case, 'post-1945 practice has been crucial in its crystallization'.[145] Thus, an armed attack must already have begun and the forcible response by all those acting in collective self-defence must comply with the principles of necessity and proportionality. In addition, as the ICJ adjudged in the *Nicaragua* case,[146] the state that is the object of an armed attack must seek action in its self-defence. The 'Good Samaritan', whose assistance has not been solicited, acts unlawfully.[147] That said, a solicitation does not need to be overly formal in nature.[148]

Although the wording of Article 51 talks specifically of an armed attack against a member state, collective self-defence against a state that is not a member of the United Nations can also be lawful.[149] Arguably, however, only the UN member states engaging in collective self-defence are required to report to the UN Security Council on the forcible measures they have taken; a non-member state that has been attacked is not.

---

[142] ibid para 235.

[143] Eritrea-Ethiopia Claims Commission, *Partial Award: Jus Ad Bellum – Ethiopia's Claims 1–8*, 19 December 2005, para 11. See Gray, *International Law and the Use of Force*, 129.

[144] ICJ, *Nicaragua* judgment, Dissenting Opinion of Judge Sir Robert Jennings, 530.

[145] Gray, *International Law and the Use of Force*, 179.

[146] ICJ, *Nicaragua* judgment, para 195.

[147] Gray, *International Law and the Use of Force*, 181.

[148] ICJ, *Nicaragua* judgment, Dissenting Opinion of Judge Sir Robert Jennings, 544–45; see Gray, *International Law and the Use of Force*, 186.

[149] Brownlie, *International Law and the Use of Force by States*, 331; Bowett, *Self-defence in International Law*, 193–94.

# 4

# United Nations Security Council Authorisation to Use Force

## I. Introduction

Under the 1945 Charter of the United Nations[1] (UN Charter), the member states confer primary responsibility for the maintenance of international peace and security upon the UN Security Council 'and agree that in carrying out its duties under this responsibility the Security Council acts on their behalf'.[2] Under Chapter VII of the Charter, the Council is empowered to 'take such action by air, sea, or land forces as may be necessary to maintain or restore international peace and security'.[3]

But political realities and the resultant practice of the organisation have acted to divert the Council away from directing the use of force by armed forces made available to it by UN member states and firmly towards authorising those members to use force in its stead.[4] In so doing, states do not violate the general *jus cogens* prohibition on interstate use of force unless they violate the terms of the authorisation. Such a violation appears to have occurred in Libya in 2011 in relation to the Security Council's authorisation to protect civilians under Resolution 1973.

Accordingly, this chapter addresses the power of the Security Council to authorise the use of force in seeking to fulfil its fundamental duties as the 'keystone of the UN system of collective security'[5] along with the duty of states to act within the limits of an authorisation. In considering the role of the UN Security Council in the maintenance of international peace and security, it describes the forms that an authorisation to use force may take. It concludes with a brief assessment of the role of regional organisations in peace enforcement.

---

[1] Charter of the United Nations; adopted at San Francisco, 26 June 1945; entered into force, 24 October 1945.

[2] UN Charter, Art 24(1).

[3] UN Charter, Art 42.

[4] This is so even though, as Christine Gray observes, 'the precise legal basis for this in the Charter is not clear'. C Gray, *International Law and the Use of Force*, 4th edn (Oxford, Oxford University Press, 2018) 343. Kolb argues that this practice has 'surely' been adopted into law. R. Kolb, *International Law on the Maintenance of Peace: Jus Contra Bellum* (Cheltenham, Edward Elgar, 2019), 167.

[5] J Crawford, *Brownlie's Principles of Public International Law*, 9th edn (Oxford, Oxford University Press, 2019) 732.

# II. The Role of the UN Security Council

In discharging its 'primary'[6] (but not exclusive[7]) responsibility for the maintenance of international peace and security, the Security Council is obligated to act in accordance with the purposes and principles of the United Nations.[8] These purposes comprise 'effective collective measures' to prevent and remove 'threats to the peace' and to suppress 'acts of aggression or other breaches of the peace', as well as to achieve international cooperation in promoting and encouraging respect for human rights.[9]

In carrying out its responsibility for the maintenance of international peace and security, the Security Council is obligated to comply with, at the least, *jus cogens* norms.[10] In 1999, the Appeals Chamber of the International Criminal Tribunal for the former Yugoslavia (ICTY), itself established by a Security Council resolution, stated that the powers of the Council are 'subject to respect for peremptory norms of international law (*jus cogens*)'.[11] This is also the view of the International Law Commission (ILC), which determined in its 2011 Draft Articles on the Responsibility of International Organizations that: 'Nothing ... precludes the wrongfulness of any act of an international organization which is not in conformity with an obligation arising under a peremptory norm of general international law'.[12]

The Security Council, as an organ of the United Nations,[13] is part of an international organisation that is a subject of international law. Thereby, as the International Court of Justice (ICJ) has explicitly found, the United Nations is 'capable of possessing rights and duties'.[14] The ICJ has further affirmed that, as a subject of international law, international organisations 'are bound by any obligations incumbent upon them under general rules of international law'.[15] According to the 2012 General Assembly Declaration on the Rule of Law, UN member states

---

[6] UN Charter, Art 24(1).

[7] This point was emphasised by the International Court of Justice (ICJ) in *Certain Expenses of the United Nations (Article 17, Paragraph 2, of the Charter)*, Advisory Opinion, 20 July 1962, 16, bit.ly/32QwiDo.

[8] UN Charter, Art 24(2).

[9] UN Charter, Art 1(1) and (3).

[10] R. Kolb, *International Law on the Maintenance of Peace: Jus Contra Bellum* (Cheltenham, Edward Elgar, 2019), 237.

[11] ICTY, Case No IT-94-1-A *Prosecutor v Duško Tadić*, Judgment (Appeals Chamber), 15 July 1999, para 296.

[12] ILC Draft Articles on Responsibility of International Organizations, Art 26 in Report of the International Law Commission, Sixty-third session (26 April–3 June and 4 July–12 August 2011), UN doc A/66/10/Add.1 (New York, 2011).

[13] UN Charter, Art 7.

[14] ICJ, *Reparation for Injuries for Injuries Suffered in the Service of the United Nations*, Advisory Opinion, ICJ Reports 1949, 179.

[15] ICJ, *Interpretation of the Agreement of 25 March 1951 Between the WHO and Egypt*, Advisory Opinion, 20 December 1980, para 37.

recognise that the rule of law applies to all states equally, and to international organisations, 'including the United Nations and its principal organs'.[16]

Thus, the obligation to comply with *jus cogens* norms prohibits the Security Council from authorising a use of force that would amount to, in particular, aggression, genocide, enslavement, racial discrimination, a crime against humanity, torture, a frustration of the right of a people to self-determination,[17] war crimes, or arbitrary deprivation of life.[18] The ICJ has further affirmed that international organisations are also 'bound by any obligations incumbent upon them … under their constitutions or under international agreements to which they are parties'.[19] This means, for instance, that the failure to respect the procedural requirement in the UN Charter to 'determine the existence of any threat to the peace, breach of the peace, or act of aggression'[20] prior to authorising the use of force (see below) would be a violation of the Charter.

Alexander Orakhelashvili affirms that 'a coherent and transparent determination under Article 39 is a precondition without which no Chapter VII measure could have a proper legal basis'.[21] Henderson seems to treat a failure to make such a determination as an automatic violation of the *jus cogens* norm itself,[22] but that is not necessarily the case. Even if the procedural obligation were violated, there may still be a substantive threat to the peace, breach of the peace, or act of aggression that the authorisation would effectively address. It is the lack of a threat to or breach of the peace, or an act of aggression, that would be fatal to any Chapter VII authorisation to use force.

Dapo Akande has argued persuasively that, both in advisory opinions and in contentious proceedings, the ICJ has the power to declare invalid Security Council decisions.[23] That said, a holding by the World Court that the UN Security Council had violated international law and, a fortiori, a 'striking down' of a Chapter VII

---

[16] UN General Assembly Resolution 67/1 ('Declaration of the High-level Meeting of the General Assembly on the Rule of Law at the National and International Levels'), adopted without a vote on 24 September 2012, para 2.

[17] That the prohibition of each of these seven acts is a *jus cogens* rule is the view of the ILC. See para 5 of the commentary to Art 26 of the ILC Draft Articles on the Responsibility of States for Internationally Wrongful Acts, adopted on 10 August 2001, contained in the annex to UN General Assembly Resolution 56/83 of 12 December 2001 (hereinafter 2001 Articles on State Responsibility).

[18] Human Rights Committee, 'General Comment No 36 (2018) on Article 6 of the International Covenant on Civil and Political Rights, on the Right to Life', UN doc CCPR/C/GC/36, 30 October 2018, para 68; African Commission on Human and Peoples' Rights, 'General Comment No 3 on the African Charter on Human and Peoples' Rights: The Right to Life (Article 4)', adopted at Banjul (57th Ordinary Session), November 2015, para 5.

[19] ICJ, *Interpretation of the Agreement of 25 March 1951 Between the WHO and Egypt*, Advisory Opinion, 20 December 1980, para 37.

[20] UN Charter, Art 39.

[21] A Orakhelashvili, *Akehurst's Modern Introduction to International Law*, 8th edn (London, Routledge, 2018) 513.

[22] C Henderson, *The Use of Force and International Law* (Cambridge, Cambridge University Press, 2018) 23.

[23] D Akande, 'The International Court of Justice and the Security Council: Is There Room for Judicial Control of Decisions of the Political Organs of the United Nations?' (1997) 46(2) *International and Comparative Law Quarterly* 309, 343.

decision would be a momentous act, potentially leading the international community into 'an ambiguous and indeterminate area'.[24] Such a decision by the ICJ is highly improbable, but not impossible.

To date, however, the ICJ has declined to strike down any Chapter VII resolution by the Security Council when called upon to do so. In its 1992 Order in the case between Libya and the UK, *Questions of Interpretation and Application of the 1971 Montreal Convention arising from the Aerial Incident at Lockerbie*, the Court rejected Libya's claim that Security Council Resolution 748 was ultra vires the Montreal Convention.[25] It held that the duty of Libya and the UK, as UN member states, to carry out the decisions of the Security Council (in accordance with Article 25 of the UN Charter) prevailed over their obligations under any other international agreement, including the Montreal Convention, on the basis of Article 103[26] of the Charter.[27]

This is an unequivocal holding without caveat. Libya subsequently argued in its 1993 written pleadings that Security Council resolutions 'must always be interpreted in light of, and in conformity with, international law',[28] but proceedings were discontinued before any further judicial consideration of the issue. Also in 1993, however, the ICJ addressed Bosnia and Herzegovina's request for provisional measures in its case against the Federal Republic of Yugoslavia for genocide. Bosnia and Herzegovina had asserted that Security Council Resolution 713 of 1991 and all subsequent relevant Council resolutions 'must not be construed to impose an arms embargo upon Bosnia and Herzegovina, as required by Articles 24(1) and 51 of the United Nations Charter and in accordance with the customary doctrine of ultra vires'.[29] The intent was to equate the inherent right to self-defence with a right to procure arms. The Court declined to pronounce on the question, declaring that this was not a request for provisional measures but was, in substance, a claim for judgment on the merits.[30] It is certain, however, that the right to self-defence does not override a mandatory UN arms embargo.

---

[24] MN Shaw, *International Law*, 8th edn (Cambridge, Cambridge University Press, 2017) 973.

[25] Convention for the Suppression of Unlawful Acts against the Safety of Civil Aviation; adopted at Montreal, 23 September 1971; entered into force, 26 January 1973.

[26] Art 103 of the UN Charter stipulates that 'In the event of a conflict between the obligations of the Members of the United Nations under the present Charter and their obligations under any other international agreement, their obligations under the present Charter shall prevail'.

[27] ICJ, *Questions of Interpretation and Application of the 1971 Montreal Convention arising from the Aerial Incident at Lockerbie (Libyan Arab Jamahiriya v United Kingdom)*, Order (Request for the Indication of Provisional Measures), 14 April 1992, para 39.

[28] ICJ, *Questions of Interpretation and Application of the 1971 Montreal Convention arising from the Aerial Incident at Lockerbie (Libyan Arab Jamahiriya v United Kingdom)*, Memorial by the Libyan Arab Jamahiriya, 20 December 1993, para 6.34.

[29] ICJ, *Case Concerning Application of the Convention on the Prevention and Punishment of the Crime of Genocide (Bosnia and Herzegovina v Yugoslavia (Serbia and Montenegro))*, Application Proceedings Submitted by the Republic of Bosnia and Herzegovina, 20 March 1993, para 135(o) and *cf* also paras 123, 125. See further Akande, 'The International Court of Justice and the Security Council', 311–12 and fn 8.

[30] ICJ, *Case Concerning Application of the Convention on the Prevention and Punishment of the Crime of Genocide (Bosnia and Herzegovina v Yugoslavia (Serbia and Montenegro))*, Order (Further Requests for the Indication of Provisional Measures), 13 September 1993, para 41.

## A. The Duty to Determine a Threat to, or Breach of, International Peace and Security or an Act of Aggression

Chapter VII of the UN Charter concerns generally 'Action with respect to threats to the peace, breaches of the peace, and acts of aggression'. As noted above, under Article 39, the first of the 14 provisions that constitute Chapter VII, the Security Council is obligated to 'determine the existence of any threat to the peace, breach of the peace, or act of aggression'. The suggestion that the lack of an accepted definition of these terms means that this is not a firm obligation but merely a preferment of responsibility within the United Nations[31] (for example, to the detriment of the General Assembly) is not persuasive. Instead, the lack of a definition equips the Council with exceptionally wide discretion to determine a threat to, or breach of, the peace or an act of aggression. Thus, James Crawford finds it 'difficult to think of realistic scenarios in which such determinations might be justiciable'.[32] Dinstein similarly calls a determination on this issue by the Council 'conclusive'.[33]

What is also clear is that a 'threat to the peace' is the broadest of the three terms. It is broader in compass than a use of force prohibited by Article 2(4) of the UN Charter[34] and, a fortiori, an armed attack. The substantive distinction between a 'breach of the peace' and an 'act of aggression' is less evident, though both certainly encompass an armed attack giving rise to the right of individual and collective self-defence.[35] The three notions are considered in turn.

### (i) Threat to the Peace

The notion of a threat to the peace is variously said to be 'mercurial'[36] and 'elastic',[37] although at 'its most basic, the concept is intended to enable a response to imminent armed conflict between states'.[38] Writing in 1950, Hans Kelsen had suggested that in determining, at the least, a threat to the peace, the Council's discretion was effectively unfettered.[39] Peter Malanczuk similarly affirmed four decades later that such a threat is 'whatever' the Council says it is.[40] In the subsequent

---

[31] Henderson, *The Use of Force and International Law*, 94.

[32] Crawford, *Brownlie's Principles of Public International Law*, 733.

[33] Y Dinstein, *War, Aggression and Self-defence*, 6th edn (Cambridge, Cambridge University Press, 2017) para 879.

[34] N White, 'The Relationship between the UN Security Council and General Assembly in Matters of International Peace and Security' in M Weller (ed), *The Oxford Handbook of the Use of Force in International Law* (Oxford, Oxford University Press, 2015) 34.

[35] See further chs 3 and 7.

[36] Crawford, *Brownlie's Principles of Public International Law*, 734.

[37] Dinstein, *War, Aggression and Self-defence*, para 881.

[38] Crawford, *Brownlie's Principles of Public International Law*, 734.

[39] H Kelsen, *The Law of the United Nations* (New York, Frederick A Praeger, 1950) 727.

[40] P Malanczuk, *Akehurst's Modern Introduction to International Law*, 7th edn (London, Routledge, 1997) 426.

edition of *Akehurst's Modern Introduction to International Law*, however, published in 2018, Alexander Orakhelashvili was considerably more circumspect in his assessment, observing that in its 'practice, the Security Council has made some political determinations that have no factual basis'.[41]

At the same time, Orakhelashvili accepts that the scope of the notion of a 'threat' to the peace is broad, remarking that there is nothing in the UN Charter to suggest that it 'necessarily connotes action by a State or a violation of international law'.[42] Thus, in recent years, the failure to respect and protect civilians within the borders of a state has been found to amount to a threat to the peace on a number of occasions. In its 2011 resolution authorising the use of all necessary measures to protect civilians in Libya, for instance, the Security Council determined that the situation 'continue[d] to constitute a threat to international peace and security'.[43] In Resolution 1975, adopted the same year, the Council considered 'that the attacks currently taking place in Côte d'Ivoire against the civilian population could amount to crimes against humanity', and similarly determined that the situation in Côte d'Ivoire continued to constitute a threat to international peace and security.[44]

## (ii) Breach of the Peace

Henderson observes that, in its practice, the Security Council has found a breach of the peace when one state has unlawfully invaded and occupied another.[45] This was the case with respect to North Korea invading South Korea in 1950;[46] Argentina invading the Falkland Islands in 1981;[47] and Iraq invading Kuwait in 1990.[48]

In the case of Resolution 82 (1950) on the situation on the Korean peninsula, the Council noted 'with grave concern the armed attack on the Republic of Korea by forces from North Korea' and determined that 'this action constitutes a breach of the peace'.[49] With respect to the invasion of Kuwait, the Council declared itself 'alarmed' and determined that, as regards that invasion, 'there exists a breach of international peace and security'.[50]

---

[41] Orakhelashvili, *Akehurst's Modern Introduction to International Law*, 513.

[42] ibid.

[43] UN Security Council Resolution 1973, adopted on 17 March 2011 by 10 votes to 0 with 5 abstentions (Brazil, China, Germany, India, and Russia), nineteenth preambular paragraph.

[44] UN Security Council Resolution 1975, adopted on 30 March 2011 by consensus, thirteenth and fourteenth preambular paragraphs.

[45] Henderson, *The Use of Force and International Law*, 96–97.

[46] UN Security Council Resolution 82 (1950), adopted on 25 June 1950 by 9 votes to 0 with 1 abstention (Yugoslavia) and 1 absentee (the Soviet Union).

[47] UN Security Council Resolution 502, adopted on 3 April 1982 by 10 votes to 1 (Panama) with 4 abstentions (China, Poland, Spain, and the Soviet Union).

[48] UN Security Council Resolution 660, adopted on 2 August 1990 by 14 votes to 0, with Yemen not voting.

[49] Resolution 82 (1950), third and fourth preambular paragraphs.

[50] UN Security Council Resolution 660, first and second preambular paragraphs.

## (iii) Act of Aggression

Each of those breaches of the peace (by North Korea, by Argentina, and by Iraq) could equally have been determined to be an 'act of aggression'. Instead, the Council has only very rarely held that an act of aggression has occurred, notably in the case of bombing or ground attacks by one state against or on the territory of another.[51] Israel's attack on the Palestine Liberation Organization headquarters in Tunis in 1985[52] and another targeting and killing Khalil al-Wazir ('Abu Jihad'), the founder of the Fatah political party, in Sidi Bou Said, also in Tunisia, in 1988[53] were both found to be acts of aggression. Resolution 573 (1985) condemned vigorously 'the act of armed aggression perpetrated by Israel against Tunisian territory in flagrant violation of the Charter of the United Nations'.[54] Resolution 611 (1988) similarly condemned vigorously 'the aggression perpetrated on 16 April 1988 against the sovereignty and territorial integrity of Tunisia in flagrant violation of the Charter of the United Nations'.[55]

Other instances where acts of aggression have been condemned by the Council concern, in particular, apartheid South Africa's actions against Angola in 1976 and 1985, and against Botswana in 1985, and Southern Rhodesia's actions against Zambia in 1979.[56] There has been no finding of an act of aggression by the Security Council since 1988.[57] A Council resolution drafted by Russia in April 2018 that would have condemned the 'aggression against the Syrian Arab Republic by the US and its allies in violation of international law and the UN Charter' did not reach the necessary nine votes to pass (but would assuredly have been vetoed had it done so). Since the entry into force of the Statute of the International Criminal Court (ICC) in 2002, a finding by the Security Council that aggression has occurred could allow the ICC Prosecutor to 'proceed with the investigation in respect of a crime of aggression'.[58]

## (iv) The Obligation to Act

Where it does duly identify a threat to the peace, breach of the peace, or act of aggression, the Council is obligated to either make 'recommendations' or 'decide' in accordance with other provisions in Chapter VII of the Charter, what coercive or forcible measures shall be taken to 'maintain or restore international peace

---

[51] Kolb, *International Law on the Maintenance of Peace: Jus Contra Bellum*, 116.

[52] UN Security Council Resolution 573, adopted on 4 October 1985 by 14 votes to 0, with the United States abstaining.

[53] UN Security Council Resolution 611, adopted on 25 April 1988 by 14 votes to 0, with the United States abstaining.

[54] UN Security Council Resolution 573 (1985), para 1.

[55] Resolution 611 (1988), para 1.

[56] Henderson, *The Use of Force and International Law*, 97.

[57] Dinstein observes that the Council has never made a definitive determination that the crime of aggression has occurred: Dinstein, *War, Aggression and Self-defence*, para 901.

[58] Rome Statute of the International Criminal Court, Art 15*bis*(7). For more on this issue, see ch 7.

and security'.[59] James Crawford avers that, in so acting, the Council is 'presumably bound by peremptory norms (though not international law more generally)'.[60]

In the case of Syria, the Council has determined, most recently in 2018, that the 'devastating humanitarian situation … continues to constitute a threat to peace and security in the region'.[61] It has, though, been unable to take significant enforcement action, in particular as a result of opposition from Russia to actions targeting the Syrian government.[62] Already in 2012, UN General Assembly Resolution 66/253B on the situation in the Syrian Arab Republic had deplored 'the failure of the Security Council to agree on measures to ensure the compliance of Syrian authorities with its decisions'.[63]

## III. The Form and Content of a Council Authorisation to Use Force

The Security Council has used alternative formulations to authorise UN member states to use force. In international legal terms, a distinction might be taken to exist between 'all necessary means' and 'all necessary measures' in a Security Council authorisation. The authorisation of 'all necessary means', first employed in Council Resolution 678 in relation to the Iraqi invasion of Kuwait,[64] continues to be generally understood as permitting the use of force.[65] The language was employed in resolutions authorising force in Somalia (Resolution 794), Rwanda (Resolution 929), and Haiti (Resolution 940), in particular.

In contrast, 'all necessary measures' seemed to fall short of allowing force to be used (other than in self-defence). In Resolution 665, the Council called upon member states co-operating with the Government of Kuwait and deploying naval forces to the area

> to use *such measures commensurate to the specific circumstances as may be necessary* under the authority of the Security Council to halt all inward and outward maritime

---

[59] UN Charter, Art 39.

[60] Crawford, *Brownlie's Principles of Public International Law*, 736.

[61] UN Security Council Resolution 2401, adopted on 24 February 2018 by consensus, twelfth preambular paragraph.

[62] For instance, a US-drafted Security Council Resolution, submitted for adoption on 10 April 2018, which would have established the UN Independent Mechanism of Investigation (UNIM) for a period of one year (with a possibility of further extension and update by the Security Council if it deemed necessary), was vetoed by Russia.

[63] UN General Assembly Resolution 66/253B, adopted on 7 August 2012 by 133 votes to 12 with 31 abstentions, sixteenth preambular paragraph.

[64] UN Security Council Resolution 678, adopted on 29 November 1990 by 12 votes to 2 (Cuba and Yemen) with 1 abstention (China), para 2, authorised UN member states, 'co-operating with the Government of Kuwait, to use all necessary means to uphold and implement Resolution 660'.

[65] Though for a suggestion that the Resolution was ambiguous as to whether it was authorising force or reflecting the continuing right of self-defence, see M Weller, *Iraq and the Use of Force in International Law* (Oxford, Oxford University Press, 2010) 266.

shipping, in order to inspect and verify their cargoes and destinations and to ensure strict implementation of the provisions related to such shipping laid down in resolution 661 (1990).[66]

China expressed its belief that this formulation did 'not contain the concept of using force'.[67]

The distinction between 'means' (authorising force) and 'measures' (authorising or calling for action short of the use of force) is not, however, a hard and fast rule. Indeed, as Niels Blokker has observed, the phrase 'all necessary measures' even became the Council's preferred formulation to authorise use of force between 2000 and 2012.[68] For instance, in its Resolution 1973 (2011), acting under Chapter VII of the Charter, the Security Council authorised 'all necessary measures to protect civilians and civilian populated areas under threat of attack in the Libyan Arab Jamahiriya, including Benghazi'.[69] It was fully understood that this authorisation encompassed the use of force.

More recently, however, 'all necessary measures' has been used to denote action short of the use of force against another state. In Resolution 2249 (2015), the Security Council called on member states with the capacity to do so

to take all necessary measures, in compliance with international law, in particular with the United Nations Charter, as well as international human rights, refugee and humanitarian law, on the territory under the control of ISIL [Islamic State of Iraq and the Levant, Islamic State] also known as Da'esh, in Syria and Iraq, to redouble and coordinate their efforts to prevent and suppress terrorist acts committed specifically by ISIL also known as Da'esh as well as ANF [al-Nusrah Front], and all other individuals, groups, undertakings, and entities associated with Al Qaeda, and other terrorist groups ... and to eradicate the safe haven they have established over significant parts of Iraq and Syria.[70]

The context of the negotiation and adoption of the Resolution, including the fact that it was not adopted by the Council acting under Chapter VII, and the reference in the operative paragraph to the UN Charter, make it evident that the use of force was not being authorised without the consent of Iraq or Syria, respectively. Indeed, as Christine Gray observes, Germany and the UK relied instead on an alleged right of self-defence to justify their use of force in Syria, and not the terms of Security Council Resolution 2249.[71]

---

[66] UN Security Council Resolution 665, adopted on 25 August 1990 by 13 votes to 0 with 2 abstentions (Cuba and Yemen), para 1 (emphasis added).

[67] UN doc S/PV.2938, 25 August 1990, 55.

[68] N Blokker, 'Outsourcing the Use of Force: Towards More Security Council Control of Authorized Operations?' in Weller, *The Oxford Handbook of the Use of Force in International Law*, 213.

[69] UN Security Council Resolution 1973 (2011), para 4.

[70] UN Security Council Resolution 2249, adopted on 20 November 2015 by consensus, para 5.

[71] Gray, *International Law and the Use of Force*, 386.

# IV. Respect for the Terms of the Authorisation

The terms of an authorisation validly given must be respected.[72] This comprises both the purpose of the actions taken and whether those actions were indeed necessary. Irrespective of whether the formulation in the authorisation refers to 'means' or 'measures', the qualifying adjective 'necessary' exists as an objective, not subjective, modifier.[73] Forcible action that is ultra vires a Security Council authorisation causes serious and potentially fatal problems for the legality of a military operation. This was the case in Libya in 2011.

## A. UN Security Council Resolution 1973 (Libya)

The Security Council authorisation in the case of Gaddafi's Libya was explicit: to use 'all necessary measures to protect civilians and civilian populated areas under threat of attack in the Libyan Arab Jamahiriya, including Benghazi'.[74] Regime change was neither envisaged nor authorised by Resolution 1973. Indeed, the resolution specifically ruled out 'a foreign occupation force of any form on any part of Libyan territory'.[75] In the explanation of vote after the passing of its resolution, India (which abstained) stated that: 'It is of course very important that there be full respect for the sovereignty, unity and territorial integrity of Libya.'[76]

South Africa (which voted in favour of the resolution) said: 'As a matter of principle, we have supported the resolution, with the necessary caveats to preserve the sovereignty and territorial integrity of Libya and reject any foreign occupation or unilateral military intervention under the pretext of protecting civilians.'[77] China (which abstained) declared that it had

> always emphasized that, in its relevant actions, the Security Council should follow the United Nations Charter and the norms governing international law, respect the sovereignty, independence, unity and territorial integrity of Libya and resolve the current crisis in Libya through peaceful means.[78]

---

[72] I Brownlie, *International Law and the Use of Force by States* (Oxford, Oxford University Press, 1963) 334–35.

[73] By analogy (as the Court was considering not the implementation of the UN Charter but the 1956 Treaty of Friendship, Commerce and Navigation between Nicaragua and the United States), in its judgment in the *Nicaragua* case, the ICJ recalled that 'whether a measure is necessary to protect the essential security interests of a party is not … purely a question for the subjective judgment of the party; the text does not refer to what the party "considers necessary" for that purpose': ICJ, *Nicaragua* judgment, para 282. See also O Corten, *The Law Against War* (Oxford, Hart Publishing, 20100 327–28.

[74] UN Security Council Resolution 1973, para 4.

[75] ibid.

[76] UN doc S/PV.6498, 17 March 2011, 6.

[77] ibid 10.

[78] ibid.

In a joint letter published in the *New York Times* on 14 April 2011, US President Barack Obama, British Prime Minister David Cameron, and French President Nicolas Sarkozy wrote that: 'Our duty and our mandate under UN Security Council Resolution 1973 is to protect civilians, and we are doing that. It is not to remove Qaddafi by force.'[79] But the three leaders then cautioned, ominously, that 'it is impossible to imagine a future for Libya with Qaddafi in power'.[80] Christine Gray suggests that the 'wide drafting' of Resolution 1973 was 'flexible enough to cover NATO's use of force as long as pro-Gaddafi forces continued to fight'.[81] But, as she concedes, there was significant opposition from some states as Operation Unified Protector progressed.[82]

Thus, in late May 2011, the Assembly of the African Union issued a Decision on the Peaceful Resolution of the Libya Crisis in which it 'stressed the obligation of all Member States of the United Nations and the other concerned international actors to fully comply with the letter and spirit' of Security Council Resolutions 1970 and 1973. The Assembly

> expressed deep concern at the dangerous precedence being set by one-sided interpretations of these resolutions, in an attempt to provide a legal authority for military and other actions on the ground that are clearly outside the scope of these resolutions, and at the resulting negative impact on the efforts aimed at building an international order based on legality.[83]

Ashley Deeks defends the use of force against Gaddafi's military and the provision of support to rebels against those forces as 'consistent' with Resolution 1973, albeit on the basis of quite scant legal assessment as to why that is the case. She cites a commentator who claims that Russia knew that it was allowing regime change to occur by allowing the Resolution to pass.[84] But, as she also observes, 'Russia may have had its own political and economic reasons to wish to see Qadaffi in power'.[85] Moreover, accepting that there would ultimately be a transition of power is not the same as authorising the use of force to destroy the military forces of the regime.

The consequences of NATO member states exceeding (and selectively applying only against pro-Gaddafi elements) the authorisation to use force to protect civilians in Libya[86] are still being felt, not least in the violent chaos that is Libya today. In September 2019, the African Union's Peace and Security Council (PSC)

---

[79] B Obama, D Cameron and N Sarkozy, 'Libya's Pathway to Peace', *New York Times*, 14 April 2011, nyti.ms/2M9000j.

[80] ibid.

[81] Gray, *International Law and the Use of Force*, 379–80.

[82] See also A Deeks, 'The NATO Intervention in Libya – 2011' in Weller, *The Oxford Handbook of the Use of Force in International Law*, 754–55.

[83] 'African Union Decision on the Peaceful Resolution of the Libyan Crisis', Extraordinary Session of the Assembly of the Union, Addis Ababa, 25 May 2011, para 7.

[84] Deeks, 'The NATO Intervention in Libya – 2011', 757.

[85] ibid.

[86] In contrast, James Crawford speaks only of 'suggestions that outright support for the rebels went beyond the limited scope of Security Council Resolution 1973': Crawford, *Brownlie's Principles of Public International Law*, 740.

issued a ministerial communiqué in which it reiterated 'its deep concern about the seriousness of the situation prevailing in Libya and its dangerous repercussions on the security and stability of the Region and the Continent as a whole'.[87]

Today, Libya's Government of National Accord (GNA) is supported by the UN, 'but its writ barely runs inside Tripoli, much less outside it. It is struggling to keep the lights on and the water running, even in the capital.'[88] Speaking to the BBC in late October 2019, Fathi Bashagha, the GNA Minister of the Interior, accused the international community of failing to support the country since 2011. 'They did not complete the project. They wanted to remove Muammar Gaddafi but they should have supported us to rebuild a country, and to rebuild the army. Instead they left us.'[89]

# V. Security Council Authorisation and Regional Organisations

The role of regional organisations was specifically envisaged in the UN Charter. Article 52(1) made it explicit that the Charter did not preclude

> the existence of regional arrangements or agencies for dealing with such matters relating to the maintenance of international peace and security as are appropriate for regional action, provided that such arrangements or agencies and their activities are consistent with the Purposes and Principles of the United Nations.[90]

As James Crawford observes, Operation Desert Storm, conceived to repel the Iraqi invasion of Kuwait in 1990, represented the 'high-water mark' of UN member state action under Security Council authorisation. 'Such a coordinated, pan-regional response,' with more than 30 contributing states, 'has not been replicated; rather, smaller coalitions of the willing have formed, often based around regional arrangements.'[91]

In 2005, in response to the World Summit Outcome document,[92] the UN Security Council adopted Resolution 1631 by consensus, in which it expressed its 'determination to take appropriate steps to the further development of cooperation between the United Nations and regional and subregional organizations in maintaining international peace and security, consistent with Chapter VIII of the United Nations Charter'.[93] However, the Charter also stipulates in its Article 52(2)

---

[87] Communiqué of the 883rd meeting of the African Union PSC at the Ministerial Level, held on 27 September 2019, on the Situation in Libya (last updated 4 October 2019), para 2, bit.ly/35LXSSI.
[88] O Guerin, 'Libya in Chaos as Endless War Rumbles On', *BBC News*, 30 October 2019, bbc.in/34ywBDh.
[89] ibid.
[90] For a discussion of the definition of regional organisation under the UN Charter, see E de Wet, 'Regional Organizations and Arrangements: Authorization, Ratification or Independent Action' in Weller, *The Oxford Handbook of the Use of Force in International Law*, 315–17.
[91] Crawford, *Brownlie's Principles of Public International Law*, 739.
[92] Gray, *International Law and the Use of Force*, 390.
[93] UN Security Council Resolution 1631, adopted on 17 October 2005 by consensus, para 1.

that 'no enforcement action shall be taken under regional arrangements or by regional agencies without the authorization of the Security Council'. In recent years, a number of states, notably including Brazil, India, and Pakistan, have reiterated that the primary authority for the maintenance of international peace and security is vested in the Council.[94]

That said, a notable precedent for regional action had already been set in Bosnia and Herzegovina in 1993. UN Security Council Resolution 836 authorised the use of force by the UN Protection Force (UNPROFOR) in defence of the decreed 'safe areas'.[95] On 10 and 11 April 1994, UNPROFOR called in air strikes by NATO[96] to protect the Goražde safe area, which led to the bombing of a Bosnian Serb military position by US combat aircraft.[97] This was the first time in NATO's history that it had attacked ground targets with aircraft.[98] Following the genocide at Srebrenica, another of the Security-Council-designated safe areas, and in direct response to the shelling of a marketplace in Sarajevo, on 30 August to 20 September 1995, NATO aircraft operating under Operation Deliberate Force conducted more than 1000 sorties against Bosnian Serb military targets.[99]

Under the 2000 Constitutive Act of the African Union, Article 4(h) explicitly ascribes a right to the Union 'to intervene in a Member State pursuant to a decision of the Assembly in respect of grave circumstances, namely: war crimes, genocide and crimes against humanity'. Such action is still subject to prior UN Security Council authorisation, as Article 52(2) of the UN Charter dictates, despite occasional suggestions to the contrary.[100] Moreover, to date, African Union enforcement action – as opposed to peacekeeping on the basis of consent – has been limited. One challenge has been political will; another has been adequate funding.[101] Although not a regional enforcement resolution, the 2011 action in the North African state of Libya, discussed above, was 'almost entirely planned and undertaken by NATO forces'.[102]

Indeed, as de Wet noted in 2015, all of the military operations carried out thus far by the African Union occurred on the basis of consent from the government,

---

[94] Gray, *International Law and the Use of Force*, 395.

[95] UN Security Council Resolution 836, adopted on 4 June 1993 by 13 votes to 0 with 2 abstentions (Pakistan and Venezuela).

[96] De Wet questions whether NATO qualifies as a regional organisation for the purpose of Article 53(1) of the UN Charter: de Wet, 'Regional Organizations and Arrangements: Authorization, Ratification or Independent Action', 316–17.

[97] 'Report of the Secretary-General Pursuant to General Assembly Resolution 53/35: The Fall of Srebrenica', UN doc A/54/549, 15 November 1999, para 131.

[98] DL Bethlehem and M Weller, *The 'Yugoslav' Crisis in International Law* (Cambridge, Cambridge University Press, 1997) 5.

[99] JA Tirpak, 'Deliberate Force', *Air Force Magazine*, October 1997, bit.ly/2ORgCti.

[100] On this issue, see Corten, *The Law Against War*, 342–44; de Wet, 'Regional Organizations and Arrangements: Authorization, Ratification or Independent Action', 318–21.

[101] Gray, *International Law and the Use of Force*, 393; de Wet, 'Regional Organizations and Arrangements: Authorization, Ratification or Independent Action', 323–25.

[102] Crawford, *Brownlie's Principles of Public International Law*, 742.

and many were 'classic peacekeeping'. The organisation remains reliant on the (Western) members of the UN for logistical, financial, and military assistance.[103] As a consequence, she concludes that 'sustainable free-standing AU peace enforcement that occurs politically, financially, and ultimately also legally independent from the UN is not likely to occur in the near future'.[104]

---

[103] de Wet, 'Regional Organizations and Arrangements: Authorization, Ratification or Independent Action', 327.
[104] ibid 328.

# 5

## Use of Force and the Law of Neutrality

## I. Introduction

The modern law of neutrality, which dates back to the eighteenth century, defines the relationship under international law between states engaged as parties to an international armed conflict and those that are not.[1] Considered by some as a throwback to an earlier era, in fact the law of neutrality continues to affect the law on interstate use of force as well as the conduct of military operations on the territory of and against other states. The rules governing neutrality, which transcend *jus ad bellum* as well as *jus in bello*, obligate a neutral state to refrain from engaging directly in an international armed conflict.[2] They further preclude a state proclaiming neutrality from providing support to the forces of warring parties in such a conflict.[3] This is so unless contrary action is required of an ostensibly neutral UN member state by the UN Security Council.[4] In this regard, the situation with respect to UN observer states and other states is less clear.[5]

A neutral state also has a duty not to discriminate in its treatment of parties to an international armed conflict: to comply with the rules of the law of neutrality, where it imposes restrictions against one party, it must also impose the same restrictions upon the others. Compliance with this latter rule is potentially complicated by, in addition to the UN Charter,[6] relevant treaty obligations, such as those

---

[1] UK Ministry of Defence, *Joint Service Manual of the Law of Armed Conflict*, Joint Service Publication 383 (2004) para 1.42. See also US Department of Defense, *Law of War Manual* (Washington DC, June 2015, updated December 2016) (hereinafter USDOD December 2016 Law of War Manual), para 15.1.1.

[2] USDOD December 2016 Law of War Manual, para 15.3.2.

[3] P Seger, 'The Law of Neutrality' in A Clapham and P Gaeta (eds), *The Oxford Handbook of International Law in Armed Conflict* (Oxford, Oxford University Press, 2014) 248. As Seger recalls, the term comes from the Latin expression *ne uter*, meaning neither one nor the other.

[4] Arts 41 and 42 of the Charter of the United Nations; adopted at San Francisco, 26 June 1945; entered into force, 24 October 1945. The Council must be acting under Chapter VII of the UN Charter. USDOD December 2016 Law of War Manual, para 15.2.

[5] The status of Permanent Observer is based purely on practice, with no provisions governing such status in the UN Charter. The practice dates from 1946, when the UN Secretary-General accepted Switzerland as a Permanent Observer to the United Nations. UN, 'About Permanent Observers', undated, bit.ly/2NIRUdU. One must assume that other states (Cook Islands and Niue) are not obligated to carry out UN Security Council instructions and therefore this exception to the general rule governing neutrality does not apply in their case.

[6] UK Ministry of Defence, *Joint Service Manual of the Law of Armed Conflict*, para 1.42.2.

set out in the 2013 Arms Trade Treaty,[7] and the rules governing state responsibility for internationally wrongful acts.[8] While this rule of non-discrimination tends towards a rule applicable *in bello*, a serious violation may have implications also *ad bellum*.

The corresponding obligations on states engaged in an international armed conflict are to not attack a neutral state as well as to ensure, to the maximum extent possible, that neutral states are not affected by the conduct of hostilities. This encompasses an obligation not to use the territory of neutral states for their military operations, or even to transit through neutral states with a view to attacking their enemy. The customary and conventional right of innocent passage through territorial seas[9] continues to apply during armed conflict, with the rules differing materially from those set out in the prohibition on transit through land or airspace. Passage may even be 'innocent' where it is effected with a view to committing a future act of aggression, as long as the aggression is not perpetrated against the coastal state.[10]

Should a party to an international armed conflict infringe its obligations to respect the neutrality of a state, for example by moving its troops on to the territory of a neutral state, that neutral state is required to take such measures as are reasonable in the circumstances to address the violation of their neutrality. In this particular case, this would demand that the neutral state intern the foreign troops in their territory for the duration of the conflict. To achieve this aim, lawful measures may extend to the use of force that is both necessary and proportionate in the circumstances. Such a use of force, which is akin to an operation of domestic law enforcement, does not amount to a violation of Article 2(4) of the UN Charter, much less to an armed attack, as described below.

## II. The Origins of the Law of Neutrality

The issue of neutrality is a long-standing one in international law and jurisprudence. While the modern law is said to find its intellectual origins in the work of the Dutch jurist Cornelius van Bynkershoek and the Swiss jurist Emmerich de Vattel, in fact Vattel had been heavily influenced by the earlier writings of

---

[7] Arms Trade Treaty; adopted at New York, 2 April 2013; entered into force, 24 December 2014. As at 1 May 2020, 106 states were party to the Treaty. See UN Treaty Section, bit.ly/2pDyXBm.

[8] International Law Commission (ILC) Draft Articles on the Responsibility of States for Internationally Wrongful Acts, adopted on 10 August 2001, contained in the annex to UN General Assembly Resolution 56/83 of 12 December 2001 (hereinafter 2001 Articles on State Responsibility), esp Draft Arts 40 and 41, as well as the associated commentary by the ILC Special Rapporteur with respect to serious breaches of a peremptory norm of international law, particularly the prohibition of aggression.

[9] Art 17 of the UN Convention on the Law of the Sea; adopted at Montego Bay, 10 December 1982; entered into force, 16 November 1994 (UNCLOS).

[10] Art 19(2) of UNCLOS makes it clear that passage is not innocent where it is effected with a view to committing aggression against the coastal state.

Hugo de Groot.[11] Prior even to Grotius, however, Machiavelli had considered the role of neutral states during wartime, while the German military historian Johann Wilhelm Neumair von Ramsla had written a dissertation on the issue five years before the publication of *De Jure Belli ac Pacis* in 1625.[12]

In his 1737 work *Quaestiones Juris Publici*,[13] van Bynkershoek argued that war should respect the territory of nations not involved in the war, and that it is the right and duty of every sovereign to both prevent and punish violations, whether they occur on land or at sea. van Bynkershoek distinguished neutrals from allies who are bound by treaty to one or both of the belligerents. Neutrals must refrain from any interference in war, he wrote, whatever the justice of the cause that may be perceived of one of the parties, and exclude all supply of troops, weapons, and even food to any of the belligerents.[14]

In his famed 1758 work *Le Droit des Gens* ('The Law of Nations'), Vattel addressed neutrality during war in a similar manner, defining neutral nations as 'those who, in time of war, do not take any part in the contest, but remain common friends to both parties, without favouring the arms of the one to the prejudice of the other'.[15] He declared that:

> As long as a neutral nation wishes securely to enjoy the advantages of her neutrality, she must in all things show a strict impartiality towards the belligerent powers: for, should she favour one of the parties to the prejudice of the other, she cannot complain of being treated by him as an adherent and confederate of his enemy. Her neutrality would be a fraudulent neutrality, of which no nation will consent to be the dupe.[16]

Vattel expounded on the duties upon a neutral state during warfare, which he summarised in two articles. The first concerns the duty to not furnish assistance to a belligerent other than when obligated to do so; the second is that the neutral state must not refuse to one of the parties that which it grants to the other:

> 1. To give no assistance when there is no obligation to give it, nor voluntarily to furnish troops, arms, ammunition, or any thing of direct use in war. I do not say, 'to give assistance equally', but 'to give no assistance': for it would be absurd that a state should at one and the same time assist two nations at war with each other; and, besides, it would be impossible to do it with equality. The same things, the like number of troops, the like quantity of arms, of stores, etc, furnished in different circumstances, are no longer equivalent succours.

---

[11] I Brownlie, *International Law and the Use of Force by States* (Oxford, Oxford University Press, 1963) 16.

[12] JWN von Ramsla, *Von der Neutralität und Assistenz oder Unpartheyligkeit und Partheyligkeit in Kriegszeiten* (Erfurt, 1620); see also H Duchhardt, 'From the Peace of Westphalia to the Congress of Vienna' in B Fassbender and A Peters (eds), *The Oxford Handbook of the History of international Law* (Oxford, Oxford University Press, 2014) 637.

[13] *Quaestiones Juris Publici* (1737) Book I, Ch VIII.

[14] ibid Book I, Ch IX. See J de Louter, 'Introduction' in *Quaestionum Juris Publici Libri Duo by Cornelius van Bynkershoek*, vol II (transl T Frank, Oxford, Clarendon Press, 1930), bit.ly/30kaii2.

[15] E de Vattel, *Le Droit des Gens*, Book III, Ch 7 ('Of Neutrality: and the Passage of Troops Through a Neutral Country'), §103, bit.ly/2JkeTLm.

[16] ibid §104.

2.  In whatever does not relate to war, a neutral and impartial nation must not refuse to one of the parties, on account of his present quarrel, what she grants to the other. This does not deprive her of the liberty to make the advantage of the state still serve as her rule of conduct in her negotiations, her friendly connections, and her commerce. When this reason induces her to give preferences in things which are ever at the free disposal of the possessor, she only makes use of her right, and is not chargeable with partiality. But to refuse any of those things to one of the parties purely because he is at war with the other, and because she wishes to favour the latter, would be departing from the line of strict neutrality.[17]

For the belligerents, Vattel declared that 'it is unlawful to attack an enemy in a neutral country, or to commit in it any other act of hostility'.[18]

## III. The Modern Law of Neutrality

The law of neutrality as we know it today developed during the late eighteenth century with a view to curtailing or confronting British naval power. The first League of Armed Neutrality was a treaty alliance of European naval powers, in force between 1780 and 1783 during the American War of Independence. Denmark devised the conceptual framework, although the written agreement was formally proclaimed by Catherine the Great of Russia on 29 February 1780.[19] It was subsequently endorsed by Sweden, along with a number of other European nations, spurred on by the United States.[20] The principles set out in the treaty included a right of neutral vessels to navigate freely from port to port and along the coasts of the nations at war, combined with a duty to respect the property of subjects of the belligerent parties present on board neutral vessels. The British, seeing the principles as an assault on their blockades of ports in rebellious colonies, roundly rejected the treaty.

The Second League of Armed Neutrality of 1800 – also known as the 'League of the North' because it was an alliance of north European naval powers Denmark–Norway, Prussia, Russia, and Sweden – was a revival of the earlier 1780 agreement. Its resurrection was a renewed attempt, encouraged this time by Napoleon Bonaparte, to create a bulwark against British naval power.[21] Again, Russia was the formal instigator of the agreement (with Paul I, Catherine the Great's son, leading the initiative this time). It took effect between 1800 and 1801, during the War of the Second Coalition, even though Russia was then engaged in fighting France alongside Britain. In 1801, British naval forces, deriding the potential repercussions

---

[17] ibid §104.

[18] ibid §132.

[19] See, eg I de Madariaga, *Britain, Russia, and the Armed Neutrality of 1780: Sir James Harris's Mission to St. Petersburg during the American Revolution* (New Haven, CT, Yale University Press, 1962).

[20] See, eg DM Griffiths, 'An American Contribution to the Armed Neutrality of 1780' (1971) 30(2) *Russian Review* 164.

[21] AA Richmond, 'Napoleon and the Armed Neutrality of 1800: A Diplomatic Challenge to British Sea Power' (1959) 104(614) *Royal United Services Institution Journal* 190.

on its relationship with Russia, attacked and defeated the Danish–Norwegian fleet in what became known as the Battle of Copenhagen.[22] The outcome of the battle forced Denmark's withdrawal from the League, which collapsed *in toto* following the assassination of Tsar Paul I in Saint Petersburg on 24 March 1801.

Also of importance in the development of international law governing neutrality were the declarations of Swiss and Belgian neutrality in the first half of the nineteenth century.[23] Switzerland's 'perpetual' neutrality was declared in 1815 (although the earliest moves towards Swiss neutrality date back to 1515, when the Swiss Confederacy suffered a devastating defeat to the French at the Battle of Marignano).[24] In 1798, however, during the Napoleonic Wars, Switzerland was invaded by France and reduced to a vassal state of Bonaparte's empire, forcing it to surrender its neutrality.

After Napoleon's defeat at Waterloo, the major European powers concluded that a neutral Switzerland could serve as a valuable buffer between France and Austria. Accordingly, at the 1815 Congress of Vienna, they signed a declaration affirming Switzerland's 'perpetual neutrality'[25] within the international community.[26] For its part, Belgium was also formally committed to a general position of neutrality (though it is no longer neutral today).[27] Under the 1839 Treaty of London,[28] the European powers recognised and guaranteed the country's independence and neutrality, with Article VII of the Treaty specifically obligating Belgium to remain 'perpetually' neutral; it 'shall be bound to observe such neutrality towards all other States'.[29] When German forces invaded Belgium in August 1914 in violation of the treaty, Great Britain declared war. Informed of this fact by the British

---

[22] R Cavendish, 'The Battle of Copenhagen' (2001) 51(4) *History Today*, bit.ly/30unlNM.

[23] D Schindler and J Toman, *The Laws of Armed Conflicts* (Leiden, Martinus Nijhoff, 1988) 942–47.

[24] E Andrews, 'Why Is Switzerland a Neutral Country?', News Item, *History Today*, 12 July 2016, bit.ly/2NItJzF.

[25] In 2018, however, Switzerland's government surprisingly suggested that in the event of a major armed conflict affecting Europe it would seek the protection of (presumably) NATO (North Atlantic Treaty Organization)'s nuclear capabilities, thereby renouncing its 'perpetual' neutral status: 'In the extreme case of self-defence against an armed attack, Switzerland would probably cooperate with other states or alliances, not least with nuclear weapon states or their allies.' Swiss Federal Department of Foreign Affairs, 'Report of the Working Group to analyse the Treaty on the Prohibition of Nuclear Weapons', English translation from the German original version, 30 June 2018, 6, bit.ly/2RRxUWZ.

[26] GE Sherman, 'The Neutrality of Switzerland' (1918) 12(2) *American Journal of International Law* 241; see also Duchhardt, 'From the Peace of Westphalia to the Congress of Vienna', 650.

[27] Seger correctly notes that 'permanent' neutrality does not connote 'perpetual' neutrality: Seger, 'The Law of Neutrality', 260.

[28] Treaty between Great Britain, Austria, France, Prussia, and Russia, on the one part, and Belgium, on the other; signed at London, 19 April 1839. The parties to the Treaty were Austria, Belgium, France, the German Confederation, Netherlands, Russia, and the UK. The German Confederation, an organisation of 39 German states, was established by the 1815 Congress of Vienna to replace the destroyed Holy Roman Empire. It was a loose political association, formed for mutual defence. Delegates met in a federal assembly dominated by Austria. 'German Confederation', *Encyclopaedia Britannica*, undated, bit.ly/2rpMGNb.

[29] See E Van Hooydonk, 'Places of Refuge: The Belgian Experience' in AE Chircop and O Lindén (eds), *Places of Refuge for Ships: Emerging Environmental Concerns of a Maritime Custom*, Publications on Ocean Development, vol 51 (Leiden, Martinus Nijhoff, 2006) 417.

Ambassador, the German Chancellor Theobald von Bethmann-Hollweg is said to have exclaimed his disbelief that Britain and Germany would be going to war over a 'scrap of paper'.[30]

In the second half of the nineteenth century, other treaties would set out and clarify the rules of neutrality that were gradually evolving through state practice. In 1856, the Paris Declaration on Maritime Law[31] included the stipulation that neutral goods at sea, 'with the exception of contraband of war, are not liable to capture under enemy's flag'. The grounds for adopting the Declaration were set out in its Preamble:

> That maritime law, in time of war, has long been the subject of deplorable disputes;
>
> That the uncertainty of the law and of the duties in such a matter, gives rise to differences of opinion between neutrals and belligerents which may occasion serious difficulties, and even conflicts.

In 1899, Article 57 of the Regulations respecting the laws and customs of war on land, annexed to Hague Convention II,[32] provided as follows:

> A neutral State which receives in its territory troops belonging to the belligerent armies shall intern them, as far as possible, at a distance from the theatre of war.
>
> It can keep them in camps, and even confine them in fortresses or locations assigned for this purpose.
>
> It shall decide whether officers may be left at liberty on giving their parole that they will not leave the neutral territory without authorization.

This duty of internment of belligerent troops passing through a neutral state persists in international law today. It applies directly *in bello*, although a serious failure to implement it dutifully may have implications also *ad bellum*, most notably when the troops proceed to commit an armed attack against another state.

By 1907, state practice had already settled most of the key issues on neutrality. The Second Hague Peace Conference adopted two treaties dedicated to issues of neutrality: the Convention on the Rights and Duties of Neutral Powers and Persons in case of War on Land (1907 Hague Convention V)[33] and the Convention concerning the Rights and Duties of Neutral Powers in Naval War (1907

---

[30] L Zuckerman, *The Rape of Belgium: The Untold Story of World War I* (New York, New York University Press, 2004) 43; 'Why Did War Break Out in 1914?', *National Archives*, undated, bit.ly/36iu9Bo.

[31] Declaration Respecting Maritime Law; adopted at Paris, 16 April 1856. As at 1 May 2020, there remained only 55 states parties to the 1856 Paris Declaration (and many are no longer states today; the full list of states parties is available on the website of the International Committee of the Red Cross (ICRC), bit.ly/2LKWUiY).

[32] Convention (II) with Respect to the Laws and Customs of War on Land and its annex: Regulations concerning the Laws and Customs of War on Land; adopted at The Hague, 29 July 1899; entered into force, 4 September 1900.

[33] Convention (V) respecting the Rights and Duties of Neutral Powers and Persons in Case of War on Land; adopted at The Hague, 18 October 1907; entered into force, 26 January 1910. A total of 34 states are party to the Convention. See the ICRC list at bit.ly/2Y3L9ed.

Hague Convention XIII).[34] The principles set out in each instrument were clear and far-reaching.

According to Article 1 of the 1907 Hague Convention V, 'The territory of neutral Powers is inviolable.'[35] Under Article 2, 'Belligerents are forbidden to move troops or convoys of either munitions of war or supplies across the territory of a neutral Power'. Article 5 obligated neutral powers to 'not allow' this and other specific acts to occur on their territory. In turn, under Article 1 of the 1907 Hague Convention XIII, 'Belligerents are bound to respect the sovereign rights of neutral Powers and to abstain, in neutral territory or neutral waters, from any act which would, if knowingly permitted by any Power, constitute a violation of neutrality'. In accordance with Article 2, 'Any act of hostility, including capture and the exercise of the right of search, committed by belligerent warships in the territorial waters of a neutral Power, constitutes a violation of neutrality and is strictly forbidden'.

Although Great Britain and a number of other states existing at the time did not adhere to the Hague Convention V, its significance *ad bellum* is seen in the fact that in the 1920s, the international arbitration tribunal in the *Naulilaa* case relied expressly on its provisions (and the 1899 Hague Regulations) in reaching its decision. The *Naulilaa* arbitration between Portugal and Germany concerned events occurring between 31 July 1914 and 9 March 1916, when war had not yet been declared between the two states and Portugal was thus still a neutral state.[36] These events comprised the killing, in 1914, of three German officers in the Angolan fortress of Naulila. Later, German colonial troops from neighbouring German South West Africa attacked and destroyed six Portuguese border fortresses inside Angola in an action it described as a 'reprisal'.[37]

In the Arbitral Award of 1928, it was stated, with particular reference to a core provision of the 1907 Hague Convention V, as follows:

> The attacks took place long before the declaration of war, which occurred on 9 March 1916. These are deliberate violations of the border of a neutral state. Since neutral territory is inviolable,[38] the action of the German forces was, in principle, contrary to the law of nations. As this action can not be justified as a reprisal, it must be recognised that the

---

[34] Convention (XIII) concerning the Rights and Duties of Neutral Powers in Naval War; adopted at The Hague, 18 October 1907; entered into force, 26 January 1910. A total of 30 states are party to the Convention. See the ICRC list at bit.ly/2G6fRsO.

[35] As the US Department of Defense has observed, 'The inviolability of neutral territory prohibits any unauthorized entry into the territory of a neutral State, its territorial waters, or the airspace over such areas by armed forces or instrumentalities of war': USDOD December 2016 Law of War Manual, para 15.3.1.1.

[36] J Pfeil, 'Naulilaa Arbitration (*Portugal v Germany*)', *Max Planck Encyclopedia of Public International Law* (last updated March 2007), bit.ly/2LdWlid.

[37] J Zollmann, 'History as a Legal Argument – The Naulilaa Case (1928)' (Berlin, WZB Center for Global Constitutionalism, October 2016), bit.ly/2S78dTI. Zollmann explains that Naulila is the correct spelling of the name of the fortress and that the extra 'a' in the word contained in the report of the Arbitral Award slipped in by mistake.

[38] *cf* 1907 Hague Convention (V), Art 1 (footnote in original).

authorities of South West Africa have contravened one of the explicit rules of positive international law.[39]

With respect to rules applicable *ad bellum* and *in bello*, the Arbitral Award referred to the 1899 Hague Regulations in declaring that a neutral state has the right to both disarm and intern armed belligerents who enter its territory.[40]

## A. The Law of Neutrality since the UN Charter

The issue of neutrality is not addressed explicitly in the UN Charter. That said, the Charter affects the law of neutrality by its imposition on each member state of the duty to implement UN Security Council decisions.[41] This rule may require a neutral state to treat one or more certain states that are party to an international armed conflict differently from other parties to that conflict.[42] It has a significant impact on the applicable rules of the law of neutrality.[43]

In its 1996 Advisory Opinion on the *Legality of the Threat or Use of Nuclear Weapons*, the International Court of Justice (ICJ) cited the submission of Nauru whereby 'The principle of neutrality, in its classic sense, was aimed at preventing the incursion of belligerent forces into neutral territory, or attacks on the persons or ships of neutrals.'[44] Nauru cites both 1907 Hague Conventions in detailing the application of the principle to nuclear weapons. The Court found that international law 'leaves no doubt that the principle of neutrality, whatever its content ... is applicable (subject to the relevant provisions of the United Nations Charter), to all international armed conflict'.[45]

---

[39] 'Les agressions ont eu lieu longtemps avant la déclaration de guerre, survenue le 9 mars 1916. Il s'agit donc de violations délibérées de la frontière d'un État neutre. Le territoire neutre étant inviolable [footnote omitted], l'action des forces allemandes était, en principe, contraire au droit des gens. Cette action ne pouvant se justifier à titre de représailles, il faut admettre que les autorités du Sud-Ouest africain ont contrevenu à l'une des règles expresses du droit des gens positif': *Responsabilité de l'Allemagne à raison des dommages causés dans les colonies portugaises du sud de l'Afrique (sentence sur le principe de la responsabilité) (Portugal c Allemagne)*, *Reports of International Arbitral Awards*, 31 July 1928, vol II, 1028–29 (author's translation), text of the award is at bit.ly/2XB7Xxn.

[40] Germany and Portugal were states parties to the Convention, both having adhered in 1900.

[41] UN Charter, Art 25.

[42] USDOD December 2016 Law of War Manual, para 15.2.3.

[43] Art 103 of the UN Charter stipulates that 'In the event of a conflict between the obligations of the Members of the United Nations under the present Charter and their obligations under any other international agreement, their obligations under the present Charter shall prevail'. This primacy given to the UN Charter over other treaties does not directly resolve the potential legal conflicts arising from the law of neutrality as much of that body of law is of a customary rather than treaty law nature. One must assume, however, that the applicable customary rules of the law of neutrality have been modified as a result of the adoption of the Charter and its adherence by 193 states.

[44] ICJ, *Legality of the Threat or Use of Nuclear Weapons*, Advisory Opinion, 8 July 1996, para 88.

[45] ibid para 89.

Writing in 1992, Maurice Torelli had claimed that the law of neutrality was 'eroding'.[46] Rather, it is true to say that, owing to the modern rules *ad bellum*, the law of neutrality has been changing.

## (i) *The Sources and Scope of Application of the Law*

The primary sources of the law of neutrality are custom and treaty.[47] The two main treaties on neutrality *ad bellum* remain the 1907 Hague Conventions V and XIII, neither of which has been amended by its states parties.[48] The key rules set out within these two instruments reflect customary international law.[49] Consonant with these instruments, the law of neutrality applies only to international armed conflict and not also to non-international armed conflict.[50]

Where an international armed conflict results from a UN Security Council authorisation to use force, it is not correct that the law of neutrality does not apply at all.[51] As noted below, the UN General Assembly's consensual recognition of Turkmenistan's permanent neutrality in 1995 was made explicitly subject to Turkmenistan's continued compliance with its obligations under the UN Charter. It is not that the law of neutrality does not apply; rather, it is that the content of the law is amended by the Charter's rules allied to the general international law duty of good faith implementation.

It is also asserted that the law only applies to international armed conflicts of 'a significant scope', by which is meant those of 'a certain duration and intensity'.[52] In making this claim, Michael Bothe was referring to the existence of an armed conflict as defined under international humanitarian law. He then linked – while slightly tempering his view on – the application of the law of neutrality in the following manner:

> the threshold of application of the law of neutrality is *probably* higher than that for the rules of the law of war relating to the conduct of hostilities and the treatment of prisoners, which are applicable also in conflicts of less intensity.[53]

---

[46] M Torelli, 'La neutralité en question' (1992) 96 *Revue générale de droit international public* 5, 9. See Seger, 'The Law of Neutrality', 251, citing (but questioning) Torelli's claim.

[47] M Bothe, 'The Law of Neutrality' in D Fleck (ed), *The Handbook of Humanitarian Law in Armed Conflicts* (Oxford, Oxford University Press, 1999) rule 1102. Bothe continues to assert that the need for a new codification of the law is 'urgent': ibid commentary para 2 on rule 1102.

[48] Ukraine adhered to both Conventions in 2015, the first state to do so for 80 years. Prior to that, the last state to adhere had been Ethiopia, back in 1935. Seger, 'The Law of Neutrality', 251.

[49] UK Ministry of Defence, *Joint Service Manual of the Law of Armed Conflict*, para 1.43; USDOD December 2016 Law of War Manual, para 15.1.4.

[50] Seger, 'The Law of Neutrality', 253.

[51] ibid.

[52] Bothe, 'The Law of Neutrality', rule 1106; approved by USDOD December 2016 Law of War Manual, para 15.2.1.2. Bothe maintains this stance in the latest edition of the Handbook: M Bothe, 'The Law of Neutrality' in D Fleck (ed), *The Handbook of Humanitarian Law in Armed Conflicts*, 3rd edn (Oxford, Oxford University Press, 2014) rule 1106 and associated commentary, para 1.

[53] Bothe, 'The Law of Neutrality', commentary para 1 on rule 1106 (emphasis added). See similarly Seger, 'The Law of Neutrality', 253.

Whether or not this is correct in relation to the law of neutrality *in bello*, it does not hold true for *jus ad bellum*. Any use of force that falls within the scope of the general prohibition on the use of force, as codified in Article 2(4) of the UN Charter, brings into play the following rules *ad bellum*.

## (ii) *The Right to Proclaim Neutrality*

It is potentially open to every state to proclaim its neutrality either on an ad hoc or on a permanent basis in case of international armed conflict. That is the case whether or not the neutral state is also a member state of the United Nations. UN General Assembly Resolution 50/80A, adopted without a vote in 1995, concerned the 'permanent neutrality' of Turkmenistan.[54] In the preamble to the Resolution, the Assembly reaffirmed 'the sovereign right of every State to determine independently its foreign policy in accordance with the norms and principles of international law and the Charter of the United Nations'.[55]

As already noted, Resolution 50/80A further recognised that Turkmenistan's adoption of a status of permanent neutrality 'does not affect the fulfilment of its obligations under the Charter'.[56] Thus, where action is required by the UN Security Council, acting under Chapter VII of the UN Charter,[57] any neutral UN member state must fulfil those obligations, even if they would otherwise contradict its duties under the law of neutrality. There are six main rules of the law of neutrality that apply *ad bellum*.

## (iii) *The* ad Bellum *Rules of the Law of Neutrality*

First and foremost, the law of neutrality prohibits a neutral state from engaging its own forces in an international armed conflict. This is the very essence of neutral status. A neutral state may not even participate in the collective self-defence of another state that is the subject of an armed attack without violating its neutrality.[58] Moreover, as the US Department of Defense has observed:

> a neutral State's acts of participation in a war of *aggression* against another member of the United Nations would likely violate not only its duties under the law of neutrality ... but also the Charter's prohibition on the unlawful use of force.[59]

Second, a neutral state may not provide significant material support to the forces of the parties to an international armed conflict. Given the UN Charter rules of *jus ad*

---

[54] UN General Assembly Resolution 50/80A, adopted without a vote on 12 December 1995.
[55] ibid second preambular paragraph.
[56] ibid seventh preambular paragraph.
[57] UN Charter, Arts 41 and 42.
[58] Bothe, 'The Law of Neutrality', commentary para 5 on rule 1101.
[59] USDOD December 2016 Law of War Manual, para 15.2.3.1 (emphasis added). See also Bothe, 'The Law of Neutrality', rule 1104 and associated commentary.

*bellum*, Ian Brownlie declared in 1963 that economic as well as military assistance to an aggressor 'will naturally constitute breaches of the law of neutrality'.[60] Such assistance must, though, be of a significant nature.[61] Ireland, for example, provides landing and refuelling to US Air Force aircraft and did so during the 2003 Gulf War, despite the unlawful nature of the US invasion.[62] Arguably, this was not illegal.

Unlawful assistance to a party to an international armed conflict will, however, engage the responsibility of the state under international law for an internationally wrongful act.[63] A serious violation of the law of neutrality may make the state a lawful target *ad bellum* following an armed attack.[64] Where, for instance, a foreign state's armaments are hosted on its territory, this may render those weapons a lawful target under *jus in bello*.[65] In this regard, Brownlie considered a scenario where an ostensibly neutral state hosts missiles belonging to a foreign state:

> If state A is attacked by state B with long-range missiles the former may find it necessary to retaliate not only against missile bases in state B but also on the territory of other states which, prior to the outbreak of hostilities, have allowed state B to set up missile bases. The actual or imminent use of these bases by state B will jeopardize the neutrality of the host states.[66]

With respect to nuclear weapons, which was at the forefront of Brownlie's concern, today this would pertain to Belgium, Germany, Italy, the Netherlands, and Turkey, all of which have US nuclear weapons present on airbases located on their respective territory.[67] Writing in the aftermath of the Cuban Missile Crisis, Brownlie had hoped that the problem would be 'academic'. He noted, however, that, at the time, the Soviet Union had 'considered it necessary to warn those states which have permitted the establishment of foreign missile bases and nuclear weapons on their territory of the grave consequences which this policy might have in the event of war'.[68]

The third main rule *ad bellum* of the law of neutrality is the corresponding set of obligations imposed on the parties engaged in an international armed conflict towards states proclaiming their neutrality.[69] The parties to the conflict are strictly obligated to neither attack a neutral state (consonant with the *jus cogens* prohibition on aggression) nor to use a neutral state's territory for its military operations.[70]

---

[60] Brownlie, *International Law and the Use of Force by States*, 369.

[61] Bothe, 'The Law of Neutrality', commentary para 1 on rule 1110.

[62] See Seger, 'The Law of Neutrality', 260.

[63] Under Draft Arts 40 and 41 of the 2001 Articles on State Responsibility, the ILC determined that no state shall 'render aid or assistance' in maintaining a serious breach of an obligation arising under a peremptory norm of general international law.

[64] UK Ministry of Defence, *Joint Service Manual of the Law of Armed Conflict*, para 1.43(a).

[65] For more on this issue see ch 7.

[66] Brownlie, *International Law and the Use of Force by States*, 314–15.

[67] HM Kristensen and RS Norris, 'Worldwide Deployments of Nuclear Weapons, 2017' (2017) 73(5) *Bulletin of the Atomic Scientists* 290, 292, bit.ly/2GbCwUA.

[68] Brownlie, *International Law and the Use of Force by States*, 315, fn 1.

[69] USDOD December 2016 Law of War Manual, para 15.3.1.2.

[70] UK Ministry of Defence, *Joint Service Manual of the Law of Armed Conflict*, para 1.43(b); USDOD December 2016 Law of War Manual, para 15.5.

This encompasses a prohibition on transiting through neutral states with a view to attacking an enemy by land or by air. The United States affirms that, in general, military aircraft of a party to an international armed conflict may not enter neutral airspace except to address violations of neutrality by enemy forces when the neutral state is 'unwilling or unable' to address such violations.[71]

The legal situation at sea is more complex. The customary and conventional right of innocent passage through territorial seas[72] continues to apply to naval forces during armed conflict. Passage is even potentially innocent where it is effected with a view to committing a future act of aggression, as long as that is not perpetrated against the coastal state.[73] The situation is clearer outside territorial seas, although there is state practice that runs counter to the applicable rule. According to the UK, erecting military installations on the continental shelf[74] of a neutral state is a violation of its neutrality.[75] The United States does not agree with the UK assessment of the law. In the December 2016 edition of its *Law of War Manual*, the US Department of Defense stated that: 'For the purpose of applying the law of neutrality, all ocean areas not subject to the territorial sovereignty of any State (i.e., all waters seaward of neutral States' territorial seas) are not considered neutral waters.'[76] The US view is persuasive, given that sovereignty is limited to territorial seas.[77]

The fourth main rule is that a state whose neutrality has been infringed must take all such measures as are reasonable in the circumstances to address the violation of their neutrality.[78] Should, for example, a party to an international armed conflict move troops on to the territory of a neutral state, the belligerent state's forces must be interned to ensure that they do not proceed or return to the armed conflict.[79] In other cases, all reasonable measures must be taken by a neutral state to defend its airspace and territorial seas, as well as its cyber infrastructure,[80]

---

[71] USDOD December 2016 Law of War Manual, para 15.10.

[72] UNCLOS, Art 17.

[73] As noted above, Art 19(2) of UNCLOS makes it clear that passage is not innocent where it is effected with a view to committing aggression against the coastal state.

[74] Under the 1982 UN Convention on the Law of the Sea, the continental shelf of a coastal state 'comprises the seabed and subsoil of the submarine areas that extend beyond its territorial sea throughout the natural prolongation of its land territory to the outer edge of the continental margin, or to a distance of 200 nautical miles from the baselines from which the breadth of the territorial sea is measured where the outer edge of the continental margin does not extend up to that distance': UNCLOS, Art 76(1).

[75] UK Ministry of Defence, *Joint Service Manual of the Law of Armed Conflict*, para 1.43(b).

[76] USDOD December 2016 Law of War Manual, para 15.7.1.

[77] In this regard, see Seger, 'The Law of Neutrality', 254.

[78] Art 25 of the 1907 Hague Convention XIII stipulated that 'A neutral Power is bound to exercise such surveillance as the means at its disposal allow to prevent any violation of the provisions of the above Articles occurring in its ports or roadsteads or in its waters'.

[79] USDOD December 2016 Law of War Manual, para 15.16.

[80] The Tallinn Manual stipulates in Rule 93 that a neutral state 'may not knowingly allow the exercise of belligerent rights by the parties to the conflict from cyber infrastructure located in its territory or under its exclusive control': M Schmitt (ed), *Tallinn Manual on the International Law Applicable to Cyber Warfare* (Cambridge, Cambridge University Press, 2013) (hereinafter 2013 Tallinn Manual), Rule 93. The Manual's commentary on this rule suggests that the phrase 'may not knowingly allow'

against intrusion.[81] To achieve this aim, lawful measures may extend to a use of force that is both necessary and proportionate in the circumstances. Such a use of force is primarily one of law enforcement within the state's own territory.[82] It does not amount to a violation of Article 2(4) of the UN Charter, much less to an armed attack.[83]

Thus, where one state 'clearly and expressly' attacks another, with operations occurring 'across the territory' of a third neutral state, and that neutral state fails to take all reasonable measures to halt the unlawful use of its territory, the state that has been attacked may take defensive measures *ad bellum* on the territory of the neutral state. According to Brownlie, this is the case 'when the object of the operations has become reasonably clear' and it is also obvious that the neutral state 'has not only failed to repel the invader but has fallen substantially under his control'.[84]

More controversially, Bruno Simma's appreciation of the law in this regard has been cited with approval by the United States Department of Defense.[85] In 1994, Simma wrote that:

> For the purpose of responding to an 'armed attack', the state acting in self-defence is allowed to trespass on foreign territory, even when the attack cannot be attributed to the state from whose territory it is proceeding. It does not follow from the fact that the right of self-defence pursuant to Art. 51 is restricted to the case of an 'armed attack' that defensive measures may only affect the 'attacker'. Thus it is compatible with Art. 51 and the laws of neutrality when a warring state fights hostile armed forces undertaking an attack from neutral territory on the territory of the neutral state, provided that the state concerned is either unwilling or unable to curb the ongoing violation of its neutrality.[86]

With respect to the test to be applied to the neutral state's response to breaches of its claimed neutrality, the 2013 *Tallinn Manual on the International Law Applicable to Cyber Warfare* stipulates that: the violation of the neutral state's territory must be serious (as judged in the circumstances ruling at the time); the hostile action on neutral territory must represent an immediate threat to the security of the 'aggrieved' party; and there must be 'no feasible and timely alternative to taking action on neutral territory'.[87] Moreover, a warning must be given prior to

---

implies a duty on the part of neutral states to take 'all feasible measures' to end the hostile action: 2013 Tallinn Manual, commentary para 6 to Rule 93. This standard of feasibility comes from the realm of international humanitarian law, applicable *in bello* amid the 'fog of war', and is too low as far as *ad bellum* duties are concerned.

[81] USDOD December 2016 Law of War Manual, para 15.4.3.

[82] Bothe, 'The Law of Neutrality', commentary para 1 on rule 1109.

[83] 2013 Tallinn Manual, commentary para 7 to Rule 93. According to Art 10 of the 1907 Hague Convention V, 'The fact of a neutral Power resisting, even by force, attempts to violate its neutrality cannot be regarded as a hostile act'.

[84] Brownlie, *International Law and the Use of Force by States*, 314.

[85] USDOD December 2016 Law of War Manual, para 15.2.3.1 and fn 40.

[86] B Simma, *The Charter of the United Nations: A Commentary* (Oxford, Oxford University Press, 1994) 673.

[87] 2013 Tallinn Manual, commentary paras 3 and 4 to Rule 94.

forcible action, giving the neutral state reasonable time to address the violation of its neutrality.[88]

In contrast, the 'unable' element of the test – as opposed to the neutral state being 'unwilling' to address the violation of its neutrality – does not reflect customary law, and in any event its application is limited. For instance, the overflight of missiles fired from one state over one or more neutral states would not automatically serve to deprive these states of their neutrality. A state has primary jurisdiction over all of its sovereign territory, which includes not just landmass, but also the airspace above that land.[89] A working definition of outer space is that it begins at the Kármán Line, often set at 100 kilometres above the earth's sea level.[90] But neutral states may not have a defence system capable of downing missiles overflying their airspace, and even if they do, they are not required by international law to shoot down the missiles if this would jeopardise their own security.[91]

With respect to the right of innocent passage through territorial seas, the duties on the neutral coastal state differ materially to those set out in the corresponding prohibition on transit through land or airspace. As the 1907 Hague Convention XIII stipulates: 'The neutrality of a Power is not affected by the mere passage through its territorial waters of warships or prizes belonging to belligerents.'[92] In contradistinction to the transit of foreign armed forces on its land, therefore, a neutral coastal state is not required to prevent a belligerent's warship from entering and passing through its territorial sea.[93] A coastal state may suspend the right of innocent passage where this is required by its national security, but it must apply the suspension equally to all foreign vessels.[94] During an international armed conflict, a partial suspension on the grounds of national security must be applied equally to all the parties to the conflict. Wolff Heintschel von Heinegg cites as evidence for the existence of this latter rule the soft-law Helsinki Principles on the Law of Maritime Neutrality adopted within the International Law Association in 1998.[95] Paragraph 2.3, on 'suspension of passage', provides as follows:

> The neutral State may suspend temporarily in specified areas of its territorial sea and archipelagic waters the innocent passage of foreign ships if such suspension is essential

---

[88] ibid commentary para 5 to Rule 94.

[89] S Casey-Maslen and T Vestner, *A Guide to International Disarmament Law* (London, Routledge, 2019) 24.

[90] This altitude is significant, as it is where aircraft have to travel at a speed greater than orbital velocity to get sufficient lift from their wings to stay in the air. Institute of Physics, 'A Brief History of Space', undated, bit.ly/2Rbsdmk.

[91] Bothe, 'The Law of Neutrality', commentary para 2 on rule 1108 and commentary para 2 on rule 1151.

[92] 1907 Hague Convention XIII, Art 10; Bothe, 'The Law of Neutrality', rule 1126. For a discussion of the term 'mere passage' and its confluence and distinction with 'innocent passage', see JD Farrant, 'Modern Maritime Neutrality Law', thesis (Durham University, 2015) 15–19, bit.ly/2K6HRi1.

[93] L Oppenheim, *International Law: A Treatise, Book II: War and Neutrality* (London, Longmans, 1906) para 325.

[94] Art 25(3), UNCLOS.

[95] W Heintschel von Heinegg, 'Maritime Warfare' in Clapham and Gaeta, *The Oxford Handbook of International Law in Armed Conflict*, 175, citing the Helsinki Principles on the Law of Maritime

for the protection of its security, provided that the principle of impartiality is observed, and the suspension is duly published.

A coastal state must prevent, using as much force as is reasonable in the circumstances, violations of the right of innocent passage.[96] Should it fail to do so, another party to the conflict may be entitled itself to take forcible action. The evidence from this comes from an interpretation of the *Altmark* incident in the Second World War.[97] In 1940, the *Altmark*, a German naval auxiliary ship,[98] was returning to Germany from the South Atlantic with some 300 British prisoners of war. She passed through Norwegian territorial waters for around 400 miles, hugging the coastline. When hailed by a Norwegian torpedo boat, the *Altmark*'s captain falsely stated that it had no members of the armed forces of any belligerent aboard. The Norwegian boat's crew were not permitted to verify the accuracy of the claim.[99] Subsequently, still within Norwegian waters, a British destroyer boarded the *Altmark* and freed the prisoners. Norway protested the violation of her sovereignty and her neutrality. Great Britain argued that the result of the *Altmark*'s choice of route was to obtain a shield against attack by virtue of Norway's neutrality.[100] Such action is not to be considered innocent passage.[101]

The fifth main rule of the law of neutrality obligates the parties to an international armed conflict to also ensure, to the maximum extent possible, that neutral states are not affected by the conduct of hostilities.[102] This obligation of due diligence – it is not one of strict liability – has implications for conventional weapons and cyber operations, but especially for the use of weapons of mass destruction. Thus, in its submission to the ICJ in connection with the 1996 Advisory Opinion on the Legality of the Threat or Use of Nuclear Weapons, Nauru stated that 'the principle of neutrality applies with equal force to transborder incursions of armed forces and to the transborder damage caused to a neutral

---

Neutrality, prepared by the ILA's Maritime Neutrality Committee. See also Bothe, 'The Law of Neutrality', commentary para 1 on rule 1137; USDOD December 2016 Law of War Manual, para 13.2.2.4.

[96] According to Art 25 of the 1907 Hague Convention XIII, 'A neutral Power is bound to exercise such surveillance as the means at its disposal allow to prevent any violation of the provisions of the above Articles occurring in its ports or roadsteads or in its waters'. See also Bothe, 'The Law of Neutrality', rule 1137.

[97] See, eg PB Walker, 'What is Innocent Passage?' (1980) 22(1) *Naval War College Review* 53; US Naval War College, *International Law Situations and Documents, 1956* (Washington DC, US Government Printing Office, 1957) 4–48.

[98] An auxiliary is a ship, other than a warship, that is owned or exclusively used by the armed forces of a state.

[99] DP O'Connell, *The Influence of Law on Sea Power* (Manchester, Manchester University Press, 1977) 41, bit.ly/2LfN1ZH.

[100] Farrant, *Modern Maritime Neutrality Law*, 18.

[101] O'Connell agrees, but contests that this gives rise to a right of an opposing party to an armed conflict to use force: 'The Altmark certainly breached international law by taking refuge in such circumstances in internal waters, but, by the same token, so did HMS Cossack by attacking her there'. O'Connell, *The Influence of Law on Sea Power*, 44.

[102] Bothe, 'The Law of Neutrality', commentary para 2 on rule 1108.

State by the use of a weapon in a belligerent State'.[103] The Court did not, however, explicitly endorse this claim.

The sixth and final main rule *ad bellum* of the law of neutrality (which also applies *in bello*) is that a neutral state must not discriminate in its treatment of parties to an international armed conflict as far as the supply or use of armaments is concerned.[104] Thus, to comply with the law of neutrality, where a neutral state imposes restrictions or prohibitions on the export of arms and munitions from companies operating within its jurisdiction against one party, it must impose similar restrictions against the other(s). It is the logical corollary of the prohibition on assistance by a neutral state to a party to an international armed conflict.

Compliance with this rule is potentially complicated by the collective security provisions of the UN Charter as well as other applicable rules of international law.[105] The Tallinn Manual cites the illustrative case where the UN Security Council has determined that a state involved in an [international] armed conflict has engaged in aggression and is conducting 'highly destructive cyber attacks'. The Council passes a resolution under Chapter VII in which it authorises all UN member states to 'employ their cyber assets and capabilities to terminate the attacks'.[106] The Manual suggests that states acting in compliance with this resolution would not be in breach of their obligations under the law of neutrality. This assertion is highly questionable. There is a major difference between being authorised to do something and being required to do something. If the Security Council requires a state to take certain action, it must comply. But an authorisation to use force is not an obligation to use force, and a neutral state that wishes to retain its neutrality should decline to engage its armed forces, including any cyber capability. It may not, of course, lawfully obstruct the actions of any states that do choose to act, but, despite claims to the contrary,[107] it is not obligated to actively assist them.

As noted above, a neutral state may certainly not assist a state engaged in aggression. This would not only violate its neutrality, it would also render the formerly neutral state complicit in the aggression.[108] This would engage the responsibility of the state under international law for an internationally wrongful act. In Article 41 of the 2001 Draft Articles on the Responsibility of States for Internationally Wrongful Acts, the ILC determined that no state shall 'render aid or assistance' in maintaining a serious breach of an obligation arising under a peremptory norm of general international law.[109] As James Crawford recalls

---

[103] ICJ, *Legality of the Threat or Use of Nuclear Weapons*, Advisory Opinion, 8 July 1996, para 89.

[104] Bothe, 'The Law of Neutrality', commentary para 3 on rule 1101.

[105] USDOD December 2016 Law of War Manual, para 15.2.

[106] 2013 Tallinn Manual, commentary para 3 to Rule 95.

[107] See P Palchetti, 'Consequences for Third States as a Result of an Unlawful Use of Force' in M Weller (ed), *The Oxford Handbook of the Use of Force in International Law* (London, Oxford University Press, 2015) 1228.

[108] See USDOD December 2016 Law of War Manual, para 15.2.3.1.

[109] Art 41 of the International Law Commission (ILC) Draft Articles on the Responsibility of States for Internationally Wrongful Acts, adopted on 10 August 2001, contained in the annex to UN General Assembly Resolution 56/83 of 12 December 2001 (hereinafter 2001 Articles on State Responsibility).

in his official commentary on the Draft Articles, 'it is generally agreed that the prohibition of aggression is to be regarded as peremptory'.[110]

More complicated is the impact of the now customary legal duty on states to cooperate to bring to an end a situation created by a serious breach of a peremptory norm. While the status of the duty under international law was previously uncertain,[111] today this is an authoritative statement of the law applicable to all states.[112] Thus, in its 2019 draft conclusions on peremptory norms of general international law, adopted on first reading, the ILC stipulates that: 'States shall cooperate to bring to an end through lawful means any serious breach by a State of an obligation arising under a peremptory norm of general international law (*jus cogens*).'[113] Implementation of this duty does not obligate a neutral state to breach its neutrality. Political and legal cooperation within the United Nations, for example,[114] is fully compatible with neutral status.

The ILC further reiterates that: 'No State shall recognize as lawful a situation created by a serious breach by a State of an obligation arising from a peremptory norm of general international law (*jus cogens*), nor render aid or assistance in maintaining that situation.'[115] This latter rule is also consistent with the rules set out on the 2013 Arms Trade Treaty. Under Article 6(1), a state party is prohibited from authorising any transfer of conventional arms and related munitions within the scope of the Treaty if the transfer would violate its obligations under measures adopted by the UN Security Council acting under Chapter VII of the UN Charter, 'in particular arms embargoes'. While the provision does not refer explicitly to aggression,[116] under Article 39 of the UN Charter, enforcement measures are adopted under Chapter VII whenever the Council considers them to be necessary to maintain or restore international peace and security, in particular where there exists any threat to the peace, a breach of the peace, or act of aggression.[117]

In other respects, the Arms Trade Treaty prohibits the authorisation of transfer by a state party of conventional arms and related munitions within the scope of the Treaty where it has knowledge at the time of authorisation that the arms or items

---

[110] Commentary para 4 on Art 40.

[111] See, eg Palchetti, 'Consequences for Third States as a Result of an Unlawful Use of Force', 1229. Palchetti notes that in 2001 the ILC viewed the duty to cooperate to bring the serious breach to an end (Art 41(1)) as a progressive development of the law.

[112] ILC, 'Third Report on Peremptory Norms of General International Law (*Jus Cogens*) by Dire Tladi, Special Rapporteur', UN doc A/CN.4/714, 12 February 2018, para 90.

[113] ILC, 'Peremptory Norms of General International Law (*Jus Cogens*). Text of the Draft Conclusions and Draft Annex Provisionally Adopted by the Drafting Committee on First Reading', UN doc A/CN.4/L.936, 29 May 2019, Conclusion 19(1).

[114] ILC, 'Third Report on Peremptory Norms of General International Law (*Jus Cogens*)', paras 90–91.

[115] ILC, 'Peremptory Norms of General International Law (*Jus Cogens*)', Conclusion 19(2).

[116] Andrew Clapham justly describes this as a 'curious omission': A Clapham, 'Commentary on Article 6(2)' in S Casey-Maslen, A Clapham, G Giacca and S Parker, *The Arms Trade Treaty: A Commentary* (Oxford, Oxford University Press, 2016) para 6.65.

[117] See, eg S Casey-Maslen and G Giacca, 'Commentary on Article 6(1)' in Casey-Maslen et al, *The Arms Trade Treaty: A Commentary*, paras 6.26 et seq.

would be used in the commission of genocide, crimes against humanity, grave breaches of the 1949 Geneva Conventions, attacks directed against civilian objects or civilians protected as such, or other war crimes as defined by international agreements to which it is a party.[118] The Treaty further prohibits the authorisation of export of conventional arms and related munitions within the scope of the Treaty where there is an overriding risk that they will be used to 'undermine peace and security' or to commit or facilitate a serious violation of international humanitarian law or international human rights law.[119] Use for the purpose of aggression would certainly undermine peace and security.

Thus, while it is explicit that the Treaty must be applied in a non-discriminatory manner,[120] in practice this may result in differing treatment of one party to an international armed conflict compared to another. This will result from the conduct of the parties, in addition to where one is committing an act of aggression, where a party is committing serious violations of IHL or human rights, while an opposing party is not. Thus, the actions of the parties to an international armed conflict impact on the content of the rules under the law of neutrality.

Finally, as the US Department of Defense recalls, violations of neutrality by belligerent or neutral states should be distinguished from the end of a state's neutral status. Only a serious violation of the law of neutrality, such as participation in an international armed conflict, will be sufficient to conclusively end a state's neutral status.[121]

---

[118] 2013 Arms Trade Treaty, Art 6(3).
[119] 2013 Arms Trade Treaty, Arts 7(1)(a) and (b)(i) and (ii) and 7(3).
[120] 2013 Arms Trade Treaty, Arts 5(1) and 7(1).
[121] USDOD December 2016 Law of War Manual, para 15.4.1. See also Bothe, 'The Law of Neutrality', rule 1107 and associated commentary.

# 6

## The Legality of Humanitarian Intervention

## I. Introduction

Once permitted by international law, unilateral intervention by force of arms in another state for humanitarian purposes has certainly been unlawful since the adoption in 1945 of the Charter of the United Nations[1] (UN Charter). A number of classical writers, including Grotius and Vattel, had argued, albeit in general terms, that a war wrought 'to punish injustice and those guilty of crimes was a just war'.[2] As Brownlie also observes, by the end of the nineteenth century most publicists had accepted that a right of humanitarian intervention existed where a state abused its sovereignty by brutal and excessively cruel treatment of those within its power.[3] The right of intervention was raised particularly in the nineteenth century 'in situations of perceived persecution of Christians in territories under Ottoman Turkish rule'.[4]

Nevertheless, 'intervention' in the internal affairs of other states was prohibited by treaty for much of the twentieth century. The 1933 Montevideo Convention on Rights and Duties of States provided that: 'No state has the right to intervene in the internal or external affairs of another'.[5] The acceptance of this text by the United States was said to be '*prima facie* evidence' of the withdrawal of its earlier claim to 'a right of intervention to protect the lives and property of nationals'.[6]

Within the UN Charter, in addition to the general prohibition on interstate use of force codified in paragraph 4 of Article 2, paragraph 7 prohibits the United Nations from intervening in matters 'essentially within the domestic jurisdiction of any state':

> Nothing contained in the present Charter shall authorize the United Nations to intervene in matters which are essentially within the domestic jurisdiction of any state or

---

[1] Charter of the United Nations; adopted at San Francisco, 26 June 1945; entered into force, 24 October 1945.

[2] I Brownlie, *International Law and the Use of Force by States* (Oxford, Oxford University Press, 1963) 338, citing H Grotius, *De Jure Belli ac Pacis*, 1625 (trans AC Campbell, London, 1814) Book II, Ch XXV, §8 and Ch XX, §38; Vattel, *Le Droit des Gens*, 1758, Book II, Ch IV, §56.

[3] Brownlie, *International Law and the Use of Force by States*, 338.

[4] N Rodley, 'Humanitarian Intervention' in M Weller (ed), *The Oxford Handbook of the Use of Force in International Law* (Oxford, Oxford University Press, 2015) 775, but *cf* also 780.

[5] Art 8 of the Convention on Rights and Duties of States; signed at Montevideo, 26 December 1933; entered into force, 26 December 1934.

[6] Brownlie, *International Law and the Use of Force by States*, 97.

shall require the Members to submit such matters to settlement under the present Charter; but this principle shall not prejudice the application of enforcement measures under Chapter VII.

Since 1945 and the adoption of the Charter, international human rights law has certainly developed so as to render many matters no longer the *domaine réservé* of states.[7] Writing in 1990, W Michael Reisman argued that where 'free elections are internationally supervised and the results are internationally endorsed as free and fair and the people's choice is clear', those 'confirmed wishes' may not be 'ignored by a local caudillo'.[8] That much may be true. But Reisman went on to claim that a 'jurist rooted in the late twentieth century' can 'hardly say' that 'an invasion by outside forces to remove the caudillo and install the elected government is a violation of national sovereignty':

> Cross-border military actions should certainly never be extolled, for they are necessarily brutal and destructive of life and property. They may well be unlawful for a variety of other reasons. But if they displace the usurper and emplace the people who were freely elected, they can be characterized, in this particular regard, as a violation of sovereignty only if one uses the term anachronistically to mean the violation of some mystical survival of a monarchical right that supposedly devolves jure gentium on whichever warlord seizes and holds the presidential palace or if the term is used in the jurisprudentially bizarre sense to mean that inanimate territory has political rights that pre-empt those of its inhabitants.[9]

While there has been a tremendous evolution in the promotion and protection of human rights, and despite Reisman's colourful use of language, it is wrong to say that this has acted to weaken the *jus cogens* bonds constricting the interstate use of force. In Roth's words, 'measures otherwise illegal cannot be made lawful by the actor's mere incantation of the language of human rights'.[10] Accordingly, as this chapter discusses, unilateral humanitarian intervention by force was a violation of *jus ad bellum* in the second half of the twentieth century, and it remains so thus far in the first half of the twenty-first.[11]

## II. The Notion of Humanitarian Intervention

There is no consensual definition under international law of what amounts to humanitarian intervention, despite copious references to it in scholarly literature.

---

[7] See, eg KS Ziegler, 'Domaine Réservé', *Max Planck Encyclopedia of Public International Law* (last updated April 2013), bit.ly/32ssUhx.

[8] WM Reisman, 'Sovereignty and Human Rights in Contemporary International Law' (1990) 84 *American Journal of International Law* 871.

[9] ibid.

[10] BR Roth, *Governmental Illegitimacy in International Law* (Oxford, Oxford University Press, 2000) 170.

[11] Rodley, 'Humanitarian Intervention', 775ff.

One proposed definition emanating from academia treats the concept as a coercive, notably military action across state borders by a state or a group of states, aimed at preventing or ending widespread and grave violations of human rights of individuals other than its own citizens, and occurring without the permission of the state in whose territory force is applied.[12] But, as the Report of the Independent International Fact-Finding Mission on the Conflict in Georgia (hereinafter the Georgia Fact-Finding Mission Report) has also noted, 'the debate on humanitarian intervention often does not distinguish between the protection of own nationals and the protection of people of a different nationality'.[13]

For the purpose of this chapter, the term 'humanitarian intervention' is construed broadly to encompass all interstate use of force for ostensibly humanitarian purposes that occurs without either the consent of the territorial state or the authorisation of the UN Security Council. Such purposes are primarily the protection of civilians, whether or not they are nationals of the intervening state or states.

## III.  Humanitarian Intervention under International Law

Under international law as it stands, intervention involving the interstate use of force for avowedly humanitarian purposes, as delineated above, is illegal.[14] This remains the case unless and until the use of force has been duly authorised by the UN Security Council acting under Chapter VII of the UN Charter. Nonetheless, an autonomous right in international law of humanitarian intervention was most recently claimed in April 2018 by the UK as a lawful response to chemical weapons attacks on civilians in Syria. The UK claims that it

> is permitted under international law, on an exceptional basis, to take measures in order to alleviate overwhelming humanitarian suffering. The legal basis for the use of force is humanitarian intervention, which requires three conditions to be met:
>
> (i)   there is convincing evidence, generally accepted by the international community as a whole, of extreme humanitarian distress on a large scale, requiring immediate and urgent relief;
> (ii)  it must be objectively clear that there is no practicable alternative to the use of force if lives are to be saved; and
> (iii) the proposed use of force must be necessary and proportionate to the aim of relief of humanitarian suffering and must be strictly limited in time and in scope to this aim (i.e. the minimum necessary to achieve that end and for no other purpose).[15]

---

[12] JL Holzgrefe, 'The Humanitarian Intervention Debate' in R Keohane and J Holzgrefe (eds), *Humanitarian Intervention* (Cambridge, Cambridge University Press, 2003) 18; see also Independent International Fact-Finding Mission on the Conflict in Georgia, Report, vol II, 2009, 283 (hereinafter Georgia Fact-Finding Mission Report).

[13] Georgia Fact-Finding Mission Report, 283.

[14] Brownlie, *International Law and the Use of Force by States*, 301.

[15] UK Prime Minister's Office, 'Syria Action – UK Government Legal Position', Policy Paper (10 Downing Street, 14 April 2018), bit.ly/2LT7owG.

The UK is wrong as a matter of international law. It is also a major change in its own appreciation of the law, as Christine Gray has pointed out.[16] In the mid-1980s, the UK was asserting that 'the best case that can be made in support of humanitarian intervention is that it cannot be said to be unambiguously illegal'.[17] Even this was a stretch. As expressed in the 1970 Declaration on Principles of International Law:

> No State or group of States has the right to intervene, directly or indirectly, for any reason whatever, in the internal or external affairs of any other State. Consequently, armed intervention and all other forms of interference or attempted threats against the personality of the State or against its political, economic, and cultural elements, are in violation of international law.[18]

Citing the 1970 Declaration in its 1986 judgment on the merits in the *Nicaragua* case, the International Court of Justice (ICJ) considered the principle of non-intervention to be 'part and parcel of customary international law'.[19] This is so even though, as the Court acknowledged, 'examples of trespass against this principle are not infrequent'.[20] The ICJ affirmed that 'while the United States might form its own appraisal of the situation as to respect for human rights in Nicaragua, the use of force could not be the appropriate method to monitor or ensure such respect'.[21]

It is true that there has been 'intense scholarly and interstate debate' during and since the NATO (North Atlantic Treaty Organization)'s intervention against the Federal Republic of Yugoslavia over Kosovo in 1999 (a case discussed in detail below).[22] But this 'has not yet led to a development of international law in favour of unilateral humanitarian interventions without a Security Council mandate'.[23] At the time, only Belgium and the UK formally advanced a right of humanitarian intervention to justify the use of force in Kosovo. Furthermore, as Yoram Dinstein observes, in the later case of Libya: 'It speaks volumes about the new

---

[16] C Gray, *International Law and the Use of Force*, 4th edn (Oxford, Oxford University Press, 2018) 40–41.

[17] 'UK Materials on International Law' (1986) 57 *British Yearbook of International Law* 614.

[18] *Declaration on Principles of International Law concerning Friendly Relations and Co-operation among States*, annexed to UN General Assembly Resolution 2625, adopted by the UN General Assembly without a vote on 24 October 1970. For similar language, see inter alia Art 18 of the 1948 Charter of the Organization of American States; signed at Bogotá, 30 April 1948; entered into force, 13 December 1951.

[19] ICJ, *Case Concerning Military and Paramilitary Activities in and against Nicaragua (Nicaragua v United States of America)*, Judgment (Merits), 27 June 1986, para 202 (hereinafter ICJ, *Nicaragua* judgment).

[20] ibid.

[21] ibid para 268.

[22] Georgia Fact-Finding Mission Report, 284. See also D. Franchini and A. Tzanakopoulos, 'The Kosovo Crisis – 1999', Chap. 47 in Weller (ed), *The Oxford Handbook of the Use of Force in International Law*, 594–622, at 594.

[23] ibid citing S. Chesterman, *Just War or Just Peace? Humanitarian Intervention and International Law*, Oxford University Press, Oxford, 2001, *esp.* 226.

state of mind prevailing in NATO that … there was no dissent from the view that any humanitarian intervention in Libya, in early 2011, must be firmly embedded in Security Council authorization.'[24]

## A. Humanitarian Intervention: The Case of Kosovo

In still recent history, the intervention by NATO member states in Kosovo is often cited as a clear instance of humanitarian intervention in practice. A review of the facts and the applicable law is therefore instructive. As NATO itself reports, it launched an air campaign, Operation Allied Force, in March 1999 'to halt the humanitarian catastrophe that was then unfolding in Kosovo'. The 'decision to intervene', it noted, 'followed more than a year of fighting within the province and the failure of international efforts to resolve the conflict by diplomatic means'.[25]

### (i) The Facts

The 1974 Constitution of the Socialist Federal Republic of Yugoslavia had decreed that Kosovo was an autonomous province of Serbia. But pressure for Kosovo's independence mounted in the 1980s after the death of Yugoslav President, Josip Broz Tito.[26] In 1987, Slobodan Milosevic, then the second in command in the hierarchy of the Serbian Communist Party, seized the opportunity to promote his career by championing the rights of ethnic Serbs in Kosovo. After becoming President of Yugoslavia in 1989, Milosevic began to remove Kosovo's autonomy, prompting ethnic Albanian legislators in the province to declare Kosovo independent from Serbia in July 1990. A year later, Albania recognised Kosovo as independent.

In 1991, ethnic Albanians inside Kosovo formed the Kosovo Liberation Army (KLA), the aim of which was to unite Kosovo in a 'Greater Albania'. An insurgency by the KLA in Kosovo against ethnic Serb police and Yugoslav forces persisted throughout the 1990s. In the summer of 1998, KLA fighters killed dozens of Serb police and civilians, while Yugoslav-backed authorities responded by driving ethnic Albanians from their homes and burning down their houses. In January 1999, after KLA fighters killed four Serbs in an attack on a police post, Yugoslav government forces cordoned off the nearby village of Racak. When international observers were able to enter, they found 45 ethnic Albanian civilians dead.[27]

---

[24] Y Dinstein, *War, Aggression and Self-defence*, 5th edn, Cambridge University Press, Cambridge, 2011, 338; see also C. Henderson, *The Use of Force and International Law*, Cambridge University Press, Cambridge, 2018, 161.

[25] NATO, 'Kosovo Air Campaign (Archived): Operation Allied Force' (last updated 7 April 2016), bit.ly/2UcugNh.

[26] BBC, 'Flashback to Kosovo's war', 10 July 2006, bbc.in/360MIdd.

[27] A. Chapple, 'Operation Allied Force: The NATO Bombing of Yugoslavia', *Radio Free Europe*, 24 March 2019, bit.ly/2r5FMMX.

A deal to end the crisis was brokered by the international community in early 1999. The plan for autonomy was reluctantly accepted by the ethnic Albanians but rejected by President Milosevic. The continued persecution of Kosovo Albanians led to the start of NATO air strikes against targets in Kosovo and Serbia in March 1999 under Operation Allied Force.[28] The first attacks occurred on the night of 24 March 1999, and involved 250 US aircraft. Thirteen other NATO member states also contributed aircraft to the Operation.[29]

During the 78-day campaign, NATO flew 10,484 strike sorties, with attacks peaking in late May and early June 1999. Operation Allied Force witnessed the first combat use of the B-2 Spirit stealth bomber and the first significant employment of remotely piloted aircraft (drones). Under threat of a ground operation, Milosevic yielded. The Military Technical Agreement that ended the conflict decreed a durable cessation of hostilities and stipulated that a phased withdrawal of Yugoslav forces from Kosovo would occur; that a NATO-led force would provide security for the province; that refugees would be allowed to return to their homes; and that Kosovo would be granted self-rule, albeit still under Yugoslav sovereignty.[30] On 10 June 1999, Yugoslavia ratified the Agreement and Serbian forces began to leave Kosovo; the next day, members of NATO's Kosovo Force began to arrive.[31]

## (ii)  The Law

In October 1998, the UN Security Council had expressed its deep alarm and concern at 'the continuing grave humanitarian situation throughout Kosovo and the impending humanitarian catastrophe', re-emphasising 'the need to prevent this from happening'.[32] Security Council Resolution 1203 further affirmed that the unresolved situation in 'Kosovo, Federal Republic of Yugoslavia' constituted 'a continuing threat to peace and security in the region'.[33] Acting under Chapter VII of the UN Charter, the Council called for 'prompt and complete investigation ... of all atrocities committed against civilians' and 'full cooperation' with the International Criminal Tribunal for the former Yugoslavia.[34] Yet, it did not authorise the use of force against Yugoslavia or Yugoslav forces. Moreover, the Council reaffirmed 'the commitment of all [UN] Member States to the sovereignty and territorial integrity of the Federal Republic of Yugoslavia'.[35]

---

[28] BBC, 'Flashback to Kosovo's war', 10 July 2006.

[29] Capt G Ball, '1999 – Operation Allied Force' (Air Force Historical Support Division, 23 August 2012), bit.ly/33B2v0B.

[30] Military Technical Agreement Between the International Security Force ('KFOR') and the Governments of Federal Republic of Yugoslavia and the Republic of Serbia, 9 June 1999, bit.ly/2K1wpX7.

[31] Ball, '1999 – Operation Allied Force'.

[32] UN Security Council Resolution 1203, adopted on 24 October 1998 by 13 votes to 0 with 2 abstentions (China and Russia), eleventh preambular paragraph.

[33] ibid fifteenth preambular paragraph.

[34] ibid operative para 14.

[35] ibid fourteenth preambular paragraph.

Ethnic Albanians in Kosovo did not represent a state, and therefore could not issue a request to NATO to come to its collective self-defence. They were also not recognised as a people struggling for self-determination, and therefore the central Yugoslav authorities were not prohibited per se from using force to repress Kosovar demands for independence. This is despite the subsequent finding by the ICJ that the unilateral declaration of independence by the province in 2008 was 'not unlawful'.[36]

Given the absence of overt Security Council authorisation, an argument was made before and during the military intervention of the existence of 'implied' authorisation in furtherance of the aims of the international community.[37] Before the ICJ, in a case in which Yugoslavia sought provisional measures against NATO member states, Belgium argued that the military intervention had an 'incontestable basis' in a series of UN Security Council resolutions.[38] It is true that the Council had recognised that the situation in Kosovo was a threat to international peace and security, and that action had been taken under Chapter VII of the UN Charter, but at no point before (or after) Operation Allied Force did the Security Council authorise the use of force. Implied authorisation to use force simply does not exist under either customary or conventional international law.

Indeed, on 26 March 1999, two days after the NATO bombing campaign had started, a draft resolution was put before the Council affirming that the unilateral use of force was a violation of Article 2(4) of the UN Charter. Only three states – China, Namibia, and Russia – voted in favour of the resolution, with the other 12 members of the Security Council (Argentina, Brazil, Canada, France, Gabon, Gambia, Malaysia, the Netherlands, Slovenia, the UK, and the United States) voting against. Speaking before the vote, the United States emphasised that military action was initiated

> only with the greatest reluctance, after all peaceful options had been thoroughly exhausted. By rejecting a peace settlement and escalating its assault on the people of Kosovo – in violation of numerous Security Council resolutions – Belgrade chose the path of war.[39]

Peter Burleigh, the US representative on the Council, further declared:

> The draft resolution before us today alleges that NATO is acting in violation of the United Nations Charter. This turns the truth on its head. The United Nations Charter

---

[36] ICJ, *Accordance with International Law of the Unilateral Declaration of Independence in Respect of Kosovo*, Advisory Opinion, 22 July 2010, para 84.

[37] Gray, *International Law and the Use of Force*, 4th edn, 46–47 and 50–51.

[38] Public sitting on 10 May 1999, Vice-President Weeramantry, Acting President, presiding in the case concerning *Legality of Use of Force (Yugoslavia v Belgium)*, Request for the indication of provisional measures, Verbatim Record, ICJ doc 99/15 (1999), 15: 'le Royaume de Belgique est d'avis que l'intervention armée trouve un fondement sans conteste dans les résolutions du Conseil de sécurité que je viens de citer. Ces résolutions du Conseil de sécurité sont claires, elles sont basées sur le chapitre VII de la Charte, constate une menace contre la paix et la sécurité internationales.'

[39] UN doc S/PV.3989, 4, bit.ly/2qd05HS.

does not sanction armed assaults upon ethnic groups, or imply that the international community should turn a blind eye to a growing humanitarian disaster.[40]

In response, Sergei Lavrov, Russia's representative on the Council, stated:

> The aggressive military action unleashed by NATO against a sovereign State without the authorization and in circumvention of the Security Council is a real threat to international peace and security and a gross violation of the United Nations Charter and other basic norms of international law. Key provisions of the Charter are being violated, in particular Article 2, paragraph 4, which requires all Members of the United Nations to refrain from the threat or use of force in their international relations, including against the territorial integrity or political independence of any State …[41]

Russia had the law on its side. After the vote had been taken and the resolution firmly rejected, the UK made the clearest statement that NATO's action in Kosovo was, in its view, based on a right of unilateral humanitarian intervention:

> Every means short of force was used to try to avert the current situation. These efforts have failed because President Milosevic has flouted the demands of the international community, including successive Security Council resolutions, allowed his forces to continue their violent oppression of civilians in Kosovo and ignored all appeals to negotiate a political settlement. He has acted in defiance of the expressed will of the Security Council … In the current circumstances, military intervention is justified as an exceptional measure to prevent an overwhelming humanitarian catastrophe.[42]

Subsequently, in its oral pleadings before the ICJ, Belgium would also make the case for humanitarian intervention as a unilateral right – and even an obligation – under international law:

> we must go further and develop the idea of armed humanitarian intervention. NATO, the Kingdom of Belgium in particular, had a genuine obligation to intervene to prevent a humanitarian catastrophe that was under way and which had been noted by Security Council resolutions.[43]

This action was taken, Belgium asserted, to safeguard 'essential values which are also at the level of *jus cogens*' including the right to life.[44] But not every violation of a *jus cogens* norm gives rise to the right to use force: 'it does not follow from the mere fact that human rights may now be *jus cogens* that this overrides the prohibition on the use of force.[45] In the words of James Crawford, 'there is simply no room' for this 'within the regulatory space established by Articles 2(4) and 51 of the Charter.[46]

---

[40] ibid 5.
[41] ibid.
[42] ibid 6–7.
[43] Public sitting on 10 May 1999, Vice-President Weeramantry, ICJ doc 99/15 (n 38) 15.
[44] ibid 15–16.
[45] Gray, *International Law and the Use of Force*, 53.
[46] J Crawford, *Brownlie's Principles of Public International Law*, 9th edn (Oxford, Oxford University Press, 2019) 728.

Along the lines of Reisman's argument to defend the US invasion of Panama in 1989, the claim was also made with respect to Kosovo that Article 2(4) of the UN Charter allows force to be used as long as it is consistent with the purposes of the UN, which include the promotion of human rights.[47] An attempt was made to narrow the scope of the *jus cogens* prohibition on interstate use of force. Thus, Belgium also claimed, the intervention in Kosovo had 'another important characteristic': NATO had 'never questioned' the political independence or territorial integrity of the Federal Republic of Yugoslavia:

> it is an intervention to save a population in peril, in deep distress. This is why the Kingdom of Belgium considers it an armed humanitarian intervention that is compatible with Article 2(4) of the Charter which only prohibits interventions directed against the territorial integrity and political independence of the State.[48]

Belgium was wrong as a matter of law. As set out above, and as discussed in chapter two, the provision in Article 2(4) is both general and broad. The wording in Article 2(4) – 'or in any other manner inconsistent with the Purposes of the United Nations' – expands the scope of the prohibition beyond the protection of territorial integrity and political independence rather than narrowing it. This is absolutely clear from the *travaux préparatoires*, from subsequent state practice, and from ICJ jurisprudence,[49] and this continues to be the case.[50] In 2014, the Seventeenth Ministerial Conference of the Non-Aligned Movement, comprising at the time 113 states, 'reiterated the rejection by the Movement of the so called "right" of humanitarian intervention, which has no basis either in the UN Charter or in international law'.[51]

Others have suggested that even if humanitarian intervention without Security Council authorisation is unlawful under international law, it can still be 'legitimate', and the NATO intervention in Kosovo in 1999 'is especially cited' in this regard.[52] This is, however, an implicit acceptance that the military action was not lawful.[53] It is not, as Nigel Rodley concluded, 'evidently on the borderline'.[54] In 2014, Germany, which flew 500 sorties during Operation Allied Force, accepted 'at last' that the military action had been illegal. Indeed, Gerhard Schröder, the Federal Chancellor at the time of the intervention, revealed publicly that Germany had been aware all along that 'formally going to war without a decision of the Security Council was a violation of international law'.[55]

---

[47] UN Charter, Art 1(3).

[48] Public sitting on 10 May 1999, Vice-President Weeramantry, ICJ doc 99/15 (n 38) 16.

[49] ICJ, *Corfu Channel case (United Kingdom v Albania)*, Judgment (Merits), 9 April 1949, 35.

[50] See Franchini and Tzanakopoulos, 'The Kosovo Crisis – 1999', 610.

[51] XVII Ministerial Conference of the Non-Aligned Movement, Algiers, 26–29 May 2014, Final Document, para 673.

[52] A Lang, 'Legal Basis for UK Military Action in Syria', Briefing Paper No 7404 (London, House of Commons Library, 1 December 2015) 21.

[53] Franchini and Tzanakopoulos, 'The Kosovo Crisis – 1999', 608.

[54] Rodley, 'Humanitarian Intervention', 787.

[55] SAG Talmon, 'At Last! Germany Admits Illegality of the Kosovo Intervention' (2014) 57 *German Yearbook of International Law* 581, citing a *Die Zeit* panel with Gerhard Schröder on 9 March 2014, bit.ly/34Esu8I; see also Gray, *International Law and the Use of Force*, 52.

In sum, the NATO military intervention in Kosovo must be considered a violation of the general prohibition on interstate use of force.[56] It is not state practice in the elaboration of a new customary rule *de lege ferenda*,[57] much less one that one day might overturn or amend the *jus cogens* prohibition on interstate use of force and permit unilateral humanitarian intervention by force of arms.[58]

## IV. The Content and Consequence of 'Responsibility to Protect'

It is also sometimes claimed that the doctrine of 'Responsibility to Protect' has become the international legal basis for a right – or even a duty – of unilateral humanitarian intervention. On closer inspection, however, this is not correct.[59] In 2005, the World Summit Outcome document, adopted by consensus, endorsed the duty of the international community not to remain silent when 'atrocity crimes' were being committed as a doctrine in its own right. As UN member states declared, the international community, through the United Nations, 'has the responsibility to use appropriate diplomatic, humanitarian and other peaceful means, in accordance with Chapters VI and VIII of the Charter, to help to protect populations from genocide, war crimes, ethnic cleansing and crimes against humanity'.[60]

However, UN member states have expressed their willingness, 'should peaceful means be inadequate' and where 'national authorities are manifestly failing to protect their populations from genocide, war crimes, ethnic cleansing and crimes against humanity', 'to take collective action, in a timely and decisive manner, through the Security Council, in accordance with the Charter, including Chapter VII'.[61] This is a significant endorsement that such international crimes may per se amount to a threat to international peace and security, requiring the UN Security Council to act, and potentially to authorise the use of force.

Thus, while the doctrine is directly relevant to the repression of international crimes, as the Georgia Fact-Finding Mission Report states:

> State practice and *opinio iuris* do not support the claims scholars have made in favour of a rule on humanitarian intervention without a Security Council mandate, and the

---

[56] As Dinstein observes, 'no State acting alone (or even jointly with like-minded allies) has a legal option of resorting to force against another State, with a view to preventing genocide, or bringing it to an end': Y Dinstein, *War, Aggression and Self-defence*, 6th edn (Cambridge, Cambridge University Press, 2017) para 209.

[57] R Cryer, D Robinson and S Vasiliev, *An Introduction to International Criminal Law and Procedure*, 4th edn (Cambridge, Cambridge University Press, 2019) 309.

[58] See on this issue S Haines, 'The influence of Operation Allied Force on the development of the *jus ad bellum*', (May 2009) 85(3), *International Affairs*, 477–90.

[59] Gray, *International Law and the Use of Force*, 60.

[60] UN General Assembly Resolution 60/1 ('2005 World Summit Outcome'), adopted without a vote on 16 September 2005, para 139.

[61] ibid.

law has not developed in the direction of the experts' proposals, however morally desirable such a rule might be. The cautious endorsement of the concept of 'responsibility to protect' by international actors barely affected the law on unilateral interventions, because the 'responsibility to protect' was quickly limited to UN-authorized operations. So the potentially emerging international principle of a 'responsibility to protect' only allows humanitarian actions authorized by the Security Council ...[62]

'Barely affected' should rather be understood as 'did not affect at all'. The doctrine of 'Responsibility to Protect' justly reinforces the critical need to take action to prevent and repress serious violations of international law. But such action does not occur by perpetrating another serious violation of international law: an act of aggression. Once more, as the 1974 Definition of Aggression holds: 'No consideration of whatever nature, whether political, economic, military or otherwise, may serve as a justification for aggression.'[63]

# V. Rescue of Nationals as Humanitarian Intervention?

If there is no right of unilateral humanitarian intervention to protect the populations of other states, the same is true where a state intervenes militarily in another state purporting to protect its own nationals. That said, a rescue operation limited in time and space may, as chapter one described, be a law enforcement action that is not prohibited by Article 2(4) of the UN Charter. This is so at the least where a grave and temporally proximate threat to the life of hostages exists.[64] The Georgia Fact-Finding Mission Report refers to the famous Entebbe airport incident in 1976 and the less well-known German action in Albania in 1997.[65] Certainly, more substantive armed operations in time and space will violate the general prohibition on interstate use of force; in such a case, either territorial state consent or UN Security Council authorisation to use force is required.

---

[62] Georgia Fact-Finding Mission Report, 284, citing 'A More Secure World: Our Shared Responsibility', Report of the High-level Panel on Threats, Challenges and Change, UN doc A759/565, 2 December 2004, para 203, and UN General Assembly Resolution 60/1, 24 October 2005, para 139. Strangely, the Georgia Fact-Finding Mission Report concludes the final sentence with the phrase 'if at all'. It is clear from Security Council practice over the last 20 years that where the Council finds a threat to international peace and security, as it increasingly does when civilians are being threatened or attacked, it may authorise the use of force. See ch 4 of the present volume.

[63] Art 5(1) of the Definition of Aggression, annexed to UN General Assembly Resolution 3314 (XXIX); adopted without a vote on 14 December 1974.

[64] See also Georgia Fact-Finding Mission Report, 286.

[65] The Report thus notes that: 'The best known case is the Entebbe incident of 1976. Here an Israeli special military unit conducted a rescue action at Entebbe airport in Uganda in order to liberate Israeli air passengers who had been taken hostage by Palestinian terrorists. Another example is the evacuation of 120 persons, among them 20 Germans, from the Albanian capital Tirana in 1997 by German military helicopters. Both incidents were limited in scope and were not condemned by the majority of states': ibid fn 202.

As chapter three noted, the argument is sometimes made by states that putting in danger and violating the rights of a state's nationals equals an 'armed attack' on those nationals. According to one possible argument, because nationals constitute one element of statehood, an 'armed attack' on nationals must be treated as analogous to an armed attack on territory and is therefore apt to trigger self-defence.[66] This argument is unpersuasive. Diplomatic protection and UN Security Council action offer more effective, pacific routes to ensure the protection of nationals abroad. Accordingly, in the specific context of Russia's military intervention in Georgia in 2008, as the Georgia Fact-Finding Mission Report declares, 'The better view therefore is that self-defence can therefore [*sic*] not be invoked on the grounds of attacks on Russian nationals in Georgia.'[67]

---

[66] Georgia Fact-Finding Mission Report, 287.
[67] ibid 288.

# 7

## Responsibility for Aggression

## I. Introduction

Aggression was first outlawed in domestic law by the French Constitution of 1791.[1] Internationally, the term was widely used in diplomatic circles in the years leading up to the First World War to mean an unprovoked military attack that involved the crossing by armed forces of an international border.[2] But the Commission on the Responsibility of the Authors of the War and on Enforcement of Penalties, established by the 1919 Paris Peace Conference, did not find that responsibility could yet be adjudged by a criminal tribunal. It did, though, conclude that: 'It is desirable that for the future penal sanctions should be provided for such grave outrages against the elementary principles of international law.'[3]

Victorious states at the Paris Peace Conference ignored the conclusions of the Commission and demanded that the former German Emperor, Wilhelm II, be put on trial for war crimes and aggression. The Treaty of Versailles included the following provision:

> The Allied and Associated Powers publicly arraign William II of Hohenzollern, formerly German Emperor, for a supreme offence against international morality and the sanctity of treaties.
>
> A special tribunal will be constituted to try the accused, thereby assuring him the guarantees essential to the right of defence. It will be composed of five judges, one appointed by each of the following Powers: namely, the United States of America, Great Britain, France, Italy and Japan.
>
> In its decision the tribunal will be guided by the highest motives of international policy, with a view to vindicating the solemn obligations of international undertakings and

---

[1] I Brownlie, *International Law and the Use of Force by States* (Oxford, Oxford University Press, 1963) 18. As Rob Cryer et al observe, the trial of Conradin von Hohenstaufen in 1268 for what would now be termed waging aggressive war must be considered a 'historical curiosity': R Cryer, D Robinson and S Vasiliev, *An Introduction to International Criminal Law and Procedure*, 4th edn (Cambridge, Cambridge University Press, 2019) 297 and fn 2.

[2] Brownlie, *International Law and the Use of Force by States* 24.

[3] Commission on the Responsibility of the Authors of the War and on Enforcement of Penalties, Report presented to the Preliminary Peace Conference, 29 March 1919, Conclusions, Point 4, bit.ly/2YLOdsw.

the validity of international morality. It will be its duty to fix the punishment which it considers should be imposed.

The Allied and Associated Powers will address a request to the Government of the Netherlands for the surrender to them of the ex-Emperor in order that he may be put on trial.[4]

The German delegate to the peace talks stated that the 'intended criminal prosecution' was 'not founded on any legal basis'.[5] Ultimately, however, Kaiser Wilhelm II would not face trial, not out of respect for the fundamental principle of *nulla poena nullum crimen sine lege previa*, but because the Dutch Government refused to comply with demands to extradite him, claiming it would compromise their neutrality.[6] Nonetheless, a precedent had still been set, and only 26 years later, German leaders would be put on trial for, inter alia, crimes against peace: namely, the planning, preparation, initiation, or waging of a war of aggression.[7]

Under contemporary international law, aggression, a crime against peace, is an international crime.[8] Indeed, in the words of the International Military Tribunal, it is the 'supreme' international crime: 'To initiate a war of aggression … is not only an international crime; it is the supreme international crime differing only from other war crimes in that it contains within itself the accumulated evil of the whole.'[9]

In November 1950, the UN General Assembly, in its Resolution 380 (V), solemnly reaffirmed, by consensus, that, 'whatever the weapons used, any aggression, whether committed openly, or by fomenting civil strife in the interest of a foreign Power, or otherwise, is the gravest of all crimes and security throughout the world'.[10] According to the 1974 Definition of Aggression, no consideration of whatever nature, whether political, economic, military, or other, may serve as a justification for aggression.[11]

In 1954, the Draft Code of Offences against the Peace and Security of Mankind stipulated that offences defined in the Code 'are crimes under international law,

---

[4] Art 227 of the 1919 Treaty of Versailles; signed at Versailles, 28 June 1919; entered into force, 10 January 1920.

[5] Observations by German delegate on 29 May 1919, in HWV Temperley (ed), *A History of the Paris Peace Conference*, vol II (London, Henry Frowde and Hodder & Stoughton, 1920) 304, text at bit.ly/2YIyE4t.

[6] E Blakemore, 'Why Kaiser Wilhelm Was Never Tried for Starting World War I', *History* (last updated 8 July 2019), bit.ly/2YG8gZf.

[7] Art 6(a) of the 1945 Charter of the International Military Tribunal (IMT), in Agreement for the Prosecution and Punishment of the Major War Criminals of the European Axis; signed at London, 8 August 1945.

[8] Art 5(2) of the Definition of Aggression adopted by UN General Assembly Resolution 3314 (XXIX), adopted without a vote on 14 December 1974 (hereinafter 1974 Definition of Aggression).

[9] *Trial of the Major War Criminals before the International Military Tribunal*, vol 22 (1948), 427.

[10] UN General Assembly Resolution 380 (V) ('Peace through Deeds'), adopted by consensus on 17 November 1950, para 1.

[11] 1974 Definition of Aggression, Art 5(1).

for which the responsible individuals shall be punished'.[12] Article 2 of the Code defined as offences against the peace and security of mankind:

> (1)   Any act of aggression, including the employment by the authorities of a State of armed force against another State for any purpose other than national or collective self-defence or in pursuance of a decision or recommendation of a competent organ of the United Nations.
>
> (2)   Any threat by the authorities of a State to resort to an act of aggression against another State.

By 1996, the Draft Code had evolved such that it now provided explicitly for individual criminal responsibility:

> An individual shall be responsible for the crime of aggression.[13]

> An individual who, as leader or organizer, actively participates in or orders the planning, preparation, initiation or waging of aggression committed by a State shall be responsible for a crime of aggression.[14]

In the official commentary on the Draft Code, it is explained that individual responsibility for the crime of aggression

> is intrinsically and inextricably linked to the commission of aggression by a State. The rule of international law which prohibits aggression applies to the conduct of a State in relation to another State. Therefore, only a State is capable of committing aggression by violating this rule of international law which prohibits such conduct.[15]

Accordingly, this chapter discusses both the international crime of aggression for which responsibility attaches to the state and the individual responsibility that attaches under international criminal law.

# II.  The Definition of Aggression

Preventing acts of aggression is one of the primary purposes of the United Nations.[16] But identifying when it has been perpetrated has long proved challenging. In 1951, the Special Rapporteur of the International Law Commission (ILC)

---

[12] Art 1 of the Draft Code of Offences against the Peace and Security of Mankind, Text adopted by the International Law Commission (ILC) at its sixth session in 1954 and submitted to the UN General Assembly, bit.ly/2JBpKzw.

[13] Art 2(2) of the Draft Code of Crimes against the Peace and Security of Mankind, Text adopted by the ILC at its forty-eighth session in 1996 and submitted to the UN General Assembly, bit.ly/2LfbdwU.

[14] 1996 Draft Code of Crimes against the Peace and Security of Mankind, Art 16 ('Crime of aggression').

[15] 1996 Draft Code of Crimes against the Peace and Security of Mankind, commentary para 4 on Art 16.

[16] Cryer et al, An Introduction to International Criminal Law and Procedure, 297.

even suggested that aggression was 'by its essence … not susceptible of definition'.[17] This position has not, though, been sustained.

First and foremost, aggression is an unlawful interstate use of force. Not every unlawful use of force, however, is an act of aggression:[18] aggression is a *grave* violation by a state of the general prohibition on the use of force codified in Article 2(4) of the UN Charter.[19] In 1974, UN General Assembly Resolution 3314 (XXIX), adopted by consensus, annexed the definition of aggression that exists under customary law today.[20] The preamble to the definition termed aggression 'the most serious and dangerous form of the illegal use of force'.[21] This clearly indicates that there are less serious forms of unlawful use of force that do not amount to aggression.

Indeed, while the 1974 UN definition largely (though not precisely) replicated the formulation in Article 2(4) of the Charter, determining that aggression 'is the use of armed force by a State against the sovereignty, territorial integrity or political independence of another State, or in any other manner inconsistent with the Charter of the United Nations',[22] it also introduced a significant caveat. The text declared that the UN Security Council

> may, in conformity with the Charter, conclude that a determination that an act of aggression has been committed would not be justified in the light of other relevant circumstances, including the fact that the acts concerned or their consequences are not of sufficient gravity.[23]

In the context of the customary law definition, acts of aggression include, but are not limited to,[24] the following conduct:

(a) The invasion or attack by the armed forces of a State of the territory of another State, or any military occupation, however temporary, resulting from such invasion or attack, or any annexation by the use of force of the territory of another State or part thereof;

---

[17] 'Second Report on a Draft Code of Offences Against the Peace and Security of Mankind by Mr J Spiropoulos, Special Rapporteur', ILC, UN doc A/CN.4/44, 12 April 1951, 69; see Cryer et al, *An Introduction to International Criminal Law and Procedure*, 299.

[18] SD Murphy, 'The Crime of Aggression at the International Criminal Court' in M Weller (ed), *The Oxford Handbook of the Use of Force in International Law* (Oxford, Oxford University Press, 2015) 538. Cryer et al distinguish an act of aggression, which engages the responsibility only of the state, from a war of aggression, which also engages individual criminal responsibility: Cryer et al, *An Introduction to International Criminal Law and Procedure*, 299.

[19] Charter of the United Nations; adopted at San Francisco, 26 June 1945; entered into force, 24 October 1945.

[20] The resolution was 'a carefully negotiated instrument that reflected current customary international law', in the words of the Special Working Group on the Crime of Aggression set up by states parties to the ICC. See ICC doc ICC-ASP/6/20/Add.1, Annex II: Report of the Special Working Group on the Crime of Aggression (June 2008), para 31; see also J Klabbers, 'Intervention, Armed Intervention, Armed Attack, Threat to Peace, Act of Aggression, and Threat or Use of Force: What's the Difference?' in Weller, *The Oxford Handbook of the Use of Force in International Law*, 498–99.

[21] 1974 Definition of Aggression, fifth preambular paragraph.

[22] 1974 Definition of Aggression, Art 1.

[23] 1974 Definition of Aggression, Art 2.

[24] 1974 Definition of Aggression, Art 4.

(b) Bombardment by the armed forces of a State against the territory of another State or the use of any weapons by a State against the territory of another State;

(c) The blockade of the ports or coasts of a State by the armed forces of another State;

(d) An attack by the armed forces of a State on the land, sea or air forces, or marine and air fleets of another State;

(e) The use of armed forces of one State which are within the territory of another State with the agreement of the receiving State, in contravention of the conditions provided for in the agreement or any extension of their presence in such territory beyond the termination of the agreement;

(f) The action of a State in allowing its territory, which it has placed at the disposal of another State, to be used by that other State for perpetrating an act of aggression against a third State;

(g) The sending by or on behalf of a State of armed bands, groups, irregulars or mercenaries, which carry out acts of armed force against another State of such gravity as to amount to the acts listed above, or its substantial involvement therein.[25]

Under Article 4 of the definition, these enumerated acts of aggression 'are not exhaustive', and the Security Council may determine that other acts constitute aggression under the provisions of the Charter. At the same time, it is stipulated under Article 7 of the 1974 Definition of Aggression that nothing in it 'could in any way prejudice the right to self-determination, freedom and independence, as derived from the Charter, of peoples ... particularly peoples under colonial and racist regimes or other forms of alien domination'. The right of such peoples 'to struggle to that end and to seek and receive support, in accordance with the principles of the Charter', is also preserved.[26]

## III. State Responsibility for Acts of Aggression

Under Article 5(2) of the 1974 Definition of Aggression, aggression 'gives rise to international responsibility'. Chapter III of the ILC's 2001 Draft Articles on the Responsibility of States for Internationally Wrongful Acts[27] (hereinafter the 2001 Draft Articles on State Responsibility) addresses serious breaches of obligations under peremptory norms of general international law. The prohibition of aggression is without doubt a *jus cogens* norm. Article 40(2) of the Draft Articles stipulates that a 'breach of such an obligation is serious if it involves a gross or systematic failure by the responsible State to fulfil the obligation'. Launching an aggressive war would, per se, constitute a serious breach of a *jus cogens* norm.

---

[25] 1974 Definition of Aggression, Art 3.

[26] Jan Klabbers remarks that although the 1974 Definition of Aggression proclaims that no consideration can justify aggression, in fact 'aggression is bad, unless done for good reasons, and those reasons remain relatively open-ended': Klabbers, 'Intervention, Armed Intervention, Armed Attack', 499.

[27] ILC Draft Articles on the Responsibility of States for Internationally Wrongful Acts, adopted on 10 August 2001, contained in the annex to UN General Assembly Resolution 56/83 of 12 December 2001 (hereinafter 2001 Articles on State Responsibility).

## A. The Duty to Make Reparation

Article 1 of the 2001 Draft Articles on State Responsibility states that: 'Every internationally wrongful act of a State entails the international responsibility of that State.' This will include a duty to pay compensation. Thus, the responsible state 'is under an obligation to make full reparation for the injury caused by the internationally wrongful act'.[28] There is state practice for the allocation of financial responsibility for an act of aggression. According to the commentary to Article 1, however, 'the award of *punitive* damages is not recognized in international law even in relation to serious breaches of obligations arising under peremptory norms'.[29]

The UN Compensation Commission (UNCC) was created to address Iraq's financial liability for its 'unlawful invasion and occupation of Kuwait' in 1990. In its Resolution 687, the UN Security Council reaffirmed that Iraq was 'liable under international law for any direct loss, damage – including environmental damage and the depletion of natural resources – or injury to foreign Governments, nationals and corporations as a result of its unlawful invasion and occupation of Kuwait'.[30] The Commission was established in 1991 as a subsidiary organ of the Security Council.[31]

The UNCC was 'neither a court nor a tribunal with an elaborate adversarial process'.[32] The total compensation it paid out amounted to some \$48 billion, which was awarded to approximately 1.5 million successful claimants.[33] Decision 11 of the Commission's Governing Council had limited the possibility of members of the Allied Coalition Armed Forces receiving compensation for loss or injury arising from their involvement in Coalition military operations against Iraq to those held as prisoners of war and whose loss or injury resulted from mistreatment in violation of the laws of armed conflict.[34] However, the UNCC's Panel of Commissioners also accepted claims from members of the Kuwaiti Armed Forces for events that occurred during the day of the invasion (2 August 1990) or on the days immediately following that of the invasion. The Panel further accepted claims on behalf of Kuwaiti members of the resistance or other military personnel who remained within Kuwaiti territory and who suffered death or personal injury due to the Iraqi invasion and occupation of Kuwait.[35]

---

[28] 2001 Draft Articles on State Responsibility, Art 31(1).

[29] 2001 Draft Articles on State Responsibility, commentary para 5 on Draft Art 1 (emphasis added).

[30] UN Security Council Resolution 687, adopted on 3 April 1991 by 12 votes to 1 (Cuba) with 2 abstentions (Ecuador and Yemen), operative para 15.

[31] UN Security Council Resolution 692 (1991), adopted on 20 May 1991 by 14 votes to 0, with 1 abstention (Cuba).

[32] UNCC, 'Claims Processing', accessed on 3 September 2013 at bit.ly/2U865PM (page no longer online).

[33] UNCC Home Page, https://uncc.ch/.

[34] Text of the Decision, bit.ly/2UcYZtw.

[35] UNCC, 'Recommendations Made by the Panel of Commissioners Concerning Individual Claims for Serious Personal Injury or Death (Category "B" Claims)', UN doc S/AC.26/1994/1, 26 May 1994, 14–15.

## B. The Duty to Cooperate to Bring to an End an Act of Aggression

Article 41(1) of the 2001 Draft Articles on State Responsibility lays down a rule whereby states are obligated to 'cooperate to bring to an end through lawful means any serious breach within the meaning of article 40'. This would concern all states (presumably even including the state that is directly responsible for the violation of the *jus cogens* norm). According to the commentary on Article 41, cooperation could be organised 'in the framework of a competent international organization, in particular the United Nations', or through non-institutionalised cooperation.[36]

It was recognised, at the time, that the provision might 'reflect the progressive development of international law',[37] meaning that it was not a binding rule of international law in 2001. In fact, it is widely agreed that such a duty is *lex lata* today.[38] That said, a legal requirement that every state *actively*[39] cooperate in the event of an aggression might be considered somewhat challenging to implement, given that, under the UN Charter, member states have effectively subcontracted the maintenance (including the restoration) of international peace and security to the UN Security Council.[40]

## C. The Prohibition on Recognising as Lawful the Result of Aggression

Article 41(2) of the 2001 Draft Articles on State Responsibility provides that no state 'shall recognize as lawful a situation created by a serious breach within the meaning of article 40, nor render aid or assistance in maintaining that situation'. The accompanying commentary on this element of the provision notes that an

> example of the practice of non-recognition of acts in breach of peremptory norms is provided by the reaction of the Security Council to the Iraqi invasion of Kuwait in 1990. Following the Iraqi declaration of a 'comprehensive and eternal merger' with Kuwait, the Security Council, in resolution 662 (1990) of 9 August 1990, decided that the annexation had 'no legal validity, and is considered null and void', and called upon all States, international organizations and specialized agencies not to recognize that annexation and to refrain from any action or dealing that might be interpreted as a recognition of

---

[36] 2001 Draft Articles on State Responsibility, commentary para 2 on Draft Art 41.

[37] 2001 Draft Articles on State Responsibility, commentary para 3 on Draft Art 41.

[38] In his report of February 2018, for instance, the ILC Special Rapporteur on peremptory norms of general international law (*jus cogens*) implied that the duty to cooperate had become reflective of customary law: ILC, 'Third Report on Peremptory Norms of General International Law (*Jus Cogens*) by Dire Tladi, Special Rapporteur', UN doc A/CN.4/714, 12 February 2018, paras 90–94.

[39] See also C Tomuschat, 'Reconceptualizing the Debate on *Jus Cogens* and Obligations Erga Omnes – Concluding Observations' in C Tomuschat and J-M Thouvenin (eds), *The Fundamental Rules of the International Legal Order* (Leiden, Martinus Nijhoff, 2006) 429.

[40] UN Charter, Art 24(1).

it, whether direct or indirect. In fact, no State recognized the legality of the purported annexation, the effects of which were subsequently reversed.[41]

This indicates that the view of the ILC was that any state which had recognised the legality of Iraq's purported annexation would itself be responsible for an internationally wrongful act. This view was supported by the 1974 Definition of Aggression, which provides that: 'No territorial acquisition or special advantage resulting from aggression is or shall be recognized as lawful.'[42]

Henderson discusses in this context the non-recognition of the Russian Federation's forcible annexation of Crimea from Ukraine in 2014. He refers to UN General Assembly Resolution 68/262 on the territorial integrity of Ukraine, in which the Assembly, by majority vote, called upon all states to 'desist and refrain from actions aimed at the partial or total disruption of the national unity and territorial integrity of Ukraine, including any attempts to modify Ukraine's borders through the threat or use of force or other unlawful means', and further 'not to recognize any alteration of the status of the Autonomous Republic of Crimea and the city of Sevastopol ... and to refrain from any action or dealing that might be interpreted as recognizing any such altered status'.[43] The passing of the resolution was opposed by 11 states: Armenia, Belarus, Bolivia, Cuba, the Democratic People's Republic of Korea, Nicaragua, the Russian Federation, Sudan, Syria, Venezuela, and Zimbabwe.

Interpreting and applying Article 41(2) of the 2001 Draft Articles on State Responsibility, these 11 states could be responsible for an internationally wrongful act. None accepted that its action in opposing the resolution was unlawful. In the explanations of vote,[44] Bolivia stated that while it was not opposing universally accepted principles, it would vote against the text to demonstrate its disagreement with major powers that were exercising double standards and threatening international security. In its remarks, Cuba stressed the importance of allowing peoples to exercise their right to self-determination and stated that it would not accept the current Ukrainian authorities because they had assumed power by overthrowing the constitutional government through violence.

The Democratic People's Republic of Korea attributed the crisis in Ukraine to interference by the United States and other Western nations. It claimed that Crimea's reunification with the Russian Federation had been conducted legitimately through a referendum and in accordance with the UN Charter. Nicaragua stated that it supported the principle of peaceful, legitimate self-determination through the ballot box and rejected unilateral methods, including political and economic sanctions against the Russian Federation, which it believed were in violation of international law. The Russian Federation itself said that the referendum had reunified Crimea with Russia and it called on 'everyone to respect that

---

[41] 2001 Draft Articles on State Responsibility, commentary para 7 on Draft Art 41.

[42] 1974 Definition of Aggression, Art 5(3).

[43] UN General Assembly Resolution 68/262 ('Territorial Integrity of Ukraine'), adopted on 27 March 2014 by 100 votes to 11 with 58 abstentions, paras 2 and 6.

[44] UN, 'General Assembly Adopts Resolution Calling upon States Not to Recognize Changes in Status of Crimea Region', Information Note, UN doc GA/11493, 27 March 2014, bit.ly/2OExDq5.

voluntary choice'. It argued that the Russian Government could not refuse Crimeans their right to self-determination.

If the rule proposed by the ILC were to be customary law without caveat, it could mean that a peace deal between state A and state B, following unlawful use of force by state A against state B, could not lawfully include or result in the cession or independence of territory previously under the jurisdiction of state B. This would seemingly be the case for all time, notwithstanding that the peace deal was freely entered into by state A without coercion. This is highly questionable from both a legal and a policy perspective. Added to this problem, how many peace agreements are actually not made on the basis of unlawful coercion? Under Article 52 of the 1969 Vienna Convention on the Law of Treaties ('Coercion of a State by the threat or use of force'), 'A treaty is void if its conclusion has been procured by the threat or use of force in violation of the principles of international law embodied in the Charter of the United Nations'.

The use of force by NATO (North Atlantic Treaty Organization) member states in Operation Allied Force[45] against the Federal Republic of Yugoslavia, which was conducted with a view to protecting ethnic Albanians in Kosovo, was unlawful under *ad bellum* rules, as discussed in the previous chapter. There was no UN Security Council authorisation to use force against Yugoslavia, and Kosovo (and a fortiori the Kosovo Liberation Army), as a non-state entity, was not entitled under international law to act forcibly in self-defence, much less to invite other states to assist it in such an endeavour.[46] Hence, Yugoslav forces were driven out of Kosovo by an unlawful use of force by the NATO member states engaged in Operation Allied Force in 24 March to 10 June 1999.

On 26 March 1999, Belarus, India, and the Russian Federation put forward a draft resolution to the Security Council which, if adopted, would have expressed deep concern that NATO used military force against Yugoslavia 'without the authorization by the Council' and would have affirmed that 'such unilateral use of force constitutes a flagrant violation of the United Nations Charter, in particular Articles 2(4), 24, and 53'. The resolution would have deemed that unilateral use of force a threat to international peace and security.[47] The resolution was rejected by the Council, attracting only three votes in favour (China, Namibia, and the Russian Federation) but 12 votes against, including three permanent members (France, UK, and the United States), with no abstentions.[48] 'War was no humanitarian solution,' Cuba stated.[49]

---

[45] NATO, 'Kosovo Air Campaign (Archived): Operation Allied Force' (last updated 7 April 2016), bit.ly/2UcugNh.

[46] See, eg The Independent International Commission on Kosovo, *The Kosovo Report: Conflict, International Response, Lessons Learned* (Oxford, Oxford University Press, 2000) esp 166–74.

[47] 'Belarus, India and Russian Federation: Draft Resolution', UN doc S/1999/328, 26 March 1999, bit.ly/2Ygkqqw. Art 24 confers primary responsibility for the maintenance of international peace and security upon the UN Security Council. Art 53 allows regional arrangements for peace enforcement, but subject to authorisation from the UN Security Council.

[48] UN, 'Security Council Rejects Demand for Cessation of Use of Force against Federal Republic of Yugoslavia', Press Release, 26 March 1999, bit.ly/2JYh0no.

[49] ibid.

Under the Military Technical Agreement of 9 June 1999 between NATO's International Security Force and the Federal Republic of Yugoslavia and Republic of Serbia, 'under no circumstances shall any Forces of the FRY [Federal Republic of Yugoslavia] and the Republic of Serbia enter into, re-enter, or remain within the territory of Kosovo'.[50] Twenty years later, Kosovo had been recognised as a state by more than 100 states. In February 2019, Kosovo President Hashim Thaci claimed that Kosovo would reach a comprehensive agreement with Serbia before the end of the year that would allow the entry of Kosovo as a state member of the European Union.[51] That aim, which had always looked overly optimistic, was not achieved.

The International Court of Justice (ICJ) was asked to rule on a narrow issue of the legality of Kosovo's 2008 declaration of independence in an Advisory Opinion. It issued its Opinion in July 2010.[52] The Court addressed briefly the issue of independence based on unlawful use of force. In so doing, it recalled that 'the principle of territorial integrity is an important part of the international legal order and is enshrined in the Charter of the United Nations, in particular in Article 2, paragraph 4'.[53] It further stated that illegality attached to earlier declarations of independence stemmed

> not from the unilateral character of these declarations as such, but from the fact that they were, or would have been, connected with the unlawful use of force or other egregious violations of norms of general international law, in particular those of a peremptory character (*jus cogens*).

It avoided detailed discussion of this issue by noting simply that, in 'the context of Kosovo, the Security Council has never taken this position'.[54]

The second part of the provision in Article 41(2) of the 2001 Draft Articles on State Responsibility concerns a prohibition on rendering aid or assistance in maintaining a situation that has resulted from a serious breach of a *jus cogens* norm. As the official commentary on this rule explains:

> This goes beyond the provisions dealing with aid or assistance in the commission of an internationally wrongful act, which are covered by article 16 [of the Draft Articles]. It deals with conduct 'after the fact' which assists the responsible State in maintaining a situation 'opposable to all States in the sense of barring erga omnes the legality of a situation which is maintained in violation of international law'.[55]

---

[50] Art I(4)(a) of the Military Technical Agreement between the International Security Force (KFOR) and the Governments of the Federal Republic of Yugoslavia and the Republic of Serbia; concluded at Kumanovo, North Macedonia (then the former Yugoslav Republic of Macedonia), 9 June 1999; entered into force, 10 June 1999, bit.ly/2K1wpX7.

[51] A Dudik and J Kuzmanovic, 'Kosovo Targets Deal with Serbia This Year to Boost EU Hopes', *Bloomberg*, 16 February 2019, bloom.bg/2OGWGsB.

[52] ICJ, *Accordance with International Law of the Unilateral Declaration of Independence in Respect of Kosovo*, Advisory Opinion, 22 July 2010.

[53] ibid para 80.

[54] ibid.

[55] Commentary para 11 on Draft Art 41, citing European Court of Human Rights, *Loizidou v Turkey*, Judgment (Merits) (Chamber), 18 December 1996, para 56, and *Cyprus v Turkey*, Judgment (Grand Chamber), 10 May 2001, paras 89–98.

The commentary further explains that the specific obligation stands discrete from the putative duty not to recognise the situation as lawful, as 'confirmed, for example, in the resolutions of the Security Council prohibiting any aid or assistance in maintaining the illegal apartheid regime in South Africa or Portuguese colonial rule'.[56] In 2018, ILC Special Rapporteur Dire Tladi endorsed the view expressed earlier by the ILC that this specific obligation was a customary rule of international law.[57] The prohibition on rendering aid or assistance in maintaining a situation resulting from a serious breach of a *jus cogens* norm would preclude the provision by any state of armed forces, arms, or other military materiel for use in holding territory claimed by aggressive use of force.

## IV. Individual Responsibility for Aggression under International Criminal Law

As is the case with all international crimes, there is individual criminal responsibility for the crime of aggression. In the famous words of the International Military Tribunal, 'Crimes against international law are committed by men, not by abstract entities, and only by punishing individuals who commit such crimes can the provisions of international law be enforced'.[58] In this scenario, the individuals are limited subjects of international law, being imbued with duties as opposed to rights.

The crime of aggression exists under customary international law and now too within the jurisdiction of the 1998 Rome Statute of the International Criminal Court[59] (ICC Statute). The two preceding ad hoc tribunals (for the former Yugoslavia and Rwanda) did not have jurisdiction to prosecute acts of aggression but only war crimes, crimes against humanity, and genocide. They did, though, help 'to break through the political log-jam holding back the creation of a permanent International Criminal Court'.[60]

The origin of individual criminal responsibility for the crime of aggression is the Charter of the International Military Tribunal. As has been alluded to, whether this was a reaffirmation of existing law or the progressive development of international law is disputed. As Ian Brownlie observed, while the American

---

[56] 2001 Draft Articles on State Responsibility, commentary para 12 on Draft Art 41, citing as examples UN Security Council Resolution 218 (1965) of 23 November 1965 on the Portuguese colonies, and Resolutions 418 (1977) of 4 November 1977 and 569 (1985) of 26 July 1985 on South Africa.

[57] ILC, 'Third Report on Peremptory Norms of General International Law (*Jus Cogens*) by Dire Tladi', paras 95–102.

[58] *Trial of the Major War Criminals before the International Military Tribunal*, vol I, Nuremberg, 1947, 223.

[59] Rome Statute of the International Criminal Court; adopted at Rome, 17 July 1998; entered into force, 1 July 2002.

[60] Murphy, 'The Crime of Aggression at the International Criminal Court', 538.

representative to the negotiation of the Charter was persuaded that aggressive war was per se criminal, the French representative, Professor Andre Gros, 'did not consider that aggressive war was a crime in existing law, and, even if it was, the criminality attached only to the state'.[61] Gros accepted the compromise included in the Charter, considering that 'the objection of retroactivity would be met if there was reference to violation of treaties and assurances'.[62] Thus, Article 6(a) of the 1945 Charter of the International Military Tribunal provides as follows:

> *Crimes against peace*: namely, planning, preparation, initiation or waging of a war of aggression, or a war in violation of international treaties, agreements or assurances, or participation in a common plan or conspiracy for the accomplishment of any of the foregoing.

Before the International Military Tribunal, Professor Dr Hermann Jahrreiss, the defence counsel for Alfred Jodl, Hitler's Chief of Staff, suggested that if an unequivocal treaty prohibition of aggressive war did exist at the outbreak of the Second World War, the violation of that treaty would be an offence against international law but that this did not connote the criminality of either states or individuals.[63]

In its judgment, the Tribunal acknowledged that the Kellogg–Briand Pact (to which Germany was a party) did not criminalise aggression, and had never intended to do so.[64] The Tribunal did, however, point out that the same was true of the prohibitions in the 1907 Hague Convention governing war on land, yet war crimes existed with individual criminal responsibility. This argument is weak, though, as, at best, it serves to underpin a claim that the prohibition of aggression *could* be criminalised, not that it *was* criminalised. To support its conclusions, the Tribunal also pointed to the references in the 1923 Draft Treaty of Mutual Assistance (which never entered into force); the 1924 Geneva Protocol for the Pacific Resolution of International Disputes (which also never entered into force); Article 227 of the Treaty of Versailles (which was never implemented); the 1927 Resolution of the Assembly of the League of Nations (where reference to a war of aggression as an international crime was in the preamble, not even in the operative text); and a resolution of the Sixth International Conference of American States in 1928 (wherein again the reference was in the preamble,[65] and this was in a resolution from a regional, not a global, body).

Taken together, this evidence is unpersuasive as a legal underpinning of the existence, in 1939, of individual criminal responsibility under customary

---

[61] Brownlie, *International Law and the Use of Force by States*, 163.

[62] ibid.

[63] ibid 170.

[64] Cryer et al, *An Introduction to International Criminal Law and Procedure*, 298.

[65] '[Whereas] ... War of aggression is an international crime against the human race ...': Papers relating to the foreign relations of the United States, 1928, vol I, 204, bit.ly/2NQ9Jer.

international law for the commission of an international crime of waging aggressive war. Nonetheless, in its judgment, the Tribunal concluded:

> All these expressions of opinion, and others that could be cited, so solemnly made, reinforce the construction which the Tribunal placed upon the Pact of Paris, that resort to a war of aggression is not merely illegal, but is criminal. The prohibition of aggressive war demanded by the conscience of the world[] finds its expression in the series of pacts and treaties to which the Tribunal has just referred.[66]

The Tribunal held that the *Anschluss* of Austria and the German administration of parts of Czechoslovakia were 'aggressive actions', while the invasions of Belgium, Denmark, Greece, Luxembourg, the Netherlands, Norway, Poland, and Yugoslavia, and attacks against the United States, were all 'aggressive wars'.[67]

Similar discussions were held on the definition of crimes against peace in the context of the International Criminal Tribunal for the Far East. With respect to that, however, the Tribunal's Charter differed from that in Nuremberg:

> *Crimes against Peace*: Namely, the planning, preparation, initiation or waging of a declared or undeclared war of aggression, or a war in violation of *international law*, treaties, agreements or assurances, or participation in a common plan or conspiracy for the accomplishment of any of the foregoing.[68]

The Tribunal stated in its judgment that aggressive war was 'a crime at international law long prior to the Declaration of Potsdam'.[69] The Declaration was a formal demand for Japan's unconditional surrender made on 26 July 1945 by China, Great Britain, and the United States. In a concurring opinion to the Tribunal's judgment, the President of the Tribunal, Sir William Webb, referred to the 1928 Kellogg–Briand Pact and affirmed that in the instance of any state that adhered to the Pact and which engages in aggressive war, 'those individuals through whom it acts, knowing as they do that their State is a party to the Pact, are criminally responsible for this delict of State'.[70]

In contrast, Judge Bernard of France stated that there was no question of criminal responsibility for a war in violation of the Pact, although he accepted that such a war 'always has been a crime in the eyes of reason and universal conscience'. Judge Röling of the Netherlands and Judge Pal of India came to similar conclusions in their own dissenting opinions.[71] These views notwithstanding, under both treaty and customary law, individual criminal responsibility attaches to a senior state official engaged in the planning, preparation, initiation or execution of an aggressive war.

---

[66] *Trial of the Major War Criminals before the International Military Tribunal*, vol I, 222.
[67] Murphy, 'The Crime of Aggression at the International Criminal Court', 536.
[68] Art 5(a) of the International Military Tribunal for the Far East; Charter dated 19 January 1946, bit.ly/2SbfWAa (emphasis added).
[69] International Military Tribunal for the Far East, Judgment, 1946, 27, bit.ly/2LJSXuW.
[70] Cited by Brownlie, *International Law and the Use of Force by States*, 173.
[71] ibid.

# A. Individual Criminal Responsibility under Conventional Law

## (i) Jurisdiction under the ICC

Article 8*bis* of the ICC Statute defines the crime of aggression for the purpose of individual criminal responsibility in the International Criminal Court. This provision states as follows:

1.  For the purpose of this Statute, 'crime of aggression' means the planning, preparation, initiation or execution, by a person in a position effectively to exercise control over or to direct the political or military action of a State, of an act of aggression which, by its character, gravity and scale, constitutes a manifest violation of the Charter of the United Nations.

2.  For the purpose of paragraph 1, 'act of aggression' means the use of armed force by a State against the sovereignty, territorial integrity or political independence of another State, or in any other manner inconsistent with the Charter of the United Nations. Any of the following acts, regardless of a declaration of war, shall, in accordance with United Nations General Assembly resolution 3314 (XXIX) of 14 December 1974, qualify as an act of aggression:

    a)  The invasion or attack by the armed forces of a State of the territory of another State, or any military occupation, however temporary, resulting from such invasion or attack, or any annexation by the use of force of the territory of another State or part thereof;

    b)  Bombardment by the armed forces of a State against the territory of another State or the use of any weapons by a State against the territory of another State;

    c)  The blockade of the ports or coasts of a State by the armed forces of another State;

    d)  An attack by the armed forces of a State on the land, sea or air forces, or marine and air fleets of another State;

    e)  The use of armed forces of one State which are within the territory of another State with the agreement of the receiving State, in contravention of the conditions provided for in the agreement or any extension of their presence in such territory beyond the termination of the agreement;

    f)  The action of a State in allowing its territory, which it has placed at the disposal of another State, to be used by that other State for perpetrating an act of aggression against a third State;

    g)  The sending by or on behalf of a State of armed bands, groups, irregulars or mercenaries, which carry out acts of armed force against another State of such gravity as to amount to the acts listed above, or its substantial involvement therein.[72]

---

[72] Amendments on the crime of aggression to the Rome Statute of the International Criminal Court; adopted at Kampala, 11 June 2010. As discussed below, the Court has been entitled to exercise jurisdiction with respect to crimes of aggression committed by states parties or nationals of states parties that have ratified or accepted the amendments since 17 July 2018. The UN Security Council may also refer a situation to the ICC for possible prosecution.

The states parties negotiating the definition resisted calls to add a limitative purpose to the definition of aggression, such as military occupation or annexation.[73] The threshold for a prosecution for the crime of aggression under the ICC Statute is, unsurprisingly, high, although the types of acts and modes of liability that may be prosecuted are numerous and the prima facie definition of aggression is seemingly broad. Indeed, it appears to equate an act of aggression with any violation of Article 2(4) of the UN Charter since the notion of gravity present in the 1974 Definition of Aggression is absent from the provision in Article 8*bis*(2) of the ICC Statute.[74] That said, a formal understanding reached at the Statute's 2010 Kampala Review Conference clarifies that, consonant with the 1974 Definition of Aggression, 'aggression is the most serious and dangerous form of illegal use of force', and further 'that a determination whether an act of aggression has been committed requires consideration of all the circumstances of each particular case, including the gravity of the acts concerned and their consequences'.[75]

Under paragraph 1 of Article 8*bis* of the ICC Statute, a senior government or military figure may be held responsible for an act of aggression if he or she were involved in its planning, preparation, initiation, or execution. The accused must have been in a position where they either 'directed or exercised effective control' over the political or military action of the state that committed an act of aggression. In Murphy's words, 'Kampala's "crime of aggression" by its terms is a leadership crime'.[76] As he recalls, in the 1948 *High Command* case (*Von Leeb and others*) after the Second World War, 13 German generals and one admiral were acquitted of the charges of crimes against peace on the ground that 'the criminality which attaches to the waging of an aggressive war should be confined to those who participate in it at the policy level'.[77]

In addition, the language used in Article 8*bis*(1) 'excludes non-governmental actors'.[78] This would mean, for instance, that the head of an armed group that was sent to carry out an act of armed aggression[79] would not be liable to prosecution by the ICC, but a senior official of the state that sent the group could be. Potentially, though, by far the most significant limiting criterion is that an aggression which has been perpetrated must have constituted, by its 'character', 'gravity', and 'scale', considered cumulatively, a manifest violation of the UN Charter.

## (ii) A 'Manifest Violation' of the UN Charter

If aggression is a grave violation of the prohibition of the interstate use of force, then only the clearest and most serious of aggressive actions would be capable of

[73] Cryer et al, *An Introduction to International Criminal Law and Procedure*, 302, 310.
[74] Murphy, 'The Crime of Aggression at the International Criminal Court', 540.
[75] ICC doc RC/Res 6, Annex III, Understanding No 6, adopted on 11 June 2010 by consensus, bit.ly/2OFt14t; see also Murphy, 'The Crime of Aggression at the International Criminal Court', 553.
[76] Murphy, 'The Crime of Aggression at the International Criminal Court', 540.
[77] See Cryer et al, *An Introduction to International Criminal Law and Procedure*, 302.
[78] Murphy, 'The Crime of Aggression at the International Criminal Court', 540.
[79] ICC Statute, Art 8*bis*(2)(g).

being lawfully prosecuted before the ICC. The three criteria of 'character', 'gravity', and 'scale' apply cumulatively, implying that only a major military operation or one that caused many casualties would come within the jurisdiction of the Court. Thus, for example, as Murphy opines, the 'unprovoked and massive invasion by one state of another state would presumably fall within the scope of the crime of aggression, such as Iraq's 1990 invasion of Kuwait'.[80]

In contrast, in a rare instance of the UN Security Council finding that an act of aggression had occurred, Resolution 611 of 1988 concerned 'the aggression perpetrated on 16 April 1988 in the locality of Sidi Bou Said', which 'caused loss of human life, particularly the assassination of Mr Khalil al-Wazir'.[81] That Israeli act of aggression would not meet the criteria of either gravity or scale required under the ICC Statute for the crime of aggression to be prosecuted. With respect to 'character', Jennifer Trahan suggests that protagonists in a humanitarian intervention (at the least where this was not a mere cover for aggression) would not be punishable by the Court.[82] Such a conclusion is, however, uncertain, as discussed further below.

## (iii) The Prosecution of the Crime of Aggression

By ratifying the amendment on the crime of aggression adopted in Kampala in 2010,[83] a state party to the ICC is potentially allowing its leaders and senior officials to be tried before the Court. As of 1 May 2020, this concerned 39 states: Andorra, Argentina, Austria, Belgium, Botswana, Chile, Costa Rica, Croatia, Cyprus, Czech Republic, Ecuador, El Salvador, Estonia, Finland, Georgia, Germany, Guyana, Iceland, Ireland, Latvia, Liechtenstein, Lithuania, Luxembourg, Malta, the Netherlands, North Macedonia, Panama, Paraguay, Poland, Portugal, Samoa, San Marino, Slovakia, Slovenia, Spain, State of Palestine, Switzerland, Trinidad and Tobago, and Uruguay.[84] This list includes a number of NATO members who participated in the unlawful attacks on Yugoslavia in 1999:[85] indeed, as noted in the previous chapter, Germany's Federal Chancellor at the time of Operation Allied Force, Gerhard Schröder, revealed publicly in 2014 that Germany had been aware at the time that 'formally going to war without a decision of the Security Council was a violation of international law'.[86]

---

[80] ibid 553.

[81] UN Security Council Resolution 611, adopted on 25 April 1988 by 14 votes to 0, with 1 abstention (United States of America), third preambular paragraph.

[82] J Trahan, 'Defining the "Grey Area" Where Humanitarian Intervention May Not Be Fully Legal, but Is Not the Crime of Aggression' (2015) 2(1) *Journal on the Use of Force and International Law* 42.

[83] Amendments on the crime of aggression to the Rome Statute of the International Criminal Court; adopted at Kampala, 11 June 2010; entered into force, 8 May 2013.

[84] See the list maintained by the UN Treaty Section, bit.ly/2rIahsm.

[85] On this issue, Murphy suggests that a state party 'might seek to opt out of the ICC's "aggression" jurisdiction solely with respect to alleged crimes arising from that state's involvement in a military operation of the NATO (North Atlantic Treaty Organization)': Murphy, 'The Crime of Aggression at the International Criminal Court', 548.

[86] SAG Talmon, 'At Last! Germany Admits Illegality of the Kosovo Intervention' (2014) 57 *German Yearbook of International Law*, citing a *Die Zeit* panel with Gerhard Schröder on 9 March 2014,

There are, though, a series of procedural hoops to pass through before any trial may take place. In accordance with Article 15*bis*, the ICC may exercise jurisdiction over any crime of aggression since 17 July 2018 with respect to states parties that have accepted the amendment to the ICC Statute.[87] With respect to a state not party to the Statute, the Court 'shall not exercise its jurisdiction over the crime of aggression when committed by that State's nationals or on its territory'.[88]

Where the ICC Prosecutor concludes a 'reasonable basis' exists to proceed with an investigation in respect of a crime of aggression, he or she must first ascertain whether the UN Security Council has made a determination of an act of aggression committed by the state concerned.[89] Where the Security Council has made such a determination, the Prosecutor may proceed with the investigation in respect of a crime of aggression.[90] Where no such determination has been made within six months of a notification to the UN Secretary-General, the Prosecutor may then proceed with his or her investigation, provided that the ICC Pre-Trial Division has authorised it and the Security Council has not decided otherwise.[91] It is explicitly clarified that a determination of an act of aggression by another 'organ' (whether the Security Council or even a judicial body such as the ICJ) 'shall be without prejudice to the Court's own findings under this Statute'.[92]

It is also possible for the UN Security Council to refer a possible case to the ICC for prosecution in accordance with Article 15*ter*. Such a referral is only possible when the Council is acting under Chapter VII of the UN Charter.[93] Again, however, a determination of an act of aggression by another 'organ' (whether the Security Council or even a judicial body such as the ICJ) 'shall be without prejudice to the Court's own findings under this Statute'.[94]

Given all of these limitations, Alex Whiting found it 'difficult to imagine an aggression prosecution at the ICC involving States Parties, at least for the time being'.[95] Writing in late 2017, he acknowledged the significance of the 'articulation and establishment of the crime', but cautioned that it might

> burden the ICC with even more expectations that cannot be fulfilled. Already, the Court can prosecute only a tiny fraction of the atrocity crimes that occur in the world, even where it has jurisdiction, leaving many supporters and victims frustrated.[96]

---

available on YouTube at bit.ly/34Esu8I; see also C Gray, *International Law and the Use of Force*, 4th edn (Oxford, Oxford University Press, 2018) 52.

[87] See, eg J Trahan, 'Activation of the International Criminal Court's Jurisdiction Over the Crime of Aggression & Challenges Ahead', *Opinio Juris*, 18 July 2018, bit.ly/2DD6Ju3.

[88] ICC Statute, Art 15*bis*(5).

[89] ICC Statute, Art 15*bis*(6).

[90] ICC Statute, Art 15*bis*(7).

[91] ICC Statute, Art 15*bis*(8).

[92] ICC Statute, Art 15*bis*(9).

[93] ICC Statute, Art 13(b).

[94] ICC Statute, Art 15*ter*(4).

[95] A Whiting, 'Crime of Aggression Activated at the ICC: Does It Matter?', *Just Security*, 19 December 2017, bit.ly/2RbQU5n.

[96] ibid.

He further warned that the Court 'might find itself spending a lot of time trying to explain why it is not prosecuting aggression cases, a dynamic that is never very good for a court's overall reputation and legitimacy'.[97]

That said, to successfully prosecute an individual charged with the crime of aggression, the updated ICC *Elements of Crimes* makes it explicit that there is no need to prove that the perpetrator had made 'a legal evaluation as to whether the use of armed force was inconsistent with the Charter of the United Nations' or even 'a legal evaluation as to the "manifest" nature of the violation' of the UN Charter (though the perpetrator must have been aware of 'the factual circumstances that established such a manifest violation').[98]

A proposal by the United States at the Kampala Review Conference that states parties include a specific exception for force used in a humanitarian intervention was not accepted.[99] Thus, writing in 2015, Harold Koh and Todd Buchwald questioned whether an act of humanitarian intervention might be caught by the threshold of a manifest violation:

> States may become unduly reluctant to risk involvement even in military actions that are lawful and appropriate, if such involvement creates an inherent and unpredictable risk of ICC investigation or prosecution. Ironically, one such result could be that the ICC ends up prolonging violence and abuses of human rights by deterring future military actions – for example, ones parallel to the intervention frequently urged in Rwanda in 1994 – aimed at stopping the commission of genocide, war crimes, and crimes against humanity, which the Rome Statute sought to eliminate. It would be hugely tragic if this chilling effect discouraged states from stopping preventable genocide, war crimes, and crimes against humanity, and thus limited states' responses to *post hoc* efforts at accountability.[100]

The obvious response to this charge is that securing UN Security Council authorisation to use force will preclude any charge of aggression. That does not address the problem where the Council is deadlocked (such as with respect to Kosovo in 1999 or Syria since 2012), but it is far from certain that unlawful unilateral uses of force over the past 50 years have proved overwhelmingly successful in protecting all civilians when the longer term consequences are factored in. In any event, Murphy fails to persuade in his claim that

> NATO's bombing campaign against Serbia [*sic*, actually the Federal Republic of Yugoslavia] in 1999 might not fall within the Kampala definition of an act of aggression because 'reasonable' people disagreed about whether that intervention was lawful, with

---

[97] ibid. In contrast, Cryer et al assert that 'if the existence of the ICC jurisdiction acts as a deterrent to even a few war-mongering presidents and prime ministers, it has the potential to save many lives': Cryer et al, *An Introduction to International Criminal Law and Procedure*, 317.

[98] ICC Elements of Crimes, 'Article 8 *bis*: Crime of Aggression', Introduction paras 2 and 4, and Elements, para 6.

[99] Cryer et al, *An Introduction to International Criminal Law and Procedure*, 311.

[100] TF Buchwald and HH Koh, 'The Crime of Aggression: The United States Perspective' (2015) 109 *American Journal of International Law* 272, bit.ly/33HP7aQ.

some arguing that it was permissible in order to protect the fundamental human rights of Kosovar Albanians.[101]

## B. Individual Criminal Responsibility under Customary International Law

As Cryer et al observe, whatever the merits of the decisions of the two Military Tribunals established at the end of the Second World War, it is now 'widely accepted' that the crime of aggression exists under customary international law.[102] This crime is 'generally regarded as being limited to participation in a "war" of aggression'.[103]

In March 2006, the UK House of Lords unanimously decided in *R v Jones (Margaret)*, in the context of the invasion of Iraq, that although the crime of aggression existed under customary international law, there was no such crime under the law of England and Wales.[104] In its 2017 judgment in *Al Rabbat v Tony Blair and others*, the High Court of Justice of England and Wales held that there was 'no prospect of the Supreme Court holding that the decision in Jones was wrong or the reasoning no longer applicable'.[105]

Yet, despite the fact that aggression has not been recognised as a crime under the law in force in England and Wales, Lord Bingham affirmed in his leading judgment for the House of Lords in *R v Jones*

> that the core elements of the crime of aggression have been understood, at least since 1945, with sufficient clarity to permit the lawful trial (and, on conviction, punishment) of those accused of this most serious crime. It is unhistorical to suppose that the elements of the crime were clear in 1945 but have since become in any way obscure.[106]

## C. The Threat of Aggression

While planning, preparing, or initiating an act of aggression is punishable under the ICC, the 'threat' to perpetrate aggression, which would violate Article 2(4) of the UN Charter and customary international law, is not. Dinstein finds this 'perhaps regrettable' insofar as a small state may be so intimidated by the threat

---

[101] Murphy, 'The Crime of Aggression at the International Criminal Court', 554.
[102] Cryer et al, *An Introduction to International Criminal Law and Procedure*, 298.
[103] ibid 309.
[104] *R v Jones (Margaret)* [2007] 1 AC 136.
[105] High Court of Justice of England and Wales, *Al Rabbat v Tony Blair and others* [2017] EWHC 1969 (Admin), para 18.
[106] UK House of Lords, *R v Jones and others* [2006] UKHL 16, para 19.

of massive force – especially by a major military power – that it prefers to give in without a fight in order to preserve the life of its citizens.[107]

## V. Concluding Remarks

It is sometimes suggested that acts of aggression occur infrequently and, a fortiori, that aggressive wars that would meet the ICC Statute threshold are few and far between. But while it is undoubtedly true that actual prosecutions for the crime of aggression within the ICC will be 'rarely ever' conducted[108] (by which is probably meant 'never'), that is not to deny that such crimes continue to be committed. In the first two decades of the twenty-first century, the world has seen the US-led aggression in Iraq in 2003;[109] the Russian aggression in the Crimea region of Ukraine in 2014;[110] and most recently, in 2019, the Turkish invasion of northern Syria.[111] Each of these cases constitutes 'an act of aggression which, by its character, gravity and scale, constitutes a manifest violation of the Charter of the United Nations' in the terms of Article 8*bis*(1) of the ICC Statute.

---

[107] Y Dinstein, *War, Aggression and Self-defence*, 6th edn (Cambridge, Cambridge University Press, 2017) para 394.

[108] See, eg Cryer et al, *An Introduction to International Criminal Law and Procedure*, 317.

[109] The Dutch Inquiry on the War in Iraq held that 'the only conclusion possible is that there was no adequate international law mandate for the unilateral military force used against Iraq by the US and UK': '*Report of the Dutch Committee of Inquiry on the War in Iraq*, ch 8 ("The Basis in International Law for the Military Intervention in Iraq")' (May 2010) 57(1) *Netherlands International Law Review* 81, 136. See also International Commission of Jurists (ICJ), 'Iraq – ICJ Deplores Moves Toward a War of Aggression on Iraq' (Geneva, 18 March 2003), bit.ly/2r8GfxL; and R. Kolb, *International Law on the Maintenance of Peace: Jus Contra Bellum* (Cheltenham, Edward Elgar, 2019), 106–07, 347.

[110] See, eg M Milanovic, 'Does the European Court of Human Rights Have to Decide on Sovereignty over Crimea? Part I: Jurisdiction in Article 1 ECHR', *EJIL: Talk!*, 23 September 2019, bit.ly/2NWDkAN.

[111] See, eg C Kreß, 'A Collective Failure to Prevent Turkey's Operation "Peace Spring" and NATO's Silence on International Law', *EJIL: Talk!*, 14 October 2019, bit.ly/35D1LJx.

# 8

## Use of Force in United Nations Peacekeeping Operations

### I. Introduction

The use of force by United Nations peacekeeping operations 'raises important and distinct issues for international law'.[1] Indeed, the deployment of peacekeeping forces under the nominal command of the UN Secretary-General was not even envisaged, much less regulated, in the Charter of the United Nations[2] (UN Charter).[3] That said, from 'modest beginnings', peacekeeping 'has become a central and indispensable activity of the organization and is now an accepted part of UN law and practice'.[4] Thus, as of February 2020, peacekeeping operations were being conducted in 13 separate operations in nine specific states by 'blue helmets' (so-called because of the light blue helmets the soldiers wear when on UN duty), as well as in Kosovo, in Western Sahara, and across the Middle East.[5]

Traditional UN peacekeeping operations are established with the consent of the parties to a dispute. They were therefore not authorised by a Chapter VII mandate emanating from the UN Security Council, but, rather, operate under Chapter VI of the UN Charter. The first armed peacekeeping operation, however, was actually authorised by the General Assembly rather than the Security Council, in an operation adopted in accordance with the 1950 'Uniting for Peace' resolution.[6]

---

[1] S Sheeran, 'The Use of Force in United Nations Peacekeeping Operations' in M Weller (ed), *The Oxford Handbook of the Use of Force in International Law* (Oxford, Oxford University Press, 2015) 347.

[2] Charter of the United Nations; adopted at San Francisco, 26 June 1945; entered into force, 24 October 1945.

[3] Sheeran, 'The Use of Force in United Nations Peacekeeping Operations', 347.

[4] ibid 347–48.

[5] Central African Republic, Cyprus, Democratic Republic of the Congo, India, Mali, Pakistan, South Sudan, Sudan, and Syria. The UN peacekeeping operations are the following: MINURSO (Mission for the Referendum in Western Sahara); MINUSCA (UN Multidimensional Integrated Stabilization Mission in the Central African Republic); MINUSMA (UN Multidimensional Integrated Stabilization Mission in Mali); MONUSCO (UN Organization Stabilization Mission in the Democratic Republic of the Congo); UNAMID (African Union – UN Hybrid Operation in Darfur); UNDOF (UN Disengagement Observer Force) (Golan Heights); UNFICYP (UN Peacekeeping Force in Cyprus); UNIFIL (UN Interim Force in Lebanon); UNISFA (UN Interim Security Force for Abyei); UNMIK (UN Interim Administration Mission in Kosovo); UNMISS (UN Mission in the Republic of South Sudan); UNMOGIP (UN Military Observer Group in India and Pakistan); UNTSO (UN Truce Supervision Organization) (Middle East).

[6] UN General Assembly Resolution 377A, adopted on 3 November 1950 by 52 votes to 5 (the Byelorussian SSR, Czechoslovakia, Poland, the Soviet Union, and the Ukrainian SSR), with 2 abstentions

Accordingly, peacekeepers were typically limited in their ability to use force to instances where they were acting in individual self-defence.[7] In this regard, Yoram Dinstein distinguishes between the 'specific right to self-defence, applicable to peacekeeping forces' and the 'much broader right to self-defence vested in States'. As he observes, a peacekeeping force's exercise of self-defence 'is more akin to a military unit's self-defence, in the context of on-the-spot reaction'.[8]

Since then, the authorisation given to UN peacekeepers to use force has evolved significantly towards a far greater permissiveness, as this chapter explains. But two of the operations in which UN peacekeepers used the highest levels of force – in the Congo in 1960–63 and in Somalia in 1993 – were 'traumatic experiences for the organization and civilians'.[9]

## II. The Evolution in Peacekeeping Use of Force: From Self-defence to the Protection of Civilians

### A. Use of Force in the First Fifty Years of UN Peacekeeping

UN Emergency Force I (UNEF I), established in 1957 by the UN General Assembly to secure and supervise the cessation of hostilities that had erupted following the nationalisation of the Suez Canal Company by Egyptian President Gamal Nasser,[10] was the first armed UN peacekeeping force. In 1958, the UN Secretary-General reported to the General Assembly that: 'UNEF troops have a right to fire in self-defence. They are never to take the initiative in the use of arms, but may respond with fire to an armed attack upon them …'.[11] This was a strict policy of allowing the use of force only to protect oneself and one's colleagues in the mission.

---

(Argentina and India), para 1. The resolution states that in any case where the Security Council is unable to act effectively, 'because of lack of unanimity of the Council's permanent members', the General Assembly shall consider the matter and may issue any recommendations it deems necessary with a view to restoring or maintaining international peace and security. If the General Assembly is not in session at the relevant time, it may convene in 'emergency special session'. See generally on the resolution C Binder, 'Uniting for Peace Resolution (1950)', *Max Planck Encyclopedia of International Law* (last updated May 2017), bit.ly/2P2PU2j.

[7] H Willmot, 'The Evolution of the UN Collective Security System' in H Willmot, R Mamiya, S Sheeran, and M Weller (eds), *Protection of Civilians* (Oxford, Oxford University Press, 2016) 126.

[8] Y Dinstein, *War, Aggression and Self-defence*, 6th edn (Cambridge, Cambridge University Press, 2017) para 939 [footnote omitted].

[9] Sheeran, 'The Use of Force in United Nations Peacekeeping Operations', 348.

[10] UN General Assembly Resolution 998 (ES – 1), adopted on 2 November 1956 by 57 votes to 0, with 19 abstentions (Albania, Australia, Austria, Bulgaria, Byelorussian SSR, Czechoslovakia, Egypt, France, Hungary, Israel, Laos, New Zealand, Poland, Portugal, Romania, Ukrainian SSR, Union of South Africa, UK, and USSR). See, eg Willmot, 'The Evolution of the UN Collective Security System', 121.

[11] 'Summary Study of the Experience Derived from the Establishment and Operation of the Force: Report of the Secretary-General', UN doc A/3943, 9 October 1958, para 70, bit.ly/2MYvlBT. See also B Oswald, 'Soldier Self-defense Symposium: The Evolution of the UN Doctrine of Self-defence in UN Peacekeeping', *Opinio Juris*, 1 May 2019, bit.ly/2pxfnGG.

In general, UN policy evolved modestly over the subsequent decade to encompass possible use of force in defence of the mission as a whole, including its property. That said, the UN Operation in the Congo (ONUC) at the beginning of the 1960s was a major departure from prevalent practice: even 'a preliminary reading of the ONUC experience clearly demonstrates that it was not "typical" of its period'.[12] UN Security Council Resolution 143 (1960) authorised the deployment of a peacekeeping operation following a request by the Government of the Congo to put down an insurrection in Katanga province in the south-east of the country.[13] But the mundane text of the resolution masked deep disquiet among several states about what appeared to have been aggression by Belgium against the Congo.[14]

In 1961, Security Council Resolution 161 urged the United Nations to 'take immediately all appropriate measures to prevent the occurrence of civil war in the Congo, including ... the use of force, if necessary, in the last resort'.[15] But, as Scott Sheeran observes,[16] just seven days later, the Council convened to further strengthen the mandate, authorising the UN Secretary-General

> to take vigorous action, including the use of the requisite measure of force, if necessary, for the immediate apprehension, detention pending legal action and/or deportation of all foreign military and paramilitary personnel and political advisers not under the United Nations Command, and mercenaries.[17]

Thus, the 'robust mandate of ONUC and how it was being implemented went well beyond the "basic principles" of UN peacekeeping from UNEF I'.[18] As Trevor Findlay recorded, the issue that provoked calls for the use of force beyond self-defence

> was the protection of civilians, both expatriates and Congolese, from ANC attacks. As in Rwanda three decades later, ONUC had to decide whether and how to use force, including beyond self-defence, to protect civilians in grave danger, whether individuals, groups or entire populations. [UN Secretary-General] Hammarskjöld's view seemed to be that ONUC should act on humanitarian grounds to protect populations at risk, even to the extent of stretching the self-defence rule ...[19]

This evolution towards authorising the use of force to protect civilians would, however, be held in abeyance for three decades. In 1964, in the case of the UN

---

[12] E Aksu, *The United Nations, Intra-state Peacekeeping and Normative Change* (Manchester, Manchester University Press, 2003) 100.

[13] UN Security Council Resolution 143, adopted on 14 July 1960 by 8 votes to 0, with 3 abstentions (Republic of China (Taiwan), France, and the UK), operative para 2.

[14] Aksu, *The United Nations, Intra-state Peacekeeping and Normative Change*, 102–03.

[15] UN Security Council Resolution 161, adopted on 14 July 1960 by 9 votes to 0, with 2 abstentions (France and the Soviet Union), operative para 1.

[16] Sheeran, 'The Use of Force in United Nations Peacekeeping Operations', 351–52.

[17] UN Security Council Resolution 169, adopted on 24 November 1961 by 9 votes to 0, with 2 abstentions (France and the UK), operative para 4.

[18] Sheeran, 'The Use of Force in United Nations Peacekeeping Operations', 352.

[19] T Findlay, *The Use of Force in UN Peace Operations* (Stockholm, Stockholm International Peace Research Institute (SIPRI)/Oxford, Oxford University Press, 2002) 67–68.

Peacekeeping Force in Cyprus (UNFICYP), the UN Secretary-General informed the General Assembly that self-defence included defence of UN posts, premises, and vehicles under armed attack, and support to other personnel of UNFICYP under armed attack.[20] This broadened the mandate slightly from one allowing the exercise of self-defence and defence of colleagues in the peacekeeping mission to one that envisaged protection of UN property. Under international law, however, the use of firearms for the purpose of law enforcement is limited to situations whether this is necessary to confront an imminent threat of death or serious injury, or a grave and temporally proximate threat to life.[21] Firearms may not be used in such scenarios purely to protect property.

Until the Somalia and Bosnia and Herzegovina missions in the 1990s, ONUC proved to be 'the most violent peacekeeping operation ever conducted by the UN'.[22] One of the lessons that Findlay drew from the UN's operation in the Congo was that the use of force 'is a blunt instrument for pursuing discrete political aims in a peace operation'.[23] Another was that the UN 'needed a doctrine for the use of force which would set out in advance the rationale for it, notably the circumstances under which it was appropriate or inappropriate to use force under varying mandates'.[24] The lessons would not be learnt the easy way.

Indeed, by the early 1990s, the traditionally consensual view of peacekeeping – and a consequentially limited scope for use of force – was under significant pressure from facts on the ground, specifically in Bosnia and Herzegovina and Somalia.[25] Following the UN Secretary-General's 1993 report, *An Agenda for Peace*, the President of the Security Council issued a statement in which he reaffirmed that the Council may authorise peacekeepers to use all means necessary 'to carry out their mandate'; this would be in addition to 'the inherent right of United Nations forces to take appropriate measures for self-defence'.[26] But this did not yet occur routinely.

The failure to extend the right to use force to an explicit authorisation to protect civilians in Rwanda would lead to genocide. In early 1994, a request for permission to act to seize arms caches stashed in preparation for coming atrocities, addressed to the UN headquarters in New York by the UN military force commander in Kigali, Canadian General Roméo Dallaire, was denied on the basis that this would be outside the Chapter VI mandate for the mission and endanger the lives of the

[20] 'Note by the Secretary-General', UN doc S/5653, 11 April 1964, para 16, bit.ly/2pxxGLS.
[21] Basic Principle 9 of the UN Basic Principles on the Use of Force and Firearms by Law Enforcement Officials, welcomed by UN General Assembly Resolution 45/166, adopted without a vote on 14 December 1990.
[22] ibid 81.
[23] ibid 82.
[24] ibid 84.
[25] See Sheeran, 'The Use of Force in United Nations Peacekeeping Operations', 353–54.
[26] Statement of the President of the UN Security Council, UN doc S/PV.3225, 28 May 1993, 3.

peacekeepers.[27] Shortly thereafter, hundreds of thousands of Tutsi and moderate Hutu civilians were exterminated by Hutu extremists. The UN's failure to act decisively to prevent the genocide, combined with a huge reluctance on the part of the United States to engage following its humiliating withdrawal from Somalia, is an indelible stain on the reputation of the global organisation's seven decades of peacekeeping.

## B. The Use of Force to Protect Civilians

The pressure to put the protection of civilians at the heart of the UN's peacekeeping work continued to build, following the failure of UN peacekeepers, even when backed by NATO (North Atlantic Treaty Organization) air support, to prevent the genocide perpetrated at Srebrenica in 1995, just a year after the massacres in Rwanda. Bosnian Serb forces summarily executed more than 8000 Bosnian Muslim men and boys after storming the eastern enclave.[28] Calls for a more robust mandate for peacekeepers to protect civilians were growing.

Thus, in its seminal Resolution 1265 of 1999 on the protection of civilians, the Council noted the importance of including in the mandates of peacemaking, peacekeeping, and peacebuilding operations special protection and assistance provisions for groups requiring particular attention, including women and children.[29] Resolution 1265 was not adopted under Chapter VII of the UN Charter, and did not authorise any use of force to protect civilians, but it did express the Security Council's 'willingness to consider how peacekeeping mandates might better address the negative impact of armed conflict on civilians'.[30] Only a month after the adoption of the Resolution, however, the Council was already authorising use of force by a peacekeeping operation explicitly to protect civilians. In its Resolution 1270 on Sierra Leone, the Council, acting under Chapter VII of the Charter, decided

> that in the discharge of its mandate UNAMSIL [United Nations Observer Mission in Sierra Leone] may take the necessary action to ensure the security and freedom of movement of its personnel and, within its capabilities and areas of deployment, *to afford protection to civilians under imminent threat of physical violence*, taking into account the responsibilities of the Government of Sierra Leone and ECOMOG [the Military Observer Group of the Economic Community of West African States].[31]

---

[27] Sheeran, 'The Use of Force in United Nations Peacekeeping Operations', 364. See also, eg K Shiffman, 'As Genocide Raged, General's Pleas for Help Ignored', *CNN*, 10 December 2008, cnn.it/2MSFqQJ.

[28] See, eg O Bowcott and J Borger, 'Ratko Mladić Convicted of War Crimes and Genocide at UN Tribunal', *The Guardian*, 22 November 2017, bit.ly/2Kjrn7E.

[29] UN Security Council Resolution 1265 (1999), adopted unanimously on 17 September 1999, para 13.

[30] ibid para 11.

[31] UN Security Council Resolution 1270 (1999), adopted unanimously on 22 October 1999, operative para 14 (emphasis added).

Despite the UN's earlier troubled experiences in the Congo, Bosnia and Herzegovina, and Somalia, a new precedent was set.[32] Even with the attached caveats of 'within its capabilities and areas of deployment', the traditional doctrine of peacekeepers only using force in self-defence or, in circumscribed cases, to ensure the safe delivery of humanitarian assistance had been largely overridden.

A mandate to use force for the 'direct physical protection' of civilians quickly became an integral component of a UN peacekeeping mission according to specific Security Council authorisation.[33] Thus, by 1 February 2020, seven of the 13 extant UN peacekeeping operations had an explicit mandate to protect civilians, as Table 1 summarises. Indeed, in recent years, 'civilian protection has become the *raison d'être* of most missions'.[34] In most cases (though not all), the authorisation to use force, where necessary, to protect civilians has been given by the Council acting explicitly under Chapter VII of the UN Charter.[35]

**Table 1** Mandates in UN Peacekeeping Operations to Protect Civilians

| UN peacekeeping operation | Security Council mandate | Mandate |
|---|---|---|
| MINURSO (Mission for the Referendum in Western Sahara) | Resolution 1979 (2011) | No mandate to protect civilians |
| MINUSCA (UN Multidimensional Integrated Stabilization Mission in the Central African Republic) | Resolution 2448 (2018), para 39(a)(i) | 'To protect ... without prejudice to the primary responsibility of the CAR Authorities and the basic principles of peacekeeping, the civilian population under threat of physical violence' |
| MINUSMA (UN Multidimensional Integrated Stabilization Mission in Mali) | Resolution 2164 (2014), para 13(a)(i) | 'To protect, without prejudice to the responsibility of the Malian authorities, civilians under imminent threat of physical violence' |

*(continued)*

---

[32] Willmot, 'The Evolution of the UN Collective Security System', 129.

[33] ibid. Willmot refers to something of a hiatus in authorising force to protect civilians between 2002 and 2006, which she ascribes to the US-led invasion of Iraq and the resultant 'strained Council dynamics' (130–31).

[34] ibid 110.

[35] UN Department of Peace Operations (DPO), *The Protection of Civilians in United Nations Peacekeeping*, DOP Policy doc 2019.17, 1 November 2019, para 16, fn 2.

**Table 1** *(Continued)*

| UN peacekeeping operation | Security Council mandate | Mandate |
|---|---|---|
| MONUSCO (UN Organization Stabilization Mission in the Democratic Republic of the Congo) | Resolution 1925 (2010), paras 12(a) and 11 | 'Ensure the effective protection of civilians, including humanitarian personnel and human rights defenders, under imminent threat of physical violence, in particular violence emanating from any of the parties engaged in the conflict'; and 'Emphasizes that the protection of civilians must be given priority in decisions about the use of available capacity and resources and authorizes MONUSCO to use all necessary means, within the limits of its capacity and in the areas where its units are deployed, to carry out its protection mandate' |
| UNAMID (African Union–UN Hybrid Operation in Darfur) | Resolution 1769 (2007), para 15(a)(ii) | 'decides that UNAMID is authorised to take the necessary action, in the areas of deployment of its forces and as it deems within its capabilities in order to … protect civilians, without prejudice to the responsibility of the Government of Sudan' |
| UNDOF (UN Disengagement Observer Force) (Golan Heights) | Resolution 350 (1974) | No mandate to protect civilians |
| UNFICYP (UN Peacekeeping Force in Cyprus) | Resolution 186 (1964) | No mandate to protect civilians (but 'to use its best efforts to prevent a recurrence of fighting and, as necessary, to contribute to the maintenance and restoration of law and order') |

*(continued)*

**Table 1**  *(Continued)*

| UN peacekeeping operation | Security Council mandate | Mandate |
|---|---|---|
| UNIFIL (UN Interim Force in Lebanon) | Resolution 1701 (2006), para. 12 | 'authorizes UNIFIL to take all necessary action in areas of deployment of its forces and as it deems within its capabilities … to protect civilians under imminent threat of physical violence' |
| UNISFA (UN Interim Security Force for Abyei) | Resolution 1990 (2011), para 3(d) | 'authorizes UNISFA within its capabilities and its area of deployment to take the necessary actions … without prejudice to the responsibilities of the relevant authorities, to protect civilians in the Abyei Area under imminent threat of physical violence' |
| UNMIK (UN Interim Administration Mission in Kosovo) | Resolution 1244 (1999), para 11(j) | No explicit mandate to protect civilians but mandate of 'Protecting and promoting human rights' |
| UNMISS (UN Mission in the Republic of South Sudan) | Resolution 2155 (2014), para 4(a)(i) | 'authorizes UNMISS to use all necessary means … to protect civilians under threat of physical violence, irrespective of the source of such violence, within its capacity and areas of deployment' |
| UNMOGIP (UN Military Observer Group in India and Pakistan) | Resolution 47 (1948) | No mandate to protect civilians |
| UNTSO (UN Truce Supervision Organization) (Middle East) | Resolution 50 (1948) | No mandate to protect civilians |

At the same time, the United Nations acknowledges the challenges its peace-keepers face in protecting civilians in practice. These include operating 'in harsh conditions and in difficult terrain, with limited resources'; 'unrealistic' expecta-tions that peacekeepers will be able to protect all civilians at all times; and the 'dynamic nature' of the places in which peacekeepers operate, meaning that the security situation can change very quickly.[36]

Another risk is that, when operating in a complex environment, UN peacekeepers may decide to act to protect civilians against attacks and abuses only from non-state armed groups, but not from state armed forces. Indeed, it is explicitly recognised in the UN's new internal policy on peacekeeping 'that a robust response to threats posed by the host state may be beyond the mission's capabilities, may result in insecurity for peacekeepers and can affect the host state's strategic consent to the mission'.[37] That said, the policy does affirm that, while the mission will, 'as far as possible, support the host state's protection efforts', it 'may act independently to protect civilians when the host state is deemed unable or unwilling to do so or where government forces themselves pose a threat to civilians'.[38]

In any event, in outlining the principles of UN peacekeeping, the United Nations cautions that:

> A UN peacekeeping operation should only use force as a measure of last resort. It should always be calibrated in a precise, proportional and appropriate manner, within the principle of the minimum force necessary to achieve the desired effect, while sustaining consent for the mission and its mandate. The use of force by a UN peacekeeping operation always has political implications and can often give rise to unforeseen circumstances.[39]

## C.   An Authorisation to 'Neutralise' Armed Groups

These principles are not, though, of universal application. To date, the most robust authorisation to use force in a UN peacekeeping operation has been provided to an Intervention Brigade of MONUSCO in the Democratic Republic of Congo (DRC). This authorisation, which emanates from a 2013 UN Security Council resolution adopted by unanimous vote, explicitly tasks the Brigade with 'the responsibility of neutralizing armed groups'.[40] This tasking of assault operations – the UN's 'first-ever "offensive" combat force'[41] – is highly controversial, potentially placing

---

[36] UN, 'Protection of Civilians Mandate', undated, bit.ly/2Bqhdf2.

[37] DPO, *The Protection of Civilians in United Nations Peacekeeping*, para 61. This one-sided approach to peacekeeping can also permeate non-forcible protection measures. As the head of protection of a UN agency in the Democratic Republic of Congo told the author several years ago, 'We are here to support the government so it would not be right to criticise them'.

[38] DPO, *The Protection of Civilians in United Nations Peacekeeping*, para 29.

[39] UN, 'Principles of Peacekeeping', undated, bit.ly/2VTa7t6.

[40] UN Security Council Resolution 2098 (2013), adopted unanimously on 28 March 2013, operative para 9. The Brigade was authorised to consist 'of three infantry battalions, one artillery and one Special force and Reconnaissance company with headquarters in Goma, under direct command of the MONUSCO Force Commander'.

[41] '"Intervention Brigade" Authorized as Security Council Grants Mandate Renewal for United Nations Mission in Democratic Republic of Congo', UN doc SC/10964, 28 March 2013, bit.ly/2r8WZ8b.

the UN in a position where it is complicit in war crimes and other serious violations of international human rights and humanitarian law committed by the DRC armed forces (FARDC). But as Dinstein observes, it also 'stretches to the limit' the meaning of the term 'peacekeeping'.[42] Is this more robust approach to peacekeeping – through a form of peacemaking – the exception that proves the rule or an augury of things to come?

The Intervention Brigade enjoyed initial success, 'earn[ing] its stripes in 2013 when it helped the DRC's army defeat the powerful Rwanda-backed M23 rebels in the east of the country'.[43] While acknowledging the problems of the Brigade, writing in 2016, Jay Benson believed that 'under the right circumstances' the Intervention Brigade model of peace enforcement 'may have the potential to be effective as a tool for civilian protection'.[44] He concluded that:

> Though this new model of UN peace operations certainly has serious drawbacks if misapplied, the need to protect civilians suffering truly horrific abuses in conflict areas means that the international community must continue to consider the use of the IB [Intervention Brigade] model as a tool for civilian protection where conditions for its success exist. The IB model will not protect all civilians all of the time, but it may be the best tool available for making long-term net improvements in civilian security.[45]

More recently, however, Rachel Sweet has been one of a number of commentators to question whether the Intervention Brigade has been successful in the DRC and therefore whether the approach should be attempted in other UN peacekeeping operations.[46] She believes that the Brigade's results 'suggest that a bigger stick isn't working', given that, five years into its military campaign, the Brigade 'has failed to eradicate the targeted rebels' [the Allied Democratic Forces, (ADF)].

> Instead, military operations provoked deadly attacks on UN peacekeepers and escalated violence in the country to its highest levels in a decade. Inaccurate assumptions about the nature of security threats contribute to these failures. Military approaches define threats as emanating from armed actors outside of the state who can be targeted with force, but corrupt networks within the national army also contribute to violence and support armed groups. The cross-infiltration of rebels and state politics creates intelligence gaps regarding the conflict that risk turning UN efforts against themselves. Military force cannot succeed in these environments.[47]

---

[42] Dinstein, *War, Aggression and Self-defence*, para 940, citing R Murphy, 'UN Peacekeeping in the Democratic Republic of the Congo and the Protection of Civilians' (2016) 21(2) *Journal of Conflict and Security Law* 209, 228.

[43] P Fabricius, 'Is the Force Intervention Brigade Still Justifying Its Existence?' (Institute for Strategic Studies, 22 June 2017), bit.ly/2RgGS3g.

[44] J Benson, 'The UN Intervention Brigade: Extinguishing Conflict or Adding Fuel to the Flames?' One Earth Future Discussion Paper (June 2016) ii, bit.ly/37XYGpA.

[45] ibid 10.

[46] R Sweet, 'Militarizing the Peace: UN Intervention Against Congo's "Terrorist" Rebels', Foreign Policy Essay, *Lawfare*, 2 June 2019, bit.ly/2YgoF7o; see also, eg A Day, 'The Best Defence Is No Offence: Why Cuts to UN Troops in Congo Could Be a Good Thing' (United Nations University, 15 May 2017), bit.ly/33LtFlx.

[47] ibid.

She concluded that the conflict 'demands a new approach with more sophisticated intelligence capabilities, an expanded role for civilian branches of UN missions in operational decision-making, and reengagement with political channels to deescalate violence'.[48]

While these points are reasonable, her criticisms of the Intervention Brigade may be overly harsh. As South African military analyst André Roux has pointed out, a specific impediment to its effectiveness is that the 'framework' forces – the other elements of MONUSCO – have not always provided the necessary support. When the FARDC and the Brigade clear out ADF forces from a camp or stronghold, the function of the framework troops should be to hold the captured ground. But this often does not happen, leading eventually to the return of the rebel forces to occupy their previous positions.[49] One of the main problems, Roux says, is that several of the governments that contribute troops to MONUSCO have given their troops strict instructions not to put themselves at any risk, so they will not defend territory.[50]

Whatever the truth may be, the people who matter the most – the civilians who the peacekeeping operation is seeking to protect – cannot be said to be satisfied with MONUSCO's efforts. In late November 2019, protests against the UN mission's failure to protect civilians from rebel attacks entered a second day in Beni, North Kivu province. At least two people were killed as security forces engaged in running street battles with protestors. In the cities of Butembo and Goma, demonstrators attempted to find their way to a UN base near the airport before being repulsed by government soldiers.[51] On 27 November 2019, the UN announced that it would open an investigation into the death of one of the demonstrators, which may have occurred at the hands of a peacekeeper.[52]

## D. The 2019 UN Policy on Protection of Civilians During Peacekeeping Operations

Set against this troubling backdrop in the DRC, UN internal policy on the protection of civilians during peacekeeping operations was being updated. *The Protection of Civilians in United Nations Peacekeeping*, issued on 1 November 2019, clarifies that UN peacekeeping operations

---

[48] ibid.

[49] In conversation with Peter Fabricius, in 'Is the Force Intervention Brigade Still Justifying Its Existence?'.

[50] ibid.

[51] J Tasamba, 'DR Congo: 2 Killed in Protests against UN Peacekeepers. Security Forces Engage in Running Street Battles with Protestors in Second Day of Unrest in Beni', *Anadolu Agency*, 27 November 2019, bit.ly/33MiCbw.

[52] BBC, 'DR Congo Protests: UN to Open Investigation into Demonstrator's Death', 27 November 2019, bbc.in/35VEJhl. Guidance on the investigation of a potentially unlawful death, including during a UN peacekeeping operation, is given in *The Minnesota Protocol on the Investigation of Potentially Unlawful Death (2016)* (New York, Office of the UN High Commissioner for Human Rights, 2017).

are guided by three inter-related and mutually reinforcing principles: consent of the parties, impartiality and non-use of force, except in self-defence and defence of the mandate. The protection of civilians is fully consonant with these principles, including the authorization of the use of force. As such, the principles of peacekeeping can never be an excuse for failure to protect civilians.[53]

This could be interpreted as stepping back from the approach used in the DRC by the Intervention Brigade. Indeed, the approach endorsed by the UN Department of Peace Operations seems to be one of positive engagement rather than armed confrontation with non-state armed groups:

> When engaging with non-state armed groups on POC [protection of civilians], the mission's aim should be to prevent or stop attacks on civilians, change a group's behaviour so that they no longer threaten civilians, seek a group's meaningful commitments to desist from attacks on civilians, and improve understanding and respect for international human rights and international humanitarian law, as well as to diffuse tensions, identify grievances and build confidence between parties to the conflict.[54]

Consonant with the UN's obligations under customary international law, the 2019 Policy explicitly reiterates that, when international humanitarian law (as the mainstay of *jus in bello*) applies to UN forces, they must comply with it. This obligation, which is independent of the protection of civilians mandate, includes, it is explicitly noted, the principles of distinction, proportionality, and precaution.[55] This would typically cover the actions of the Intervention Brigade in the DRC. Furthermore, as the Policy also stipulates, protection of civilians mandates

> are a manifestation of the international community's determination to prevent the most serious violations of international humanitarian law, international human rights law and international refugee law and related standards and must be implemented in both the letter and spirit of these legal frameworks.[56]

This has implications for the use of force, particularly potentially lethal force. As the Policy decrees, in a law enforcement scenario, 'the use of force should be graduated, unless this would place the civilians to be protected or mission personnel themselves at risk of death or serious bodily injury, or clearly be ineffective in the circumstances'.[57] Where 'armed force' is employed, though, 'it must be limited in its intensity and duration to that necessary to ensure that civilians are protected and civilian casualties avoided or at least minimized'.[58] Nonetheless, as the Policy instructs, UN peacekeepers must be ready 'at all times to act swiftly and decisively' and with 'the full degree of force which is needed to protect civilians and avoid or minimize casualties among them'.[59]

---

[53] DPO, *The Protection of Civilians in United Nations Peacekeeping*, 1 November 2019, para 30.
[54] ibid para 50.
[55] ibid para 22.
[56] ibid para 27.
[57] ibid para 57.
[58] ibid.
[59] ibid.

## III. The International Legal Basis for Use of Force by UN Peacekeepers

The UN Charter has been interpreted as giving a right to both the UN General Assembly and the UN Security Council to mandate a UN peacekeeping operation where this operates with the consent of the territorial state. Only a UN Security Council mandate, however, can authorise a broader use of force beyond the right of personal self-defence that inheres in everyone. This mandate applies principles similar to those authorising states to use all necessary means in order to enforce the will of the Security Council; again, the approach is outside the scenario explicitly envisaged in the UN Charter.[60]

Where a UN peacekeeping operation is taking place in accordance with Chapter VI of the UN Charter with the consent of the territorial state, peacekeepers rely first and foremost on the exercise of the individual right of self-defence for the legal basis of their use of force. This exists for every individual, wherever they may be, as a general principle of law.[61] But peacekeepers are also operating, outside the conduct of hostilities, in a manner akin to law enforcement officials.[62] In so doing, they are operating not only with the consent of the territorial state, but also as its *de jure* agent.[63] Unquestionably, their scope of authority is markedly reduced from the police of the territorial state, but they are still entitled to use necessary and proportionate force to prevent the commission of certain crimes, notably by defending property that falls within the scope of the mission, including humanitarian relief, and by using potentially lethal force to confront an imminent threat of death or serious injury or, exceptionally, a grave and temporally proximate threat to the life of any person within the mission.[64]

---

[60] Under Art 43(1), member states 'undertake to make available to the Security Council, on its call and in accordance with a special agreement or agreements, armed forces, assistance, and facilities, including rights of passage, necessary for the purpose of maintaining international peace and security'.

[61] JA Hessbruegge, *Human Rights and Personal Self-Defense in International Law* (Oxford, Oxford University Press, 2017) 3–4. But *cf* Sheeran, who describes the concept of use of force in self-defence as 'fraught' and inherently clear in legal scope and foundation': Sheeran, 'The Use of Force in United Nations Peacekeeping Operations', 360. However, in his reference to the Capstone Doctrine on peacekeeping (in his fn 87), he appears to mix self-defence and defence of the mandate, which are two very different things materially and from a legal perspective. He also omits to consider the notion of use of force at the 'tactical' level to which the Capstone Doctrine specifically refers. See *United Nations Peacekeeping Operations Principles and Guidelines* (New York, UN, 2008) 34, bit.ly/2P709kQ.

[62] In accordance with the commentary on Art 1 of the 1979 UN Code of Conduct for Law Enforcement Officials, 'the term "law enforcement officials" includes all officers of the law, whether appointed or elected, who exercise police powers, especially the powers of arrest or detention. In countries where police powers are exercised by military authorities, whether uniformed or not, or by State security forces, the definition of law enforcement officials shall be regarded as including officers of such services.'

[63] Sheeran takes a slightly different position, asserting that the host state does not consent to the use of force per se, but rather to a UN peacekeeping operation 'as a whole package and on the basis that it may use force in self-defence, even against the host state': Sheeran, 'The Use of Force in United Nations Peacekeeping Operations', 362. He argues that it is also possible for self-defence 'to be understood as a right under customary law for UN peacekeeping operations' (363).

[64] See, eg *Leuven Manual on the International Law Applicable to Peace Operations* (Cambridge, Cambridge University Press, 2017) Rule 12.3; Hessbruegge, *Human Rights and Personal Self-Defense in International Law*, 148 and fn 251.

With respect to the protection of civilians more broadly, however, a Chapter VII authorisation from the UN Security Council is needed if this power to use force is to apply not only to civilian colleagues in the UN mission but also to the protection of any and all civilians who are wholly independent of it.[65] Thus, the 'presumed' authority to protect civilians that the 2000 Brahimi Report identified[66] is not persuasive as a matter of international law. In its 2009 judgment in the *Sesay* case, the Special Court for Sierra Leone stated that:

> the Security Council empowered UNAMSIL pursuant to Chapter VII of the UN Charter to take 'necessary action' to ensure the security of its personnel and the freedom of movement of its personnel and to protect civilians under threat of physical violence. We consider this ... as the 'trigger' which empowered UNAMSIL personnel to use force, but only in these specific and defined circumstances.[67]

The Special Court further affirmed, equally correctly, that 'the personnel of a peacekeeping mission are entitled to the protection afforded to civilians only insofar as the peacekeepers are not taking a direct part in hostilities'.[68] But, the Court also held that 'the use of force by peacekeepers in self-defence and in the discharge of their mandate ... does not constitute direct participation in hostilities'.[69]

This last holding is partially open to contestation. If there is intense and sustained armed violence between peacekeepers and an organised armed group, even if this is limited to the aim of protecting civilians, an armed conflict may be occurring. Accordingly, a Chapter VII authorisation of 'all necessary means' from the UN Security Council is at least advisable – and arguably is necessary – to render legal the use of significant military force against armed groups. This is unquestionably the case where offensive operations are envisaged as these are highly likely to involve direct participation in hostilities by the blue helmets.

Moreover, operating in such a scenario, without the express consent of the territorial state and absent a Chapter VII authorisation, by directly participating in hostilities, the UN would be violating the general prohibition on interstate use of force codified in Article 2(4) of the UN Charter. This general prohibition *ad bellum* applies both to the national troop contingents on the basis of their state allegiances and also to the United Nations *qua* international organisation. When UN peacekeepers are engaged directly in hostilities, they must also comply with the *jus in bello* (particularly international humanitarian law).[70] In such a scenario, as is well understood, the risks to all UN personnel are markedly augmented. Complex environments bring exceptionally complex challenges for peacekeepers.

---

[65] Otherwise, the self-defence norm is 'stretched and ultimately broken': Findlay, *The Use of Force in UN Peace Operations*, 356; see also Sheeran, 'The Use of Force in United Nations Peacekeeping Operations', 365.

[66] *Report of the Panel on United Nations Peace Operations*, UN doc A/55/305 and S/2000/809, 2000, para 62; see also Sheeran, 'The Use of Force in United Nations Peacekeeping Operations', 367–68.

[67] Special Court for Sierra Leone, Case No SCSL-04-15-T *Prosecutor v Issa Hassan Sesay, Morris Kallon, and Augustine Gbao*, Judgment (Trial Chamber), 2 March 2009, para 1908.

[68] ibid para 1906.

[69] ibid para 1925.

[70] *Leuven Manual on the International Law Applicable to Peace Operations*, Rule 12.6.

# 9

# Rights and Obligations of Non-state Actors *ad Bellum* and *in Bello*

## I. Introduction

The existence and nature of an extraterritorial right to self-defence under *jus ad bellum* against an armed attack from a non-state actor is sharply disputed, as chapter three discussed. International law, as reflected in the preponderance of state practice, demands that the acts be attributable in some manner to the territorial state from where an armed attack was launched, either because the state sent the armed group to attack another state or because it was complicit in the actions of an armed group prior to the use of force amounting to an armed attack or ex post facto.[1] What is generally accepted, however, is that non-state actors do not themselves benefit from the right to self-defence under international law.

This chapter first discusses the definitions of 'non-state actor' and 'non-state armed group' before turning to consideration of their status as a 'subject' of international law, which would entitle them to rights as well as obligations and to enter into legal relations that are binding under international law. This is important to clarify because, under classical legal theory, while anyone can be an object of international law, 'Since the law of nations is based on the common consent of individual States, and not of individual human beings, States solely and exclusively are subjects of international law'.[2] While international law has developed since

---

[1] Under Art 2 ('Elements of an internationally wrongful act of a State') of the 2001 Draft Articles on State Responsibility, there is an internationally wrongful act of a state when conduct consisting of an action or omission is attributable to the State under international law: International Law Commission (ILC), *Draft Articles on Responsibility of States for Internationally Wrongful Acts, with commentaries*, UN doc A/56/10 (New York, 2001) Art 2(a). In the *United States Diplomatic and Consular Staff in Tehran* case, the initial seizure of the hostages by militant students (not at that time acting as organs or agents of the state) was attributable to the combination of the students' own independent action and the failure of the Iranian authorities to take necessary steps to protect the embassy. International Court of Justice (ICJ), *United States Diplomatic and Consular Staff in Tehran* case *(United States v Iran)*, Judgment, 24 May 1980, 29–32; see 2001 Draft Articles on State Responsibility, commentary para 12 on Draft Art 31. What was significant was that the failure of the Iranian Government to take the necessary steps to protect US embassies 'was due to more than mere negligence or lack of appropriate means': ICJ, *United States Diplomatic and Consular Staff in Tehran* case, Judgment, para 63.

[2] L Oppenheim, *International Law. A Treatise*, 2nd edn (London, Longmans, 1912) vol 1, 19.

Lassa Oppenheim wrote those words in 1912, other subjects of international law still possess only 'limited or functional legal personality'.[3]

## II. 'Non-state Actor' and 'Non-state Armed Groups' Defined

There is no accepted definition of a non-state actor under customary international law, although the term is certainly broad in scope, potentially encompassing any entity that is not formally an organ of a government. In its Resolution 1540, adopted by unanimous vote by the UN Security Council in 2004, the term 'non-state actor' was described as an 'individual or entity, not acting under the lawful authority of any State in conducting activities which come within the scope of this resolution'. It was further specified that the descriptor was for the purpose of Resolution 1540 only.[4]

That said, where the conduct of an ostensibly non-state actor occurs under the direction, instigation, or control of an organ of a government, it becomes an agent of the state and is no longer to be considered a non-state actor under international law *ad bellum*. In contrast, as a state agent *ad bellum*, it retains the principal attributes of a non-state actor under *jus in bello*. Nonetheless, in certain circumstances, it may also benefit from protections generally accorded only to the armed forces of a state, notably as far as the right to prisoner-of-war status in an international armed conflict is concerned.[5]

With respect to non-state armed groups, few definitions exist in international law. In the 2000 Optional Protocol to the Convention on the Rights of the Child on the involvement of children in armed conflict,[6] to which 170 states were party as of writing,[7] reference is made simply to 'Armed groups that are distinct from the armed forces of a State'.[8] Under *jus in bello*, however, the criteria for a non-state armed group to be a party to a non-international armed conflict are more stringent. A group must be 'armed' and 'organised',[9] and it must engage, *qua* group, in significant[10] armed violence with a state or with another similarly armed and

---

[3] A Orakhelashvili, *Akehurst's Modern Introduction to International Law*, 8th edn (London, Routledge, 2018) 111, para 6.1.

[4] UN Security Council Resolution 1540, adopted by unanimous vote on 28 April 2004, footnote.

[5] See Art 4 of the Convention (III) relative to the Treatment of Prisoners of War; adopted at Geneva, 12 August 1949; entered into force, 21 October 1950.

[6] Optional Protocol to the Convention on the Rights of the Child on the involvement of children in armed conflict; adopted at New York, 25 May 2000; entered into force, 12 February 2002 (hereinafter 2000 Optional Protocol to the CRC).

[7] As at 1 May 2020.

[8] 2000 Optional Protocol to the CRC, Art 4(1).

[9] See, eg German Ministry of Defence, *Law of Armed Conflict Manual*, Joint Service Regulation (ZDv) 15/2 (Berlin, 2013) para 210.

[10] Termed awkwardly in the leading jurisprudence on the issue, 'protracted'. International Criminal Tribunal for the former Yugoslavia (ICTY), Case No IT-94-1 *Prosecutor v Tadić (aka 'Dule')*, Decision on the Defence Motion for Interlocutory Appeal on Jurisdiction (Appeals Chamber), 2 October 1995, para 70.

organised group.[11] The notion of organisation means that such groups are military or paramilitary forces operating hierarchically, and some of their members must be equipped with, at least, firearms. Such armed groups must also be capable of mounting military operations, but they do not need to possess uniforms, nor do they need to actively (or even passively) control territory.[12]

## A.   A State Agent is Not a Non-state Actor *ad Bellum*

As an agent of the state, an erstwhile non-state actor is no longer considered as such under *jus ad bellum*. In particular, 'armed bands, groups, irregulars or mercenaries, which carry out acts of armed force against another State', when they are sent 'by or on behalf of a State',[13] do not fall to be considered as either a non-state actor or a non-state armed group. In its 2001 Draft Articles on the Responsibility of States for Internationally Wrongful Acts, the International Law Commission (ILC) determined that:

> The conduct of a person or group of persons shall be considered an act of a State under international law if the person or group of persons is in fact acting on the instructions of, or under the direction or control of, that State in carrying out the conduct.[14]

In his commentary on the provision, the ILC Special Rapporteur, James Crawford, affirmed that conduct carried out 'under the direction or control' of a state will only be attributable to the state 'if it directed or controlled the specific operation and the conduct complained of was an integral part of that operation'.[15] With respect to the conduct of non-state armed groups, the approach taken by the ILC followed that laid down by the International Court of Justice (ICJ) in its judgment in 1986 on the merits in the *Nicaragua* case.[16] The ICJ held that, to give rise to the legal responsibility of the United States for their conduct, acts by members of the Contras would have to be committed while under its 'effective control'.[17]

Thus, the Court also saw 'no reason to deny' that, under customary international law,

> the prohibition of armed attacks may apply to the sending by a State of armed bands to the territory of another State, if such an operation, because of its scale and effects, would have been classified as an armed attack rather than as a mere frontier incident had it been carried out by regular armed forces.[18]

---

[11] ibid.

[12] S Casey-Maslen, *Hague Law Interpreted: The Conduct of Hostilities under the Law of Armed Conflict* (Oxford, Hart Publishing, 2018) 52ff.

[13] Art 3(g) of the 1974 Definition of Aggression, annexed to UN General Assembly Resolution 3314 (XXIX), adopted without a vote on 14 December 1974 (hereinafter 1974 Definition of Aggression).

[14] *Draft Articles on Responsibility of States for Internationally Wrongful Acts, with commentaries*, Art 8 ('Conduct directed or controlled by a State').

[15] 2001 Draft Articles on States Responsibility, commentary para 3 on Art 8.

[16] ICJ, *Case Concerning Military and Paramilitary Activities in and against Nicaragua (Nicaragua v United States of America)*, Judgment (Merits), 27 June 1986 (hereinafter ICJ, *Nicaragua* judgment).

[17] ibid para 115.

[18] ibid para 195.

But with this in mind, the supply of weapons and logistical support alone would not amount to an armed attack.[19]

In its 2009 report, the Independent International Fact-Finding Mission on the Conflict in Georgia found that the 'pre-conditions for an armed attack by Russia through the "sending" of North Caucasian and other fighters' in the sense of Article 3(g) of the 1974 UN Definition of Aggression were 'not fulfilled'.[20] The Report further stated that: 'It does not seem that the armed attack by South Ossetia on Georgia could be imputed to Russia under any other type of "effective control" of South Ossetian militia.'[21]

# III. Non-state Actors' Rights and Obligations under International Law

The Report of the Independent International Fact-Finding Mission on the Conflict in Georgia (hereinafter the Georgia Fact-Finding Mission Report) assesses the actions of the breakaway territories of Abkhazia and South Ossetia against the obligations laid down in Article 2 of the 1945 Charter of the United Nations[22] (UN Charter), treating them as if they had the same obligations with respect to the use of force as states. The Report describes a number of incidents, including the threat or use of force by individuals or groups within Abkhazia and South Ossetia prior to the outbreak of force between Russia and Georgia:

> It is unclear to what extent these incidents formed part of a concerted effort directed against Georgia which was orchestrated or actively condoned by the de facto authorities of the two breakaway territories. With regard to South Ossetia, the publicly-announced intention to attack Georgian cities suggests this was the case, while in Abkhazia's case, the public claim to have downed Georgian spy planes would serve the same purpose. Both breakaway regions sought the assistance of Russia in the hope that they would receive support should armed hostilities break out, and consequently undermined efforts to defuse the crisis. In this sense, their behaviour is hardly consistent with the provisions of Art. 2(3) of the UN Charter, namely the obligation to seek the settlement of disputes by peaceful means, and also, at least potentially in contradiction to Art. 2(4).[23]

It explained this asserted application of *jus ad bellum* rules in the following terms.

First, it argued that a 1992 political agreement between Georgia and Russia had brought into effect *ad bellum* rights and obligations not only for these two

---

[19] Ibid; C Gray, *International Law and the Use of Force*, 4th edn (Oxford, Oxford University Press, 2018) 184.

[20] Independent International Fact-Finding Mission on the Conflict in Georgia, Report, vol II, September 2009, 261.

[21] ibid.

[22] Charter of the United Nations; adopted at San Francisco, 26 June 1945; entered into force, 24 October 1945.

[23] Independent International Fact-Finding Mission on the Conflict in Georgia, Report, vol II, 236.

states, but also for the regions of Abkhazia and South Ossetia. It did so on the basis that the Sochi Agreement concluded in 1992 between Georgia and the Russian Federation[24] reaffirms in its preamble 'the commitment to the UN Charter and the Helsinki Final Act'.[25] This clause, the Report asserts, 'is a clear indication that Georgia accepts the applicability of the prohibition of the use of force in its conflict with South Ossetia'.[26]

The Georgia Fact-Finding Mission believed that this was the case, despite the fact that South Ossetia is not a party to the Sochi Agreement, because the purpose of the Agreement, as set out in its preamble, was to 'bring about the immediate cessation of bloodshed and achieve comprehensive settlement of the conflict between Ossetians and Georgians'. The reference to the UN Charter, the report asserted,

> would not make any sense if it did not include the prohibition of the use of force, as this is the centrepiece of the Charter. This interpretation is also in line with the spirit of the Sochi Agreement aiming at the termination of hostilities between the opposing parties, i.e. between Georgia and South Ossetia.[27]

Equally, however, the reference to the UN Charter can also be viewed purely as reflecting the obligation upon Georgia and Russia not to use force against each other. This is fully in line with the nature of the Agreement and the UN Charter itself.

The second argument advanced by the Fact-Finding Mission in its 2009 Report is that a

> legal obligation of Georgia to refrain from the use of force in its relations with South Ossetia is enshrined in the 1994 Agreement 'On the further development of the process of the peaceful regulation of the Georgian-Ossetian conflict and on the Joint Control Commission'.[28]

As the Agreement states: 'The Parties to the conflict reiterate pledged commitments to settle all the issues in dispute exclusively by peaceful means, without resort to force or threat of resort to force.'

This reads as a reiteration of a prior political promise not to use force against South Ossetia rather than the recognition of the imposition of the Charter rules

---

[24] Agreement on Principles of Settlement of the Georgian–Ossetia Conflict of 24 June 1992.

[25] The Helsinki Final Act stipulates, in part, that 'The participating States will refrain in their mutual relations, as well as in their international relations in general, from the threat or use of force against the territorial integrity or political independence of any State, or in any other manner inconsistent with the purposes of the United Nations and with the present Declaration. No consideration may be invoked to serve to warrant resort to the threat or use of force in contravention of this principle … Accordingly, the participating States will refrain from any acts constituting a threat of force or direct or indirect use of force against another participating State': Conference on Security and Co-operation in Europe, *Final Act* (Helsinki, 1975) Part I, s II.

[26] Independent International Fact-Finding Mission on the Conflict in Georgia, Report, vol II, 240.

[27] ibid.

[28] ibid.

upon Georgia in that regard. Indeed, the Georgia Fact-Finding Mission Report acknowledges that the 'legal nature of the document is not that of a treaty in its own right'.[29] It avers, though, that the 1994 Agreement builds on and supplements the 'compromise reached in 1992' and can therefore be qualified as 'subsequent practice in the application of the treaty which establishes the agreement of the parties regarding its interpretation' in the sense of the 1969 Vienna Convention on the Law of Treaties.[30]

Again, this is unpersuasive. This reiteration of commitments can just as easily be explained as a political agreement between the four parties to the 1994 Agreement (Georgia, Russia, South Ossetia, and North Ossetia), whose status under international law differs markedly:

> While Georgia and Russia are full subjects of international law, North Ossetia is, under Russian constitutional law, part of a federation with limited competence to conclude international treaties.[31] South Ossetia, as a party to an armed conflict, has limited treaty-making power to conclude international treaties related to the military conflict, especially armistices[32].[33]

The third and final instrument cited by the Georgia Fact-Finding Mission Report is the Memorandum on Measures to Provide Security and Strengthen Mutual Trust between Sides in the Georgian–South Ossetian Conflict of 16 May 1996. In it, the parties to the Memorandum (Georgia, South Ossetia, and North Ossetia) explicitly agree to 'denounce application of force or threat of force'. A reference to the UN Charter is again incorporated, as is one to 'universally recognized norms of international law'. Despite the difference in parties, the Fact-Finding Mission declares that the Memorandum 'indicates how the original 1992 Agreement must be understood'. It further notes that the UN Security Council condemned the use of force in the Georgian-Abkhaz conflict on two occasions.[34]

The Memorandum is not a binding treaty under international law. It could be considered, as the Georgia Fact-Finding Mission Report suggests, as guidance in

---

[29] ibid.

[30] See Art 31(3)(b) of the Vienna Convention on the Law of Treaties; adopted at Vienna, 23 May 1969; entered into force, 27 January 1980.

[31] According to Article 72(n) of the Russian Constitution, the constituent entities of the Russian Federation may establish their own 'international and foreign economic relations', ie are granted limited treaty-making power at least in those areas where they have exclusive jurisdiction. The coordination of these activities falls within the joint jurisdiction of the Federation and the constituent entities.

[32] A Peters, 'Treaty-Making Power' in R Wolfrum (ed), *Max Planck Encyclopedia of Public International Law* (Oxford, Oxford University Press, 2009) paras 61–62.

[33] Independent International Fact-Finding Mission on the Conflict in Georgia, Report, vol II, 240 (footnotes included in original).

[34] UN Security Council Resolution 876 demanded that 'all parties refrain from the use of force' and condemned violations of the ceasefire agreement between Georgia and forces in Abkhazia: UN Security Council Resolution 876, adopted unanimously on 19 October 1993, paras 4 and 2. Five years later, in its Resolution 1187, the Security Council called upon the parties 'to refrain from the use of force': UN Security Council Resolution 1187, adopted unanimously on 30 July 1998, para 11. See also Independent International Fact-Finding Mission on the Conflict in Georgia, Report, vol II, 241.

the interpretation of the 1992 Agreement, but is better considered discretely on its own merits. It is therefore a huge leap of faith to assert that both Article 2(4) and Article 51 of the UN Charter are thereby brought into force in protection of South Ossetia. Georgia was not according the right of self-defence to South Ossetia, which remained legally a part of its sovereign territory in the view of the government.[35] To do so, it would have had to have explicitly undertaken in a legally binding agreement to grant South Ossetia the right to use force in its own protection (which could prove tantamount to a right to secede). This it did not do.

The ICJ has explicitly rejected the suggestion that a 'general right of intervention, in support of an opposition within another State, exists in contemporary international law'.[36] Later in its judgment on the merits in the *Nicaragua* case, the Court declares that:

> Indeed, it is difficult to see what would remain of the principle of non-intervention in international law if intervention, which is already allowable at the request of the government of a State, were also to be allowed at the request of the opposition. This would permit any State to intervene at any moment in the internal affairs of another State, whether at the request of the government or at the request of its opposition. Such a situation does not in the Court's view correspond to the present state of international law.[37]

The Court's appreciation of the law in 1986 continues to be one that is accurate today.

## A.  The Treaty-Making Capacity of Non-state Actors

That non-state actors can ever conclude agreements with binding force under international law is disputed. The better view is that, under certain circumstances, they can, but this is more readily admitted under *jus in bello* than it is under *jus ad bellum*. For instance, states recognise that parties to a non-international armed conflict not only can but 'should further endeavour to bring into force, by means of special agreements', all or part of the other provisions of the 1949 Geneva Conventions aside from Common Article 3.[38] Such agreements, which seek to bind the parties under international law as well as, potentially, under domestic law, are achieved without affecting the legal status of the parties to the conflict.[39]

The Special Court of Sierra Leone, however, gainsaid the proposition that non-state actors are capable of concluding instruments with a state that have force under international law. In particular, it held that the Lomé Accord that sought to end hostilities in Sierra Leone did not bind the government to an amnesty that it had

---

[35] ibid 241–42.
[36] ICJ, *Nicaragua* judgment, para 209.
[37] ibid para 246.
[38] Art 3 common to the 1949 Geneva Conventions.
[39] ibid.

promised to grant the Revolutionary United Front (RUF).[40] The conclusion of the Appeals Chamber was thus that the Lomé Agreement 'created neither rights nor obligations capable of being regulated by international law'.[41] Its argumentation was as follows.

> The RUF had no treaty-making capacity so as to make the Lomé Agreement an international agreement.

> The conclusion seems to follow clearly that the Lomé Agreement is neither a treaty nor an agreement in the nature of a treaty. However, it does not need to have that character for it to be capable of creating binding obligations and rights between the parties to the agreement in municipal law. The consequence of its not being a treaty or an agreement in the nature of a treaty is that it does not create an obligation in international law.[42]

This is a conclusory argument. The Appeals Chamber cites as evidence Lindsay Moir, who had written about the treaty call upon parties to a non-international armed conflict to seek to bring into force, by means of special agreements, all or part of the other provisions of the Geneva Conventions aside from Common Article 3. He had claimed that the provision 'underlines the fact that parties to an internal conflict are bound only to observe Article 3, remaining free to disregard the entirety of the remaining provisions in each of the Convention'.[43] But that is only true if no special agreement is concluded. As the International Committee of the Red Cross (ICRC) wrote in 2008, special agreements

> can provide a plain statement of the law applicable in the context – or of an expanded set of provisions of IHL beyond the law that is already applicable – and secure a clear commitment from the parties to uphold that law.[44]

It approved this statement in its 2016 commentary on Article 3 in the 1949 Geneva Convention I.[45] This clearly indicates the view of the ICRC that the parties can bring into force additional obligations of *jus in bello* under international law. That is akin to a treaty-making capacity. In its new commentary of Geneva Convention III, published in June 2020, the ICRC stated, in a footnote,[46] that: 'Whether or not they constitute treaties under international law, special agreements concluded between Parties to non-international armed conflicts arguably create obligations under international law.' It is, however, unclear how international legal obligations would be created if it were not considered a treaty.

The Appeals Chamber of the Special Court further asserts that the final clause of Common Article 3, which provides that nothing in the article affects the legal

[40] SCSL, *Prosecutor v Kallon and Kamara*, Decision on Challenge to Jurisdiction: Lomé Accord Amnesty (Appeals Chamber), 13 March 2004, paras 42 et seq.

[41] ibid para 42.

[42] ibid paras 48 and 49.

[43] L Moir, *The Law of Internal Armed Conflict* (Cambridge, Cambridge University Press, 2002) 63–64.

[44] ICRC, 'Increasing Respect for International Humanitarian Law in Non-International Armed Conflicts' (Geneva, February 2008) 16.

[45] Commentary on 1949 Geneva Convention I, para 842, bit.ly/2ViDpiL.

[46] Commentary on Geneva Convention III, 2020, note 848, bit.ly/3hyEDmn.

status of the parties to the conflict, 'indicates that the insurgents may still be made subject to the State's municipal criminal jurisdiction'.[47] That is undeniably a correct statement of fact and law, but it is not the same as averring that a non-state actor has no rights and obligations under international law. In fact, what this final clause does is reiterate that being a party to a non-international armed conflict does not transform a non-state actor into a state, with its concomitant rights and obligations.

Moir himself, as cited by the Appeals Chamber in the relevant footnote, acknowledged that 'scholars have since argued that … Article 3 must confer a measure of international legal personality upon the insurgents, at least they become the holders of rights and obligations under the Article', but condemns them on the basis that they are ignoring 'the obvious intention of the framers of the Conventions'.[48] His all-or-nothing approach is mistaken. The ICRC has it right, in its 2016 commentary on Geneva Convention I, whereby

> it cannot be deduced that the recognition of the capacity to conclude special agreements bringing into force additional obligations in the Conventions implies recognition of belligerency or in any way signifies that the non-State Party to the agreement possesses full international legal personality.[49]

But when a state enters into a formal agreement with a non-state actor that is party to an armed conflict, it is perfectly possible and rational that the agreement may have binding force under international law. This occurred, for instance, with the agreements concluded between the parties to the armed conflicts in Bosnia and Herzegovina in 1992, which brought into force many provisions of the Geneva Conventions and some provisions of the Additional Protocols, and called for the prosecution of those who violated those provisions.[50] This agreement was cited by the Appeals Chamber of the International Criminal Tribunal for the former Yugoslavia (ICTY), which held that 'the conclusion is warranted that the conflicting parties in Bosnia-Herzegovina had clearly agreed at the level of treaty law to make punishable breaches of international humanitarian law occurring within the framework of that conflict'.[51]

Accordingly, in the case of the RUF, the better – and legally correct – approach would have been for the Appeals Chamber to acknowledge that the Lomé Accord had binding force under international law, but then to hold that the decision of

---

[47] SCSL, *Prosecutor v Kallon and Kamara*, Decision on Challenge to Jurisdiction: Lomé Accord Amnesty (Appeals Chamber), 13 March 2004, para 46.

[48] Moir, *The Law of Internal Armed Conflict*, 65.

[49] ICRC Commentary on 1949 Geneva Convention I, para 860, citing R van Steenberghe, 'Théorie des sujets' in R van Steenberghe (ed), *Droit international humanitaire: un régime spécial de droit international?* (Brussels, Bruylant, 2013) 51–65.

[50] See, eg Bosnia and Herzegovina, Agreement No 1 of 22 May 1992, bit.ly/2Honnim.

[51] ICTY, Case No IT-94-1 *Prosecutor v Tadić*, Decision on the Defence Motion for Interlocutory Appeal on Jurisdiction (Appeals Chamber), paras 73, 136. See also the ICRC's discussion in a footnote to its 2016 commentary on Common Art 3: ICRC Commentary on Article 3 of the 1949 Geneva Convention I (2016) fn 819, bit.ly/2DNLYvH.

the RUF to return to violence, which it did, was a material breach that entitled the Government of Sierra Leone to no longer respect the promise of immunity from prosecution. Boiled down to its core, the Lomé Accord was little more than an exchange of amnesty in return for peace. Indeed, in the letter of 12 June 2000 from the President of Sierra Leone to the UN Security Council, which called for the establishment of the Special Court for Sierra Leone, Alhaji Ahmad Tejan Kabbah declared that:

> In July 1999, my Government and the leadership of the RUF signed the Lomé Peace Agreement. The aim of this Agreement was to bring peace and a permanent cessation to those atrocities and the conflict. As a prize for such peace, my Government even conceded to the granting of total amnesty to the RUF leadership and its members in respect of all the acts of terrorism committed by them up to the date of the signing of that Peace Agreement.

> But the RUF leadership have since reneged on that Agreement, and have resumed their atrocities ... In the process, the RUF have committed crimes against Sierra Leonean and international law and it is my Government's view that the issue of individual accountability of the leadership of the RUF for such crimes should be addressed immediately and that it is only by bringing the RUF leadership and their collaborators to justice in the way now requested that peace and national reconciliation and the strengthening of democracy will be assured in Sierra Leone.[52]

Despite the Appeal Chamber's holding, it is actually the case that there was an agreement between the Government of Sierra Leone and the RUF that had the force of international law. The RUF remained a non-state actor (its legal status unchanged), but its material breach of the bilateral agreement to which it was party allowed Sierra Leone, as the other party, to seek the prosecution of RUF commanders and leaders. This is because the principles of the 1969 Vienna Convention on the Law of Treaties – though obviously not the letter – would apply to this material breach.[53]

## B. Obligations under *Jus in Bello* on Non-state Armed Groups

While the Special Court for Sierra Leone did not find that armed groups had sufficient international legal personality to enter into binding relations under international law, it had no difficulty affirming that such groups are directly bound by international humanitarian law. In 2004, the Appeals Chamber held, though without offering strong supporting evidence, that 'it is well settled that all parties

---

[52] Letter cited in SCSL, *Prosecutor v Kallon and Kamara*, Decision on Challenge to Jurisdiction: Lomé Accord Amnesty (Appeals Chamber), 13 March 2004, para 9.

[53] According to the Vienna Convention, 'A material breach of a bilateral treaty by one of the parties entitles the other to invoke the breach as a ground for terminating the treaty or suspending its operation in whole or in part': Art 60(1) of the Vienna Convention on the Law of Treaties; adopted at Vienna, 23 May 1969; entered into force, 27 January 1980.

to an armed conflict, whether states or non-state actors, are bound by international humanitarian law, even though only states may become parties to international treaties'.[54]

Notwithstanding this clear affirmation, there persists a distinct lack of clarity as to how, as a matter of legal theory, non-state armed groups are bound by international law. A widely advanced argument to justify this conclusion is that Common Article 3 to the 1949 Geneva Conventions (which governs situations of non-international armed conflict) explicitly states that the provision binds 'each Party to the conflict', a formulation understood to encompass non-state actors. A major drawback of this approach, though, is that it implies that where a treaty does not use such express language, as is the case, for instance, with the 1977 Additional Protocol II to the Geneva Conventions, it would logically not bind a non-state actor that is party to the non-international armed conflicts governed by that instrument.[55]

Another argument, known as the doctrine of legislative jurisdiction, asserts that the rules of international humanitarian law bind any private individuals, including armed groups, through domestic law. This occurs by means of domestic implementation of international legal rules in national legislation or as a result of the direct applicability in a monist state of self-executing norms. This theory is also problematic, since what is questioned is not whether armed groups are subjects of domestic law (which they clearly are), but whether and, if so, how and to what extent their acts are directly regulated by international law.[56]

Another approach is to argue that international law binds non-parties to a treaty as a result of their consent. It is true that the general principle of law whereby treaties cannot bind third parties (*pacta tertiis nec nocent nec prosunt*) does not apply where the consent of the third party is secured. But applying this principle to a non-international armed conflict would demand that in each case the consent of the non-state armed group is secured in a manner that binds them. This is scarcely a likely prospect in practice.[57]

Far more persuasive is the argument that non-state actors are bound by customary international law. Thus, with respect to Common Article 3 to the Geneva

---

[54] Special Court for Sierra Leone, Case No SCSL-2004-14-AR72(E) *Prosecutor v Sam Hinga Norman*, Decision on Preliminary Motion Based on Lack of Jurisdiction (Appeals Chamber), 31 May 2004, para 22.

[55] Moir's argument in response is, primarily, that it would be 'bizarre' if Common Art 3 were legally binding but Additional Protocol II, which complements and supplements it, were not. This is, however, scarcely a persuasive legal argument. The omission of the reference to 'each Party to the conflict' is not insignificant, and as Cassese (whom Moir cites) acknowledged, several negotiating states clearly believed that insurgent groups would not be bound by the Protocol they were elaborating. See Moir, *The Law of Internal Armed Conflict*, 97.

[56] Y Sandoz, C Swinarski and B Zimmermann (eds), *Commentary on the Additional Protocols of 8 June 1977 to the Geneva Conventions of 12 August 1949* (Geneva, ICRC/Dordrecht, Martinus Nijhoff, 1987) 1345; S Sivakumaran, 'Binding Armed Opposition Groups' (2006) 55 *International and Comparative Law Quarterly* 369, 381.

[57] It would also potentially fall foul of the Special Court's view on non-state actors' inability to contract legal relations that are binding on the international plane.

Conventions, the Special Court's Appeals Chamber asserted that 'there is now no doubt that this article is binding on states and insurgents alike, and that insurgents are subject to international humanitarian law'. A 'convincing theory', it stated, is that insurgents 'are bound as a matter of customary international law to observe the obligations declared by Common Article 3 which is aimed at the protection of humanity'.[58] This is the best approach in legal theory as to how non-state armed groups are bound by *jus in bello*. That said, it is also not without its problems.

First, it is unclear at what precise point in time the rules set out in Common Article 3 became binding as a matter of custom. In 1986, the International Court of Justice implied, but did not make it explicit, that they amounted to customary law by then: 'There is no doubt that, in the event of international armed conflicts, these rules also constitute a minimum yardstick, in addition to the more elaborate rules which are also to apply to international conflicts'.[59] Second, however, and following on directly from the first issue of concern, was the question of what the legal situation vis-à-vis non-state armed groups was prior to the instant at which the rules became custom. Were they not bound as a matter of law?

In its 2016 commentary on the 1949 Geneva Convention I, the ICRC advocates both the customary and treaty-based arguments for the application of Common Article 3. It affirms that 'it is today accepted that common Article 3 is binding on non-State armed groups, both as treaty and customary law'.[60] It duly acknowledges, however, that the 'exact mechanism by which common Article 3 becomes binding on an entity that is not a High Contracting Party to the Geneva Conventions is the subject of debate'.[61] It summarises the different positions on the means by which armed groups are legally bound by international humanitarian law, but, surprisingly, does not identify which it finds the most persuasive.[62] It concludes by simply declaring:

> A variety of these legal theories have been advanced to explain how non-State armed groups are bound by common Article 3, but it is undisputed that the substantive provisions of common Article 3 bind all such armed groups when they are party to an armed conflict.[63]

---

[58] Special Court for Sierra Leone, Case Nos SCSL-2004-15-AR72(E) and SCSL-2004-16-AR72(E) *Prosecutor v Morris Kallon and Brima Buzzy Kamara*, Decision on Challenge to Jurisdiction: Lomé Accord Amnesty (Appeals Chamber), 13 March 2004, paras 45–47.

[59] ICJ, *Nicaragua* judgment, para 218. In 1995, the ICTY approved this finding. With respect to the 1977 Additional Protocol II, it held: 'Attention must also be drawn to Additional Protocol II to the Geneva Conventions. Many provisions of this Protocol can now be regarded as declaratory of existing rules or as having crystallised emerging rules of customary law or else as having been strongly instrumental in their evolution as general principles': ICTY, Case No IT-94-1 *Prosecutor v Tadić*, Decision on the Defence Motion for Interlocutory Appeal on Jurisdiction (Appeals Chamber), paras 98, 117.

[60] ICRC Commentary on Article 3 of the 1949 Geneva Convention I (2016), para 505, bit.ly/2OQn9Wf.

[61] ibid para 507.

[62] ibid.

[63] ibid para 508.

# 10

## The Interrelationship between
## *Jus ad Bellum* and *Jus in Bello*

### I. Introduction

The traditional theory of the interrelationship between *jus ad bellum* and *jus in bello* is simply that these bodies of international law exist and apply entirely separately. Certainly, it remains true to say that a violation of the law on inter-state use of force has no impact whatsoever on the duty to respect international humanitarian law (IHL, also called the law of armed conflict, the mainstay of *jus in bello*). Thus, the 'aggressor' and the 'aggressee' are both equally constrained by *in bello* rules, and the 'justice' of the cause has no bearing on this legal reality.[1] But while the application of the two distinct branches of international law may indeed be in parallel – at least, for certain periods of time and in relation to the same events – the nature of the relationship between them is more complex than initially appears.

First and foremost, application of the rules of *jus ad bellum* may determine whether there is an armed conflict between two states or between a state and an armed group, and therefore whether IHL even applies. Critical to this determination is the notion of consent by the territorial state to the use of force on its territory by a foreign state. If consent has not been provided prior to the use of force, an international armed conflict will exist between the two states.

Second, as discussed in greater detail in chapter five, the law of neutrality transcends *jus ad bellum* and *jus in bello*. This law imposes clear obligations on both states engaged in an international armed conflict and other states that adopt a permanent or ad hoc position of neutrality. As discussed in that chapter, a serious violation of the law of neutrality during an armed conflict may also be an unlawful act *ad bellum*.

Third, certain seemingly identical legal terms apply in international law both *ad bellum* and *in bello*, but with a markedly different meaning. The most obvious of these is 'proportionality'.[2] The exercise of the right of self-defence is subject to the

---

[1] International Committee of the Red Cross (ICRC), 'Jus ad Bellum and Jus in Bello' (29 October 2010), bit.ly/2NxAB0u.

[2] Independent International Fact-Finding Mission on the Conflict in Georgia, Report, vol II, September 2009, 272, fn 163.

principle of proportionality,[3] meaning that only that force which is proportionate to the aim of repelling an armed attack may be used. In contrast, under IHL, the rule of proportionality in attack stipulates that when targeting a lawful military objective, the incidental civilian harm expected to result must not be excessive compared with the concrete and direct military advantage anticipated.[4]

Fourth, and of direct relevance to the issue of proportionality, it is disputed when the application of *ad bellum* rules ends during a given armed conflict (as defined by rules *in bello*). IHL applies throughout any armed conflict to all acts with a sufficient nexus to it (and also beyond the end of the conflict, if, for instance, prisoners of war are detained after the cessation of active hostilities). Arguably, however, the assessment of proportionality *ad bellum* looks only at the intent of the state acting in self-defence through the lens existing at the time it was planning its armed response. Action to repel the armed attack is lawful; regime change is not. If, though, the aggressor continues to fight on after its forces have been successfully repelled, ultimately it may be lawful *ad bellum* to overturn the government as the only means to ensure the safety and security of the aggressee state.

Fifth – and far more controversial – is the issue of whether the legality of targeting under IHL affects the legality of an exercise of self-defence *ad bellum*, taking into account the controversial dicta of the International Court of Justice (ICJ) in the *Oil Platforms* case.[5] IHL clearly outlaws attacks against civilians and civilian objects, which are generally a serious violation of the law and a war crime. But are such attacks also a violation of *jus ad bellum*?

# II. The Relevance of *ad Bellum* Rules to an Application of *Jus in Bello*

Whether or not an armed conflict exists under IHL depends in part on the interpretation and application of *ad bellum* rules to a particular set of facts. If state A uses force on the territory of state B, or if it sends its troops onto that territory without first securing the valid, express consent of the territorial state *ad bellum*, an international armed conflict will exist between the two states. That is so irrespective of whether the foreign military action is actively opposed by the armed forces of the territorial state. The resultant armed conflict will be regulated by the rules of IHL applicable to international armed conflict, with the specific rules of military occupation governing the actions of foreign occupying troops exercising effective control over an area and/or a populace of the territorial state.

---

[3] International Court of Justice (ICJ), *Case Concerning Military and Paramilitary Activities in and against Nicaragua (Nicaragua v United States of America)*, Judgment (Merits), 27 June 1986 (hereinafter ICJ, *Nicaragua* judgment), para 194.

[4] ICRC, Customary IHL Study Rule 14 ('Proportionality in Attack'), bit.ly/2k9mrHh.

[5] ICJ, *Case Concerning Oil Platforms (Islamic Republic of Iran v United States of America)*, Judgment (Merits), 6 November 2003 (hereinafter ICJ, *Oil Platforms* judgment), para 51.

Under *ad bellum* rules, the use of force without consent will in all likelihood fall within the ambit of the general prohibition on the use of force codified in Article 2(4) of the 1945 Charter of the United Nations[6] (UN Charter). In order to be lawful *ad bellum*, the state using force must be acting either in lawful self-defence against an armed attack or pursuant to (and within the terms of) a UN Security Council authorisation to use force. In contrast, if state A has secured the valid, express consent of territorial state B for its forcible extraterritorial action, there is no *ad bellum* violation and no armed conflict.

The issue arises today especially with respect to air strikes, in particular those using remotely piloted vehicles (drones) in pursuit of an extraterritorial counterterrorism strategy. In its 1949 judgment in the *Corfu Channel* case – the first contentious case adjudged by the ICJ after its creation – the Court affirmed that: 'Between independent States, respect for territorial sovereignty is an essential foundation of international relations.'[7] Accordingly, in 1985, Israel's aerial attack on the Palestine Liberation Organization (PLO) headquarters outside Tunis,[8] for which Israel clearly did not have Tunisian consent, was 'condemn[ed] vigorously' by the UN Security Council. In its Resolution 573, the Council further declared it an 'act of armed aggression … in flagrant violation' of the UN Charter.[9] A brief international armed conflict also occurred between Israel and Tunisia that was regulated by IHL, with the strike itself governed by the rules on the conduct of hostilities.

The Council urged other states 'to take measures to dissuade Israel from resorting to such acts against the sovereignty and territorial integrity of all States',[10] implicitly rejecting Israel's argument before the Council that a state 'cannot claim the protection of sovereignty when it knowingly offers a piece of its territory for terrorist activity against other nations'.[11] That said, Christian Tams has suggested that how the UN Security Council would respond were it to hear the same argument again today 'remains a matter for speculation'. He observes that

> the underlying legal claim argument – that states aiding and abetting terrorists abuse their sovereignty and must accept some form of counter-action – has become a standard formula of modern debates and would probably meet with approval of some and tacit agreement of many states.[12]

---

[6] Charter of the United Nations; adopted at San Francisco, 26 June 1945; entered into force, 24 October 1945.

[7] ICJ, *The Corfu Channel Case*, Judgment (Merits), 9 April 1949, 35.

[8] Operation Wooden Leg was an attack carried out by Israel on 1 October 1985 against the PLO headquarters in Hammam Chott, a town 12 miles from the Tunisian capital. The attack, which used modified F-15 combat aircraft, was the longest distance air strike in Israeli Air Force history. D Leone, 'The True History of Israel's Operation Wooden Leg and the Longest-Range F-15 BAZ Strike Ever Made', *The National Interest*, 9 July 2019, bit.ly/2K6UxFw.

[9] UN Security Council Resolution 573, adopted on 4 October 1985 by 14 votes to 0 with 1 abstention (United States), operative para 1. See CJ Tams, 'The Use of Force against Terrorists' (2009) 20(2) *European Journal of International Law* 359, 367.

[10] UN Security Council Resolution 573, para 3.

[11] UN doc S/PV.2615, 87; see Tams, 'The Use of Force against Terrorists', 393.

[12] Tams, 'The Use of Force against Terrorists', 393.

Nonetheless, even if a particular drone strike can be justified *ad bellum* as an act of lawful self-defence, there is still an international armed conflict in existence between the state using force and the territorial state owing to the lack of consent. As the International Committee of the Red Cross (ICRC) has stated: 'Should the third State's intervention be carried out without the consent of the territorial State, it would amount to an international armed conflict between the intervening State and the territorial State.'[13] Determining whether valid consent has been given to foreign use of force is, as chapter two reviewed, a challenging endeavour. But, for the application (or not) of *jus in bello*, it remains critical to establish in fact and law whether consent has been validly secured.

## III. Neutrality *ad Bellum* and *in Bello*

When an international armed conflict exists, the relationship between the parties to the conflict and all other states is governed by the law of neutrality as well as the rules of *jus ad bellum*.[14] As chapter five described, the law of neutrality prohibits a neutral state from engaging in an international armed conflict.[15] Should it violate this rule, it will become a party to the conflict and thereby be bound by *jus in bello*. The law of neutrality further precludes neutral states from providing support to the forces of warring parties in such a conflict.[16]

A neutral state also has a duty not to discriminate in its treatment of parties to an international armed conflict: where it imposes restrictions against one party, to comply with the rules of the law of neutrality, it must impose the same restrictions against the others. Compliance with this latter rule is potentially complicated by other rules of international law, as chapter five describes. For instance, action against one of the parties to an armed conflict may be required of an ostensibly neutral UN member state by the UN Security Council. Indeed, while the duty of non-discrimination imposed upon neutral states tends towards a rule *in bello*, a serious violation may have implications also *ad bellum*, potentially even rendering a state complicit in an act of aggression in certain circumstances.

The corresponding obligations imposed by the law of neutrality on states engaged in an international armed conflict are to not attack a neutral state and to ensure, to the maximum extent possible, that neutral states are not affected by the conduct of hostilities. Should a party to an international armed conflict infringe

---

[13] ICRC Commentary on 1949 Geneva Convention I, 2016, para 260, bit.ly/2NVube4.

[14] UK Ministry of Defence, *Joint Service Manual of the Law of Armed Conflict*, Joint Service Publication 383 (2004) para 1.42. See also US Department of Defense, *Law of War Manual* (Washington DC, June 2015, updated December 2016) (hereinafter USDOD December 2016 Law of War Manual), para 15.1.1.

[15] USDOD December 2016 Law of War Manual, para 15.3.2.

[16] P Seger, 'The Law of Neutrality' in A Clapham and P Gaeta (eds), *The Oxford Handbook of International Law in Armed Conflict* (Oxford, Oxford University Press, 2014) 248. As Seger recalls, the term comes from the Latin expression *ne uter*, meaning neither one nor the other.

its obligations to respect the neutrality of a state, for example by moving troops onto its territory, that neutral state is obligated to take such measures that are reasonable in the circumstances to address the violation of their neutrality. In this particular case, this would require the neutral state to intern the foreign troops on their territory for the duration of the conflict.

To achieve this aim, lawful measures may extend to the use of force that is both necessary and proportionate in the circumstances. Such a use of force, which is akin to an operation of domestic law enforcement, does not amount to a violation of Article 2(4) of the UN Charter, much less an armed attack. It may, though, lead to the application of IHL, whereby a separate international armed conflict exists between the territorial state and the state that has violated its neutrality.

# IV. Proportionality *ad Bellum* and *in Bello*

The principle of proportionality *ad bellum* restricts action that may be taken when a state is exercising its inherent right of self-defence.[17] This means that only that force which is proportionate to the aim of repelling an armed attack may be used. Thus, as the Independent International Fact-Finding Mission on the Conflict in Georgia affirmed, a 'reaction is proportionate if there is a reasonable relationship between the measures employed and the objective, the only permissible objective being the repulsion of the armed attack'.[18]

As discussed in chapter three, 'what matters in this respect is the result to be achieved by the "defensive action", and not the forms, substance and strength of the action itself'.[19] If, for instance, foreign troops have invaded, the territorial state is entitled to use such force as is required to drive the invaders out. That may involve targeting military and logistical support abroad. Similarly, if a foreign state's air force has bombarded the territorial state, that state may attack, among other military targets, the air force as well as their bases abroad.[20]

The legality of the response *ad bellum* must be determined by looking primarily at the planning and conduct of the initial response in self-defence and judging it against the scale and nature of the armed attack. Being the victim of an armed attack does not justify regime change as an automatic response in self-defence. Only, for instance, where the armed attack has already been successfully repelled

---

[17] ICJ, *Nicaragua* judgment, para 194.

[18] Independent International Fact-Finding Mission on the Conflict in Georgia, Report, vol II, 249.

[19] R Ago, ILC Special Rapporteur, 'Addendum to the Eighth Report on State Responsibility' (1980) II(1) *United Nations Yearbook of the International Law Commission* 69, para 121.

[20] In its judgment in the *Armed Activities* case, the ICJ stated, obiter, that 'The Court cannot fail to observe, however, that the taking of airports and towns many hundreds of kilometres from Uganda's border would not seem proportionate to the series of transborder attacks it claimed had given rise to the right of self-defence, nor to be necessary to that end': ICJ, *Case Concerning Armed Activities on the Territory of the Congo (Democratic Republic of the Congo v Uganda)*, Judgment, 19 December 2005, para 147.

and the aggressee state continues to fight – and especially where the erstwhile victim state subsequently attempts to install a puppet regime as the government of its enemy – compliance with *ad bellum* rules should be judged over the course of the entire military campaign.

In contrast, under IHL, the rule of proportionality applicable throughout the conduct of hostilities stipulates that when targeting a lawful military objective in each planned attack, the incidental civilian harm expected to result must not be excessive compared with the concrete and direct military advantage anticipated.[21] Such civilian harm is explicitly defined as encompassing deaths or injuries to civilians; destruction of or damage to civilian objects; 'or a combination thereof'. It is important to reiterate that the assessment of likely civilian harm is made by the attacker in advance of the attack and projecting forward in time. This is another potential distinction with the principle of proportionality *ad bellum*. Proportionality *in bello* is never an ex post facto analysis based on the extent of any civilian casualties or damage to civilian objects actually inflicted (though clearly such casualties or damage may justify a timely review of compliance with the rule of proportionality in attack).

The challenge in applying the proportionality rule *in bello* centres on the inherent imprecision of the term 'excessive'. As Yoram Dinstein has observed, the rule is a balancing act: the greater the anticipated military advantage, the greater the extent of foreseeable civilian harm that may not be unlawful.[22] As the US Department of Defense cautioned in 2015: 'The weighing or comparison between the expected incidental harm and the expected military advantage does not necessarily lend itself to empirical analyses.'[23] This statement was not repeated in the revised edition of the *Law of War Manual*, issued by the Department of Defense in December 2016. In any event, the legal review assesses what a reasonable military commander, put in the position of the commander who served at the time, with the same knowledge at his or her disposal, would be expected to do (or refrain from doing).

# V.  The Legality of Targeting under *Jus in Bello* and its Influence on the Legality of Action in Self-defence

In its 2003 judgment in the *Oil Platforms* case, the ICJ referred to what appears to be a new condition for the exercise of self-defence *ad bellum* that exists either as

---

[21] ICRC, Customary IHL Study Rule 14 ('Proportionality in Attack'), bit.ly/2k9mrHh.

[22] Y Dinstein, *The Conduct of Hostilities under the Law of International Armed Conflict*, 2nd edn (Cambridge, Cambridge University Press, 2010) 131.

[23] US Department of Defense, *Law of War Manual* (June 2015) para 5.12.4, citing in turn International Criminal Tribunal for the former Yugoslavia (ICTY), *Final Report to the Prosecutor by the Committee Established to Review the NATO Bombing Campaign Against the Federal Republic of Yugoslavia*, 13 June 2000, para 48.

part of, or in addition to, the principles of necessity and proportionality. This is that the targets of the use of force in self-defence must be lawful military objectives under *jus in bello*. The Court stated that: 'The United States must also show that its actions were necessary and proportional to the armed attack made on it, *and* that the platforms were a legitimate military target open to attack in the exercise of self-defence.'[24]

Article 48 of the 1977 Additional Protocol I sets out the basic rule governing the conduct of hostilities:

> In order to ensure respect for and protection of the civilian population and civilian objects, the Parties to the conflict shall at all times distinguish between the civilian population and combatants and between civilian objects and military objectives and accordingly shall direct their operations only against military objectives.[25]

This fundamental IHL rule represents customary international law applicable to all armed conflicts and is also a norm of *jus cogens*.[26]

According to the 1977 Additional Protocol I:

> In so far as objects are concerned, military objectives are limited to those objects which by their nature, location, purpose or use make an effective contribution to military action and whose total or partial destruction, capture or neutralization, in the circumstances ruling at the time, offers a definite military advantage.[27]

This definition similarly exists as a matter of custom in all armed conflicts.[28]

The definition of civilians is a little more complicated. According to the ICRC, under customary IHL, 'Civilians are persons who are not members of the armed forces. The civilian population comprises all persons who are civilians.'[29] The ICRC further affirms that:

> State practice establishes this rule as a norm of customary international law applicable in international armed conflicts. It also applies to non-international armed conflicts although practice is ambiguous as to whether members of armed opposition groups are considered members of armed forces or civilians.[30]

In fact, there is also further complexity in an international armed conflict. A *levée en masse* is where 'inhabitants of a non-occupied territory' (ie civilians) spontaneously take up arms to resist an approaching enemy. They thereby lose their civilian

---

[24] ICJ, *Oil Platforms* judgment, para 51 (emphasis added).

[25] Art 48 of the Protocol Additional to the Geneva Conventions of 12 August 1949, and Relating to the Protection of Victims of International Armed Conflicts (Protocol I), of 8 June 1977 (hereinafter 1977 Additional Protocol I).

[26] See, eg ICJ, *Legality of the Threat or Use of Nuclear Weapons*, Advisory Opinion, 8 July 1996, paras 78 and 79; 'Fourth Report on Peremptory Norms of General International Law (*Jus Cogens*) by Dire Tladi, Special Rapporteur', UN doc A/CN.4/727, 31 January 2019, paras 117–21.

[27] 1977 Additional Protocol I, Art 52(2).

[28] ICRC Customary IHL Rule 8 ('Definition of Military Objectives'), at: bit.ly/2X2mHqu.

[29] ICRC Customary IHL Rule 5 ('Definition of Civilians'), bit.ly/34KPPVO.

[30] ibid.

immunity but are entitled to prisoner-of-war status 'provided they carry arms openly and respect the laws and customs of war'.[31]

The view of the ICJ whereby attacking the civilian population or civilian objects cannot be a lawful act of self-defence *ad bellum* has been criticised by a number of leading publicists. Foremost among them is Yoram Dinstein (writing in 2016),[32] who cites James Green (writing in 2004).[33] Green does describe the implication that an 'extra hurdle must be cleared' in exercising self-defence as 'disconcerting',[34] but he also affirms that it 'seems highly unlikely that an attack against non-military targets could amount to a necessary action in self-defence'.[35] In 2015, Green further argued that 'military targeting is inherent in the proportionality requirement'.[36] Olivier Corten has argued that 'if the target has no military role, its destruction cannot prove effective and therefore necessary in repelling the attack'.[37]

But what if the armed attack giving rise to the right of self-defence was made against civilians? Let us say for the sake of argument that the attacks on US soil on 11 September 2001 were indeed an armed attack. While the Pentagon was a legitimate military objective under IHL, the World Trade Centre was a civilian object and the overwhelming majority of those in the Twin Towers were unquestionably civilians. Could the United States not have struck back in self-defence against civilians linked to al-Qaeda under *jus ad bellum*? After all, it is often said that the law on interstate use of force is 'weapon-neutral'.[38]

Clearly, attacks on civilians are generally a serious violation of IHL and, when conducted with the requisite *mens rea*, are also a war crime under *jus in bello*. This argument can be harnessed to advocate that targeting issues are adequately dealt with under *jus in bello* and therefore that there is no need to also consider them *ad bellum*. That said, reprisals against civilians in the conduct of hostilities, while

---

[31] Art 4(6) of the Convention (III) relative to the Treatment of Prisoners of War; adopted at Geneva, 12 August 1949; entered into force, 21 October 1950.

[32] Y Dinstein, *War, Aggression and Self-defence*, 6th edn (Cambridge, Cambridge University Press, 2017) para 490.

[33] JA Green, 'The Oil Platforms Case: An Error in Judgment?' (2004) 9(3) *Journal of Conflict and Security Law* 357.

[34] ibid 381.

[35] ibid.

[36] JA Green and CPM Waters, 'Military Targeting in the Context of Self-defence Actions' (2015) 84(1) *Nordic Journal of International Law* 3.

[37] O Corten, *The Law Against War: The Prohibition on the Use of Force in Contemporary International Law* (Oxford, Hart Publishing, 2010) 488.

[38] N Hayashi, 'Using Force by Means of Nuclear Weapons and Requirements of Necessity and Proportionality *ad Bellum*' in G Nystuen, S Casey-Maslen and A Golden Bersagel (eds), *Nuclear Weapons under International Law* (Cambridge, Cambridge University Press, 2014) 15.

ostensibly outlawed under the 1977 Additional Protocol I, which governs international armed conflict (despite reservations by a number of states parties to this provision),[39] are not explicitly regulated in a situation of non-international armed conflict.[40] When the Protocol can be exercised, however, there are certainly strict conditions imposed for any reprisals to be lawful.

---

[39] 1977 Additional Protocol I, Art 51(6). See S Casey-Maslen with S Haines, *Hague Law Interpreted: The Conduct of Hostilities under the Law of Armed Conflict* (Oxford, Hart Publishing, 2018) 341–42.

[40] For a discussion of practice, scholarship, and jurisprudence on this issue, see Casey-Maslen with Haines, *Hague Law Interpreted*, 343–44.

# 11

## The Interrelationship between International Human Rights Law and *Jus ad Bellum*

### I. Introduction

In its most recent General Comment on the right to life, published at the end of October 2018, the Human Rights Committee affirmed that states parties to the 1966 International Covenant on Civil and Political Rights (ICCPR)[1] that engage in acts of aggression which result in deprivation of life 'violate ipso facto' the right to life protected in Article 6 of the Covenant.[2] The Committee further asserts, more tentatively, that states that fail to take all reasonable measures to settle their international disputes by peaceful means 'might fall short of complying with their positive obligation to ensure the right to life'.[3] Is the Committee engaging in judicial activism, or merely reflecting the notion of 'arbitrariness' inherent in a substantive violation of the right to life?

### II. The Substantive Prohibition under the Right to Life

Article 6(1) of the ICCPR provides as follows: 'Every human being has the inherent right to life. This right shall be protected by law. No one shall be arbitrarily deprived of his life.' In its 2018 General Comment, the Human Rights Committee has reaffirmed that the right to life 'is the supreme right from which no derogation is permitted',[4] and specifically notes that this is so 'even in situations of armed conflict'.[5]

---

[1] International Covenant on Civil and Political Rights; adopted at New York, 16 December 1966; entered into force, 23 March 1976.

[2] Human Rights Committee, 'General Comment No 36 (2018) on Article 6 of the International Covenant on Civil and Political Rights, on the Right to Life', UN doc CCPR/C/GC/36, 30 October 2018, para 70 (hereinafter Human Rights Committee General Comment 36 on the Right to Life).

[3] ibid.

[4] ibid para 2; Human Rights Committee, General Comment No 6 (1982), para 1 (hereinafter Human Rights Committee General Comment 6 on the Right to Life). See also Human Rights Committee, General Comment No 14 (1984), para 2.

[5] Human Rights Committee General Comment 36 on the Right to Life, para 2.

Attention naturally focuses on the scope of the term 'arbitrary' in Article 6(1). In its 1982 General Comment on the right to life (now formally superseded by General Comment 36 of 2018), the Committee had considered that

> States have the supreme duty to prevent wars, acts of genocide and other acts of mass violence causing arbitrary loss of life. Every effort they make to avert the danger of war, especially thermonuclear war, and to strengthen international peace and security would constitute the most important condition and guarantee for the safeguarding of the right to life.[6]

This was not an explicit affirmation that aggression violates the right to life, though it is strongly implied by the notion that wars cause 'arbitrary loss of life'.

In its 2018 General Comment on the right to life, the Human Rights Committee clarifies that deprivation of life 'is, as a rule, arbitrary if it is inconsistent with international law or domestic law'.[7] In its corresponding General Comment on the right to life under Article 4 of the 1981 African Charter on Human and Peoples' Rights,[8] the African Commission on Human and Peoples' Rights similarly affirmed that: 'A deprivation of life is arbitrary if it is impermissible under international law, or under more protective domestic law provisions.'[9]

This sets out the ground rule for a consideration of the interrelationship between *jus ad bellum* and international human rights law. Where an act of violence by one state against another breaches the rules of *jus ad bellum*, that breach will not only constitute a violation of the law on interstate use of force, it will also violate the human rights of those harmed by the unlawful violence. Thus, if they are killed, they potentially have a claim for a remedy for a right to life against the state that has acted unlawfully *ad bellum*. Accordingly, no human rights liability *ad bellum* will attach to a state that is lawfully exercising its inherent right of self-defence, or which is using force pursuant to (and within the terms of) an authorisation from the UN Security Council acting under Chapter VII of the UN Charter.

As discussed elsewhere in this work, an act of aggression is a serious violation ('the most serious and dangerous form')[10] of the general prohibition on interstate use of force. It is defined in the UN General Assembly Resolution 3314 (the 1974 Definition of Aggression) in similar terms to its codification in Article 2(4) of the Charter of the United Nations[11] (UN Charter) as the 'use of armed force by

---

[6] Human Rights Committee General Comment 6 on the Right to Life, para 2.

[7] Human Rights Committee General Comment 36 on the Right to Life, para 12.

[8] 1981 African Charter on Human and Peoples' Rights; adopted at Nairobi, 27 June 1981; entered into force, 21 October 1986.

[9] African Commission on Human and Peoples' Rights, General Comment No 3 on the African Charter on Human and Peoples' Rights: The Right to Life (Article 4); adopted during the 57th Ordinary Session of the African Commission on Human and Peoples' Rights, held from 4 to 18 November 2015 in Banjul, The Gambia, para 12.

[10] Definition of Aggression, annexed to UN General Assembly Resolution 3314 (XXIX); adopted without a vote on 14 December 1974 (hereinafter 1974 Definition of Aggression), fifth preambular paragraph.

[11] Art 51 of the Charter of the United Nations; adopted at San Francisco, 26 June 1945; entered into force, 24 October 1945.

a State against the sovereignty, territorial integrity or political independence of another State, or in any other manner inconsistent with the Charter of the United Nations'.[12] This is duly qualified by the affirmation that use of armed force by a state in contravention of the UN Charter

> shall constitute prima facie evidence of an act of aggression although the Security Council may, in conformity with the Charter, conclude that a determination that an act of aggression has been committed would not be justified in the light of other relevant circumstances, including the fact that the acts concerned or their consequences are not of sufficient gravity.[13]

Article 3 of the 1974 Definition of Aggression then sets out the acts that thereby qualify as an act of aggression:

(a) The invasion or attack by the armed forces of a State of the territory of another State, or any military occupation, however temporary, resulting from such invasion or attack, or any annexation by the use of force of the territory of another State or part thereof;

(b) Bombardment by the armed forces of a State against the territory of another State or the use of any weapons by a State against the territory of another State;

(c) The blockade of the ports or coasts of a State by the armed forces of another State;

(d) An attack by the armed forces of a State on the land, sea or air forces, or marine and air fleets of another State;

(e) The use of armed forces of one State which are within the territory of another State with the agreement of the receiving State, in contravention of the conditions provided for in the agreement or any extension of their presence in such territory beyond the termination of the agreement;

(f) The action of a State in allowing its territory, which it has placed at the disposal of another State, to be used by that other State for perpetrating an act of aggression against a third State;

(g) The sending by or on behalf of a State of armed bands, groups, irregulars or mercenaries, which carry out acts of armed force against another State of such gravity as to amount to the acts listed above, or its substantial involvement therein.

In its 1996 Advisory Opinion on the Legality of the Threat or Use of Nuclear Weapons,[14] the International Court of Justice (ICJ) addressed the application of *jus ad bellum* to the use of nuclear weapons and the protection of the right to life under the ICCPR in situations of international armed conflict. It affirmed that, 'In principle, the right not arbitrarily to be deprived of one's life applies also in hostilities', and declared that the use of force *in bello* was to be 'determined by the applicable *lex specialis*, namely, the law applicable in armed conflict which is designed to regulate the conduct of hostilities'.[15] Thus, the scope of arbitrary deprivation of life drew on a different branch of international law (IHL)

---

[12] 1974 Definition of Aggression, Art 1.
[13] 1974 Definition of Aggression, Art 2.
[14] ICJ, *Legality of the Threat or Use of Nuclear Weapons*, Advisory Opinion, 8 July 1996.
[15] ibid para 25.

to consider its respect during a situation of armed conflict. It did not, though, consider whether and, if so, how international human rights law would be breached by an unlawful use of nuclear weapons *ad bellum*.

The approach to the right to life under the 1950 European Convention on Human Rights[16] differs substantially from that taken in other regional and global human rights instruments, but nonetheless endorses the understanding of the fundamental interrelationship between *jus ad bellum* and international human rights law. Article 2(2) of the European Convention does not prohibit 'arbitrary' deprivation of life, but limits use of force by the state to that which is 'absolutely necessary':

(a)   in defence of any person from unlawful violence;
(b)   in order to effect a lawful arrest or to prevent the escape of a person lawfully detained;
(c)   in action lawfully taken for the purpose of quelling a riot or insurrection.

Article 15(2) addresses the use of force in a situation of international armed conflict,[17] specifying that no derogation may be made from Article 2, 'except in respect of deaths resulting from lawful acts of war'. As William Schabas observes: 'Historically, the term "act of war" had significance in the context of the *jus ad bellum*.'[18] Furthermore, prior to the adoption of the European Convention, the legality of a use of force by one state against another had already 'been confined to the exceptional circumstances' set out in the UN Charter.[19] He concludes that

> to avail of the 'lawful acts of war' exception to killing in the course of armed conflict, the use of force itself must be consistent with international law. In other words, a declaration of derogation from the right to life by a State with respect to the use of force against another State that is not in the exercise of the inherent right of self-defence or authorized by the Security Council would be ineffective.[20]

The use of force *ad bellum* has not been litigated directly before the European Court of Human Rights. In its judgments in 1995 and 1996 in the *Loizidou* case, the Grand Chamber did not address the legality of the Turkish invasion of northern Cyprus. In its judgment on the preliminary objections, the Grand Chamber stated simply:

> Bearing in mind the object and purpose of the Convention, the responsibility of a Contracting Party may also arise when as a consequence of military action – *whether lawful or unlawful* – it exercises effective control of an area outside its national territory.[21]

---

[16] Convention for the Protection of Human Rights and Fundamental Freedoms; adopted at Rome by the Council of Europe, 4 November 1950; entered into force, 3 September 1953.

[17] An insurrection, as referred to in Art 2(2)(c), is a form of non-international armed conflict.

[18] W Schabas, *The European Convention on Human Rights: A Commentary* (Oxford, Oxford University Press, 2017) 601.

[19] Schabas, *The European Convention on Human Rights: A Commentary*, 602.

[20] ibid.

[21] European Court of Human Rights, *Loizidou v Turkey*, Judgment (Preliminary Objections) (Grand Chamber), 23 March 1995, para 62 (emphasis added); affirmed in *Loizidou v Turkey*, Judgment (Merits) (Grand Chamber), 18 December 1996, para 52.

In May 2018, the Court held a Grand Chamber hearing in the case of *Georgia v Russia (II)*, which concerned the armed conflict between Georgia and the Russian Federation in August 2008 and its aftermath.[22] The case concerned alleged violations of the right to life only *in bello*, however, and not also those *ad bellum*, and is thus not expected to elucidate further the interrelationship between the rules of *jus ad bellum* and the protection of the right to life under the 1950 European Convention on Human Rights.

More recently, on 11 September 2019, the European Court of Human Rights' Grand Chamber held oral hearings on the admissibility of an interstate claim by Ukraine against Russia regarding Crimea.[23] Marko Milanovic has asked whether the European Court should pronounce on whether Ukraine or Russia is the rightful sovereign of Crimea. He affirms that the legal response is not difficult to determine: 'Russia's annexation of Crimea was as clearly illegal as anything can be.'[24] But he cautions against international human rights bodies pronouncing on 'issues which, while capable of legal determination, are not part of their central mission of human rights protection and may negatively affect that mission'. He even suggests that any such pronouncement 'would provoke [an] intense backlash, even possibly leading to Russia's withdrawal from the Council of Europe'.[25]

At the oral hearings, the judges asked the two states parties whether they believed that the Court should address the issue of sovereignty over Crimea and any UN Charter violations on the part of Russia, in order to establish whether Russia had jurisdiction over Crimea in the sense of Article 1 of the European Convention. Russia responded that the Court should not pronounce itself on the sovereignty dispute between the parties, arguing that this was a purely political issue over which the Court did not have jurisdiction. In contrast, Ukraine called on the Court to rule that Crimea remained Ukrainian territory. It did so on the basis that this would be in accordance with the general position taken within the international community and that the Court needed to define whether the juridical nature of Russia's jurisdiction was territorial or extraterritorial. As Milanovic observes, however, this latter argument

> rests on a fallacy – partly one of the Court's own making, from *Banković* onwards – that there is some kind of profound difference in nature between Article 1 jurisdiction which is territorial and that which is extraterritorial. On the contrary, both should be regarded as being of the same, factual nature – based in the exercise of control over territory, rather than in the right to exercise such control.[26]

---

[22] European Court of Human Rights, *Georgia v Russia* (II) App No 38263/08 (Grand Chamber hearing, 30 May 2018).

[23] European Court of Human Rights, *Ukraine v Russia* App No 20958/14 (Grand Chamber hearing, 11 September 2019).

[24] M Milanovic, 'Does the European Court of Human Rights Have to Decide on Sovereignty over Crimea? Part I: Jurisdiction in Article 1 ECHR', *EJIL: Talk!*, 23 September 2019, bit.ly/2NWDkAN.

[25] ibid.

[26] ibid.

Milanovic recommends that the Court follow its approach in the *Loizidou* case and accept that Russia has control, and thus jurisdiction, over Crimea, regardless of whether it obtained that control lawfully or unlawfully. As he notes, Russia does not dispute that it has jurisdiction.

> The Court could then add for even more clarity that its finding of jurisdiction is not an implicit determination of the sovereignty dispute between the parties. This is in my view the most sensible way in which the Article 1 applicability question should be resolved.[27]

He does acknowledge, though, that the precise moment in time at which Russia obtained control over Crimea will demand some assessment of the facts. Indirectly, it may also call for a legal assessment, potentially including when a military occupation existed in the peninsula. The legality of the occupation is irrelevant for any obligations *in bello* under international humanitarian law, but were the Court to make such a finding, it might be at the least implicit in any finding of jurisdiction that the occupation was unlawful *ad bellum.*[28]

Also contentious on the nature of the interrelationship between *jus ad bellum* and human rights, but for a different reason, is the Human Rights Committee's assertion that the failure by states to take all reasonable measures to settle their international disputes by peaceful means 'might fall short of complying with their positive obligation to ensure the right to life'.[29] It is true that, under Article 2(3) of the UN Charter, all member states are obligated 'to settle their international disputes by peaceful means in such a manner that international peace and security, and justice, are not endangered'. This obligation, though, is subject to the inherent right of states to exercise individual and collective self-defence against an armed attack. Thus, we return to the primary rule *ad bellum* as codified in Article 2(4) of the UN Charter. State practice does not support the crystallisation of a rule of customary international law whereby recourse is required to the ICJ to resolve disputes between states concerning, for example, the delineation of borders or the prohibition of support for armed groups within another state.

## III.  Identifying and Remedying a Violation of the Right to Life *ad Bellum*

Two main objections may be raised to the notion that an act of aggression will violate not only *jus ad bellum*, but also international human rights law. First, that

---

[27] ibid.

[28] In a further blog post, Milanovic suggests that there is no need for the Court to make a determination of military occupation. He also discusses the problems engendered by alleged violations of human rights by the mass automatic naturalisation of Ukrainian citizens in Crimea by Russia, and respect for the right of each person to enter their own country, which might demand an assessment of the legality of Russian action *ad bellum*. M Milanovic, 'Does the European Court of Human Rights Have to Decide on Sovereignty over Crimea? Part II: Issues Lurking on the Merits', *EJIL: Talk!*, 24 September 2019, bit.ly/33XYc0p.

[29] Human Rights Committee General Comment 6 on the Right to Life, para 70.

a human rights body will not have the requisite expertise to make a determination of legality of the use of force *ad bellum*. Second, that should such a body find a violation of the right to life, it could potentially award huge sums of compensation. Neither objection is persuasive.

With respect to the first criticism, human rights bodies, including the regional courts, apply different bodies of international and domestic law on a routine basis. The judges and jurists are not or may not be experts in environmental law, but they nonetheless apply environmental standards and norms to the interpretation and protection of human rights. They can undertake this task (and sometimes do) for *jus ad bellum*. Likewise, judges in domestic courts are not experts in *jus ad bellum*, but they have considered allegations of acts of aggression in recent years in a number of cases.[30] A suggestion that, for instance, the European Court of Human Rights would somehow be incapable of correctly adjudicating the legality of an interstate use of force must be rejected.

With respect to the second criticism (on the existence of suitable remedies adequate to the task), there are potentially at least two distinct issues to consider, depending on whether the body in question has the power to award compensation. If, for example, the Human Rights Committee makes an adjudication of legality *ad bellum* in its views rendered on a particular communication from an individual under the ICCPR,[31] there is no possibility of any compensation being awarded. There is, rather, a determination of whether one or more violations of the Covenant have occurred that is not formally binding on the state (though it is nonetheless influential).

If, in contrast, it is a regional human rights court that is issuing a binding judgment, that court may impose a duty to make reparation. Under the European Convention on Human Rights, for instance, if the Court finds that there has been a violation of the Convention, and if the internal law of the state party concerned allows only partial reparation to be made, the Court shall, if necessary, afford just satisfaction to the injured party.[32] There is a corresponding obligation on each state party to 'undertake to abide by the final judgment of the Court in any case to which they are parties'.[33]

Here, a massive financial award could potentially be made, whether in an interstate case or to a huge number of applicants in a joined set of individual applications. While such an award is highly unlikely to be made, it is not outside the realm of the possible. One of a number of objections could concern the

---

[30] See, eg *R v Jones (Margaret)* [2007] 1 AC 136; *R (on the application of Al Rabbat) v Westminster Magistrates' Court (HM Attorney General intervening)* [2017] EWHC 1969 (Admin). See also, eg A Orakhelashvili, 'The High Court and the Crime of Aggression' (2018) 5(1) *Journal on the Use of Force and International Law* 3, bit.ly/33YviNt.

[31] Art 5(4) of the Optional Protocol to the International Covenant on Civil and Political Rights; adopted at New York, 16 December 1966; entered into force, 23 March 1976.

[32] 1950 European Convention on Human Rights, Art 41 (Just satisfaction).

[33] 1950 European Convention on Human Rights, Art 46(1).

practicality of adjudicating and implementing the Court's award. That should not, though, be the basis for outright objection of the notion. Is it suggested that a finding of genocide or crime against humanity (and corresponding award of compensation) should not be made in a judgment on the basis that its implementation would be administratively demanding? That is surely not the case.

There is, though, a third and more imposing objection. As Milanovic has suggested, adjudicating the legality of an interstate use of force could politicise a court or create a dangerous backlash, but without advancing the cause of human rights. This is a valid concern, and where a court has no need to address the legality of an interstate use of force, it is clearly in a position to decide not to do so in its judgment. There may, though, be occasions where a determination of legality *ad bellum* is required in order to adjudicate a case correctly. In such a circumstance, the court has no justification in eschewing a good faith interpretation and application of the relevant convention to the facts at hand. Legal jiggery-pokery to avoid consideration of *ad bellum* rules could also risk the politicisation of the court.

# BIBLIOGRAPHY

## Books

Aksu, E, *The United Nations, Intra-state Peacekeeping and Normative Change* (Manchester University Press, Manchester, 2003).

Bethlehem, DL and Weller, M, *The 'Yugoslav' Crisis in International Law* (Cambridge, Cambridge University Press, 1997).

Bowett, DW, *Self-Defence in International Law* (Manchester, Manchester University Press, 1958).

Brownlie, I, *International Law and the Use of Force by States* (Oxford, Oxford University Press, 1963.

Cadoux, CJ, *The Early Christian Attitude to War* (London, Headley Bros, 1919).

Casey-Maslen, S (ed), *Weapons Under International Human Rights Law* (Cambridge, Cambridge University Press, 2014).

Casey-Maslen, S, *The Treaty of the Prohibition of Nuclear Weapons: A Commentary* (Oxford, Oxford University Press, 2019).

Casey-Maslen, S with Haines, S, *Hague Law Interpreted: The Conduct of Hostilities under the Law of Armed Conflict* (Oxford, Hart Publishing, 2018).

Casey-Maslen, S and Vestner, T, *A Guide to International Disarmament Law* (London, Routledge, 2019).

Casey-Maslen, S, Clapham, A, Giacca, G and Parker, S, *The Arms Trade Treaty: A Commentary* (Oxford, Oxford University Press, 2016).

Cassese, A, *International Law*, 2nd edn (Oxford, Oxford University Press, 2005).

Chesterman, S, *Just War or Just Peace? Humanitarian Intervention and International Law* (Oxford, Oxford University Press, 2001).

Cicero, MT, *De Officiis*.

Clapham, A, *Brierly's Law of Nations*, 7th edn (Oxford, Oxford University Press, 2012).

Clapham, A and Gaeta, P (eds), *The Oxford Handbook of International Law in Armed Conflict* (Oxford, Oxford University Press, 2014).

Corten, O, *The Law Against War: The Prohibition on the Use of Force in Contemporary International Law* (Oxford, Hart Publishing, 2010).

Crawford, J, *Brownlie's Principles of Public International Law*, 9th edn (Oxford, Oxford University Press, 2019).

Cryer, R, Friman, H, Robinson, D and Wilmshurst, E, *An Introduction to International Criminal Law and Procedure*, 2nd edn (Cambridge, Cambridge University Press, 2010).

Cryer, R, Robinson, D, and Vasiliev, S, *An Introduction to International Criminal Law and Procedure*, 4th edn (Cambridge, Cambridge University Press, 2019).

de Groot, H, *De Jure Belli ac Pacis* (1625).

de Vattel, E, *Le Droit des Gens* (1758).

de Madariaga, I, *Britain, Russia, and the Armed Neutrality of 1780: Sir James Harris's Mission to St. Petersburg during the American Revolution* (New Haven, CT, Yale University Press, 1962).

de Victoria, F, *Relectiones Theologicae* (1557).

Dinstein, Y, *The Conduct of Hostilities under the Law of International Armed Conflict*, 2nd edn (Cambridge, Cambridge University Press, 2010).

Dinstein, Y, *War, Aggression and Self-defence*, 6th edn (Cambridge, Cambridge University Press, 2017).

Findlay, T, *The Use of Force in UN Peace Operations* (Stockholm, Stockholm International Peace Research Institute (SIPRI)/Oxford, Oxford University Press, 2002).

Fleck, D (ed), *The Handbook of Humanitarian Law in Armed Conflicts* (Oxford, Oxford University Press, 1999).

Fleck, D (ed), *The Handbook of Humanitarian Law in Armed Conflicts*, 3rd edn (Oxford, Oxford University Press, 2014).

Gray, C, *International Law and the Use of Force*, 4th edn (Oxford, Oxford University Press, 2018).

Hallaq, WB, *Sharia: Theory, Practice, Transformations* (Cambridge, Cambridge University Press, 2009).

Hessbruegge, JA, *Human Rights and Personal Self-Defense in International Law* (Oxford, Oxford University Press, 2017).

The Independent International Commission on Kosovo, *The Kosovo Report: Conflict, International Response, Lessons Learned* (Oxford, Oxford University Press, 2000).

Henderson, C, *The Use of Force and International Law* (Cambridge, Cambridge University Press, 2018).

*Keesing's Record of World Events*, vol 36 (August 1990).

Kelsen, H, *Principles of International Law* (New York, Rinehart & Co, 1952).

Kelsen, H, *The Law of the United Nations* (New York, Frederick A Praeger, 1950).

Kelsen, H, *General Theory of Law and State* (trans A Wedberg, New York, Russell & Russell, 1961).

Keynes, JM, *The Economic Consequences of the Peace. Collected Writings of JM Keynes*, vol II (Cambridge, Cambridge University Press, 1971).

Keynes, JM, *The Economic Consequences of the Peace* (reprinted by Freeland Press, 2017).

Khadduri, M, *The Law of War and Peace in Islam* (London, Luzac & Co, 1940).

Kilmuir, Lord, *Political Adventures: The Memoirs of the Earl of Kilmuir* (London, Weidenfeld & Nicolson, 1964).

Kolb, R, *Ius contra bellum. Le droit international relatif au maintien de la paix*, 2nd edn (Basel, Helbing Lichtenhahn/Brussels, Bruylant, 2009).

Kolb, R, *International Law on the Maintenance of Peace: Jus Contra Bellum* (Cheltenham, Edward Elgar, 2019).

Lauterpacht, L (ed), *Oppenheim's International Law: A Treatise, vol II: Disputes, War and Neutrality*, 7th edn (1952).

*Leuven Manual on the International Law Applicable to Peace Operations* (Cambridge, Cambridge University Press, 2017).

Malanczuk, P, *Akehurst's Modern Introduction to International Law*, 7th edn (London, Routledge, 1997).

Moir, L, *The Law of Internal Armed Conflict* (Cambridge, Cambridge University Press, 2002).

Murray, W and Lacey, J, *The Making of Peace: Rulers, States, and the Aftermath of War* (New York, Cambridge University Press, 2009).

Mutalib, H, *Islam in Malaysia: From Revivalism to Islamic State?* (Singapore, NUS Press, 1993).

Numelin, R, *The Beginnings of Diplomacy* (New York, Copenhagen, 1950).

Nystuen, G, Casey-Maslen, S and Golden Bersagel, A (eds), *Nuclear Weapons under International Law* (Cambridge, Cambridge University Press, 2014).

O'Connell, DP, *The Influence of Law on Sea Power* (Manchester, Manchester University Press, 1977).

O'Connell, R, *Of Arms and Men. A History of War, Weapons, and Aggression* (New York, Oxford University Press, 1990).

Oppenheim, L, *International Law: A Treatise, Book II: War and Neutrality* (London, Longmans, 1906).

Oppenheim, L, *International Law. A Treatise*, 2nd edn, vol 1 (London, Longmans, 1912).

Orakhelashvili, A, *Akehurst's Modern Introduction to International Law*, 8th edn (London, Routledge, 2018).

Phillipson, C, *The International Law and Custom of Ancient Greece and Rome*, vols I and II (London, Macmillan and Co, 1911).

Qureshi, WA, *The Use of Force in Islam* (Islamabad, National Book Foundation, 2017).

Roth, BR, *Governmental Illegitimacy in International Law* (Oxford, Oxford University Press, 2000).

Ruys, T, *'Armed Attack' and Article 51 of the UN Charter: Evolutions in Customary Law and Practice* (Cambridge, Cambridge University Press, 2010).

Ruys, T and Corten, O with Hofer, A (eds), *The Use of Force in International Law: A Case-Based Approach* (Oxford, Oxford University Press, 2018).

Sandoz, Y, Swinarski, C and Zimmermann, B (eds), *Commentary on the Additional Protocols of 8 June 1977 to the Geneva Conventions of 12 August 1949* (Geneva, ICRC/Dordrecht, Martinus Nijhoff, 1987).

Schabas, W, *The European Convention on Human Rights: A Commentary* (Oxford, Oxford University Press, 2017).

Schindler, D and Toman, J, *The Laws of Armed Conflicts* (Leiden, Martinus Nijhoff, 1988).

Schmitt, M (ed), *Tallinn Manual on the International Law Applicable to Cyber Warfare* (Cambridge, Cambridge University Press, 2013).

Shaw, MN, *International Law*, 8th edn (Cambridge, Cambridge University Press, 2017).

Simma, B, *The Charter of the United Nations: A Commentary* (Oxford, Oxford University Press, 1994, p. 673).

Simma, B, Khan, D-E, Nolte, G and Paulus, A (eds), *The Charter of the United Nations: A Commentary, vol I, Oxford Commentaries on International Law*, 3rd edn (Oxford, Oxford University Press, 2012).

Stürchler, N, *The Threat of Force in International Law* (Cambridge, Cambridge University Press, 2007).

Taylor, T, *The Anatomy of the Nuremberg Trials* (London, Bloomsbury, 1993).

Temperley, HWV (ed), *A History of the Paris Peace Conference*, vol II (London, Henry Frowde and Hodder & Stoughton, 1920).

Tomuschat, C and Thouvenin, J-M (eds), *The Fundamental Rules of the International Legal Order* (Leiden, Martinus Nijhoff, 2006).

van Bynkershoek, C, *Quaestionum Juris Publici*, vol II (trans T Frank, Oxford, Clarendon Press, 1930).

Van der Molen, GHJ, *Alberico Gentili and the Development of International Law* (Amsterdam, HJ Paris, 1937).

van Steenberghe, R (ed), *Droit international humanitaire: un régime spécial de droit international?* (Brussels, Bruylant, 2013).

von Ramsla, JWN, *Von der Neutralität und Assistenz oder Unpartheyligkeit und Partheyligkeit in Kriegszeiten* (Erfurt, 1620).

Walzer, M, *Just and Unjust Wars*, 2nd edn (London, Basic Books, 1992).

Weller, M, *Iraq and the Use of Force in International Law* (Oxford, Oxford University Press, 2010).

Weller, M (ed), *The Oxford Handbook of the Use of Force in International Law* (Oxford, Oxford University Press, 2015).

Willmot, H, Mamiya, R, Sheeran, S and Weller, M (eds), *Protection of Civilians* (Oxford, Oxford University Press, 2016).

Wrangham, R and Peterson, D, *Demonic Males: Apes and the Origins of Human Violence* (London, Bloomsbury, 1996).

Zuckerman, L, *The Rape of Belgium: The Untold Story of World War I* (New York, New York University Press, 2004).

# Monographs, Articles, Blog Posts, and Chapters in Edited Volumes

Akande, D, 'The International Court of Justice and the Security Council: Is There Room for Judicial Control of Decisions of the Political Organs of the United Nations?' (1997) 46(2) *International and Comparative Law Quarterly* 309.

Ali, SS and Rehman, J, 'The Concept of Jihad in Islamic International Law' (2005) I *Journal of Conflict and Security Law* 321.

Alland, D, 'International Responsibility and Sanctions: Self-Defence and Countermeasures in the ILC Codification of Rules Governing International Responsibility' in M Spinedi and B Simma (eds), *United Nations Codification of State Responsibility* (New York, Oceana Publications, 1987).

Andrews, E, 'Why is Switzerland a Neutral Country?', *History Today*, 12 July 2016, bit.ly/2NItJzF.

Ball, Capt G, '1999 – Operation Allied Force' (Air Force Historical Support Division, 23 August 2012), bit.ly/33B2v0B.

Bannelier-Christakis, K, 'Military Interventions against ISIL in Iraq, Syria and Libya, and the Legal Basis of Consent' (2016) 29(3) *Leiden Journal of International Law* 743.

Benson, J, 'The UN Intervention Brigade: Extinguishing Conflict or Adding Fuel to the Flames?' One Earth Future Discussion Paper (June 2016), bit.ly/37XYGpA.

Bílkov, V, 'The Use of Force by the Russian Federation in Crimea' (2015) 75 *ZaöRV* 27, bit.ly/2rpTcmR.

Blakemore, E, 'Why Kaiser Wilhelm Was Never Tried for Starting World War I', *History*, last updated 8 July 2019, bit.ly/2YG8gZf.

Blokker, N, 'Outsourcing the Use of Force: Towards More Security Council Control of Authorized Operations?' in Weller (ed), *The Oxford Handbook of the Use of Force in International Law* 202–26.

Bothe, M, 'The Law of Neutrality' in Fleck (ed), *The Handbook of Humanitarian Law in Armed Conflicts*, 1999.

Bothe, M, 'The Law of Neutrality' in Fleck (ed), *The Handbook of Humanitarian Law in Armed Conflicts*, 3rd edn, 2014.

Buchan, R, 'Cyber Attacks: Unlawful Uses of Force or Prohibited Interventions?' (2012) 17(2) *Journal of Conflict & Security Law* 211.

Buchwald, TF and Koh, HH, 'The Crime of Aggression: The United States Perspective' (2015) 109 *American Journal of International Law* 272, text available at bit.ly/33HP7aQ.

Buys, E and Garwood-Gowers, A, 'The (Ir)Relevance of Human Suffering: Humanitarian Intervention and Saudi Arabia's Operation Decisive Storm in Yemen' (2019) 24(1) *Journal of Conflict and Security Law* 1.

Byers, M, 'The Intervention in Afghanistan – 2001–' in Ruys et al (eds), *The Use of Force in International Law: A Case-Based Approach* 625–38.

Catechism of the Catholic Church, 1992.

Cavendish, R, 'The Treaty of Westphalia' (1998) 48(10) *History Today*, bit.ly/2POh6Tr.

Cavendish, R, 'The Battle of Copenhagen' (2001) 51(4) *History Today*, bit.ly/30unlNM.

Cengiz, S, 'Why Is the 1998 Adana Pact between Turkey and Syria Back in the News?' *Arab Monitor*, 25 January 2019, bit.ly/2XKbwDf.

Chalmers, M, 'Which Rules? Why There is No Single "Rules-Based International System"', RUSI Occasional Paper (London, Royal United Services Institute for Defence and Security Studies, April 2019), bit.ly/2OeuMWe.

'Combined Joint Task Force Operation Inherent Resolve', Doc APO AE 09306, bit.ly/2OHg2ye.

Cooper, T and Fontanellaz, A, 'In 1977, 80 Mercenaries Nearly Took Over Benin', *War is Boring*, 25 January 2018, bit.ly/2OSGyVg.

Cox, R, 'Expanding the History of the Just War: The Ethics of War in Ancient Egypt' (2017) 61(2) *International Studies Quarterly* 371.

Day, A, 'The Best Defence Is No Offence: Why Cuts to UN Troops in Congo Could Be a Good Thing' (United Nations University, 15 May 2017), bit.ly/33LtFlx.

D'Amato, A, 'Israel's Airstrike upon the Iraqi Nuclear Reactor' (1983) 77(3) *American Journal of International Law* 584, bit.ly/2CIfXFl.

D'Amato, A, 'Israel's Air Strike Against the Osiraq Reactor: A Retrospective', Faculty Working Papers (Chicago, Northwestern University School of Law, 2010), bit.ly/2FGuDW9.

Deeks, A, 'Consent to the Use of Force and International Law Supremacy' (2013) 54(1) *Harvard International Law Journal* 1.

Deeks, A, 'The NATO Intervention in Libya – 2011' in Weller (ed), *The Oxford Handbook of the Use of Force in International Law* 749–59.

de Hoogh, A, 'Jus Cogens and Armed Force' in Weller (ed), *The Oxford Handbook of the Use of Force in International Law* 1161–86.

de Wet, E, 'Regional Organizations and Arrangements: Authorization, Ratification or Independent Action' in Weller (ed), *The Oxford Handbook of the Use of Force in International Law* 314–28.

Doswald-Beck, L, 'The Legal Validity of Military Intervention by Invitation of the Government' (1985) 56(1) *British Yearbook of International Law* 189–252.

Duchhardt, H, 'From the Peace of Westphalia to the Congress of Vienna' in B Fassbender and A Peters (eds), *The Oxford Handbook of the History of international Law* (Oxford, Oxford University Press, 2014) ch 26.

Farrant, JD, 'Modern Maritime Neutrality Law', thesis (Durham University, 2015), bit.ly/2K6HRi1.

Fabricius, P, 'Is the Force Intervention Brigade Still Justifying Its Existence?' (Institute for Strategic Studies, 22 June 2017), bit.ly/2RgGS3g.

Fine, HA, 'The Liquidation of World War II in Thailand' (1965) 34(1) *Pacific Historical Review* 65.

Fortin, K, 'Unilateral Declaration by Polisario under API Accepted by Swiss Federal Council', 2 September 2015, bit.ly/2NcA0lb.

Franchini, D and Tzanakopoulos, A, 'The Kosovo Crisis – 1999' in Weller (ed), *The Oxford Handbook of the Use of Force in International Law* 594–622.

Franck, T, 'Who Killed Article 2(4)? or: Changing Norms Governing the Use of Force by States' (1970) 64(5) *American Journal of International Law* 809.

Franck, T, 'What Happens Now? The United Nations After Iraq' (2003) 97(3) *American Journal of International Law* 607.

Freedman, L, 'The Falklands War Explained', *History Extra*, text originally published in 2007, bit.ly/2SzLQqf.

Frostad, M, 'The Kellogg–Briand Pact – Nearing the 90th Anniversary for the Outlawing of War' (Kellogg College Oxford, 3 July 2017), bit.ly/2DbrRbM.

German Ministry of Defence, *Law of Armed Conflict Manual*, Joint Service Regulation (ZDv) 15/2 (Berlin, 2013).

Green, JA, 'Questioning the Peremptory Status of the Prohibition of the Use of Force' (2011) 32 *Michigan Journal of International Law* 215.

Green, JA, 'The Oil Platforms Case: An Error in Judgment?' (2004) 9(3) *Journal of Conflict and Security Law* 357.

Green, JA and Waters, CPM, 'Military Targeting in the Context of Self-defence Actions' (2015) 84(1) *Nordic Journal of International Law* 3.

Griffiths, DM, 'An American Contribution to the Armed Neutrality of 1780' (1971) 30(2) *Russian Review* 164.

Haines, S 'The influence of Operation Allied Force on the development of the *jus ad bellum*', (May 2009) 85(3), *International Affairs*, 477.

Hammond, JR, 'Newly Disclosed Documents Shed More Light on Early Taliban Offers, Pakistan Role', *Foreign Policy Journal*, 20 September 2010, bit.ly/2YaDt5v.

Harris, E, 'Pain but Not Harm: Some Classical Resources toward a Hindu Just War Theory' in P Robinson (ed), *Just War in Comparative Perspective* (London, Routledge, 2016).

Hashmi, SH, 'War and Peace' in R Peters and P Bearman (eds), *Ashgate Research Companion to Islamic Law* (London, Routledge, 2014).

Hayashi, N, 'Using Force by Means of Nuclear Weapons and Requirements of Necessity and Proportionality *ad Bellum*' in Nystuen et al (eds), *Nuclear Weapons under International Law*, ch 1.

Hayashi, N, 'Legality under jus ad bellum of the threat of use of nuclear weapons' in Nystuen et al (eds), *Nuclear Weapons under International Law*, ch 2.

Heathcote, G, 'Feminist Perspectives on the Law on the Use of Force' in M Weller (ed), *The Oxford Handbook of the Use of Force in International Law* 114–28.

Heindel, RH, Kalijarvi, TV and Wilcox, FO, 'The North Atlantic Treaty in the United States Senate' (1949) 43(4) *American Journal of International Law* 633.

Heintschel von Heinegg, W, 'Maritime Warfare' in Clapham and Gaeta (eds), *The Oxford Handbook of International Law in Armed Conflict* 145–81.

Hofer, A, 'The Suez Crisis – 1956' in Ruys and Corten with Hofer (eds), *The Use of Force in International Law: A Case-Based Approach* 36–47.

Holzgrefe, JL, 'The Humanitarian Intervention Debate' in R Keohane and J Holzgrefe (eds), *Humanitarian Intervention* (Cambridge, Cambridge University Press, 2003).

Institute of Physics, 'A Brief History of Space', undated, bit.ly/2Rbsdmk.

Jorgensen, M, 'International Law Cannot Save the Rules-Based Order', *The Interpreter*, 18 December 2018, bit.ly/2OGm2HD.

Keck, Z, 'India's Nuclear Blunder', *The National Interest*, 26 August 2013, bit.ly/2WAyl5m.

Kenny, C, 'Alberico Gentili, De Jure Belli Libri Tres (1588–1599)', *Classics of Strategy and Diplomacy*, 7 July 2015, bit.ly/2L91CaR.

Kenny, C, 'Hugo Grotius, The Law of War and Peace (1625)', *Classics of Strategy and Diplomacy*, 27 July 2015, bit.ly/2Pm2rPQ.

Klabbers, J, 'Intervention, Armed Intervention, Armed Attack, Threat to Peace, Act of Aggression, and Threat or Use of Force – What's the Difference?' in Weller (ed), *The Oxford Handbook of the Use of Force in International Law* 488–506.

Koplow, DA, 'Nuclear Kellogg–Briand Pact: Proposing a Treaty for the Renunciation of Nuclear Wars as an Instrument of National Policy' (2014–15) 42 *Syracuse Journal of International Law and Commerce* 123.

Kreß, C, 'A Collective Failure to Prevent Turkey's Operation "Peace Spring" and NATO's Silence on International Law', *EJIL: Talk!*, 14 October 2019, bit.ly/35D1LJx.

Kristensen, HM and Norris, RS, 'Worldwide Deployments of Nuclear Weapons, 2017' (2017) 73(5) *Bulletin of the Atomic Scientists*, bit.ly/2GbCwUA.

Kritsiotis, D, 'The Legality of the 1993 US Missile Strike on Iraq and the Right of Self-Defence in International Law' (1996) 45(1) *International and Comparative Law Quarterly* 162.

Kritsiotis, D, 'Close Encounters of a Sovereign Kind' (2009) 20(2) *European Journal of International Law* 299.

Lagerwall, A, 'Threats of and Actual Military Strikes against Syria – 2013 and 2017' in Ruys et al (eds), *The Use of Force in International Law: A Case-Based Approach* 828–54.

Lang, A, 'Legal Basis for UK Military Action in Syria', Briefing Paper No 7404 (London, House of Commons Library, 1 December 2015).

Latty, F, 'Founding "Fathers" of International Law: Recognizing Christine de Pizan', *EJIL: Talk!*, Blog post, 15 January 2019, bit.ly/3a8hH9h.

Leone, D, 'The True History of Israel's Operation Wooden Leg and the Longest-Range F-15 BAZ Strike Ever Made', *The National Interest*, 9 July 2019, bit.ly/2K6UxFw.

Lesaffer, R, 'Kellogg-Briand Pact (1928)', *Max Planck Encyclopedia of Public International Law* (last updated October 2010), bit.ly/2YrjnEX.

Lesaffer, R, 'From War as Sanction to the Sanction of War' in Weller (ed), *The Oxford Handbook of the Use of Force in International Law* 35–55.

McNair, AD, 'The Legal Meaning of War, and the Relation of War to Reprisals' (1925) 11 *Transactions of the Grotius Society* 29.

Mancini, M, 'The Effects of a State of War or Armed Conflict' in M Weller (ed), *The Oxford Handbook of the Use of Force in International Law* 988–1013.

Mark, JJ, 'War: Definition', *Ancient History Encyclopedia*, 2 September 2009, bit.ly/2qzIPsM.

Marston, G, 'Armed Intervention in the 1956 Suez Canal Crisis: The Legal Advice Tendered to the British Government' (1998) 37(4) *International and Comparative Law Quarterly* 773.

Masters, J, 'Russia, Trump, and the 2016 US Election', Council on Foreign Relations, United States (last updated 26 February 2018), on.cfr.org/2M1xOws.

Meron, T, 'Common Rights of Mankind in Gentili, Grotius and Suarez' (1991) 85 *American Journal of International Law* 110.

Milanovic M, 'Does the European Court of Human Rights Have to Decide on Sovereignty over Crimea? Part I: Jurisdiction in Article 1 ECHR', *EJIL: Talk!*, 23 September 2019, bit.ly/2NWDkAN.

Milanovic, M, 'Does the European Court of Human Rights Have to Decide on Sovereignty over Crimea? Part II: Issues Lurking on the Merits', *EJIL: Talk!*, 24 September 2019, bit.ly/33XYc0p.

Mills, C, 'Operation Peace Spring: A Timeline', *Geopolitical Monitor*, 18 October 2019, bit.ly/2KUyRgl.

Murphy, R, 'UN Peacekeeping in the Democratic Republic of the Congo and the Protection of Civilians' (2016) 21(2) *Journal of Conflict and Security Law* 209.

Murphy, SD, 'The Eritrean-Ethiopian War (1998–2000)' (Washington DC, George Washington University Law School, 2016), bit.ly/2KPyqUu.

Murphy, SD, 'The Crime of Aggression at the International Criminal Court' in Weller (ed), *The Oxford Handbook of the Use of Force in International Law* 533–60.

NATO, 'Kosovo Air Campaign (Archived): Operation Allied Force' (last updated 7 April 2016), bit.ly/2UcugNh.

Office of the Director of National Intelligence, 'Background to "Assessing Russian Activities and Intentions in Recent US Elections": The Analytic Process and Cyber Incident Attribution' (Washington DC, 6 January 2017), bit.ly/2Lx1SAm.

Office of the Historian, United States Department of State, 'The Suez Crisis, 1956', Milestones in the History of US Foreign Relations, US Department of State, bit.ly/2NOdNMq.

Office of the Historian, 'The Kellogg–Briand Pact, 1928', Milestones in the History of US Foreign Relations, US Department of State, bit.ly/2DuSIAr.

Office of the Historian, 'U-2 Overflights and the Capture of Francis Gary Powers, 1960', Milestones in the History of US Foreign Relations, US Department of State, bit.ly/2LVj4PA.

Orakhelashvili, A, 'The High Court and the Crime of Aggression' (2018) 5(1) *Journal on the Use of Force and International Law* 3, bit.ly/33YviNt.

Oswald, B, 'Soldier Self-Defense Symposium: The Evolution of the UN Doctrine of Self-Defence in UN Peacekeeping', *Opinio Juris*, 1 May 2019, bit.ly/2pxfnGG.

Pfeil, J, 'Naulilaa Arbitration (Portugal v Germany)', *Max Planck Encyclopedia of Public International Law* (last updated March 2007), bit.ly/2LdWlid.

Plaut, M, 'The Conflict and Its Aftermath' in D Jacquin-Berdal and M Plaut (eds), *Unfinished Business: Ethiopia and Eritrea at War* (Trenton, NJ, Red Sea Press, 2004).

Quigley, J, 'The United States Invasion of Grenada: Stranger than Fiction' (1986–87) 18(2) *University of Miami Inter-American Law Review* 271.

Palchetti, P, 'Consequences for Third States as a Result of an Unlawful Use of Force' in Weller (ed), *The Oxford Handbook of the Use of Force in International Law* 1224–38.

Peters, A, 'Treaty-Making Power' in R Wolfrum (ed), *Max Planck Encyclopedia of Public International Law* (Oxford, Oxford University Press, 2009).

Randelzhofer, A and Dörr, O, 'Article 2(4)' in Simma et al (eds), *The Charter of the United Nations: A Commentary*, 3rd edn, vol I.

Randelzhofer, A, 'Article 42' in Simma (ed), *The Charter of the United Nations: A Commentary*, vol I, 2002.

Randelzhofer, A, 'Article 51' in B Simma (ed), *The Charter of the United Nations: A Commentary*, vol I, 2002.

Reisman, WM, 'Sovereignty and Human Rights in Contemporary International Law' (1990) 84 *American Journal of International Law* 871.

Richmond, AA, 'Napoleon and the Armed Neutrality of 1800: A Diplomatic Challenge to British Sea Power' (1959) 104(614) *Royal United Services Institution Journal*.

Rodley, N, 'Humanitarian Intervention' in Weller (ed), *The Oxford Handbook of the Use of Force in International Law* 775–96.

Roscini, M, 'Cyber Operations as a Use of Force' in N Tsagourias and R Buchan (eds), *Research Handbook on International Law and Cyberspace* (Cheltenham, Edward Elgar, 2015) 233–54.

Ruys, T, 'The Meaning of "Force" and the Boundaries of the Jus ad Bellum: Are "Minimal" Uses of Force Excluded from UN Charter Article 2(4)?' (2014) 108(2) *American Journal of International Law* 159.

'St Thomas Aquinas Discusses the Three Conditions for a Just War (1265–74)', *The Portable Library of Liberty*, 2013, bit.ly/2PSWvNO.

Sadurska, R, 'Threats of Force' (1988) 82(2) *American Journal of International Law* 239.

'Salisbury Incident', Statement by the Prime Minister (Mrs Theresa May), in *Hansard* HC Vol 637 (14 March 2018), bit.ly/2Q8Ol1L.

Schachter, O, 'The Legality of Pro-democratic Invasion' (1984) 78(3) *American Journal of International Law* 645.

Schrijver, N, 'The Ban on the Use of Force in the UN Charter' in M Weller (ed), *The Oxford Handbook of the Use of Force in International Law* 465–87.

Schwebel, SM, 'Aggression, Intervention and Self-Defence in Modern International Law' (1972 – II) 136 *Hague Recueil des Cours*.

Seger, P, 'The Law of Neutrality' in Clapham and Gaeta (eds), *The Oxford Handbook of International Law in Armed Conflict* 248–70.

Shabaneh, G, 'Operation Decisive Storm: Objectives and Hurdles', Report (Al Jazeera Centre for Studies, 12 April 2015), bit.ly/37umCk6.

Sheeran, S, 'The Use of Force in United Nations Peacekeeping Operations' in Weller (ed), *The Oxford Handbook of the Use of Force in International Law* 347–74.

Sherman, GE, 'The Neutrality of Switzerland' (1918) 12(2) *American Journal of International Law* 241.

Sivakumaran, S, 'Binding Armed Opposition Groups' (2006) 55 *International and Comparative Law Quarterly* 369.

Statement of President George W Bush, National Security Strategy of the United States of America, Washington DC, September 2002, bit.ly/2Xrp9p6.

Sweet, R, 'Militarizing the Peace: UN Intervention Against Congo's "Terrorist" Rebels', *Lawfare*, 2 June 2019, bit.ly/2YgoF7o.

Swiss Federal Department of Foreign Affairs, 'Report of the Working Group to Analyse the Treaty on the Prohibition of Nuclear Weapons', English translation from the German original version, 30 June 2018, bit.ly/2RRxUWZ.

Steinberg, JW, 'Was the Russo-Japanese War World War Zero?' (2008) 67(1) *The Russian Review*.

Taft, WH, IV, 'Self-defense and the Oil Platforms Decision' (2004) 29 *Yale Journal of International Law* 295, bit.ly/2YkzO9o.

Talmon, SAG, 'At Last! Germany Admits Illegality of the Kosovo Intervention' (2014) 57 *German Yearbook of International Law*.

Tams, CJ, 'The Use of Force against Terrorists' (2009) 20(2) *European Journal of International Law* 359.

Tirpak, JA, 'Deliberate Force', *Air Force Magazine*, October 1997, bit.ly/2ORgCti.

Torelli, M, 'La neutralité en question' (1992) 96 *Revue générale de droit international public* 5.

Trahan, J, 'Defining the "Grey Area" Where Humanitarian Intervention May Not Be Fully Legal, but Is Not the Crime of Aggression' (2015) 2(1) *Journal on the Use of Force and International Law* 42–80.

Trahan, J, 'Activation of the International Criminal Court's Jurisdiction Over the Crime of Aggression & Challenges Ahead', *Opinio Juris*, 18 July 2018, bit.ly/2DD6Ju3.

Trapp, K, 'Can Non-state Actors Mount an Armed Attack?' in Weller (ed), *The Oxford Handbook of the Use of Force in International Law* 679–96.

Tunkin, G, 'Is General International Law Customary Law Only?' [1993] *European Journal of International Law* 534.

Turkish Ministry of Foreign Affairs, 'Minutes of the Agreement Signed by Turkey and Syria in Adana (Unofficial Translation)–20 October 1999', bit.ly/37ye2kl.

UK Ministry of Defence, *Joint Service Manual of the Law of Armed Conflict*, Joint Service Publication 383 (2004).

'UK Materials on International Law' (1986) 57 *British Yearbook of International Law* 614.

UK Prime Minister's Office, 'Syria Action – UK Government Legal Position', Policy Paper (10 Downing Street, 14 April 2018), bit.ly/2LT7owG.

US Department of Defense, *Law of War Manual* (Washington DC, June 2015, updated December 2016).

US Naval War College, *International Law Situations and Documents, 1956* (Washington DC, US Government Printing Office, 1957).

US Senate, Report of the Committee on Foreign Relations on the North Atlantic Treaty, Executive Report No 8.

Van Hooydonk, E, 'Places of Refuge: The Belgian Experience' in AE Chircop and O Lindén (eds), *Places of Refuge for Ships: Emerging Environmental Concerns of a Maritime Custom*, Publications on Ocean Development, vol 51 (Leiden, Martinus Nijhoff, 2006) ch 15.

Villani, U, 'The ECOWAS Intervention in Liberia – 1990–97', in Ruys et al (eds), *The Use of Force in International Law: A Case-Based Approach* 442–55.

Vermeer, Z, 'Intervention with the Consent of a Deposed (but Legitimate) Government? Playing the Sierra Leone Card', *EJIL Talk!*, 6 March 2014, bit.ly/35Dt0Ea.

Walker, PB, 'What is Innocent Passage?' (1980) 22(1) *Naval War College Review* 53.

White, N, 'The Relationship between the UN Security Council and General Assembly in Matters of International Peace and Security' in Weller (ed), *The Oxford Handbook of the Use of Force in International Law* 293–313.

Whiting, A, 'Crime of Aggression Activated at the ICC: Does it Matter?', *Just Security*, 19 December 2017, bit.ly/2RbQU5n.

XVII Ministerial Conference of the Non-Aligned Movement, Algiers, 26–29 May 2014, Final Document.

Ziegler, KS, 'Domaine Réservé', *Max Planck Encyclopedia of Public International Law* (last updated April 2013), bit.ly/32ssUhx.

Zollmann, J, 'History as a Legal Argument – The Naulilaa Case (1928)' (Berlin, WZB Center for Global Constitutionalism, October 2016), bit.ly/2S78dTI.

# Permanent Court of Arbitration

Award delivered on 24 February 1911 by the Arbitral Tribunal Appointed to Decide the 'Case of Savarkar', bit.ly/30BsYtP.

'Arrest and Return of Savarkar (France/Great Britain)', undated but accessed 1 July 2019 at: bit.ly/2LlCnBY.

*Responsabilité de l'Allemagne à raison des dommages causés dans les colonies portugaises du sud de l'Afrique (sentence sur le principe de la responsabilité) (Portugal c. Allemagne)*, Reports of International Arbitral Awards, 31 July 1928, vol II, 1011–33, bit.ly/2XB7Xxn.

# Permanent Court of International Justice

## Contentious Cases

*SS Lotus (France v Turkey)*, Judgment, 7 September 1927.

## Advisory Opinions

*Status of the Eastern Carelia*, Advisory Opinion No 5, 23 July 1923.

# United Nations Documents and Materials

## Human Rights Committee

### Concluding Observations

Concluding Observations on the Fourth Periodic Report of the United States of America, UN doc CCPR/C/USA/CO/4, 23 April 2014.

### General Comments

General Comment No 6 (1982).

General Comment No 14 (1984).

'General Comment No 36 (2018) on Article 6 of the International Covenant on Civil and Political Rights, on the Right to Life', UN doc CCPR/C/GC/36, 30 October 2018.

# International Court of Justice

## Contentious Cases

*Corfu Channel case (United Kingdom v Albania)*, Judgment, 9 April 1949.

*Nuclear Tests Case (New Zealand v France)*, Judgment, 20 December 1974.

*Case Concerning United States Diplomatic and Consular Staff in Tehran (United States v Iran)*, Judgment, 24 May 1980.

*Case Concerning Military and Paramilitary Activities in and against Nicaragua (Nicaragua v United States of America)*, Judgment (Merits), 27 June 1986.

*Questions of Interpretation and Application of the 1971 Montreal Convention arising from the Aerial Incident at Lockerbie (Libyan Arab Jamahiriya v United Kingdom)*, Order (Request for the Indication of Provisional Measures), 14 April 1992.

*Questions of Interpretation and Application of the 1971 Montreal Convention arising from the Aerial Incident at Lockerbie (Libyan Arab Jamahiriya v United Kingdom)*, Memorial by the Libyan Arab Jamahiriya, 20 December 1993.

*Case Concerning Application of the Convention on the Prevention and Punishment of the Crime of Genocide (Bosnia and Herzegovina v Yugoslavia (Serbia and Montenegro))*, Application Proceedings Submitted by the Republic of Bosnia and Herzegovina, 20 March 1993.

*Case Concerning Application of the Convention on the Prevention and Punishment of the Crime of Genocide (Bosnia and Herzegovina v Yugoslavia (Serbia and Montenegro))*, Order (Further Requests for the Indication of Provisional Measures), 13 September 1993.

*Case Concerning East Timor (Portugal v Australia)*, Judgment, 30 June 1995.

*Case Concerning the Gabčikovo-Nagymaros Project (Hungary v Slovakia)*, Judgment, 25 September 1997.

*Fisheries Jurisdiction case (Spain v Canada)*, Judgment (Jurisdiction of the Court), 4 December 1998.

*Case Concerning Legality of Use of Force (Yugoslavia v Belgium)*, Request for the indication of provisional measures, 1999.

*Case Concerning the Land and Maritime Boundary Between Cameroon and Nigeria (Cameroon v Nigeria, Equatorial Guinea intervening)*, Judgment, 10 October 2002.

*Case Concerning Oil Platforms (Islamic Republic of Iran v United States of America)*, Judgment, 6 November 2003.

*Case Concerning Armed Activities on the Territory of the Congo (Democratic Republic of the Congo v Uganda)*, Judgment, 19 December 2005.

*Case Concerning Armed Activities on the Territory of the Congo (Democratic Republic of the Congo v Rwanda)*, Judgment, 19 December 2005.

## Advisory Opinions

*Reparation for Injuries for Injuries Suffered in the Service of the United Nations*, Advisory Opinion, 11 April 1949.

*Certain Expenses of the United Nations (Article 17, Paragraph 2, of the Charter)*, Advisory Opinion, 20 July 1962.

*Western Sahara*, Advisory Opinion, 16 October 1975.

*Interpretation of the Agreement of 25 March 1951 Between the WHO and Egypt*, Advisory Opinion, 20 December 1980.

*Legal Consequences of the Construction of a Wall in the Occupied Palestinian Territory*, Advisory Opinion, 9 July 2004.

*Accordance with International Law of the Unilateral Declaration of Independence in Respect of Kosovo*, Advisory Opinion, 22 July 2010.

# General Assembly Decisions and Documents

## Resolutions

Resolution 2625 (XXV) ('Declaration on Principles of International Law concerning Friendly Relations and Co-operation among States in accordance with the Charter of the United Nations') (1970).

Resolution 290 (IV) ('Essentials of Peace') (1949).

Resolution 380 (V) ('Peace through Deeds') (1950).

Resolution 377A ('Uniting for Peace') (1950).

Resolution 998 (ES – 1) (1956).

Resolution 1514 (XV) ('Declaration on the Granting of Independence to Colonial Countries and Peoples') (1960).

Resolution 3070 (XXVIII) ('Importance of the universal realization of the right of peoples to self-determination and of the speedy granting of independence to colonial countries and peoples for the effective guarantee and observance of human rights') (1973).

Resolution 34/47 (1979).

Resolution 38/7 (1983).

Resolution 45/166 (1990).

Resolution 50/80A (1995).

Resolution 60/1 ('2005 World Summit Outcome') (2005).

Resolution 67/1 ('Declaration of the High-level Meeting of the General Assembly on the Rule of Law at the National and International Levels') (2012).

Resolution 66/253B (2012).

Resolution 68/262 ('Territorial Integrity of Ukraine') (2014).

## Press Releases

'General Assembly Adopts Resolution Calling upon States Not to Recognize Changes in Status of Crimea Region', Information Note, UN doc GA/11493, 27 March 2014, bit.ly/2OExDq5.

General Assembly Special Committee on Decolonization, 'Ensuring Non-Self-Governing Territories Can Address Challenges Key to Moving Decolonization Efforts Forward, Secretary-General Tells Regional Seminar', UN doc GA/COL/3320, 10 May 2018, bit.ly/2DsZqFm.

## Reports of the Secretary-General

'Report of the Secretary-General Pursuant to General Assembly Resolution 53/35: The Fall of Srebrenica', UN doc A/54/549, 15 November 1999.

# International Law Commission Documents

'Second Report on a Draft Code of Offences Against the Peace and Security of Mankind by Mr. J Spiropoulos, Special Rapporteur', ILC, UN doc A/CN4/44, 12 April 1951.

Draft Code of Offences against the Peace and Security of Mankind, Text adopted by the ILC at its sixth session in 1954 and submitted to the UN General Assembly.

Draft Code of Crimes against the Peace and Security of Mankind, Text adopted by the ILC at its forty-eighth session in 1996 and submitted to the UN General Assembly.

Ago, R, ILC Special Rapporteur, 'Addendum to the Eighth Report on State Responsibility' (1980) II(1) *United Nations Yearbook of the International Law Commission*.

*Draft Articles on Responsibility of States for Internationally Wrongful Acts, with commentaries*, UN doc A/56/10 (New York, 2001).

Draft Articles on Responsibility of International Organizations, in Report of the International Law Commission, Sixty-third session (26 April–3 June and 4 July–12 August 2011), UN doc A/66/10/Add.1, New York, 2011.

'First Report on *Jus Cogens* by Dire Tladi, Special Rapporteur', UN doc A/CN4/693, 8 March 2016.

'Third Report on Peremptory Norms of General International Law (*Jus Cogens*) by Dire Tladi, Special Rapporteur', International Law Commission, UN doc A/CN4/714, 12 February 2018.

'Fourth Report on Peremptory Norms of General International Law (*Jus Cogens*) by Dire Tladi, Special Rapporteur', UN doc A/CN4/727, 31 January 2019.

'Peremptory Norms of General International Law (*Jus Cogens*). Text of the draft Conclusions and Draft Annex Provisionally Adopted by the Drafting Committee on First Reading', UN doc A/CN4/L936, 29 May 2019.

# Permanent Court of Arbitration

Arbitral Tribunal Constituted Pursuant to Article 287, and in Accordance with Annex VII, of the United Nations Convention on the Law of the Sea in the Matter of an Arbitration Between Guyana and Suriname, Award of the Arbitral Tribunal, The Hague, 17 September 2007.

# Security Council Decisions and Documents

## *Resolutions*

Resolution 82 (1950).
Resolution 143 (1960).
Resolution 161 (1960).
Resolution 169 (1961).
Resolution 218 (1965).
Resolution 405 (1977).
Resolution 418 (1977).
Resolution 419 (1977).
Resolution 487 (1981).
Resolution 502 (1982).
Resolution 569 (1985).
Resolution 573 (1985).
Resolution 611 (1988).
Resolution 660 (1990).
Resolution 665 (1990).
Resolution 678 (1990).
Resolution 687 (1991).

Resolution 692 (1991).
Resolution 836 (1993).
Resolution 876 (1993).
Resolution 940 (1994).
Resolution 1187 (1998).
Resolution 1203 (1998).
Resolution 1265 (1999).
Resolution 1270 (1999).
Resolution 1333 (2000).
Resolution 1368 (2001).
Resolution 1373 (2001).
Resolution 1540 (2004).
Resolution 1631 (2005).
Resolution 1973 (2011).
Resolution 1975 (2011).
Resolution 2098 (2013).
Resolution 2216 (2015).
Resolution 2249 (2015).
Resolution 2401 (2018).


## Letters, Reports, and Statements

Letter to the President of the UN Security Council from John D Negroponte, US Permanent Representative to the United Nations in New York, UN doc S/2001/946, 7 October 2001.
'Identical Letters dated 26 March 2015 from the Permanent Representative of Qatar to the United Nations addressed to the Secretary-General and the President of the Security Council', UN doc S/2015/217, 27 March 2015.
'Identical Letters dated 17 September 2015 from the Permanent Representative of the Syrian Arab Republic to the United Nations addressed to the Secretary-General and the President of the Security Council', UN doc S/2015/719, 21 September 2015, bit.ly/34lNPUb.
Letter dated 9 October 2019 from the Permanent Representative of Turkey to the United Nations addressed to the President of the Security Council, UN doc S/2019/804, 9 October 2019, bit.ly/37yrvc9.
Report of the Security Council Special Mission to the People's Republic of Benin Established under Resolution 404 (1977), UN doc S/12294/Add.1, 8 March 1977.
Statement of Vitaly Churkin before the UN Security Council, UN doc S/PV.7125, 3 March 2014.
Statement of Stephanie Power before the UN Security Council, UN doc S/PV.7125, 3 March 2014.
Statement of Sir Mark Lyall Grant before the UN Security Council, UN doc S/PV.7125, 3 March 2014.
Statement of the President of the UN Security Council, UN doc S/PV.3225, 28 May 1993.


## Press Releases

'Belarus, India and Russian Federation: draft resolution', UN doc S/1999/328, 26 March 1999, bit.ly/2Ygkqqw.
'"Intervention Brigade" Authorized as Security Council Grants Mandate Renewal for United Nations Mission in Democratic Republic of Congo', UN doc SC/10964, 28 March 2013, bit.ly/2r8WZ8b.
'Security Council Rejects Demand for Cessation of Use of Force against Federal Republic of Yugoslavia', Press Release, 26 March 1999, bit.ly/2JYh0no.

# United Nations Claims Commission

UNCC Home Page, https://uncc.ch/.
UNCC, 'Recommendations Made By the Panel of Commissioners Concerning Individual Claims for Serious Personal Injury or Death (Category "B" Claims)', UN doc S/AC26/1994/1, 26 May 1994.


# Other UN Documents

'A More Secure World: Our Shared Responsibility', Report of the High-level Panel on Threats, Challenges and Change, UN doc A759/565, 2 December 2004.
Department of Peace Operations, *The Protection of Civilians in United Nations Peacekeeping*, DOP Policy doc 2019.17, 1 November 2019.
*Capstone Doctrine*, United Nations Peacekeeping Operations Principles and Guidelines, UN, New York, 2008, bit.ly/2P709kQ.
*Report of the Panel on United Nations Peace Operations*, UN doc A/55/305 and S/2000/809, 2000.
*The Minnesota Protocol on the Investigation of Potentially Unlawful Death (2016)*, Office of the UN High Commissioner for Human Rights, New York/Geneva, 2017.
'Protection of Civilians Mandate', undated, bit.ly/2Bqhdf2.
'Principles of Peacekeeping', undated, bit.ly/2VTa7t6.
'Summary Study of the Experience Derived from the Establishment and Operation of the Force: Report of the Secretary-General', UN doc A/3943, 9 October 1958, para. 70, bit.ly/2MYvlBT


# African Commission on Human and Peoples' Rights

## General Comments

General Comment No 3 on the African Charter on Human and Peoples' Rights: The Right to Life (Article 4); adopted during the 57th Ordinary Session of the African Commission on Human and Peoples' Rights, held from 4 to 18 November 2015 in Banjul, The Gambia.


# African Union

'African Union decision on the peaceful resolution of the Libyan crisis', Extraordinary Session of the Assembly of the Union, Addis Ababa, 25 May 2011.
Communiqué of the 883rd meeting of the African Union PSC at the Ministerial Level, held on 27 September 2019, on the Situation in Libya (last updated 4 October 2019), bit.ly/35LXSSI.


# Court of Justice of the European Union

Case C-104/16 P, Judgment (Grand Chamber), 21 December 2016.
*R (on the application of Western Sahara Campaign UK) v HMRC and DEFRA*, Opinion of Advocate-General Wathelet, 10 January 2018.

# Eritrea-Ethiopia Claims Commission

*Partial Award: Jus Ad Bellum – Ethiopia's Claims 1–8*, 19 December 2005.

# European Court of Human Rights

*Loizidou v Turkey*, Judgment (Preliminary Objections) (Grand Chamber), 23 March 1995.
*Loizidou v Turkey*, Judgment (Merits) (Grand Chamber), 18 December 1996.
*Cyprus v Turkey*, Judgment (Grand Chamber), 10 May 2001.
App No 38263/08 *Georgia v Russia (II)* (Grand Chamber hearing), 30 May 2018.
App No 20958/14 *Ukraine v Russia* (Grand Chamber hearing), 11 September 2019.

# Independent International Fact-Finding Mission on the Conflict in Georgia

Independent International Fact-Finding Mission on the Conflict in Georgia, Report, Vol II, September 2009.

# International Criminal Tribunal for the Former Yugoslavia (ICTY)

Case No IT-94-1 *Prosecutor v Tadić (aka 'Dule')*, Decision on the Defence Motion for Interlocutory Appeal on Jurisdiction (Appeals Chamber), 2 October 1995.
Case No IT-95-17/1-T *Prosecutor v Anto Furundžija*, Judgment, 10 December 1998.
Case No IT-94-1-A *Prosecutor v Duško Tadić*, Judgment (Appeals Chamber), 15 July 1999.
*Final Report to the Prosecutor by the Committee Established to Review the NATO Bombing Campaign Against the Federal Republic of Yugoslavia*, 13 June 2000.

# International Committee of the Red Cross (ICRC)

'Jus ad Bellum and Jus in Bello' (29 October 2010), bit.ly/2NxAB0u.
Commentary on 1949 Geneva Convention I, 2016.
'Final Act of the International Peace Conference. The Hague, 29 July 1899' (Geneva, ICRC, 2016), bit.ly/2Fa2ycF.
Increasing Respect for International Humanitarian Law in Non-International Armed Conflicts', Geneva, February 2008.

# Customary Study of International Humanitarian Law

Rule 5 ('Definition of Civilians').
Rule 8 ('Definition of Military Objectives').
Rule 14 ('Proportionality in Attack').

# International Military Tribunal

*Trial of the Major War Criminals before the International Military Tribunal*, Vol I, Nuremberg, 1947.
International Military Tribunal for the Far East; Charter dated 19 January 1946, bit.ly/2SbfWAa.

# Special Court for Sierra Leone (SCSL)

Case Nos SCSL-2004-15-AR72(E) and SCSL-2004-16-AR72(E) *Prosecutor v Morris Kallon and Brima Buzzy Kamara*, Decision on Challenge to Jurisdiction: Lomé Accord Amnesty (Appeals Chamber), 13 March 2004.
Case No SCSL-2004-14-AR72(E) *Prosecutor v Sam Hinga Norman*, Decision on Preliminary Motion Based on Lack of Jurisdiction (Appeals Chamber), 31 May 2004.
Case No SCSL-04-15-T *Prosecutor v Issa Hassan Sesay, Morris Kallon, and Augustine Gbao*, Judgment (Trial Chamber), 2 March 2009.

# National Jurisprudence

## United Kingdom

*R v Jones (Margaret)* [2007] 1 AC 136.
*R (on the application of Al Rabbat) v Westminster Magistrates' Court (HM Attorney General intervening)* [2017] EWHC 1969 (Admin).
UK House of Lords, *R v Jones and others* [2006] UKHL 16.

# Media Articles and Press Releases

'G20 Leaders' Declaration: Building Consensus for Fair and Sustainable Development', Buenos Aires, 1 December 2018, bit.ly/37uUz3X.
'Enemy Tactics at Versailles', *The Times*, 10 May 1919, bit.ly/2JhahH1.
Associated Press, 'North Korea Threatens to Reduce US and South Korea to "Flames and Ash"', *The Guardian*, 7 March 2016, bit.ly/2FNlzi6.
Baker, P and Sang-Hun, C, 'Trump Threatens "Fire and Fury" against North Korea if It Endangers US', *New York Times*, 8 August 2017, bit.ly/2Ew8ooq.
BBC, 'Flashback to Kosovo's War', 10 July 2006, bbc.in/360MIdd.
BBC, 'Crimea Referendum: Voters "Back Russia Union"', 16 March 2014, bbc.in/33m9fPR.
BBC, 'Crimea Profile', 17 January 2018, bbc.in/2DfPmz4.
BBC, 'Western Sahara Profile', 14 May 2018, bbc.in/2NcxpYA.

BBC, 'Syrian President Bashar al-Assad: Facing Down Rebellion', 3 September 2018, bbc.in/34htIGG.

BBC, 'DR Congo Protests: UN to Open Investigation into Demonstrator's Death', 27 November 2019, bbc.in/35VEJhl.

BBC, 'Indian and Chinese troops "clash on border" in Sikkim', 10 May 2020, bbc.in/3g45w0L.

Bowcott, O and Borger, J, 'Ratko Mladić Convicted of War Crimes and Genocide at UN Tribunal', *The Guardian*, 22 November 2017, bit.ly/2Kjrn7E.

Chapple, A, 'Operation Allied Force: The NATO Bombing of Yugoslavia', *Radio Free Europe*, 24 March 2019, bit.ly/2r5FMMX.

Dudik, A and Kuzmanovic, J, 'Kosovo Targets Deal with Serbia This Year to Boost EU Hopes', *Bloomberg*, 16 February 2019, bloom.bg/2OGWGsB.

Ensor, J, Sawer, P and Vahdat, A, 'British Warship Was an Hour from Tanker Seized by Iran in "Hostile Act"', *Daily Telegraph*, 20 July 2019, bit.ly/2xXueeD.

Gannon, K, 'Pakistan, Saudis, UAE Join US–Taliban Talks', *AP News*, 17 December 2018, bit.ly/2y9tMtO.

Guerin, O, 'Libya in Chaos as Endless War Rumbles On', *BBC News*, 30 October 2019, bbc.in/34ywBDh.

'Hadi Urges Saudi Intervention to Stop UAE Support for Separatists', *Al Jazeera*, 29 August 2019, bit.ly/2XKEOBy.

International Commission of Jurists (ICJ), 'Iraq – ICJ Deplores Moves toward a War of Aggression on Iraq', Geneva, 18 March 2003, bit.ly/2r8GfxL.

Landay, JS, Strobel, WP and Walcott, J, 'Doubts Cast on Efforts to Link Saddam, al-Qaida', *Knight-Ridder*, 3 March 2004, bit.ly/2KZH4j9.

Milner, L, 'The Suez Crisis', *BBC* (last updated 3 March 2011), bbc.in/2LJyDKd.

Nichols, M, 'Britain Says Iran Approached Tanker in Omani Waters: Letter to UN', *Reuters*, 21 July 2019, reut.rs/2ZcpkGF.

Obama, B, Cameron, D and Sarkozy, N, 'Libya's Pathway to Peace', *New York Times*, 14 April 2011, nyti.ms/2M9000j.

'Officials Tell AP Ban Prompted by Enmity between Hadi and UAE, Which is Part of Saudi-Led Coalition Fighting Yemen War', *Al Jazeera*, 7 November 2017, bit.ly/34jZAuo.

Ragozin, L, 'Annexation of Crimea: A Masterclass in Political Manipulation. Ukraine's Revolution Had the Potential to Dig Putin's Political Grave, but He Managed to Turn the Situation on Its Head', *Al Jazeera*, 16 March 2019, bit.ly/35AUObY.

'Saudi Arabia: Yemen's President Hadi Arrives in Saudi Capital Riyadh', *Huffington Post*, 26 March 2015.

Shiffman, K, 'As Genocide Raged, General's Pleas for Help Ignored', *CNN*, 10 December 2008, cnn.it/2MSFqQJ.

'Superpowers Unite over Iraqi Invasion of Kuwait – Archive, 1990', *The Guardian*, 3 August 1990, bit.ly/2pSEKDq.

Tasamba, J, 'DR Congo: 2 Killed in Protests against UN Peacekeepers. Security Forces Engage in Running Street Battles with Protestors in Second Day of Unrest in Beni', *Anadolu Agency*, 27 November 2019, bit.ly/33MiCbw.

'The Kellogg–Briand Pact: World Treaty to Outlaw War – Archive, 1928', *The Guardian*, 14 June 2018, bit.ly/2STqP9T.

'UK Defence Sec: "This Was a Hostile Act"', *Sky News*, 20 July 2019, bit.ly/2xX6Y0h.

'UK Tells UN: Iran's Seizure of British-Flagged Tanker "Constitutes Illegal Interference"', *Sky News*, 20 July 2019, bit.ly/2M3E0UM.

UK Government, 'Release of the Stena Impero', Press Release, 27 September 2019, bit.ly/33hJbFg.

Uras, U, 'Turkey's Operation Peace Spring in Northern Syria: One Month On', *Al Jazeera*, 8 November 2019, bit.ly/33prvIc.

Wintour, P, 'Saudi Arabia Brokers Deal between Warring Sides in South Yemen', *The Guardian*, 25 October 2019, bit.ly/2OgbOhU.

Wyatt, T and Osborne, S, 'Iran Tensions: UK Oil Tanker Was Seized in Oman Waters in "Hostile Act"', *The Independent*, 20 July 2019, bit.ly/2YkPYzA.

'Yemeni President Hadi Resigns from Office', *Al Arabiya*, 22 January 2015, bit.ly/33fOZ23.

'Yemen's President Retracts Resignation after Escape from House Arrest', *The Guardian*, 24 February 2015, bit.ly/2KTDC9I.

# INDEX

9/11 attacks  43, 63, 64, 70, 73, 173
Abkhazia  157, 158, 159 n 34
Abu Jihad  82
Additional Protocol I (1977)  32
Afghanistan  42–43, 63, 64, 72, 73
  President (Burhanuddin Rabbani)
    42, 43
African Charter on Human and Peoples'
    Rights (1981)  176
African Commission on Human and
    Peoples' Rights  176
African Union (AU)  32, 86, 88, 89
  Constitutive Act (2000)  88
  Decision on the Peaceful Resolution of the
    Libya Crisis  86
  Peace and Security Council (PSC)  86
Aggression  14, 21, 26, 29, 54, 59, 60, 61,
    62, 77, 78, 82, 106, **Chap 7**, 175,
    176, 177
  Definition of  122–24
  Individual responsibility for  130–38
  State responsibility for  124–29
  Threat of  138–39
Ago, Roberto  70, 73
Akande, Dapo  78
Albania  36, 112, 118
All necessary means  83–84
All necessary measures  83–84
al-Nusrah Front  84
al-Qaeda  63, 70, 72, 84
*Altmark* incident  104
Angola  82
*Anschluss*  52, 132
Aquinas, St Thomas  3
Argentina  12, 28, 70, 81
Armed attack  57*ff*, 91, 118, 173
  Definition  57
  Imminent  65–66
Armed conflict (*see also Jus in bello*)  39, 90,
    98, 99, 100, 104, 164, 167, **Chap 10**
Arms embargo  79
Arms Trade Treaty (2013)  91, 106, 107

Assassination  29, 59, 94
Augustine, St  2, 3

Badme  27, 28
Bahrain  49, 55
Bakassi Peninsula  28
Barbados  13
Belarus  128
Belgium  94, 100, 111, 114, 115
Benin  62
Benson, Jay  149
Bin Laden, Osama  4, 70
Blockade, naval  22
Blokker, Niels  84
Bolivia  12, 127
Bosnia and Herzegovina  79, 88, 143, 145, 162
Bothe, Michael  98
Botswana  82
Bowett, Derek  68
Brazil  88
Breach of the peace  77
Brownlie, Ian  2, 10, 12, 22, 34, 37, 51,
    57, 62, 66, 69, 100, 102, 130
Brownlie formula  36–37
Buergenthal, Thomas  71
Burma  52

Cameroon  28
Caroline Test  6–7
Catherine the Great  48, 93
Catholic Church  3
Charter of the Organization of American
    States (1948)  60
Chemical weapons  110
China  36, 59, 85, 114, 128
Congress of Vienna (1815)  94
Consent (to use of force)  34, **Chap 2**
  Donor of  40–41
Consent (to treaty)  128
Convention on the Rights of the Child, 2000
    Optional Protocol to  155
Copenhagen, Battle of  94

Corten, Olivier   24, 173
Countermeasure   20
Court of Justice of the European Union
   (CJEU)   32
Covenant of the League of Nations (1919)
   9, 11
Crawford, James   6, 51, 80, 83, 86 n 86, 87,
   105, 115, 156
Crimea   46, 47, 127, 128, 139, 180
Crimes against humanity   76, 88, 107, 130,
   182
Cryer, Robert   120 n 1, 123 n 18, 137 n 97,
   138
Cuba   128
Cuban Missile Crisis   100
Customary law (*see also Jus cogens*)   15,
   19, 20, 23, 29, 51, 57, 151, 156,
   164–65, 172, 180
Cyber operations   22
Cyprus   143, 178

D'Amato, Anthony   26
da Legnano, Giovanni   3
da Pizan, Christine   3
Dallaire, Roméo   143
de Groot, Hugo *see* Grotius
de Vattel, Emmerich   91, 92, 93, 108
de Wet, Erika   88
Deeks, Ashley   44, 86
Democratic People's Republic of Korea
   21, 81, 127
Democratic Republic of Congo   53, 54, 65,
   141, 142, 145, 148–49
Denmark   93, 94
Dinstein, Yoram   7, 11, 23, 57, 59, 61, 62, 63,
   71, 74, 111, 138, 141, 149, 171, 173
Disputes, settlement of   10, 11, 15
Doswald-Beck, Louise   17 n 6, 41 n 15
Draft Code of Offences against the Peace
   and Security of Mankind
   (1954)   121, 122
Dutch Republic *see* Netherlands, the

Economic Community of West African
   States (ECOWAS)   43, 44
Economic measures (not force)   68
ECOWAS Monitoring Group
   (ECOMOG)   43, 44, 144
Egypt   49, 67
   President Gamal Abdel Nasser   67, 141
El Salvador   12
Entebbe   118

Eritrea   27, 75
Eritrea-Ethiopia Claims Commission   27,
   58, 75
Ethiopia   27, 28
European Convention on Human Rights
   (1950)   178, 181
European Court of Human Rights   178, 179,
   180, 181
European Union   32, 48

Falkland Islands   28, 70, 81
Findlay, Trevor   142, 143
First World War   9, 10, 120
Fitzmaurice, Sir Gerald   67
Foch, Marshal Ferdinand   9
Force, nature of   22
France   52, 63, 67, 128
   President (Nicolas Sarkozy)   86

Geneva Convention III (1949)   42
Geneva Conventions (1949)   107, 160, 161
   Common Article 3   160, 161, 164, 165
Genocide   78, 79, 88, 107, 130, 143, 144, 182
Gentili, Alberico   5
Georgia   33–34, 37, 38, 66, 67, 119, 157,
   159, 179
Germany   9, 84, 94, 96, 100, 104, 116, 118,
   132
Gray, Christine   45, 49, 55, 58, 59, 64, 84, 86,
   111
Great Britain *see* United Kingdom
Green, James   173
Grenada   41
Grotius   5, 6, 92, 108
Gulf Cooperation Council (GCC)
   48, 49, 55
Guyana   21

Hague Convention I on the Pacific
   Settlement of International
   Disputes (1899)   7
Hague Convention II on Warfare on Land
   (1899)   95
Hague Convention III on the Opening of
   Hostilities (1907)   8
Hague Convention V on Neutrality during
   Land Warfare (1907)   95, 96, 97
Hague Convention XIII on Neutrality
   during Naval Warfare (1907)   95,
   96, 103
Hague Peace Conference (1899)   7
Hague Peace Conference (1907)   8

Haines, Steven   117
Haiti   41
Helsinki Final Act   158
Helsinki Principles on the Law of Maritime
    Neutrality (1998)   103
Henderson, Christian   23, 24, 68, 72, 78, 81,
    127
Higgins, Rosalyn   71
Hofer, Alexandra   69
Honduras   36
Houthi   48–49
Human rights (*see also* International Human
    Rights Law)   77
Human Rights Committee   55, 175, 176,
    180, 181
    General Comment No 36 on the right to
        life   55, 175, 176
Humanitarian intervention   Chap 6

Independent International Fact-Finding
    Mission on the Conflict in
    Georgia   23, 29, 33, 35, 37, 54, 60,
    66, 73, 110, 117, 118, 119, 157, 158,
    159, 170
India   2, 36, 128
Innocent passage, right of   91, 101
International Committee of the Red Cross
    (ICRC)   52, 161, 165, 169
International Court of Justice (ICJ)   17, 20,
    28, 57, 64, 77, 78, 79, 111, 129, 156,
    160, 165, 167, 171, 177, 180
    *Accordance with International Law of
        the Unilateral Declaration of
        Independence in Respect of Kosovo*
        (Advisory Opinion)   50, 114, 129
    *Armed Activities* case (*Democratic Republic
        of Congo* v *Uganda*)   40, 53, 63,
        65, 66
    *Cameroon* v *Nigeria*   28–29
    *Corfu Channel* case   36, 168
    *Fisheries Jurisdiction* case   24
    *Legal Consequences of the Construction
        of a Wall in the Occupied
        Palestinian Territory* (Advisory
        Opinion)   30–31
    *Legality of the Threat or Use of Nuclear
        Weapons* (Advisory Opinion)   34,
        35, 36, 37, 97, 104, 177
    *Nicaragua* case   17, 18, 19, 20, 23, 36, 50,
        58, 61, 64, 73, 74, 75, 111, 156, 160
    *Oil Platforms* case   58, 59, 71, 72, 73, 167,
        171

*Questions of Interpretation and Application
    of the 1971 Montreal Convention
    arising from the Aerial Incident at
    Lockerbie*   79
    *United States* v *Iran*   62
    *Western Sahara* (Advisory Opinion)
        31–33
International Covenant on Civil and Political
    Rights (1966) (ICCPR)   55, 175,
    177, 181
International Criminal Court   133*ff*
International Criminal Tribunal for the
    Far East   52, 132
International Criminal Tribunal for the
    former Yugoslavia (ICTY)   19, 77,
    130, 162
International Crisis Group   65
International humanitarian law *see Jus in
    bello*
International Human Rights Law   Chap 11
International law, sources of   14–15
International Law Commission (ILC)
    19, 77, 106, 122, 127
    Draft Articles on the Law of State
        Responsibility for Internationally
        Wrongful Acts   19, 48, 50, 52, 53,
        91, 105, 106, 124–30, 156
    Draft Articles on the Responsibility of
        International Organizations
        (2011)   77
Intervention Brigade (MONUSCO)
    148, 151
Iran   25, 49, 62, 71
Iraq   26, 63, 81, 84, 87, 125, 126, 135, 139
Ireland   41, 100
    President (Michael D Higgins)   41, 60
    Taoiseach   41
Islam   4
Islamic State   45, 84
Israel   82, 168
Israeli Air Force   26
Italy   27, 100

Japan   8, 21, 52
Jericho   2
Jordan   49
*Jus cogens*   18, 19, 20, 21, 30, 39, 50, 56, 57, 76,
    77, 78, 106, 109, 115, 116, 117, 124,
    126, 129, 130, 172
*Jus in bello*   7, 32, 42, 43, 70, 72, 90, 91, 98,
    151, 153, Chap 9, Chap 10
Just War (doctrine)   2, 3

Kaiser Wilhelm II    120, 121
Kármán Line    103
Kellogg–Briand Pact (1928)    11–13, 132
Kellogg, Frank    13
Kelsen, Hans    41, 80
Keynes, John Maynard    9
Kilmuir, Lord    67, 68
Klabbers, Jan    60
Koh, Harold    137
Kolb, Robert    16, 20 n 27, 24 n 54, 35, 44,
    61 n 38, 76 n 4
Kosovo (War)    59, 111, **112–17**, 129, 137
Kosovo Liberation Army    112, 128, 129
Kreß, Claus    46
Kuwait    43, 49, 60, 81, 83, 87, 125, 126, 135

Law enforcement    151, 152
League of Armed Neutrality    93
League of Nations (*see also* Covenant of the
    League of Nations (1919))    9, 10,
    11, 16, 131
Liberia    43
    President (Samuel Doe)    43
    President (Charles Taylor)    43
Libya    24, 76, 79, 84, 85–87, 88, 111, 112
    Government of National Accord (GNA)    87
Lloyd George, David    9
Lomé Accord    160, 162

Machiavelli    92
Malanczuk, Peter    80
Malaya    52
Malvinas *see* Falkland Islands
Manchurian crisis    10
Mauritania    31
Milanovic, Marko    179, 180, 182
Military occupation    26–29
Milosevic, Slobodan    112, 113
Moir, Lindsay    161, 162
Montevideo Convention on Rights and Duties
    of States (1933)    13, 108
Morocco    31, 32, 33, 49, 62, 63
Mullah Omar    43
Murphy, Sean D    135, 137

Namibia    114, 128
Napoleon Bonaparte    93, 94
*Naulilaa* (arbitration)    96
Nauru    97, 104
Necessity (*ad bellum*)    69–72
Necessity (*in bello*)    69
Netherlands, the    6, 100

Neutrality    24, **Chap 5**, 169–70
Nicaragua    18, 127
Nigeria    28
Non-Aligned Movement    57, 66, 116
Non-intervention, duty of    16
Non-state actor (*see also* **Non-state armed
    group**)    23, 62, 64, **Chap 9**
    As subject of international law    160–63
    Definition    155–57
Non-state armed group (*see also* **Non-state
    actor**)    45, 124, 148–50, **Chap 9**
    As subject of international law    160–63
    Definition    155–57
Northern Alliance    42, 43
North Atlantic Treaty (1949)    62
North Atlantic Treaty Organization
    (NATO)    59, 86, 88, 111, 112, 113,
    114, 115, 117, 128, 135, 144
North Korea *see* Democratic People's Republic
    of Korea
Norway    104
Nuclear reactor    26
Nuclear weapons    7, 21, 38, 100
    Testing    36
Nulla poena nullum crimen principle    121
Nuremberg Trials    12, 52, 130, 131

Operation Allied Force    112, 113, 116, 128
Operation Decisive Storm    49
Operation Deliberate Force    88
Operation Desert Storm    87
Operation Inherent Resolve    45
Operation Peace Spring    45, 46
Operation Unified Protector    86
Operation Urgent Fury    41
Oppenheim, Lassa    155
Orakhelashvili, Alexander    78, 81
Organization of African Unity    28
Osirak    26

*Pacta tertiis nec nocent nec prosunt*
    principle    164
Pakistan    36, 39, 42, 49
Panama, Invasion of    116
Palestine Liberation Organization (PLO)    30,
    82, 168
Paris Declaration on Maritime Law (1856)    95
Peremptory norm *see* **Jus cogens**
Permanent Court of International Justice    10
    *Eastern Carelia* Advisory Opinion    10
    *Lotus* case    10
Polisario Front    31, 32

Pope Jean Paul II   3
Portugal   96, 130
Proportionality (*ad bellum*)   73–74, 167,
    170–71
Proportionality (*in bello*)   167, 170–71
Protection of civilians (*see also* UN Policy
    on Protection of Civilians During
    Peacekeeping Operations)   76,
    **144–48**
UN mandates   145 Table 1
Putin, Vladimir   47

Qatar   49
Quran   4
Qureshi, WA   4

Regime change (*see also* Libya)   74, 170
Regional organisations   87–89
Reisman, W Michael   109, 116
Reprisals (*ad bellum*)   68
Reprisals (*in bello*)   173, 174
Rescue (of hostages)   24, 25, 118
Rescue (of nationals)   118–19
Responsibility to Protect   117–18
Revolutionary United Front (RUF)   161, 163
Rodley, Nigel   116
Rome Statute of the International Criminal
    Court (1998)   18, 82, 130, 134
Roth, Brad R   33, 109
Roux, André   150
Russia   8, 17, 24, 37, 38, 46, 47, 48, 60, 66, 82,
    86, 93, 114, 115, 119, 127, 128, 139,
    157, 159, 179, 180
Rwanda   53, 143, 144

Sadurska, Romana   34, 35
Saharan (or Sahrawi) Arab Democratic
    Republic (SADR)   31
Salisbury   60
Saudi Arabia   42, 48, 49, 50, 55
*Savarkar* case   52
Schabas, William   178
Schröder, Gerhard   116, 135
Second World War   10, 131, 134, 138
Self-defence (*see also* Necessity (*ad bellum*);
    Proportionality (*ad bellum*))   14,
    27, 37, Chap 3
Interceptive   7, 67
Self-determination, right (of peoples) to   27,
    29, **30–33**, 50–51, 78, 124
Sierra Leone (*see also* Special Court for Sierra
    Leone)   144, 161

Simma, Bruno   63, 102
Skripal, Sergei   24, 60
Somalia   141, 143, 144, 145
South Africa   82, 130
South Korea   21, 81
South Ossetia   33, 157, 158, 159, 160
Southern Rhodesia   82
Spain   6
Special Court for Sierra Leone   153, 160,
    161, 163
Srebrenica   88, 144
States (number of)   14
Statute of the International Court of Justice
    (1945)   14
*Stena Impero*   25
Stürchler, Nikolas   21
Subject (of international law)   77, 154–55,
    160–63
Sudan   49
Suez Canal   67, 68
Suez Crisis   67–68, 69
Suriname   21
Sweet, Rachel   149
Switzerland   94
Swiss Federal Council   32
Syria   44–46, 82, 84, 110, 137, 139
President Bashar al-Assad   44

Taliban   42, 63, 64, 70, 72
Tallinn Manual on the International Law
    Applicable to Cyber Warfare
    (2013)   92, 105
Tams, Christian   168
Taylor, Charles   43
Thailand   52
Threat of force   18, 20, 21, 22, 23,
    **34–38**, 67
Definition   34–35
Tacit   35
Threat to the peace   77, **80–81**
Tladi, Dire   130
Torelli, Maurice   98
Torture   78
Trahan, Jennifer   135
Transfer (of weapons)   23, 130
Treaty of London (1839)   94
Treaty of Versailles (1919)   9, 120, 131
Treaty of Westphalia (1648)   6
Tsar (Russian)   7, 93, 94
Tunisia   82
Turkey   45, 46, 100, 139
Turkmenistan   99

U-2 plane   23
Uganda   53, 65
Ugandan People's Defence Force (UPDF)
   54, 65
Ukraine   46–48, 127
UNCLOS *see* United Nations, Convention on
   the Law of the Sea
United Arab Emirates   42, 49, 50
United Kingdom   6, 47, 50, 52, 67, 70, 84, 101,
   104, 110, 111, 128
   High Court (of England and Wales)   138
   House of Lords   138
   Prime Minister (Theresa May)   24
   Prime Minister (David Cameron)   86
   Queen Elizabeth II   41, 60
   Secretary of State for Defence (Penny
      Mordaunt)   25
   Secretary of State for Foreign and
      Commonwealth Affairs (Dominic
      Raab)   25
   Secretary of State for Foreign and
      Commonwealth Affairs   42
United Nations
   Charter (1945)   6, 7, 13, 14, 16, 39, 76, 90,
      97, 99, 105, 108, 123, 126, 134, 152,
      158, 176
      Article 2   157
      Article 2(3)   14, 157, 180
      Article 2(4)   14, **Chap 1**, 91, 102, 118,
         123, 129, 134, 157, 160, 168, 170
      Article 2(7)   108
      Article 24   79
      Article 25   79
      Article 42   14
      Article 51   14, 27, **Chap 3**, 160
      Article 52   87, 88
      Article 103   79
      Chapter VI   117, 143, 152
      Chapter VII   14, 51, Chap 4, 105, 110,
         113, 117, 153, 176
      Chapter VIII   87, 117
   Compensation Commission (UNCC)   125
   Convention on the Law of the Sea
      (1982)   18, 91 n 10
   Department of Peace Operations   151
   General Assembly   15, 140
      Declaration on Principles of International
         Law on Friendly Relations among
         States (1970)   15, 17, 18, 30, 31, 111
      Declaration on the Granting of
         Independence to Colonial Countries
         and Peoples   31
      Declaration on the Rule of Law
         (2012)   77
      Definition of Aggression (1974)   22, 26,
         29, 54, 59, 118, 121, **123–24**, 133,
         134, 157, 176, 177
      Resolution 380 (V)   121
      Resolution 34/47   32
      Resolution 38/7   41
      Resolution 50/80A   99
      Resolution 66/253B   83
      Resolution 68/262   127
      Uniting for Peace resolution   140
      World Summit Outcome   87, 117
   Peacekeeping   **Chap 8**
      MONUSCO   148–50
      Use of force, legal basis for   152–53
   Policy on Protection of Civilians During
      Peacekeeping Operations   150–51
   Secretary-General   136, 140
   Security Council   8, 25, 26, 41, 44, 45, 46,
      49, 59, 63, 67, 69, 72, 73, 74, 75,
      **Chap 4**, 90, 98, 99, 105, 110, 113,
      114, 116, 126, 129, 135, 136, 140,
      152, 163, 168
      Resolution 143 (1960)   142
      Resolution 405 (1977)   62
      Resolution 419 (1977)   62
      Resolution 487 (1981)   66
      Resolution 573 (1985)   82
      Resolution 611 (1988)   82, 135
      Resolution 665 (1990)   83–84
      Resolution 713 (1991)   79
      Resolution 836 (1993)   88
      Resolution 876 (1993)   159 n 34
      Resolution 1203 (1998)   113
      Resolution 1265 (1999)   144
      Resolution 1333 (2000)   42
      Resolution 1368 (2001)   63
      Resolution 1373 (2001)   63
      Resolution 1540 (2004)   155
      Resolution 1970 (2011)   86
      Resolution 1973 (2011)   76, 84, **85–87**
      Resolution 2098 (2013)   148
      Resolution 2216 (2015)   49 n 62
      Resolution 2249 (2015)   84
United States   6, 18, 21, 39, 41, 43, 45, 55, 63,
   70, 71, 73, 100, 101, 114, 128, 139,
   144
   Department of Defense   45, 99, 101, 107, 171
   President (Donald Trump)   45
   President (Barack Obama)   86
   President (George HW Bush)   60

presidential election (2016)  17
 Vice-President Dick Cheney  63
**Uruguay**  12

**van Bynkershoek, Cornelius**  91, 92
**von Heinegg, Wolff Heintschel**  103
**von Ramsla, Johann Wilhelm Neumair**  92
**Vattel** *see* de Vattel
**Vienna Convention on the Law of Treaties
 (1969)**  18, 128, 159, 163

**Walzer, Michael**  4
**Waterloo, Battle of**  94
**War crimes**  78, 88, 107, 117, 120, 121, 130,
 131, 137, 149

**Weapons** (*see also* **Chemical weapons;
 Transfer**)  22, 38, 106, 173
**Western Sahara**  31–33, 62
**Whiting, Alex**  136
**World War Zero**  8

**Yanukovych, Victor**  46, 47
**Yemen**  48–50
 President (Ali Abdullah Saleh)  48
 President (Abdrabbuh Mansur Hadi)  48,
  49, 50
**Yugoslavia, Federal Republic of**  79, 111,
 112–17, 128

**Zambia**  82

www.ingramcontent.com/pod-product-compliance
Lightning Source LLC
Chambersburg PA
CBHW061154220326
41599CB00025B/4481